# Supervision Modules to Support Educators in Collaborative Teaching

# Supervision Modules to Support Educators in Collaborative Teaching

*Helping to Support & Maintain Consistent Practice in the Field*

edited by

**Kathryn L. Lubniewski**
*Monmouth University*

**Debbie F. Cosgrove**
*Elmhurst College*

**Theresa Y. Robinson**
*Elmhurst College*

A research-based handbook used to facilitate productive practices, critical analysis, reflection, and monitoring of educators in the field. Modules can be used in any order and are organized to effectively support teacher pairs or teams as they collaborate and grow professionally.

INFORMATION AGE PUBLISHING, INC.
Charlotte, NC • www.infoagepub.com

**Library of Congress Cataloging-in-Publication Data**

A CIP record for this book is available from the Library of Congress
http://www.loc.gov

ISBN:  978-1-64113-584-9 (Paperback)
       978-1-64113-585-6 (Hardcover)
       978-1-64113-586-3 (ebook)

Copyright © 2019 Information Age Publishing Inc.

All rights reserved. No part of this publication may be reproduced, stored in a retrieval system, or transmitted, in any form or by any means, electronic, mechanical, photocopying, microfilming, recording or otherwise, without written permission from the publisher.

Printed in the United States of America

# Contents

Introduction ................................................................................................ vii
Acknowledgments ........................................................................................ xi

## PART I
### UNDERSTANDING YOURSELF AND OTHERS

**Module 1: Knowing Yourself and Your Colleague** ............................................................. 3
  Debbie F. Cosgrove

**Module 2: Effective Communication** ............................................................................ 25
  Kathryn L. Lubniewski and Kirstin Natale

**Module 3: Culturally Relevant Pedagogy** ..................................................................... 39
  Ayanna F. Brown

## PART II
### DISCOVERING THE CONTEXT

**Module 4: Knowledge of Students** ............................................................................. 55
  Theresa Y. Robinson

**Module 5: Partnering With Families** .......................................................................... 69
  Linda Dauksas

**Module 6: Knowing the Community and Utilizing Its Resources** ........................................ 83
  Theresa Y. Robinson

# PART III
## PUTTING IT ALL TOGETHER

**Module 7: Creating a Positive Climate in the Classroom** ................................................. 97
Wendy A. Harriott

**Module 8: Using the Co-Teaching Models** ................................................................. 113
David Hoppey, Keri Haley, and Megan Robinson

**Module 9: Promoting Engagement and Positive Behavior** ............................................ 131
Jaime L. Zurheide

**Module 10: Using Individualized Interventions for Challenging Behaviors** ................. 147
Mary B. Haspel

**Module 11: Collecting Student Data and Assessment** ................................................. 163
Kathryn L. Lubniewski

**Module 12: Collaborative Planning for Instruction** ..................................................... 177
Debbie F. Cosgrove

**Module 13: Differentiating Your Instruction** .............................................................. 199
Lisa Burke

**Module 14: Responsible Digital Citizenship** ............................................................... 211
Tracy Mulvaney

**Module 15: Using Video to Facilitate Peer Coaching and Problem Solving With Pairs** ..... 225
A. Brooke Blanks

# PART IV
## ENHANCING PROFESSIONAL PRACTICE

**Module 16: Teachers and the Law** ............................................................................... 255
Paul R. Klenck, Bernard F. Bragen Jr., and Debbie F. Cosgrove

**Module 17: Professional Dispositions** ........................................................................ 279
LuEllen Doty and Jeanne White

**Module 18: Supporting the Job Hunt** ......................................................................... 289
Courtney Miller

About the Contributors ................................................................................................. 303
Index ........................................................................................................................... 309

# Introduction

It all began at a small, private college outside of Chicago. Three women faculty discovered that they had a similar passion—to create a new student teaching model. They began to imagine models that upheld collaboration, reflective practice, professional growth, and meaningful supervision. Out of shared training, research, conversation, and questioning, *The Collaborative Student Teaching Model* (CSTM) was born.

The aim of this model is to incorporate robust collaboration among the cooperating teacher, teacher candidate, and supervisor. CSTM is a mentoring process where the supervisor supports the cooperating teacher and the teacher candidate to foster and develop a strong teaching relationship through the development and use of communication, collaboration, planning, and reflection in order to provide shared instruction for all learners. Both teachers utilize co-teaching models and are actively involved and engaged in all aspects of the teaching process (planning, instruction, and assessment).

The mentoring process requires that the student teaching supervisor understands how to effectively guide the pair as they co-plan, co-teach, and co-assess together. After close analysis of the "triad" in action (i.e., college supervisor, teacher candidate, and cooperating teacher), the researchers identified the need for a structured field-based handbook of resources for student teaching supervisors to use when guiding each pair. Additionally, they found that the support that teacher candidates received from their supervisors needed to be grounded in research that supported best practices in teaching and learning. There was minimal practical support for those who supervise and mentor student teachers, or novice teachers, especially in more collaborative settings. This need for a comprehensive supervisory resource that could be easily used by the student teaching supervisor prompted the writing of this work, *Supervision Modules to Support Educators in Collaborative Teaching*.

After being encouraged by the success of the *Collaborative Student Teaching Model* during 3 years of pilot projects and implementation, the researchers have now expanded CSTM to include pairs and teams of teachers and licensed service providers (e.g., reading interventionists, ESL specialists, speech pathologists, physical therapists, occupational therapists) in meaningful dialogue with a variety of supervisor types (e.g., college supervisor, teacher leader, department chair, school administrator). This new and more fully-developed model—the

*Collaborative Teaching Model* (CTM)—is applicable to both preservice and in-service teacher development. In this collaborative model, the supervisor plays a critical role in the development of the teaching pair or team through specific engagements in communication, collaboration, planning, and reflection on practice. Collaborative teaching, where teachers are actively engaged in all aspects of instruction, is basic to the model from start to finish. The *Supervision Modules to Support Educators in Collaborative Teaching* provides supervisors with relevant, collaborative, activity-based professional development to support and mentor preservice or in-service teachers.

## *What Is This Handbook Used For?*

The purpose of this PreK–12 module-based handbook is to support the supervisor or administrator as they guide teacher pairs or teams in instructional practice. This is accomplished through the use of module topics that were originally identified through focus groups of preservice teachers, school administrators, college supervisors, and professors of education. These stakeholders helped to identify common areas of difficulty often experienced during teaching. Once supervisors or administrators choose a module topic, they are supported with foundational knowledge of the most current research; discussion questions about the topic; productive practices that they can suggest; questions to deepen understanding; reflective professional growth activities; and monitoring, follow-up, and goal setting to be used with the teaching pair or team. *Supervision Modules to Support Educators in Collaborative Teaching* is designed to promote on-going, supervisory practice that meets teacher development needs in collaborative teaching contexts.

## *What Are the Implementation Goals?*

The essential implementation goals of the supervision modules are:

- to provide an organizational, research-based tool to support mentor teachers, teacher candidates, and collaborative pairs or teams;
- to strengthen the supervisor or administrator's knowledge base and general awareness of best practices by providing a variety of theory, discussion questions, productive practices, reflective professional growth activities, monitoring strategies, and goal setting suggestions; and
- to increase communication skills, collaboration, and reflection on practice through field-based professional development activities.

## What Is the Purpose of the Modules?

The handbook is organized in modules that one can use in any order. The modules are applicable for use with any teacher or collaborative teaching pair or team at all grade levels preschool through twelve (PK–12). Within each of the modules, you will find an overview of the topic; theory/conceptual framework; discussion questions; productive practices; "What Would You Do?" questions for discussion; reflective professional growth activities; and monitoring, follow-up, and goal setting suggestions that include monitoring and follow-up of teaching practice.

## *What Are the Different Sections in Each Module?*

**Theory/Conceptual Framework:** This section includes the relevant research and theory on the topic.

**Discussion Questions:** Questions that the supervisor or administrator may ask to guide collaboration and reflection between the pair or among team members.

**Productive Practices:** A list of useful suggestions that the pair or team can use in the learning environment, and during teaching and learning.

**What Would You Do? (WWYD):** A list of questions that are relevant to any school setting. The supervisor or administrator poses the question and allows time for each teacher to individually answer and share their thinking with the pair or team. You can find suggested responses in the appendix of each module for the different questions.

**Reflective Professional Growth Activities (RPGA):** These professional growth activities promote reflection between the teaching partners or among the team members. The supervisor or administrator will choose one or several of these activities to help facilitate the process of reflection on practice in order to develop a deeper understanding of a particular topic.

**Goal Setting, Monitoring, and Follow-Up:** The choice of the *Reflective Professional Growth Activity* will determine the selection of the follow-up activity. The numbers are aligned so that the number you choose under RPGA is the same number you choose for the follow-up activity.

**Resources:** Module resources include topic-related materials that will support the supervisor. These supports can also be shared with the pair or team. You will find technology resources, checklists, charts, and diagrams.

**Appendix:** Here you will find examples or templates of the materials that are discussed within the module. The templates can be reproduced and used with pairs or teams to provide extended opportunities for the users to think about and write their responses before sharing them in a group setting.

## How Do You Start?

1. Read the Table of Contents in the handbook to familiarize yourself with the module topics.
2. Read through each of the module descriptions and the theory/conceptual framework.
3. Observe your teacher pair or team.
4. Identify a module topic based on the evidence that you gather from teacher observations, questions, and discussions.
5. Schedule a meeting with the teaching pair or team.
6. Start the discussion by asking one or more of the "Discussion Questions."
7. Share the "Productive Practices" (be sure to ask if the teacher(s) has any questions).
8. Pose one or more of the "What Would You Do?" questions to your teacher pair or team. Openly discuss the different responses to the scenario, and be sure to provide them with the suggested response after the discussion.
9. Choose one "Reflective Professional Growth Activity" that you will guide the pair or team through and discuss.
10. Choose one "Monitoring, Goal Setting, and Follow-Up" idea that you will revisit with the teacher pair or team during your next observation.
11. Schedule a time when your teacher, pair, or team will share the results with you from the "Monitoring, Follow-Up, and Goal Setting Activity."

12. Before beginning your next observation, ask the teacher pair or team if they have any further questions or issues about the module topic, activity or goal setting process. You may decide to choose another "Reflective Professional Growth Activity" if the pair or team needs additional support with the topic (repeat steps 9–10).

# Acknowledgments

This project could not have been accomplished without the support of the faculty, supervisors, and staff of the Departments of Education at Elmhurst College and Monmouth University. The Elmhurst College Department of Education supported the piloting of a student teaching model that utilized co-teaching strategies (2013–2014). The college provided two faculty research grants to further the implementation of the model with selected teachers across programs. This research led to the design of a faculty adopted co-teaching model for student teaching that developed into the *Collaborative Student Teaching Model* that is currently used at Elmhurst College. Monmouth University supported the project by providing faculty seminars in publishing. Additionally, the dean of the School of Education, John Henning, provided insight and support of the publication process for this project.

We are grateful to Drs. Teresa Heck and Nancy Bacharach, both from the Academy for Co-Teaching and Collaboration at St. Cloud State University. Their research and training on the use of co-teaching strategies during student teaching were foundational to the success of this project.

The completion of this project could not have been accomplished without the contributions of the authors in specialized module writing and participation in a collaborative, internal, peer-review process. The authors built on their research and expertise to make this a practical field-based resource for student teaching supervisors, school administrators, and educators. We can't thank them enough!

We also owe a great debt to our families for their patience, encouragement, and unwavering support. We cannot name you all. *But we thank you all.*

# PART I

*Understanding Yourself and Others*

# MODULE 1

# Knowing Yourself and Your Colleague

Debbie F. Cosgrove

*Elmhurst College*

*As a teacher and then as principal, I learned over and over again that the relationship among adults in the schoolhouse has more impact on the quality and character of the school—and on the accomplishment of youngsters—than any other factor.*
—Roland Barth

*None of us are to be found in sets of tasks or lists of attributes, we can be known only in the unfolding of our unique stories within the context of everyday events.*
—Vivian Gussin Paley

## MODULE DESCRIPTION

A critical component of teaching is to know and understand yourself and your teaching beliefs. When teachers work in a collaborative classroom context, it is important for them to learn about and communicate with those with whom they teach. Differences in thoughts and expectations always exist among collaborating team members. This module provides support so that supervisors can facilitate an ongoing conversation about varying beliefs and expectations with the teaching pair or team. Specifically, the module offers guided questions and resources to support teachers as they learn more about each other, build trust, and develop the skills to communicate and collaborate successfully.

## Theory/Conceptual Framework

Discovering and sharing one's knowledge of self and others are essential to collaboration in teaching. Teachers begin their relationship on a social level and then move into knowing each other on a professional level as they discuss and negotiate differences and commonalities related to teaching expectations and instructional practice. To collaborate instructionally, it is important for them to know one another both personally and professionally.

Charlotte Danielson reminds us that "When it comes to professional learning, it's all about the conversation" (Danielson, 2015). Before engaging students, the teaching pair or team should discuss instructional issues, differing viewpoints or potential conflicts, written plans, communication skills, cultural differences, committing to using differences as learning opportunities, and acknowledging that no pair or team is perfect (Conderman, 2010; DeBoer, 1995; DeBoer & Fister-Mulkey, 1998; Ploessl, D., Rock, M., Schoenfeld, N., & Blanks, B., 2010). As the relationship develops through consistent communication, the pair or team identifies shared commonalities and also unique differences in what they believe about how students learn and what pedagogies to use to address individual learning needs. Reflective, ongoing conversations— including identification and discussion of concerns or conflicts in priorities or educational beliefs—help the pair or team to set a team purpose and embrace shared goals. This reflection process also builds trust, an essential element in maintaining a culture of collaboration.

Trust is the cornerstone of the collaborative-teaching relationship (Searle & Swartz, 2015; Erkens, C., et al., (2008). Building trust requires attentiveness to behaviors that can threaten trust-building efforts. Combs, Edmonson, and Harris (2013; Combs, Harris, & Edmonson, 2015) identify four "trust-busters," behaviors that are detrimental to the trust-building process: (a) not listening, (b) saving time at the expense of others (i.e., failing to communicate with all stakeholders), (c) saying one thing but doing another, and (d) breaking confidence through gossiping. The authors recommend that teacher pairs or teams practice counter-behaviors: (a) listening actively, (b) maintaining consistency in expectations, (c) monitoring self-reactions to different situations, (d) demonstrating an awareness regarding the social consequences of behavior, (e) showing empathy and appreciation of others, and (f) displaying transparency in emotions and intentions (i.e., revealing what you really think and feel; sharing what goals and values are important to you). Each of these is essential to fostering and maintaining trust.

Collaboration, or "co-laboring"—working together—occurs when a teaching pair or team identifies a shared vision, goals, and teaching objectives and successfully accomplishes these together through hard work. Collaborators cooperate—"operate together"—with each other, which demands effective communication, effort, and patience from all stakeholders (Conderman & Johnston-Rodriguez, 2012). Collaboration and communication do not happen automatically. They must be identified and practiced (DeBoer & Fister-Mulkey, 1998; Friend, 2017).

Creating effective relationships among co-teachers and team members is a developmental process that moves through a series of stages toward productive collaborative practice (Gately & Gately, 2001; Villa, Thousand, & Nevin, 2004; Tuckman, 1965). Bruce Tuckman, in his model of team formation (Tuckman, 1965, 2001) describes five stages of team development: (a) *Forming* (learning about each other both personally and professionally), (b) *Storming* (negotiating the difficult issues), (c) *Norming* (reaching consensus and common understandings/expectations), (d) *Performing* (effective collaborative teaching, which includes reflection "in" and "on" practice) (Schön, 1983), and (e) *Adjourning* (planning for the departure of team members and welcoming new members at the end of the team's work together as a unit). Pairs or teams progress through the five stages as they mature in their work and strengthen their collaboration toward a common purpose. They "co-labor"—work diligently together toward a common goal.

It is important to provide novice teachers with opportunities to learn from seasoned professionals who have successfully co-taught for a longer period of time. In fact, researchers hold that it is important to learn about co-teaching through "hands on experiences with a wide range of collaborative interactions" (Austin, 2001; Kluth & Straut, 2003). These collaborative interactions should always include a reflection of what actual professionals do to inform their practice (Schön, 1983). In this relationship, the power and accountability lie largely with the cooperating teacher (Friend, Embury & Clark, 2014; Robinson, Cosgrove & Servilio, 2015). It is important to note, however, that it is not enough to focus solely on developing a supportive relationship in co-teaching in order to be successful. Rather, other critical elements, that need to be explicitly taught, help to assure the success of the pair or team: communication, classroom applications of co-teaching, and a knowledge base of co-teaching itself (Bacharach, Heck, & Dahlberg, 2008).

## Specific Questions to Guide Discussion

1. What commonalities and differences can you identify as you share your personal "stats" or brief biographical statements, professional identities, and teaching beliefs with each other? Does your pair or team know of your gifts, talents, and skills? (Forming stage)

2. What are your individual and shared visions for your pair or team? What is your individual and pair/team vision? Can you state this vision in one sentence? In a hashtag? (Forming stage)

3. What topics, perceptions, expectations, or opinions (i.e., class procedures, discipline expectations, grading, annoyances) do you have individually that may differ considerably from your pair or team? (Storming stage)

4. Is there confusion on the pair or team about general expectations, routines, grading, discipline and roles? (Storming stage)

5. What process and tools do you plan to use to communicate and negotiate difficult truths with your pair or team? (Storming stage)

6. What steps do you plan to take— or have already taken— in order to strengthen your understanding of how to create a culture of collaboration with your co-teaching pair

or team? Is pair or team leadership shared? Is there parity of voice among members? (Norming stage)

7. What specific communication skills will you focus on as a pair or team as you plan and reflect on your collaborative teaching practice? Do team members affirm each other and the contributions that each member makes? (Performing stage)

## Productive Practices

1. *Be intentional about your efforts to collaborate.* Be intentional about creating a collaborative culture of teaching that incorporates communication, trust, affirmation, negotiation, and shared goals.
2. *Identify your personal teaching beliefs.* Identify and discuss your personal beliefs or "I believe..." tenets about teaching and learning. Look for commonalities within your pair or team in the belief statements that each member holds.
3. *Identify and share your commonalities and differences.* Identify and share your commonalities (How are we alike?) and differences (How are we different?) that contribute to your unique lives as individuals and educators.
4. *Brainstorm, affirm, and question to shape a shared vision.* Engage in frequent brainstorming, sharing of difficult truths, and questioning to provide opportunities to practice communication skills that affirm each teacher's voice. These practices encourage equitable contribution of ideas to support a shared vision of the pair or team. Use *Affinity Mapping* with the pair or team to brainstorm, categorize, and reach consensus for group norms. For an example of affinity mapping, please watch www.youtube.com/watch?v=UynxDyrOlAo (1.28 minutes in length).
5. *Agree on a consistent time and place for pair/team collaboration to occur.* Agree on a consistent time and place for pair or team communication and collaboration to occur. Schedule a time at the beginning and end of the week to plan and reflect on your practice together. This is a minimal expectation. Ideally, pairs should meet on a daily basis to support the need for ongoing communication. Make sure that you have face-to-face opportunities to communicate and collaborate with each other, which can also include the use of virtual interactions through Skype, Zoom, FaceTime or Google Hangouts.
6. *Identify and practice communication and collaboration skills in your work.* It is important that the pair or team has a shared understanding of the different types of communication and collaboration skills. Individual and group recognition and reflection on these skills will help teachers to more effectively collaborate or "co-labor" together.

## What Would You Do?

Ask your team or pair the following questions. For suggested responses to questions, see Appendix A.

1. What would you do if your co-teacher's expectations are very different from yours regarding classroom management, grading, or any other instructional topic?

2. What would you do if one of the pair or team members is reticent to share any personal information and appears disinterested in getting to know others on the pair or team on a personal level?

3. What would you do if the school does not provide adequate time for you to talk and plan with your pair or team during the school day?

## Reflective Professional Growth Activities

Consider these ideas or activities to facilitate and foster teacher growth and reflection. Select one or two ideas to help facilitate this reflection process that will help the teacher, pair, or team to understand the importance of knowing themselves and their colleagues. The activity should be selected in view of the personalities of the team members and what would be the most effective for them.

### *Idea 1: What are Your Teacher Stats? (Professional) Share Your Story (Individual)*

Teachers have unique professional backgrounds, schooling, and training that often remain hidden from their colleagues. Many teachers are even reluctant to share the individual experiences they have had that have helped to shape their own teaching identities. To help the co-teaching pair or team form a shared teaching identity, it is important for each member to tell their unique story. To start this conversation, ask each person in the pair or team to create a listing of their educational preparation, professional experiences, specialization areas of expertise, and personal interests. This list of personal experiences and/or professional "stats" should then be shared and affirmed by the other pair member or team.

Figure 1.1 is an example of a teacher stats list for a first year educator:

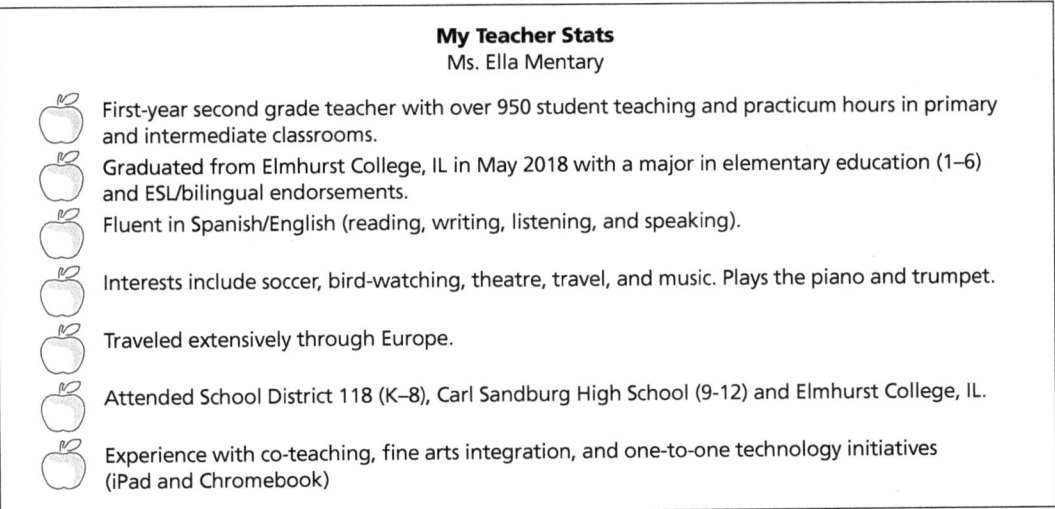

**Figure 1.1** Example of a teacher stats list for Ms. Ella Mentary.

After sharing their individual "stats" with one another, ask the pair or team members to answer several questions that will help them to tell their personal stories as to why they chose teaching as a career. This conversation will be much more personal than the reading of the "stats" as the pair or team begin telling their unique stories and sharing their individual belief statements about teaching and learning with each other.

Use the following questions for the story-telling part of this professional growth activity:

1. What personal experience(s) have you had that have shaped your identity as a teacher?
2. What are three essential tenets or belief statements that guide your teaching practice? Begin each of your tenets with "I believe..." (e.g., I believe that students learn best with others who believe in their potential, hold high expectations with them, and never give up on their success; I believe that to maximize student potential, instruction should build on prior knowledge, interest, and learning preference).

Provide time for the pair or team to share their personal stories and belief statements with one another.

**Evidence:** (a) Individual completion of the Teacher Stats activity, (b) individual preparation of the teacher identity-shaping experiences and belief statements, and (c) sharing of personal identity-shaping experiences and three belief statements with the pair and or team.

### *Idea 2: Create Your Cornerstone: What Is Your Sentence? What Is Your Hashtag?*

The cornerstone serves as the foundational brick in a building. It is the setting stone from which the other bricks are placed. Located at the corner of a building, the cornerstone unites two intersecting walls as one structure. Often, the cornerstone provides space inside of the brick for a time capsule that carries historical artifacts from the time of the building's construction. In this professional growth activity, the cornerstone will be used as a metaphor to represent the foundational stone for the pair or team as members work to build relationships, set a common vision, and plan for collaboration in teaching and learning. This activity is adapted from the ASCD publication *Teacher Teamwork* (Searle & Swartz, 2015, pp. 6–7).

Follow these steps to complete the activity based on *Drive* (2009), the best-selling motivational book by Daniel Pink.

1. Watch the Daniel Pink video *What's My Sentence?* (see www.youtube.com/watch?v=AyRu7k70Jhc [2:02])
2. Compose individual vision sentences and share.
3. Using affinity mapping, (see, https://youtu.be/UynxDyr0lAo (1:28) brainstorm ideas about what the pair or team will accomplish to have an impact on student learning.
4. Look for commonalities among brainstormed ideas and categorize into groups (i.e., instructional strategies, parental support, data-driven assessment, higher-order thinking). The categories will serve as norming "buckets" to be used for the pair or team's exploration during the Norming stage.

5. Now, write one inspiring sentence that represents the pair or team's vision or purpose. Translate this vision/purpose in sentence form to a hashtag for your pair/team (e.g., #co-laboringforimpact, #strongertogether4growth, #teachreflectgrow). Transfer the hashtag to a larger-sized paper and decorate it to display in the classroom.
6. Transfer the pair or team's vision sentence, or inscription, to a rectangular piece of colored or painted poster board (11" × 18"). Write down the date that the pair or team was established. On the back of the cornerstone, list the strengths, talents, and skills that each member will contribute to the collaborative teaching effort. These lists represent the inner time capsule of the pair or team's cornerstone.
7. Post the pair or team's cornerstone and hashtag in a prominent place in the classroom.

**Evidence:** Completion of individual and group vision sentences; completion of a pair/team hashtag; completion of one cornerstone to represent the pair or team vision, member skills, and establishment date of the pair or team.

## *Idea 3: Collaboration Self-Assessment Survey*

Collaboration or co-laboring toward a common end does not happen naturally. In fact, collaboration skills are often not strategically taught in many teacher preparation programs. The *Collaboration Self-Assessment Survey* is an effective tool to use with co-teaching pairs and also teacher teams to help members identify and reflect on the various elements that contribute to a collaborative climate. The *Collaboration Self-Assessment Survey* takes ten minutes to take. Each member of the pair or team will complete the survey, reflect on their individual responses, and discuss their individual results with the pair or team. The survey also links intrapersonal (occurs within the individual) and interpersonal (occurs among persons) skill development with the eight collaborative elements (see Appendix B for *Collaboration Self-Assessment Survey*).

**Evidence:** Individual completion and discussion of the *Collaboration Self-Assessment Survey* results.

## *Idea 4: NEED–HEED–SUCCEED!: Goal Setting Planner (Cosgrove, 2017)*

To effectively communicate with your pair or team, it is important for each team member to openly share individual needs and concerns so that the pair or team can successfully communicate and collaborate together. Participation in this activity will help team members to navigate through the *Storming* stage (Tuckman, 1965, 2001) where difficult truths are typically shared.

First, each individual should fill out the *NEED* and *HEED* sections of the flow chart. After filling out the sections, the pair or team should take time to discuss each section together (see Figure 1.2). Finally, in the *SUCCEED* section, the pair or team should work together to craft specific steps to address the voiced needs and concerns. This exercise should be completed biweekly for any teaching pair or team and kept as a record to document shared communication and problem solving tactics (see example in Figure 1.3). See Appendix C for the NEED–HEED–SUCCEED! tool.

**Evidence:** The pair or team should complete the NEED–HEED–SUCCEED! exercise together on a biweekly basis (use the template in Appendix C). The responses should be kept as a record to document the pair or team's shared communication and problem-solving strategies.

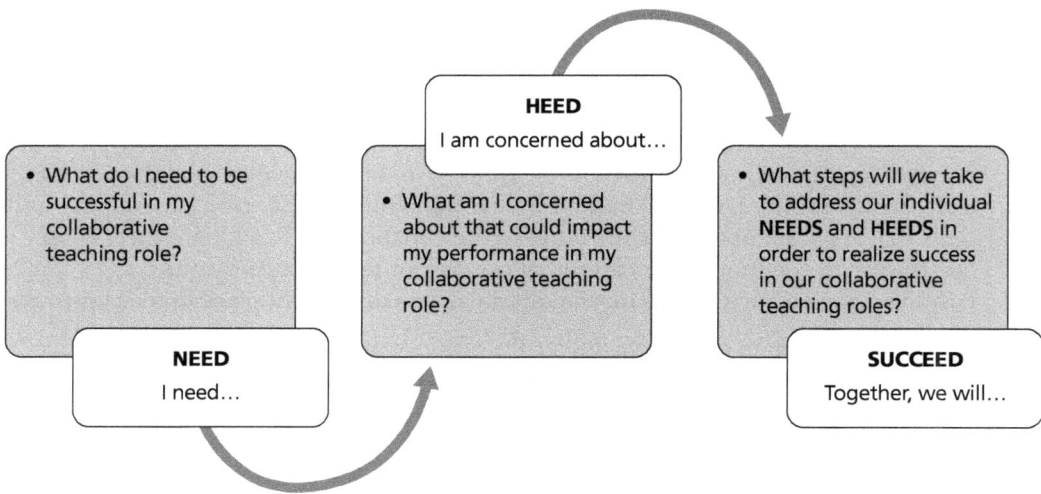

**Figure 1.2** NEED–HEED–SUCCEED! flow chart.

| **NEED**<br>I need... | • I need to more clearly understand how the grade level team approaches lesson planning in science and social science.<br>• I need more guidance from my cooperating teacher about the academic needs of the English language learners in the class. |
|---|---|
| **HEED**<br>I am concerned about... | • How can I demonstrate my ability to lesson plan when plans are completed by a team of five veteran teachers?<br>• How do I identify what levels my ELLs are in the class? How can I connect class instruction with the lesson planning goals of the ESL specialist? |
| **SUCCEED**<br>Together, we will... | • We will reach consensus with the 5th grade team regarding teacher candidate lesson planning, contributions, and responsibilities. We will clearly identify planning done in the classroom that will be completed by the teacher candidate. We will agree on all expected planning dates and keep detailed notes of our meetings.<br>• We will schedule a time on Monday to review ELL student eligibility data and proficiency levels with the ESL specialist. |

**Figure 1.3** Example of NEED–HEED–SUCCEED! exercise (Cosgrove, 2017).

## Idea 5: Practice Your Communication Skills

Teachers vary in the types of communication skills that they use to communicate in pair and team settings. Recognition of communication skills and practice of them help pairs or teams to successfully collaborate with one another. Poor communication will almost always lead to ineffective collaboration.

Review examples (see Figure 1.4) of communication skills as suggested by Conderman, Johnston-Rodriguez & Hartman (2009). Each educator should choose several of these communication skills to use during a pair or team planning session. These personal selections should not be disclosed. At the end of the planning session, the pair or team should discuss what skills they observed each other using.

| Communication Skill | Purpose of Skill | What does it sound like? |
|---|---|---|
| I-message | To speak from the first person in order to designate ownership of feeling, opinion, and rationale for thinking. | *I am impressed by how you were able to analyze the exit slips, formulate skill groups, and differentiate the lesson to more effectively meet the needs of each learner.*<br><br>*I am frustrated that you are not contributing to the group planning meeting when you have so many good ideas to share.* |
| Paraphrase | To restate something that is written or spoken by someone else in order to clarify or check accuracy of the message. | *To clarify, each teacher will design a station activity that will address a selected multiple intelligence (Gardner). We will have the stations designed and ready to share with the team by November 15.* |
| Summarize | To outline the main ideas of a conversation or discussion. | *To summarize our pair meeting today, we have agreed to use the parallel teaching strategy to teach point of view with our selected leveled texts.* |
| Open-ended questions | To encourage a substantial, lengthier response that incorporates a person's knowledge and feelings. | *How did you think our co-taught lesson went today? Can you suggest any ways that we can improve on it when we teach together tomorrow? What do you think that our formative assessments suggest that may alter our teaching plans?* |
| Closed question | To seek a short single word answer like a "yes" or "no" response. | *Can we schedule a team meeting next Wednesday at 3:00pm? Did you speak to the principal about taking a grade level field trip next month?*<br><br>*Do you have the student roster lists for the different station skill-reinforcement activities?* |
| Seed Planting | To raise the possibility of revisiting a topic at a later date. | *I need to attend a professional development meeting today after school but I really want you to think about which research topics we can recommend for our students as we continue to study the ecosystems. We can talk more about this tomorrow morning at our collaborative planning meeting.* |
| Response to Observed Affect | To respond to or question a perception about another person's feelings. | *I noticed that you appeared angered by the parental response that you received regarding John's incomplete assignment. What kind of parent feedback did you receive?* |
| Visualization | To communicate by using a visual, simile, or metaphor. | *Our grade level planning is much like a quartet. We each have our own individual melody but when we put our parts together, a beautiful song emerges!* |
| Sandwich Technique | To position a sensitive issue or statement between two other positive or factual statements. | *Your science lesson today had many opportunities for student engagement.*<br><br>**I observed, however, your frustration during the lesson that students were not always on task with the planned activities.**<br><br>*Why don't you take some time to reflect on the lesson tonight and we will discuss it tomorrow at our pair meeting.* |

**Figure 1.4** Use of communication skills in collaborative teaching contexts. Adapted from Conderman, Bresnahan, & Pedersen (2008).

**Evidence:** Each member of the pair or team will select several of the communication skills to use during a collaborative planning session or after teaching a co-taught lesson. At the end of the meeting or co-taught lesson reflection, the other member(s) will identify which communication skills they observed and provide the rationale for each skill. The pair or team will evaluate the group's communication skills and identify any skills that were not present in order to strengthen productive communication.

## Follow-Up, Monitoring, and Goal Setting

Complete the follow-up questions for the selected reflective professional growth activity.

### Idea 1: What Are Your Teacher Stats? (Professional) Share Your Story (Individual)

- Did you find any similarities in experience among the team?
- What differences are there among the Teacher Stat lists that speak to the uniqueness of each person on the pair or team?
- Did you share any commonalities in your voiced belief statements about teaching and learning?
- How has this activity helped you to form a deeper relationship with your teaching partner as you plan, teach, and assess together in co-teaching?

### Idea 2: Create Your Cornerstone: What Is Your Vision Sentence? What Is Your Hashtag?

- How does the pair or team's shared vision sentence and hashtag represent something that is important to each member?
- What strengths, skills, and talents has each member identified to be used during collaborative teaching?
- How will the pair or team's instructional practice impact student growth and professional development?
- Are there any teacher skills that need to be strengthened in order for the pair or team to realize its shared vision and goals?

### Idea 3: Collaboration Self-Assessment Survey

- What did you learn about your own collaboration skills and developmental levels?
- What did you learn about each other's use of collaboration skills and interpersonal/intrapersonal skills?
- What experiences can you plan to help you to improve the collaboration skills measured on this instrument?
- How is each collaboration skill on this tool important to the collaborative teaching process?

## Idea 4: NEED–HEED–SUCCEED!: Goal Setting Planner

- How did you feel when you shared your *Needs* and *Heeds* with your co-teaching partner or team?
- What communication or collaboration skills did you use as a pair or team to set some shared goals for the *Succeeds* portion of the goal setting planner?
- Were you aware of the content expressed by individual teachers in the *Needs* and *Heeds* portions before the content was shared with the pair or the team?
- How can you continue to use this goal setting tool to strengthen communication in the co-teaching pair or team?

## Idea 5: Practice Your Communication Skills

- What communication skills were you able to use during the group planning session?
- Which was the most difficult communication skill to use with your co-teacher or team?
- What non-verbals are important to use that compliment the use of the voiced communication skills?
- Which communication skills are most important to implement in your pair or team in order to improve communication and collaborate more effectively?

# Resources

## Articles

### A Theoretical Framework of Teacher Collaboration

Shakenova discusses literature about teacher collaboration in education. The article includes benefits, drawbacks, and recommended factors to improve collaboration.

Shakenova, L., (2017). The theoretical framework of teacher collaboration. *Khazar Journal of Humanities and Social Sciences, 20*(2), 34–48.

## Journals

### Communication Skills for Leaders

This issue of *Educational Leadership* focuses entirely on communication skills. Many of the articles can be used to teach pairs or teams about strategies for effective communication. Members of ASCD can read the archived issue at www.ascd.org. The journal can also be purchased at http://www.ascd.org/publications/educational-leadership/apr15/vol72/num07/toc.aspx

ASCD (2015, April). Communication skills for leaders. *Educational Leadership, 72*(7).

### Co-Teaching: Making It Work

This issue of *Educational Leadership* includes thirteen feature articles on co-teaching. Numerous articles provide insights for the school administrator or supervisor on facilitating collaborative instructional practice in schools. Members of ASCD can read the archived issue at www.ascd.org. The journal can also be purchased at http://www.ascd.org/publications/educational-leadership/dec15/vol73/num04/toc.aspx

ASCD (2015, December). Co-teaching: Making it work. *Educational Leadership, 73*(4).

## Books

### Mentoring Teacher Candidates Through Co-Teaching: Collaboration That Makes a Difference

Both the *Collaboration Self-Assessment Tool (CSAT) and Resources for Co-Teaching* are found in this book. Members of pairs and teams can use the *CSAT* to understand each person's interpersonal and intrapersonal collaboration skill development (see Idea 3 in this module for directions). The *Collaboration Self-Assessment Tool* is located on pages 114–117 of this book. The book also includes many resource activities to use with pairs or teams as they co-teach. Original research for this book was funded by the U.S. Department of Education, Teacher Quality Enhancement Partnership Grant. St. Cloud, MN.

Heck, T., & Bacharach, N. (2010). *Mentoring teacher candidates through co-teaching: Collaboration that makes a difference.* St. Cloud, MN: St. Cloud State University.
The Academy for Co-Teaching and Collaboration. (2013). *Collaboration self-assessment tool* (CSAT). St. Cloud State University, MN.

### Leading the Co-Teaching Dance: Leadership Strategies to Enhance Team Outcomes

This book is an excellent resource for teachers and administrators for establishing and maintaining successful co-teaching relationships. The authors provide helpful strategies on how to promote a collaborative school climate including scheduling strategies to support this goal.

Murawski, W. W., & Dieker, L. A. (2013). *Leading the co-teaching dance: Leadership strategies to enhance team outcomes.* Alexandria, VA: Council for Exceptional Children.

### The Co-Teaching Book of Lists

This book offers many practical suggestions for teachers engaged in co-teaching. It is especially helpful for teachers who are in the Norming stage of their co-teaching relationship. Topics include determining roles and responsibilities, setting up the classroom, establishing classroom climate, selecting effective accommodations and modifications for students, setting goals, negotiating conflicts, and solving scheduling issues.

Perez, K. (2012). *The co-teaching book of lists.* San Francisco, CA: Jossey-Bass.

## Web Resources

### Affinity Mapping

This group-processing tool will help pairs or teams to brainstorm thoughts and ideas, categorize them, and reach group consensus regarding teaching expectations and goals.

Drumm, J. (2015, May 26). *Affinity mapping.* Retrieved from https://youtu.be/UynxDyr0lAo (1:28)

### Center for Teaching and Learning (CTL)

The Center for Teaching and Learning is part of the Michael D. Eisner College of Education at California State University Northridge (CSUN). The website offers a designated page to co-teaching research highlighting Dr. Wendy Murawski's work in this area.

California State University, Northridge (n.d.). *Co-teaching*. Retrieved from https://www.csun.edu/center-teaching-learning/co-teaching

### *Co-Teaching Core Competency Framework*

This framework will provide the supervisor or administrator with a tool to evaluate twenty-two core competencies of co-teaching as distributed among four different domains 1) the learner and learning, 2) the task at hand, 3) instructional practice, and 4) professional responsibility. The competencies under domain 4 describe communication, collaboration, problem-solving, and professional practices that apply to Module 1: Knowing Yourself and Your Colleague. The *Co-Teaching Core Competency Framework* can be downloaded from the 2teachllc.com website.

Murawski, E., & Lochner, W. (2014). *Co-teaching core competency framework*. Retrieved from https://2teachllc.com/

### Tuckman's Model of Team Formation

This website provides a summary of Tuckman's developmental stages for team formation including a flow-chart with indicators under each stage.

Wageningen University and Research. (2012). *Tuckman (forming, norming, storming, performing, adjourning)*. Retrieved from http://www.mspguide.org/tool/tuckman-forming-norming-storming-performing

### Tools to Support Collaborative Team Structures

This web-based resource or toolkit provides helpful information to collaborative teams as they determine roles, goals, and analyze student performance data. The toolkit includes four different sections with team activities 1) introduction, 2) self-assessment, 3) foundational level for supporting collaborative teams, and 4) advanced level for supporting collaborative teams.

State of New Jersey, Department of Education. (2015). *Collaborative teams toolkit: Tools to support collaborative team structures and evidence-based conversations in schools*. Retrieved from http://www.state.nj.us/education/AchieveNJ/teams/Toolkit.pdf

### The Academy for Co-Teaching and Collaboration

This academy is part of St. Cloud State University in St. Cloud, MN. It is co-directed by Drs. Heck and Bacharach. The website includes information on the National Co-Teaching Conference and other resources to assist teachers and administrators as they implement co-teaching practices.

St. Cloud State University. (2018). *The academy for co-teaching and collaboration*. Retrieved from https://www.stcloudstate.edu/soe/coteaching/

**16** ▪ *Supervision Modules to Support Educators in Collaborative Teaching*

**What's My Sentence? Project**

This activity is taken from Daniel Pink's book *Drive* (2009). Pink shares examples to help others determine their individual purpose and personal goals. He also presents one sentence vision examples from children and adults from around the world. Video clips describing the *What's My Sentence? Project* can be used to help pairs or teams determine individual purpose or shared goals. This activity is used in Idea 2 of Module 1: Knowing Yourself and Your Colleague.

Penguin Books, USA (2010, January 6). *Drive, Daniel Pink*. Retrieved from www.youtube.com/watch?v=AyRu7k70Jhc (2:02)

Pink, D. (2011, January 1). *What's your sentence?* Retrieved from https://www.youtube.com/watch?v=xjBmnfI4Tn4 (2:10)

## Key Terms and Definitions

**Adjourning:** This is the fifth stage of team formation (Tuckman) where the pair or team reaches the end of their work together. This will typically occur at the end of the semester or school year. The pair or team reflects on their successes together, recognizes any team members who will be leaving, and plans for welcoming new team members in the future.

**Collaboration:** Collaboration focuses on the process of working together (co-laboring) toward a shared goal and outcome. It requires active participation of all members of a pair or team.

**Cooperation:** Cooperation refers to the process one uses to work together and participate toward completing a task or a shared goal. When cooperating, groups work together to achieve an objective rather than working individually to compete.

**Communication:** Communication is the process used to exchange information through verbal, non-verbal, or written means.

**Forming:** The first stage of Tuckman's team formation model where the pair or team gets to know and learn about each other.

**Norming:** The third stage of Tuckman's team formation model where the pair or team reaches consensus about routines, procedures, expectations, assessment practices, and general instructional practice in a co-taught or team context.

**Open-ended questions:** Responses to these types of questions require more thinking and multiple phrases or sentences to answer. Open-ended questions demand more than a "yes" or "no", or one word response. (Example: Instead of asking "Does the learning plan incorporate a cooperative activity?" which requires a "yes" or "no" response, ask "How will the learners demonstrate their understanding during the Pair-Share activity?").

**Performing:** The fourth stage of Tuckman's team formation model where the pair or team works successfully as one unit. The pair or team successfully implements and sustains shared goals to complete projects and tasks. This stage often overlaps with the Norming stage if new shared decision-making and consensus-reaching need to occur.

**Storming:** The second stage of Tuckman's team formation model where the pair or team shares difficult truths, negotiates conflict, and challenges members with differing views. In this stage the pair or team works to resolve any conflicts and/or tensions.

**Teacher stats:** Brief biographical notes written by an educator to inform others (e.g., colleagues, parents) about personal interests, schooling, and experiences in teaching.

# Appendix A

## *What Would You Do? Questions With Suggested Responses*

1. What would you do if your co-teacher's expectations are very different from yours regarding classroom management, grading, or any other instructional topic?
   **Suggested Response 1:** It takes much time, effort, and dialogue to know and understand the instructional expectations of your pair or team members. Prior to teaching together, the pair or team should express their individual thoughts regarding instructional expectations. They should share these thoughts candidly with each other and then work to reach consensus regarding shared expectations (i.e., classroom management, grading procedures, class routines). Working through this process helps the pair or team to set norms for their work together. Remember that keeping silent so as not to offend will only hinder the collaboration process.
   
   Make a point to discuss expectations early on in the collaborative relationship in order to negotiate and work toward a shared understanding. This process occurs during the *Forming* stage in the relationship. If there is disagreement and it is difficult to reach consensus or agreement, then the team or pair enters the *Storming* stage of group development. When consensus is reached, the pair or team transitions to the *Norming* stage. If a member of the pair or team senses a difference in individual expectations that can threaten effective collaboration, then the concern(s) should be voiced immediately during a planning meeting when the pair or team reflects on their practice together. It is critical that every team member voices their thoughts. Every pair or team should recognize parity in voice.

2. What would you do if one of the pair or team members is reticent to share any personal information and appears disinterested in getting to know others on the pair or team on a personal level?
   **Suggested Response 2:** For the most part, teachers enjoy sharing about their lives with others in the school. However, if you find it difficult to connect personally with a pair or team member, look for things that you have in common. Exploring topics like family, interests, and schooling usually help surface areas of commonality. Sharing things about yourself sometimes helps the other person to reciprocate. Ask specific (but not intrusive) questions in a way that shows genuine interest. It is also helpful to get to know someone in a context other than school. Invite the reticent team member out to lunch or coffee. Continue to reach out to the person and show interest in getting to know about them at a deeper personal level.

3. What would you do if the school does not provide adequate time for you to talk and plan with your pair or team during the school day?
   **Suggested Response 3:** The lack of time to plan threatens the success of any collaborative pair or team. If you believe that the cornerstone of collaboration is trust and that the development of trust requires consistent communication and nurturing of relationships, then the pair or team must have protected time to develop these important elements throughout the week. Meet with the school administrator or supervisor and explain the frustration that you are having with not having adequate time to develop important collaboration elements in your pair or team. Possible solutions may be the use of a floating internal or scheduled substitute to provide additional times for the pair or team to collaborate. It is important that the pair or team not rely solely on email or text to communicate with each other. Instead, be sure that each collaborator's face, not only text, appears. Pairs or teams may want to explore available video call applications (e.g., Skype, FaceTime, Google Hangouts, OoVoo, Jitsi or Tox) to meet this goal.

# Appendix B*

## Instructions for Administration of The Collaboration Self-Assessment Tool (CSAT)

It is often assumed that people know how to collaborate. However, collaboration skills are rarely identified, let alone taught. When collaborative efforts become strained or are successful, it is important to evaluate our own role in the process.

- There is a difference between cooperation and collaboration. Collaboration is a philosophy of interactions with the focus on the process of working together; cooperation stresses the product of such work (Myers, 1991).
- This is a self-assessment tool. If you are not honest with yourself, it will not help you. The benefit you get is directly related to how honest you are when rating yourself (You do not have to share your scores).
- Think of a specific collaborative relationship or team you are involved with and have the understanding that your scores may differ in other settings.
- For each category there are 4 descriptors: read them thoughtfully and honestly identify your score. If you are not sure what is meant by a certain word or specific terminology, define it in the way that makes most sense to you.
- Your rating should reflect where you are today, not where you want to be or where you would like others to think you are. There are no right and wrong answers.
- Use the explanation box at the end of each category to jot down the thoughts you might have about your rating in that category
- When you have completed each item, total your score.
- The beauty of a self-assessment tool is that we can identify those areas in which we can improve in an effort to become better collaborators.

You may begin... (Approximately 10 minutes) When finished, consider the following:

- What have you learned about yourself by completing this rubric?
- When collaboration is ineffective, the following issues are often voiced to justify the situation:
    1. Personal style
    2. Size of the group
    3. Designated role in the group (facilitator, recorder, etc.)
    4. Group history

We challenge you to ask yourself: What is at the heart of these issues? Could citing these variables possibly be a smoke screen to hide the fact that you are not using skills needed for successful collaboration?

## Interpersonal Versus Intrapersonal Skills

Consider the gray and white scoring boxes. Interpersonal skills include contribution, team support, problem solving, team dynamics, and interactions with others (gray boxes).

---

* Copyright 2017, TWH Consulting and *The Academy for Co-Teaching and Collaboration* at St. Cloud State University. Original research funded by a U.S. Department of Education, Teacher Quality Enhancement Partnership Grant.

## Collaboration Self-Assessment Survey

| Category | 1 | 2 | 3 | 4 | Explanation | Score |
|---|---|---|---|---|---|---|
| **Contribution** | I tend not to share ideas, information or resources. | I share ideas, information and resources upon request. | I usually share ideas, information, and resources. | I freely share ideas, information, and resources. | | |
| **Motivation/ Participation** | I tend not to participate or remain engaged when a project moves away from my own immediate interests. | I sometimes make an effort to participate and remain engaged when a project moves away from my own immediate interests. | I often make an effort to participate and remain engaged even when a project moves away from my own immediate interests. | I can be relied on to participate and remain engaged even when a project moves away from my own immediate interests. | | |
| **Quality of Work** | My work reflects very little effort and often needs to be checked and/or redone by others to ensure quality. | My work reflects some effort but occasionally needs to be checked and/or redone by others to ensure quality. | My work reflects a strong effort. I self-monitor to improve the quality of my work. | My work reflects my best efforts. I continuously make small changes to improve the quality of my work. | | |
| **Time Management** | I rarely get things done by the deadline and others often have to adjust deadlines or work responsibilities. | I tend to procrastinate, meaning others may have to adjust deadlines or work responsibilities. | I usually use time well to ensure that things are done so others do not have to adjust deadlines or work responsibilities. | I routinely use time well to ensure things are done on time. | | |
| **Team Support** | I am often critical of the team or the work of fellow group members when I am in other settings. | Occasionally I am critical of the team or the work of fellow group members when I am in other settings. | I usually represent the team and the work of fellow group members in a positive manner when I am in other settings. | I represent the team and the work of fellow group members in a positive manner when I am in other settings. | | |
| **Preparedness** | I forget or lose materials needed to work. | I make an effort to bring or find materials needed to work, but often misplace things. | I usually bring needed materials and come ready to work. | I consistently bring needed materials and come ready to work. | | |

*(continued)*

## Collaboration Self-Assessment Survey (continued)

| Category | 1 | 2 | 3 | 4 | Explanation | Score |
|---|---|---|---|---|---|---|
| **Problem Solving** | I usually do not participate in group problem solving with an open mind. I either tend not to share my thoughts and ideas or I inhibit the contributions of others. | I make an effort to participate in group problem solving with an open mind. I generally share my thoughts and ideas, but I sometimes inhibit the contributions of others. | I usually participate in group problem solving with an open mind, sharing thoughts and ideas without inhibiting the contributions of others. | I consistently participate in group problem solving with an open mind, sharing thoughts and ideas without inhibiting the contributions of others. | | |
| **Team Dynamics** | I do not know how to gauge my own impact on the group, and am generally unaware of team dynamics. | I occasionally know how to gauge my own impact on the group and am somewhat aware of team dynamics. | I often know how to gauge my own impact on the group and am generally aware of team dynamics. | I consistently know how to gauge my own impact on the group and am routinely aware of team dynamics. | | |
| **Interactions with Others** | I rarely listen to, respect, acknowledge, or support the efforts of others. I allow conflict or personal differences to interfere with communication. | I sometimes listen to, respect, acknowledge and support the efforts of others, but at times allow conflict or personal differences to interfere with communication. | I usually listen to, respect, acknowledge, and support the efforts of others. I occasionally allow conflict or personal differences to interfere with communication. | I consistently listen to, respect, acknowledge, and support the efforts of others. | | |
| **Role Flexibility** | I like to either lead or follow but am uncomfortable when functioning outside my perceived role. | I am uncomfortable with role flexibility, but attempt to move outside my perceived role. | I can assume both roles (leader and follower) but am more comfortable in one role than the other. | I can easily move between leader and follower, assuming either role as needed to accomplish the task. | | |
| **Reflection** | I rarely engage in self-reflection after collaborative activities but tend to focus on the behavior of others. | Self-reflection occurs after collaborative activities when prompted or reminded by others. | Self-reflection usually occurs after collaborative activities, but most often when things don't go well. | I consistently use self-reflection after collaborative activities. | | |

**Total Score** (Maximum score: 44 points):

Intrapersonal skills include motivation/participation, quality of work, time management, preparedness, role flexibility, and reflection (white boxes).

Intrapersonal skills involve those centered on the internal aspects of a person, such as self-confidence, preparedness, and reflection. In situations where an individual has excellent interpersonal skills, but is lacking in necessary intrapersonal skills, there are bound to be collaborative difficulties. Likewise, if the balance is tipped in favor of intrapersonal skills, collaboration will also be strained. How balanced are you?

## *Guide to Scoring:*

10–25: Collaboration skills are emerging
26–34: Collaboration skills are developing
35–44: Collaboration skills are established

## *Personal Reflection:*

What have you learned about yourself by completing this rubric?

What skill areas do you want to target for personal improvement?

What one thing could you do tomorrow to begin your skill enhancement?

## *Interpersonal Versus Intrapersonal skills:*

Shaded boxes represent–interpersonal skills
Clear score boxes represent–intrapersonal skills.
Interpersonal score _____
Intrapersonal score _____

*Note:* The scores will most likely be different as there are unequal numbers of boxes. Copyright 2017, TWH Consulting and The Academy for Co-Teaching and Collaboration at St. Cloud State University. Original research funded by a U.S. Department of Education, Teacher Quality Enhancement Partnership Grant.

# Appendix C

## *NEED–HEED–SUCCEED! Tools*

### Debbie F. Cosgrove (2017)

To effectively communicate with your pair or team, it is important for each team member to openly share individual needs and concerns so that the pair/team can successfully teach together.

First, *individually* fill out the "Need" and "Heed" sections of the flow chart. Then take time to discuss each section together. Finally, in the "Succeed" section, *work together* to craft specific steps to address the voiced needs and concerns.

## *NEED–HEED–SUCCEED! Flow Chart*

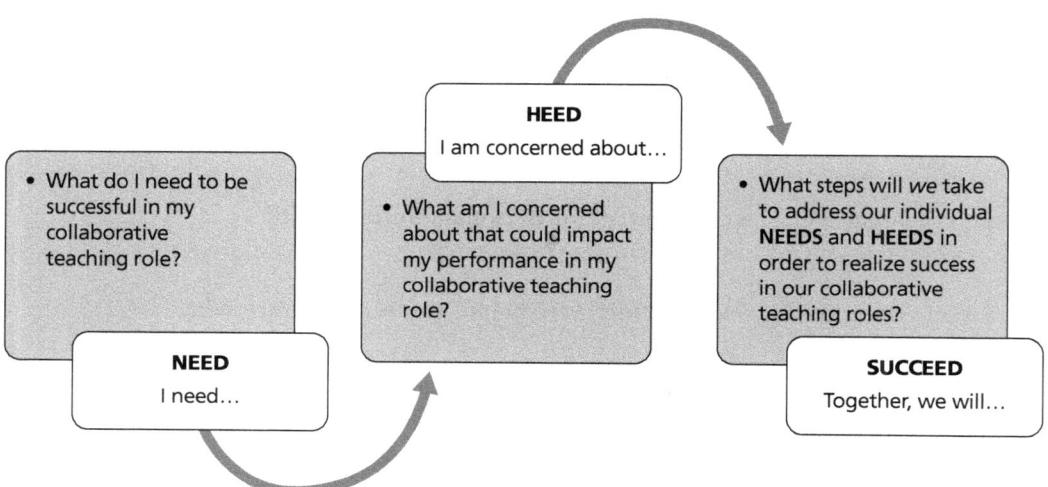

## *Template for NEED–HEED–SUCCEED! Exercise*

| **NEED**<br>I need... | **HEED**<br>I am concerned about... | **SUCCEED**<br>Together, we will... |
|---|---|---|
|  |  |  |

# Appendix D

## *Use of Communication Skills in Collaborative Teaching Contexts*

| Communication Skill | Purpose of Skill | What does it sound like? |
|---|---|---|
| **I-message** | To speak from the first person in order to designate ownership of feeling, opinion, and rationale for thinking. | |
| **Paraphrase** | To restate something that is written or spoken by someone else in order to clarify or check accuracy of the message. | |
| **Summarize** | To outline the main ideas of a conversation or discussion. | |
| **Open-ended questions** | To encourage a substantial, lengthier response that incorporates a person's knowledge and feelings. | |
| **Closed question** | To seek a short single word answer like a "yes" or "no" response. | |
| **Seed Planting** | To raise the possibility of revisiting a topic at a later date. | |
| **Response to Observed Affect** | To respond to or question a perception about another person's feelings. | |
| **Visualization** | To communicate by using a visual, simile, or metaphor. | |
| **Sandwich Technique** | To position a sensitive issue or statement between two other positive or factual statements. | |

Source: Adapted from Conderman, Bresnahan, & Pedersen (2008).

# References

Austin, V. L. (2001). Teachers' beliefs about co-teaching. *Remedial and Special Education, 22*, 245–255.
Bacharach, N., Heck, T., & Dahlberg, K. (2008). What makes co-teaching work? Identifying the essential elements. *The College Teaching Methods and Styles and Journal, 4*, 43–48.
Combs, J. P., Edmonson, S. L., & Harris, S. (2013). *The trust factor: Strategies for school leaders.* New York, NY: Routledge.
Combs, J., Harris, S., & Edmonson, S. (2015). Four essential practices for building trust. *Educational Leadership, 72*(7), 18–22.
Conderman, G. (2010). Methods for addressing conflict in co-taught classrooms. *Intervention in School and Clinic, 46*, 221–229.
Conderman, G., Bresnahan, V., & Pedersen, T. (2008). *Purposeful co-teaching: Real cases and effective strategies.* Thousand Oak, CA: Corwin Press.
Conderman, G., & Johnston-Rodriguez, S., (2012). Beginning teachers' views of their collaborative roles. *Preventing School Failure, 53*, 235–244.
Conderman, G., Johnson-Rodriguez, S., & Hartman, P. (2009). Communicating and collaborating in co-taught classrooms. *TEACHING Exceptional Children Plus, 5*(5), 1–17.
Danielson, C. (2015). Framing discussions about teaching. *Educational Leadership, 72*(7), 38–41.
DeBoer, A. (1995). *Working together: The art of consulting and communicating.* Longmont, CO: Sopris Press.
DeBoer, A., & Fister-Mulkey S. (1998). *Working Together: Tools for collaborative teaching:* Longmont, CO: Sopris Press.
Erkens, C., Jakicic, C., Jessie, L., King, D., Kramer, S., Many, T., . . . Twadell, E. (2008). *The Collaborative Teacher: Working together as a professional learning community.* Bloomington, IN: Solution Tree Press.
Friend, M., & Cook, L. (2017). *Interactions: Collaboration skills for school professionals* (8th ed.). London, England: Pearson.
Friend, M., Embury, D., & Clarke, L. (2014). Co-teaching versus apprentice teaching: An analysis of similarities and differences. *Teacher Education and Special Education, 49*(1), 1–9.
Gately, S., & Gately, F. (2001). Understanding co-teaching components. *Teaching Exceptional Children, 33*(4), 40–47.
Heck, T., & Bacharach, N. (2010). *Mentoring teacher candidates through co-teaching: Collaboration that makes a difference.* St. Cloud, MN: Authors.
Kluth, P., & Straut, D. (2003) Do as we say and as we do. *Journal of Teacher Education, 54*(3), 228–240.
Paley, V. G. (1990). *The boy who would be a helicopter.* Cambridge, MA: Harvard University Press.
Ploessl, D., Rock, M., Schoenfeld, N., & Blanks, B. (2010). On the same page: Practical techniques to enhance co-teaching interactions. *Intervention in School and Clinic, 45*, 158–168.
Robinson, T., Cosgrove, D., & Servilio, K. (2015, January). *Determining the impacts of a co-teaching model of student teaching in the K–12 context.* The Clute Institute: 2015 Conference Proceedings of the International Education Conference, Maui, HI.
Schön, D. A. (1983). *The reflective practitioner: How professionals think in action.* New York, NY: Basic Books.
Searle, M., & Swartz, M., (2015). *Teacher teamwork: How do we make it work?* Alexandria, VA: ASCD.
Tuckman, B. W. (1965). Developmental sequence in small groups. *Psychological Bulletin, 63*(6), 384–399.
Tuckman, B. (2001). Developmental sequence in small groups. *Group Facilitation: A Research and Applications Journal, 3*, 71–72.
Villa, R., Thousand, J., & Nevin, A. (2004). *A guide to co-teaching: Practical tips for facilitating student learning.* Thousand Oaks, CA: Corwin.

# MODULE 2

# Effective Communication

**Kathryn L. Lubniewski**
*Monmouth University*

**Kirstin Natale**
*Monmouth University*

*Words are singularly the most powerful force available to humanity. We can choose to use this force constructively with words of encouragement, or destructively using words of despair. Words have energy and power with the ability to help, to heal, to hinder, to hurt, to harm, to humiliate and to humble.*
—Yehuda Berg

## MODULE DESCRIPTION

The way in which one communicates is critical in both personal and professional success. This module will provide support for the supervisor of teachers and teaching teams so that they can facilitate a foundational understanding of communication along with guided questions and resources to support effective communication.

## Theory/Conceptual Framework

Communication is a crucial part of every relationship whether it is professional, personal, or simply informative. At its most mechanical level, communication can be described as a series of inputs and outputs in order to relay a message (Losee, 1999). However, communication requires skills that typically vary from person to person usually based on background and level of experience communicating with others (Friend & Cook, 2016; Newey, 2016). In communication that is positively functioning, all participants are actively engaged, regardless of their level of communication skills (Losee, 1999). Skills that contribute to successful communication include empathy, conciseness, active listening, and the ability to choose the correct channel of communication to relay a message (Sharma & Sharma, 2014). The combination of communication skills among two or more individuals or parties working towards the same goal produce effective communication. According to Sharma and Sharma (2014), "effective communication is an interpersonal process in which verbal symbols (e.g., words, sentences) and nonverbal symbols (e.g., body postures, facial gestures) are shared and understood by people" (p. 3151). When using effective communication, it is important to have a positive attitude about what the message is, while practicing empathy and being in touch with the emotional component of communication. For example, although all messages are not positive in nature, maintaining a positive attitude about communicating the message is crucial.

Communication is a key feature in the process of collaboration and the completion of a shared goal with a partner or team. Research has shown that teams or groups with proven high performances provide and exchange information frequently through various mediums of communication (Butchibabu, Sparano-Huiban, Sonenberg, & Shah, 2016). These high performing teams collaborate on chosen expectations in order to complete tasks rather than blindly asking a fellow collaborator to perform a task. The skills that are required for productive communication include, but are not limited to, listening skills, articulation, ability to be direct, and openness to feedback or criticism. Deeper communication skills could include the ability to intentionally delegate tasks based on expertise within a group or dyad, as well as effectively explaining said task (Fay & Kline, 2012). The formation of communication skills should be constantly reinforced and fine-tuned in order to remain effective. Communication skills that are effective evolve throughout the course of a project based on the changing needs and overall dynamics of the group.

In addition to communication regarding students, lesson plans, and further tasks as a member in a teaching team, it is important for each member to get to know one another in order to build rapport and comfortability within the teaching relationship (Schoonover, n.d.). Communicating likes, dislikes, and interests may appear to be phatic communication, or small talk, however research has proven that there is an important underlying function to this line of communication; it shows the connectedness as people as well as educators (Placencia, 2004). A deep sense of fellowship is established through communicating outside of typical daily expectations. According to Pratt, Imbody, Wolf, and Patterson (2017), a strong relationship between professionals not only benefits communication within that team, but it also positively impacts student learning outcomes because the team is reflecting and communicating about student progress. Building connectedness on various levels and topics can transpire through either informal communication or formal communication. An example of informal communication surrounds topics other than work such as the weather, personal business, or holidays, using shortened wording or slang terms. In contrast, formal communication is work, or project related, and uses proper terms and professional levels of expression.

Researchers have concluded that through personal connectedness, collaborators have the ability to overcome obstacles that they may be faced with in terms of personal or professional disagreements (Fay & Kline, 2012). Despite the importance of informal communication, scholars recommend the use of formal communication in order to minimize the risk of rumors, inconsistencies, and conflicts due to misunderstandings or personal interests (Nwogbaga, Nwankwo, & Onwa, 2015). There are, undoubtedly, significant benefits to using both informal and formal communication techniques (Nwogbaga, Nwankwo, & Onwa, 2015). Both aspects contribute to the flow of information as well as meeting the social needs of collaborators.

Furthermore, the anticipation of what needs to be communicated on a regular basis is important to establish early on (Butchibabu et al., 2016). For example, communicating long and short term goals, student accommodations, who will be teaching which points of the lessons, and the various teaching models that will be used in the relationship should be decided before students are in the classroom (Pratt et al., 2017). Continuing professional development in terms of communication strategies is also necessary when working with each teacher, pair, or team (Lindeman & Magiera, 2014). Research has recommended that teaching teams attend the same professional development meetings in order to acquire a shared vocabulary and understanding of a given aspect of education. Collaboration through professional development can be virtual or in person if available.

Technology advances have had a significant impact on the way educators, administrators, and families communicate today (Sharma & Sharma, 2014; Charles & Dickens, 2012). It is imperative that communication techniques that are implemented through the help of technology are explained in detail. Technological advances have negated several constraints on communication such as time or space to communicate (Yumurtaci, 2017). Research has shown, however, that even though using technology in order to communicate is becoming increasingly more productive and easier, there is a significant value in using technology in conjunction with in-person communication skills to best complete a project (Yumurtaci, 2017). Making oneself available through email, social media, or other technological methods increases the collaboration on various platforms. The previously mentioned communication skills (i.e., active listening, articulation, directness) should also be incorporated in technological communication. An important aspect that is lost through most forms of technological communication, however, is the ability to provide nonverbal cues or acknowledgement. A significant concern surrounding communication via technology, such as email, is understanding the audience receiving the email. Tone can easily be misinterpreted through email and the message can be lost. Overall, technology provides users with the opportunity to increase connectedness within an educational community of all stakeholders.

Additionally, it is imperative to consider the audience, or receiver of information, as well as their ultimate goals (Copa et al., 2011). In education, there are several stakeholders involved in the overall achievement of students. Some stakeholders involved in the educational communication process beyond teachers include families, administrators, paraprofessionals, board members, school counselors, social workers, and other support staff (NASP, 2017). To be efficient when communicating on a large scale to several stakeholders, it is important to be clear as to where information will be presented or displayed, and for whom the message is intended. Furthermore, while communicating to each stakeholder, it is important for the sender, or the individual who is putting forth information, to consider the background and level of investment each respective stakeholder has to the given subject. For example, a parent of a young student is not likely to have the same background and understanding of educational jargon compared to a tenured educator. The act of perspective taking in terms of effective communication calls on the communication skill of empathy in order to best reach all parties involved.

Finally, reflection on how effectively the communication strategies used over the period of a chosen time is recommended (Lindeman & Magiera, 2014). This reflection should be set after a previously chosen amount of time in order to alter communication methods, if necessary, in order to best meet the needs of the students and the teachers. Previous research has noted that the act of communication is a process that is constantly changing (Sharma & Sharma, 2014). Professionals who are actively looking to improve their communication are likely to have success in meeting desired goals within a team setting. Communication skills undoubtedly play a significant role on the success of the learning dynamic. From the initial planning on a large scale to the day-to-day lesson planning, it is certain that effective communication is necessary when taking on the role of an educator.

## Specific Questions to Guide Discussion

1. Do you have a specific time when you communicate with your teaching partner? If so, when does that occur?

2. Can you describe how you typically communicate with your teaching partner? How does your partner typically communicate with you?

3. What do you feel are your strengths in the area of communication?

4. What are some areas for improvement?

5. What are some tips about communication that you would give to a new professional?

## Productive Practice: Tips to Improve Communication Skills

1. *Be aware.* It is necessary to acknowledge the differences in a given situation, and among individuals, while tailoring your style to meet the needs of the relationship. Awareness is intentional. This does not typically come naturally and, as a professional, it is important to self-reflect on awareness skills. Furthermore, communication skills are positively impacted by creating practical expectations of individuals. Should a participant be unrealistic with expectations, the lines of communication could suffer. The use of silence is also key. Taking pauses between statements or questions show the other party involved that you are taking the time to listen and understand what is being communicated.

2. *Be open.* Not only should one be listening, it is also important to answer with a response of active exploration or encouragement. This shows that all who are communicating are invested in accomplishing a singular goal or goals. Openness includes

providing key contact information (e.g., best phone number, e-mail address) to those who will be in regular communication. It is important to share good news with a team as well. Often when things are going well, we neglect to properly address the positivity and focus solely on what needs to be completed or what is going wrong.
3. *Be intentional.* Making a point to communicate in person is important for collaborating in a team environment. By utilizing in-person communications, individuals who are collaborating can utilize their non-verbal communication skills and pick up on others' reactions. Try to communicate in person as much as possible. Clear expectations must be set for effective communication. If one person in the group does not feel completely clear about what the expectations are, asking direct questions for clarification is needed. It is important to respond even if you do not know the answer simply to let the team know you are looking into it.
4. *Be brief and to the point.* Less is sometimes more when collaborating for a common goal. Being brief and direct, without using educational jargon and acronyms can facilitate the communication process. This provides a positive learning environment for teams who have familiarity with different educational language.
5. *Stick to the facts.* If you do not know the answer to something, it is okay to say you don't know and that you'll get back to the person with an answer. This way you are not giving incorrect information or unintentionally ignoring the statement made. On this point, it is important to be sure you are following up if you claim that you will look into something you are unfamiliar with at the time.

## What Would You Do?

Ask your team or pair the following questions. For suggested responses to questions, see Appendix A.

1. What would you do if you and your teaching partner have decided that on Monday mornings you are going to arrive early to school to collaborate on the lesson plans for the week but your teaching partner is showing up late or not showing up at all? When asked about it, she apologizes but nothing changes.

2. What would you do if you have sent home multiple emails and notes to the Jones family about their child, Bethany, a student who you are having difficulty with in the class and the family is not responding to your emails and notes?

3. What would you do if a parent asks your paraprofessional (or other teacher) about the progress of their student, Tim? The paraprofessional shares details with the parent about how Tim is struggling and not achieving well in reading. The parent then approaches you and asks, "What's going on with Tim? I heard that he wasn't progressing in reading and that he's really struggling. Why didn't you tell me?"

## Reflective Professional Growth Activities

Consider these ideas or activities to facilitate and foster teacher growth and reflection. Select one or two ideas to help facilitate this reflection process that will help the teacher, pair, or team to understand how to effectively communicate. Remember that you know the individuals best so be sure to choose an activity that would be the most effective.

### Idea 1: Communication Survey

Utilize a survey method in order to identify ways in which stakeholders like to be communicated with, at what times, and messages that need to be received. According to Natale and Lubniewski (2018), the results of a survey distributed within an educational context with questions surrounding communication preferences and perceptions on communication among all stakeholders could be used for positive change in communication patterns among educators, administrators, and families.

**Evidence:** Create/distribute a communication survey with questions regarding what communication methods are currently being used, if they are perceived as effective, how they could be changed, and any advice moving forward. Analyze the data to see why, and with whom, communication may be lacking. According to the various stakeholders' preferences, a formal communication agreement could be determined.

### Idea 2: Acknowledging and Building on Differences

Compile a short list of three or four differences that you feel may be the primary distinctions between the two of you (e.g., philosophy, most valued relationships, views on most important things in life). First compare your lists to see which items, if any, you agreed on and what were your greatest areas of difference. Then, take turns making speculations about why those differences exist. Begin to clarify the differences and possible reasons for them. The more you discuss the more you will be drawn to reconsider the impressions that you have on each other and why you formed those impressions.

**Evidence:** Write out the impressions that you may have formed about your partner and impressions that your partner may have about you. Respond to how you are going to address these impressions and make changes.

### Idea 3: The Power of Silence

The power of silence or pauses can improve communication greatly. Yet almost everyone needs to practice allowing the silence, and using silence during interactions. Challenge yourself to provide longer pauses during some conversations. So, after someone is speaking, allow an ever so slight pause before you begin speaking. As you do this, reflect on how this impacts your interactions, your pace, and comfort with the conversation.

**Evidence:** Complete a journal entry that includes the date/time of when you focused on improving your communication. Identify what you did during that time and express how these changes impacted your communication.

## Idea 4: Evaluating the Various Forms of Communication

Evaluate the various types of communication within your classroom (e.g., e-mail, assignment notebook, classroom website, *Twitter*).

**Evidence:** Create a chart of all of the types of communication. Be sure to include: Does it include other types of communication than written? Do you need technology to assess this type of communication? How can you improve the communication with other teachers, families, and the community?

# Follow-Up, Monitoring, and Goal Setting

Complete the follow-up questions for the selected reflective professional growth activity.

## Idea 1: Communication Survey
- What types of questions did you ask in your survey?
- What did you learn about your communication? What were some ways that were effective? What are some ways that you are going to change your current ways of communication?
- What are some specific steps that you are going to take to ensure that these changes are made or continued?
- Do you have anything else that you want to share in the area of communication before we move on to the next topic?

## Idea 2: Acknowledging and Building on Differences
- What impressions did you and your partner find out about each other?
- How has this information helped you to communicate more effectively?
- How has your communication changed since the last observation?
- What are some specific steps that you are going to take to ensure that communication improves?
- Do you have anything else that you want to share in the area of communication before we move on to the next topic?

## Idea 3: The Power of Silence
- How did adding in pauses or silence work for you?
- Did you receive a reaction from the person with whom you were communicating?
- How has this impacted your practice?
- What are some specific steps that you are going to take to ensure that this continues?
- Do you have anything else that you want to share in the area of communication before we move on to the next topic?

## Idea 4: Evaluating the Various Forms of Communication
- After you reviewed your classroom communication, what did you find?
- What are some ways that you can improve your communication with teachers? Families? The community? How has this impacted your practice?
- What are some specific steps that you are going to take to ensure that this continues?
- Do you have anything else that you want to share in the area of communication before we move on to the next topic?

## Resources

### *Applications (Apps)*

**Accessible Communication Tool**

AppleTree is a free classroom communication tool that can provide access to information for teachers, families, and students. Typical communication on *AppleTree* is information regarding classroom updates, homework assignments, or classroom events.

Chatter, Inc. (2018). *AppleTree.* Retrieved from https://www.goappletree.com/

**Parent Communication Tool**

Bloomz provides a platform to aid in the communication among teachers, families, and students when appropriate. Class updates, calendars, reminders, and protected two-way communication is typical when using this application.

Bloomz. (2016). *One app for all of your parent communication.* Retrieved from https://www.bloomz.net/

**Scheduling Tool**

Doodle is a scheduling tool that can assist any educator with scheduling events or making appointments with various stakeholders. Doodle can link with several calendars without disclosing events to others that are not pertinent to the respective team.

Doodle. (n.d.). *Get together with Doodle for free: A simple way to decide on dates, places and more.* Retrieved from http://doodle.com/

**Web Conferencing Tool**

Anymeeting is a web conferencing tool to be utilized in circumstances when a teacher's schedule will not accommodate an in-person meeting.

Anymeeting. (2011–2018). *Everything you need to hold engaging and effective webinars.* Retrieved from https://www.anymeeting.com/

### *Graphics*

**Communication Styles in Appropriate Situations**

Based on the situation, find the appropriate communication style in Figure 2.1. The chart has examples for written, verbal, and nonverbal communication.

**Communication Styles in Appropriate Situations**

| Informal | Mode of Communication | Formal |
|---|---|---|
| Text Messages<br>Social Media Posts<br>To-Do Lists | Written Communication | Memo to Supervisor<br>Résumé<br>Individualized Education Plan |
| Video Chatting<br>Club Meeting<br>Socializing at Dinner | Verbal Communication | Job Interview<br>Research Presentation<br>Parent–Teacher Conferences |
| Watching a TV Show<br>High-Fiving a Friend<br>Hugging a Sibling | Nonverbal Communication | Viewing Academic Presentation<br>Shaking Hands with Supervisor<br>Eye Contact During Interview |

**Figure 2.1** Informal Communication versus Formal Communication. Adapted from: https://www.pinterest.com/pin/499618152392959836

Module 2: Effective Communication ■ 33

## *Templates*

### Communication Log

Use this log (Figure 2.2) to collect information on who you talk to, when you talk to them, and what you discussed (see Appendix B for blank template).

**Student Name:** Jasmine Rodriquez
**Parent/Guardian(s):** Carlos Rodriquez
**Preferred Method of Contact:** cell phone
**Best Day/Time:** afternoon
**Cell Phone:** (312) 632-9876   **Home Phone:** (718) 813-1234   **E-mail:** crodriquez@msn.net

| Date | Time | Method & Contact | Objective | Discussion & Action (if applicable) |
|---|---|---|---|---|
| January 16, 2019 | 2:35 p.m. | Carlos Rodriquez's cell phone | Share progress in reading | Achieving at a grade-level above in reading fluency and comprehension. Teacher is going to continue charting progress and review in a month. |
| | | | | |
| | | | | |

**Figure 2.2**   Communication log.

### Communication Program Plan

Use this log (Figure 2.3) for a larger scale program that may involve several stakeholders at once (see Appendix C for blank template).

| Communication Plan ||||||
|---|---|---|---|---|
| Stakeholder or Group of Stakeholders | Objectives (actions desired) | Message Content | Delivery Method | When? (Date & Time) |
| IEP Team | Adjust goals for Teron B. (has met 2 out of 4) | Shared data about goals, added 2 new goals; 1 for math and 1 for transition | IEP meeting in MH 212 | February 26, 2019 12:05 p.m. |
| | | | | |
| | | | | |
| | | | | |

**Figure 2.3**   Communication program plan.

## Videos

### Active Listening

This video is a great model to learn tips on how to be more of an active listener.

MindTools. (2015). *Active listening: Hear what people really are saying.* Retrieved from https://www.mindtools.com/CommSkll/ActiveListening.htm

### Improving Your Listening Skills

In this TED talk, Julian Treasure discusses five ways individuals can improve their listening skills. These listening skills will ultimately improve your communication methods and overall techniques.

TED Talk. (2017) *Julian Treasure: 5 Ways to Listen Better.* Retrieved from https://www.ted.com/talks/julian_treasure_5_ways_to_listen_better?language=en

### Think Fast, Talk Smart: Communication Techniques

Watch this video to learn skills to improve your spontaneous interactions.

Stanford Graduate School of Business. (2014, December 4). *Effective speaking in spontaneous situations.* Retrieved from https://www.youtube.com/watch?v=HAnw168huqA

## Web Resources

### Assessing Communication Skills

Go to page 10 and 11 and use the assessment tools to self-evaluate your communication skills.

Deakin University. (n.d.). *Communication skills.* Retrieved from http://www.deakin.edu.au/__data/assets/pdf_file/0014/21326/communication-skills.pdf

### Common Sense Education: Educational Application Search and Review

The link below provides teachers and teaching teams with a multitude of applications that can be utilized in the classroom and shared with families in order to provide a consistent channel of communication.

Common Sense Education. (n.d.). *Reviews and ratings.* Retrieved from https://www.commonsense.org/education/reviews/all

### Common Sense Education: Family Connection Toolbox

This link provides families with additional resources to effectively communicate with their child about school related topics. This improved communication within the family can ultimately improve communication between families and educators.

Common Sense Education (n.d.). *Connecting Families.* Retrieved from https://www.commonsense.org/education/connecting-families/share

## Key Terms and Definitions

**Active listening:** Active listening is a state of listening in which one is actively trying to secure information from another party. Three steps to active listening include comprehending, retaining, and appropriately responding. Active listening can include verbal and nonverbal communication, as well as general reassuring statements of rephrasing.

**Communication tools:** Communication tools are any device or medium used to transmit information to another person or group. These tools can be digital or in print. Choosing the appropriate communication tool, as well as adapting the tool if needed, is crucial to the success of a project.

**Cooperative teaching:** Cooperative teaching is multiple educators working towards one common goal or classroom task. Common cooperative teaching dyads include a special education teacher with a general education teacher, a paraprofessional and a lead teacher, a social worker and an educator, or an elective educator and a general or special education teacher. Cooperative teaching can be encouraged on a regular basis to meet requirements for an Individualized Education Plan. Cooperative teachers are typically placed together to enhance the learning experience for all learners and can be found throughout all grade levels.

**Effective communication:** Effective communication is a skill in which collaborators share information in direct and clear points. The message being sent out to others should be easily understood by other collaborators.

**Medium:** Medium refers to the method in which information, or a message, is being sent between a sender and receiver during communication. Examples of communication mediums include verbal discussion, written dialogue, or through the use of technology.

**Message:** The message is the sign and/or symbol that is being relayed to the receiver of information during communication. This message can be sent across various mediums depending on the method chosen by the sender and receiver.

**One-way communication:** One-way communication refers to a communication style in which the sender is solely responsible for sending the message while the receiver only receives the message. There is no exchange in message or changing of roles.

**Nonverbal communication:** Nonverbal communication refers to responses that are unspoken such as posture, a head nod, facial expressions, or hand gestures. It is important to acknowledge the various cultural and environmental considerations before presuming appropriate nonverbal communications.

**Rapport:** Rapport is a functional, harmonious relationship in which those involved understand their partner's points, concerns, and emotional state. Ways to build rapport are through verbal and nonverbal communication. Another term for rapport could include a "working alliance."

**Two-way communication:** Two-way communication style is the way in which the sender and receiver of information serve dual purposes in exchanging messages. In two-way communication, the receiver is responsible for providing feedback to the sender to acknowledge that the message was taken appropriately.

# Appendix A

## *What Would You Do? Questions with Suggested Responses*

1. What would you do if you and your teaching partner have decided that on Monday mornings you are going to arrive early to school to collaborate on the lesson plans for the week but your teaching partner is showing up late or not showing up at all? When asked about it, she apologizes but nothing changes.

   **Suggested Response 1:** The teacher should ask the teaching partner if there is a better time to meet. Think of other options to provide the teacher (i.e., meeting over the phone, different day, different time). Be understanding of personal influences that may be impacting the situation that you do not know about and keep an open mind.

2. What would you do if you have sent home multiple emails and notes to the Jones family about their child, Bethany, a student who you are having difficulty with in the class and the family is not responding to your emails and notes?

   **Suggested Response 2:** Use a different form of communication. Call them on the phone. You may not know the situation at home and it could be that the parents cannot read, cannot write, or do not receive the messages. Talking with the family over the phone helps you to understand the situation and determine the best way to communicate with the family moving forward.

3. What would you do if a parent asks your paraprofessional (or other teacher) about the progress of their student, Tim. The paraprofessional shares details with the parent about how Tim is struggling and not achieving well in reading. The parent then approaches you and asks, "What's going on with Tim? I heard that he wasn't progressing in reading and that he's really struggling. Why didn't you tell me?"

   **Suggested Response 3:** First, ask the family to come in so that you can sit down and talk with them about Tim's progress. Ask the parents for a convenient time for them to meet with you. During the meeting, be sure to share work samples and data about Tim's progress. Be very clear with the family about why this information was not shared with them earlier. Invite your teaching partner to this meeting as well, so you can be on the same page. Also, be sure to talk with your paraprofessional about sharing information. Be sure that the paraprofessional(s) understand that they are not allowed by law to share confidential information like student progress with families. Remind them that when questions like this occur that they should be directed to one of the teachers in the classroom. If the teaching partner shared this information with the family, express to the teacher that it would be helpful to know the content shared during the conversation so that the pair can be more prepared for the conference with the family. One way to support communication between the teaching partners is to document conversations on the communication log (see Resources section in this module).

Module 2: Effective Communication ■ 37

# Appendix B
*Blank Template for Communication Log*

| Student Name: | | | | |
|---|---|---|---|---|
| Parent/Guardian(s): | | | | |
| Preferred Method of Contact: | | | | |
| Best Day/Time: | | | | |
| Cell Phone:     Home Phone:     E-mail: | | | | |

| Date | Time | Method & Contact | Objective | Discussion & Action (if applicable) |
|---|---|---|---|---|
|  |  |  |  |  |
|  |  |  |  |  |
|  |  |  |  |  |

# Appendix C
*Blank Template for Communication Program Plan*

| Communication Plan ||||| 
|---|---|---|---|---|
| Stakeholder or Group of Stakeholders | Objectives (actions desired) | Message Content | Delivery Method | When? (Date & Time) |
|  |  |  |  |  |
|  |  |  |  |  |
|  |  |  |  |  |
|  |  |  |  |  |

# References

BrainyQuote. (n.d.). *Yehuda Berg Quotes*. Retrieved from http://www.brainyquote.com/quotes/quotes/y/yehudaberg536651.html

Butchibabu, A., Sparano-Huiban, C., Sonenberg, L., & Shah, J. (2016). Implicit coordination strategies for effective team communication. *Human Factors, 58*(4), 595–610. doi:10.1177/0018720816639712

Charles, K. J., & Dickens, V. (2012). Closing the communication gap: "Web 2.0 tools for enhanced planning and collaboration". *TEACHING Exceptional Children, 45*(2), 24–32.

Copa, N., Nayak, N., Holdren, D., Danforth, W., Wheeler, T., McGrew, C...Taylor, R. (2011, May). *SLDS best practices brief*. Washington, DC: National Center for Education Statistics. Retrieved from https://nces.ed.gov/programs/slds/pdf/best_practices.pdf

Fay, M. J., & Kline, S. L. (2012). The influence of informal communication on organizational identification and commitment in the context of high-intensity telecommuting. *Southern Communication Journal, 77*(1), 61–76. doi:10.1080/1041794x.2011.582921

Friend, M., & Cook, L. (2013). *Interactions: Collaboration skills for school professionals* (7th ed.). Upper Saddle River, NJ: Pearson.

Lindeman, K. W., & Magiera, K. (2014). A co-teaching model: Committed professionals, high expectations, and the inclusive classroom. *Odyssey: New Directions in Deaf Education, 15*, 40–45.

Losee, R. (1999). Communication defined as complementary informative processes. *Journal of Information, Communication and Library Science.* 5(3), 1–15.

Newey, J. (2016, May 19). *Communicate effectively with diverse groups and other stakeholders*. Retrieved from www.pinterest.com/pin/499618152392959836.

NASP. (2017). National Association of School Psychologists. Retrieved from https://www.nasponline.org

Natale, K., & Lubniewski, K. (2018). Use of communication and technology among educational professionals and families. *International Electronic Journal of Elementary Education, 10*(3), 377–384.

Nwogbaga, D. E., Nwankwo, O. U., & Onwa, D. O. (2015). Avoiding school management conflicts and crisis through formal communication. *Journal of Education and Practice, 6*(4), 33–36.

Placencia, M. E. (2004). Rapport-building activities in corner shop interactions. *Journal of Sociolinguistics, 8*(2), 215–245. doi:10.1111/j.1467-9841.2004.00259.x

Pratt, S. M., Imbody, S. M., Wolf, L. D., & Patterson, A. L. (2017). Co-planning in co-teaching: A practical solution. *Intervention in School & Clinic, 52*(4), 243–249.

Schoonover, M. (n.d.). *Communication tips for teachers*. Pattonville School-Community Relations. St. Ann, MO: Pattonville School District. Retrieved from http://www.nspra.org/files/CommTipsforTeachers.pdf

Sharma, S., & Sharma, R. (2014). Effective communication. *Scholarly Research Journal for Interdisciplinary Studies.* 3(17), 3151–3156.

Stanford Graduate School of Business (2014, December 4). Effective speaking in spontaneous situations. Retrieved from https://www.youtube.com/watch?v=HAnw168huqA

Yumurtaci, O. (2017). A re-evaluation of mobile communication technology: A theoretical approach for technology evaluation in contemporary digital learning. *Turkish Online Journal of Distance Education, 18*(1), 213–223.

# MODULE 3

# Culturally Relevant Pedagogy

Ayanna F. Brown
*Elmhurst College*

*I began by saying that one of the paradoxes of education was that precisely at the point when you begin to develop a conscience, you must find yourself at war with society.*
—James Baldwin

## MODULE DESCRIPTION

Culturally Relevant Pedagogy (CRP) is described as a "pedagogy of opposition," (Ladson-Billings, 1995, 2017) where teachers engage in deliberate building of community with students and their families, contextualized by a sense of knowing and believing. Culturally Relevant Pedagogy works to unveil and disrupt the "biases and stereotyping about race, ethnicity, and social class that affect everyone, even the most well intentioned, and unless teachers and administrators make a concerted effort to face and change these biases, they may unintentionally act on them" (Nieto, 2013, p. 12). The module operationalizes CRP to assist educators in reflective practices as well as a planning that situates CRP as a set of beliefs about the role of learning and teaching practices as a transformative educational endeavor.

## Theory/Conceptual Framework

Over the past twenty-five years, scholarship on Culturally Responsive Pedagogy (CRP) has served to spark new questions in teacher education and teacher practice about the nature of pedagogy, foremost, and primarily how might teacher practices change learning experiences for children of color and African American children, specifically. Since the 1990s, CRP continues to shape and challenge discussions of teaching and learning including school learning environments, planning, and assessment (Harding-DeKam, 2014; Aguirre & Zavala, 2013). However, the application of CRP has not always included all of its components (Ladson-Billings, 2017; Gay, 2013; Sleeter, 2012) and in some cases, erasure of the sociocultural and sociopolitical dimensionality of what it means to respond to the hegemony of education for children of color. There are discourses related to CRP that are a part of the community of language related to centering the identities, needs, and power of students who have been systematically failed by educational institutions. These discourses include terms like cultural competence, culturally responsiveness, culturally congruent, and recently, culturally sustaining pedagogies (hereafter CSP), which comprehensively challenge us to think about how we situate culture in schools as understanding how students live and think.

Culturally Responsive Pedagogy is as much a philosophy of teaching as it is a set of methodological instructional approaches. However, the methodologies are dependent upon core beliefs. As a philosophy of teaching, the beliefs about student learning are contextualized in understanding race, equity and privilege, and how deficiency paradigms have framed the conversation about learning, specifically when discussing the educational needs of Black and Brown children. For example, Kumar and Hamer (2012) posit, "Many White teachers experience some ambivalence toward minority and immigrant students and doubt their efficacy in teaching students whose cultural backgrounds differ from their own" (p. 162). A CRP philosophy of teaching uses liberatory pedagogy as a discussion of educational equity. As a methodological approach, CRP teachers are able to plan and think about students' identities and needs as fundamental components to intellectually rigorous and valuable learning that goes beyond standardized test scores, which are consequential to a CRP philosophy. However, teacher education programs, schools, supervisors, and administrators must support and model these CRP. For example, coursework and field experiences must be coupled with the expectation that students reflect on their practices and then build improved learning opportunities that align with the principle tenets of CRP. Not merely reflecting on lesson plans, but questioning how pedagogy contributes to a way of thinking about learning. In so doing, teachers might reverse the frequently experienced feelings of being unprepared. Lack of preparation to "meet the academic and psychosocial needs" of nonwhite students contribute to teachers' lack of understanding and limited planning in building a pedagogy that contributes to academic success" (Kumar & Hamer, 2012, p. 162). Pedagogically, this also includes critical reflection that is also connected to discussions of race and community, not assuming that shared racial identity equates shared culture (Brown, Bloome, Morris, Power-Carter, & Willis, 2017; Brown 2010).

As a counter-narrative, a key aspect of critical race theory (CRT), challenges the notion that low achievement of African American children is a result of a "culture of poverty" and or the lack of resources (assuming economic and cultural) and a familial and community "value" for education within the African American community (Vavrus, 2015). These phrasings used to build a typological framing for Black communities, while subtle and oftentimes coded, reflect historical and long-held racial beliefs about the Black community (Morris, 2015). While CRP has been impactful in assisting teachers to think about students' culture as active-living practices that guide the ways in which they see the world, CRP also continues to promote a deconstruction of racial ideologies that have historically driven the learning experiences of students of color. Howard (2003) writes, "teacher educators must be able to help pre-service teachers critically analyze important issues such as race, ethnicity, and culture, and recognize how these important concepts shape the learning experiences for many students (p. 195)." Can all teachers be culturally responsive? Indeed, developing culturally responsive practices is a process that is guided by a mindset; however, fundamental to culturally responsive practices is the teacher's willingness to embrace personal identities and ideologies in relationship to the lives of the students and the practices that build academic success with students and their communities. I describe four critical components of CRP and brief academic notes that have contributed to its development in the field of education.

## *Critical Component 1: Academic Success and Achievement*

All students must experience academic success and achievement. While this idea may seem obvious, culturally responsive teachers develop practices and experiences for students where their achievement is the point. As such, CRP is not a set of activities, an event, game, gimmick or a "day," where student empowerment takes on a cultural, ethnic, or linguistic lens. Academic success is guided by students being able to contribute to the learning and construct knowledge during the learning process in active and meaningful ways. Ladson-Billings (2017) describes achievement as "intellectual growth," where students' opportunities to develop reasoning and problem solving enable them to be more complex thinkers, which is different from test scores and short-term assessments. Academic achievement is located in students' ability to see the results of the successes that transfer from one subject to another and into their own living experiences, where their knowledge is identified as valuable and a contributing factor for academic achievement. Kim and Slapac (2015) suggest "teachers create spaces where students are allowed and encouraged to draw on multiple funds of knowledge to make meaning, and, therefore, the transformative pedagogy is achieved in the context of interactive collaborations between teachers and students" (p. 19). For example, encouraging students to question the contexts for how language is used in texts and under what circumstances might help students see language as dynamic and contextually bound. Simultaneously, students can be encouraged to validate their own uses of language and framings for how to understand content material as equally dynamic and appropriate.

## *Critical Component 2: Cultural Competence*

Students must be supported in exploring and knowing their own cultural identities (i.e., racial, ethnic, linguistic, familial, economic) that allow their identities to be perceived and maintained as healthy and good. And yet, cultural competence invites students to learn and explore the lives and perspectives of others as a means of building a larger global community. Unlike the ominous ideologies of "colorblindness," teachers and students actively see their communities and the values that make them important and not cultural artifacts reduced to celebrations, idiomatically bounded as static representations of cultural groups. Paris and Alim (2017) forward the notion of "relevant pedagogies," arguing that culturally sustaining pedagogy (CSP) does not limit culture to linguistic features of "Black talk" or "Latino Speak," that are deterministic, but embodies cultural competencies as "understanding culture as dynamic and fluid, while also allowing for past and present to be seen as merging, a continuum, or distinct, depending on how young people and their communities live race/ethnicity, language, and culture" (p. 8). CSP as a pedagogy of activism, builds in culture as a "necessary good" to accomplish a resistance to dominant narratives that subversively undermine pluralism. Therefore, cultural competencies are an investment in youth culture, academically situated as rich complex work.

Brown (2013) includes cultural competencies as teacher exploration and knowing the teacher's own culture in relationship to society and privilege, through a framework of racial literacy. Moreover, cultural competency can be foreclosed from many teachers, and White teachers in particular because of "the absence of opportunity to develop a racial analytic lens" in schooling and especially during teacher preparation (Milner, 2003; Howard, 2003). Assuming cultural competencies enrich students' learning about themselves and the world, teachers must also engage in a willingness to do the same, not assume their "world view" is the standard and inarguably correct.

### *Critical Component 3: Critical Consciousness*

Paris and Alim's (2017) "critique forward" of CRP embraces Hip Hop language and culture as a key example of "dynamic dexterity" through translanguaging and building transnational communities. CSP can be described as a pedagogy that embraces and fortifies the languages and perspectives of youth as a democratic project, toward a generative effort to truly develop a pluralistic society. Therefore, in effort to unpack critical consciousness and as a reflection of CSP's advancement of CRP, I use #staywoke, as a 21st century nod to digital, youth, and Hip Hop cultures, as it is a call for sociopolitical activism within CRP. What is "woke?" Critical consciousness is an awareness and an awakening of pedagogy that answers the question, "learning for what?" As a pedagogy of activism or opposition, teachers must consider how students are encouraged and equipped to reconceptualize the world and their role in its development. Teacher planning and practice invites learning to accomplish meaningful tasks—learning that takes on "messy" and unpredictable variables so that students can see their intellectual work as relevant to the lives they live and want to live. Critical consciousness considers learning happening within the classroom and outside of it. Examples of this are service learning opportunities and participation in restorative justice practices that lead to student leadership. As a tenet, critical consciousness ignites students to "wake-up" and #staywoke.

Ladson-Billings (2017) describes critical consciousness as "the neglected dimension" of CRP (p. 145). Arguably, in my work with teachers, they discuss not wanting to experience confrontations with parents or wanting to avoid tensions with administrators because of their political views; they don't see teaching as "political," much less activating students' voices that lead to critical consciousness into the curriculum. Asking the question, "Learning for what?" encourages teachers to talk to their students about the concerns in their lives, community, and society so that teachers can build learning experiences that respond to these issues. Moreover, CRP teachers find ways that students' intellectual labor builds leadership skills so they can respond to the same concerns and see meaning in their learning. For example, I think about the schools in Flint, Michigan, and the 2016 water crisis where contaminated water created health risks and forms of loss that disproportionately devastated poor and overwhelming Black and Brown communities. I think about what type of academic work could have occurred in academic content areas like biology, math, social science, and art that may have helped students answer "learn for what?"

## *Critical Component 4: Challenging the Status Quo*

Much like critical consciousness, challenging the status quo operationalizes the question "learning for what?" However, challenging the status quo is action-oriented pedagogy, different from consciousness or asset awareness pedagogical work. Souto-Manning & Martell (2017) argue that teaching critical consciousness includes, "challenging injustices with children" (p. 252). Injustices take many shapes and forms and the opportunity to use content area instruction as "a means to an end" accomplishes what challenging the status quo encourages. McCarty and Lee (2014) and their focus on indigenous Native American communities typifies a critical approach to culturally situated pedagogy as asset pedagogy because to study the fullness of indigenous communities requires decentering and normalizing whiteness and the status quo.

Culturally relevant pedagogy has changed discussions in education and equity conversations in tremendous ways, especially for teachers who recognize that good intentions and great content area preparation do not necessarily equate to "good teaching" (cf. Ladson-Billings, 1995, 2017).

## Specific Questions to Guide Discussion

1. What practices have you developed to get to know your students outside of the classroom learning community?

2. How have you reflected on your own identities (i.e., race, ethnicity, language, gender, and religion) and the belief systems that may align with them?

3. Describe how your pedagogy builds student achievement while adding to their knowledge of their own identities.

4. How do students contribute to your planning and designing of learning events?

5. Describe an activity where students were able to teach you about their ways of seeing the world and the information was integrated into your instruction.

## Productive Practices

1. *Build Perspectives*
   a. Ask yourself whose perspective is being developed in the learning and how might various types of texts and representations develop a more rich representation of ideas?
   b. Seek out texts that reflect the images, languages, and values that build cultural competency and validate students' lives.

      c. Counter the dominant narrative in choosing materials. Evaluate if and how stereotypical images are present and consider how to help your students see those stereotypes- be bold in not simply avoiding the stereotypes but developing critical discourse practices where students learn to talk about them.
2. *Collect Data*
   a. Use ongoing observations of your students to become informed about who they are and what they value. Families should be invited to and should feel as if they can share and add to their children's learning.
   b. Build in interest-inventories to your practices so topics in class connect to concepts to which students can relate.
   c. Experience student or local communities to gather information about community resources and needs.
3. *Get Out of the School*
   a. Revisit the resources and opportunities in the community that allow the students to see the wealth and value in where they live and how these resources add value to their lives.
   b. Create learning activities that include exploration of self and community that require the use of content area knowledge and skill development, but not at the expense of students' cultural competencies.
   c. Build global connections with communities using digital resources. Technology tools permit students to communicate, research, and learn with other communities that can add to their understandings in the world.

## What Would You Do?

Ask your team or pair the following questions. For suggested responses to questions, see Appendix A.

1. You decide to attend a social or cultural event that is held within the community of your students. You take your boyfriend or girlfriend with you. How do you "behave" with your boyfriend or girlfriend during the event or activity? Also, if your students mention to other students, publicly, that they saw you at the event with your significant other, how do you respond?

2. What do you do when your students develop leadership roles in school and take on addressing school policies?

3. How do you encourage families to build and connect with what you are doing in your classroom?

# Reflective Professional Growth Activities

There are three core reflective practices that can serve as benchmarks for CRP/CSP. Each of them begins with a self-assessment. Encourage the teacher, pair or team to complete each self-assessment and share the results (triumphs and challenges) with you and among each other.

## Idea 1: Complete a CRP/CSP Self-Assessment

The Culturally Relevant Pedagogy Self-Assessment Tool (Figure 3.1) can be used as a reflective tool to support teachers who are interested in deepening their pedagogy toward

| CRP Teacher Behaviors | Rate Yourself<br>1—No<br>2—Need help<br>3—Attempting<br>4—Experienced<br>5—Excellent | **Reflection**<br>What do you think you need to move up one level on the rating scale? |
|---|---|---|
| 1. Uses students' cultures to help them create meaning for content and learning. | | |
| 2. Emphasizes social and cultural success. | | |
| 3. Attempts creative approaches to teaching and learning. | | |
| 4. Sees themselves as a part of the communities in which they teach. | | |
| 5. Helps students make connections between their identities and the world. | | |
| 6. Develops scaffolding for students, constantly increasing student skills through more difficult ideas, etc. | | |
| 7. Develops a process where students set short-term and long-term learning goals that students can revisit. | | |
| 8. Encourages students to take a critical view of ideas and express their perspectives. | | |
| 9. Models and creates opportunities for students to read texts taking both a sociocultural and a critical view of ideas, themes, positioning, etc. | | |
| 10. Empowers students to explore their own funds of knowledge in various ways and use those knowledges as forms of evidence for their learning. | | |
| 11. Plans learning experiences for students to use their content knowledge to study local, regional, national, or global issues. | | |
| 12. Communicates to students how their content area learning specifically responds to local, regional, national, or global issues. | | |

**Figure 3.1** Culturally relevant pedagogy teacher self-assessment tool.

CRP. It can also be used to help teachers think about planning for instruction at differing axis points. For example, during the school year, a teacher can revisit their CRP Self-Assessment to determine their own growth or remaining challenges.

Each item listed in the CRP Self-Assessment Tool aligns with the core tenets of CRP. These tenets are operationalized as proposed things teachers can do in their classrooms and through their planning and reflection. These items do not represent an exhaustive list of teacher practices.

**Using the Tool**

I created this tool as a part of ongoing research I've been conducting with teachers on discussions of race and racial literacy (Brown, et al., 2017). For each item, rate yourself 1 through 5. After each rating, reflect on your practice and consider the third column as a place to think about moving forward. Who can you collaborate with to help you advance your CRP practices? Are there forms of professional development, reading, or institutional support with Professional Learning Communities (PLC's) that might help you? Be specific and try to name what you need to move to a higher level.

**Evidence:** Completion of *Culturally Relevant Pedagogy Self-Assessment Tool*

## *Idea 2: Develop Action Steps From the Culturally Relevant Pedagogy Teacher Assessment Tool*

What do you believe you need to do to move a "1" or "2" rating on the *Culturally Relevant Pedagogy Teacher Self-Assessment Tool?* Write down at least two action steps that you can take to move each of the items that were rated at a "1" or "2." In writing down your action steps, determine if your steps require professional development support or if they require you to "take a chance." Professional development support suggests that you need help and there are ideas you are seeking to gather. "Taking a chance" suggests that you have the skills but you need to "will" to move. Consider what it takes to be bold in your practice and how these action steps might add to your professional identity. In "taking a chance," write out your ideas for your step and share them with your supervisor or teacher colleagues. In sharing, choose an audience of professional peers who believe in your CRP/CSP vision. The wrong audience can convince you to remain at a level "1" or "2."

**Evidence:** Completion of written action steps from survey data.

## *Idea 3: Set Personal Goals*

As you consider how you can move the "1" or "2" levels to "3," also push yourself to think about how your practice can move from a "3" to a "4." Set some instructional goals and consider how your instructional practices also encourage developing your students' self-awareness. Create weekly journal writing opportunities where students can write about who they are, their goals for learning, and their expectations from you that can assist them in appreciating and sustaining their identities. Develop direct writing prompts that target specific opportunities for students to share with you how you can best serve them. For example, a prompt might inquire for students to share information about their preferred language to speak at home or preferred style of writing when brainstorming ideas. Another example for a journal prompt might ask students to share what excites them about learning or what experiences have they had in school that frustrate them about learning. Provide guidelines for writing. For example, can students use any discourse they choose? Are these graded or are there free spaces for communication? Can students draft, revise, edit, and publish their favorite entries?

**Evidence:** Completion of instructional goals that can help to further student self-awareness; Completion of student writing prompts to elicit information on how you can best serve your students.

## Follow-Up, Monitoring, and Goal Setting

Choose from the following questions to monitor the progress of the pair or team related to the module activity or idea that you have recommended for them to complete. Each idea stems from an analysis of the self-assessment data. Using the data and understandings gained from the *Culturally Relevant Teacher Self-Assessment Tool,* complete the following before you begin your next observation.

### *Idea 1: Self-Awareness*

The supervisor should ask the following questions and learn how the teacher, pair or team worked to build understanding through awareness of self. Some helpful questions are:

- When you examined the survey results and the data you collected about yourself, was there a question or questions where you self-rated at '1' or '2?' Discuss what these areas are and why you believe these ratings are low?
- Do you believe these ratings can move up to a '3' with support?
- Tell me about the students in your classroom and some of the approaches you have used to learn more about them?
- How have you approached learning more about their families and communities?
- What approaches have you taken to reflect on your own identity (e.g., race, socio-economic status, gender, language, ability) and how those identities interfaced with your own K–12 education?
- How does your knowledge about your experiences relate or not relate to your students?

### *Idea 2: Action Steps for Curriculum and CRP*

- What resources and tools have you sought out that support your students' funds of knowledge? How do you invite your students to connect with content?
- How are students empowered to respond to society or to critique society in their learning?
- What are your ideas for service learning that are connected both to your content area and student empowerment?

### Idea 3: Setting Personal Goals to Move Forward

- How does the *Culturally Relevant Pedagogy Teacher Self-Assessment Tool* help you to think about your ambitions as a CRP teacher?
- How do you see this tool informing you about planning for instruction?
- What information have you gathered about your strengths while using this tool?

## Resources

### Web Resources

**Response to Intervention as a Culturally Responsive Framework**

Culturally responsive RTI frameworks have the potential to help solve the problem of disproportionate representation for diverse students in classes. Teachers are provided access to curriculum and instructional practice that are based on considering the important role of culture in teaching and learning to ensure positive results of special education programs.

Response to Intervention as a Culturally Responsive Framework. (2016). Retrieved from http://www.nccrest.org/professional/culturally_responsive_response_to_intervention.html

**Energizing Your Curriculum**

In *BaFa' BaFa'* participants come to understand the powerful effects that culture plays in every person's life by experiencing it themselves. It may be used to help participants prepare for living and working in another culture or to learn how to work with people

Simulation Training Systems. (2001–2017). *Energizing your curriculum.* Retrieved from https://www.simulationtrainingsystems.com/schools-and-charities/products/bafa-bafa/?gclid=EAIaIQobChMIysGq_Pnk2gIVW7nACh1SigkuEAAYAyAAEgJJZ_D_BwE

**Diversity ToolKit**

NEA offers an overview of cultural competence for educators. They include the skill areas, main issues, and strategies.

National Education Association. (2002–2017). Diversity ToolKit. Retrieved from http://www.nea.org/tools/30402.htm

**Definitions**

Wisconsin has compiled critical definitions in the area of CRP based on their framework for multi-level systems of support. These terms are helpful to understanding CRP in the educational context.

Wisconsin Department of Public Instruction. (n.d.). Equitable multi-level system of supports: Definitions. Retrieved from https://dpi.wi.gov/rti/definitions

## Key Terms and Definitions

**Asset awareness:** Asset awareness is understanding student and family funds of knowledge and how cultural perspectives, ways of thinking, and living contribute as assets to learning.

**Critical consciousness:** Critical consciousness is developing awareness and involvement to understand how power and the status quo serve to maintain dominance in both the social, cultural, economic, and political landscapes of schooling. A critical consciousness helps to build pedagogy that seeks to unveil and create opportunities for students to act and counteract dominance.

**Cultural competence:** Cultural competence is awareness of self as a cultural person while also learning other cultural perspectives and frames of reference.

**Cultural frame of reference:** Cultural frame of reference refers to the ways in which people are informed by their experiences in the world that create a position or stances for how they relate to the world or others.

**Deficiency paradigm:** Deficiency paradigm is a pejorative way of thinking used to rationalize how or why an individual or a group engages as a means to justify what one observes. Framing individuals or groups of people as if conditions are traits, inherent and bounded by a naturalistic process.

**Equity:** Equity is access or opportunities based on the needs of a community or individual, intended to fortify or improve conditions that have prevented success.

**Sociohistorical:** Sociohistorical is an issue related to society and history, where contextualizing history and historical issues supports an understanding of society.

**Sociopolitical:** Sociopolitical is an issue related to society and politics, systems, and the law, where political issues are embedded into societal structures.

**Translanguaging:** Translanguaging is the act performed by bilinguals to access different linguistic features or various modes of what are described as autonomous languages, in order to maximize communicative potential.

# Appendix A

## *What Would You Do? Questions with Suggested Responses*

1. You decide to attend a social or cultural event that is held within the community of your students. You take your boyfriend or girlfriend with you. How do you "behave" with your boyfriend or girlfriend during the event or activity? Also, if your students publicly mention to other students that they saw you at the event with your significant other, how do you respond?

   **Suggested Response 1:** As an educator, you are always functioning in society as a representative of the profession; however, we must actively humanize ourselves as teachers as we should humanize our students. First, in attending the event, be authentic to who you are but also be tasteful in how you comport yourself. This includes your clothing choices, beverage choices, and interactions with people, as they add or subtract value to how you will be perceived. In attending the event, make an effort to seek out your students and their families so you can introduce yourself to them in the context of their space. The goal is to experience the event and them in the context of the event. Introduce your friend to your students and their families in a professional way, which brings integrity to your interaction rather than secrecy or embarrassment. Secondly, if and when your students mention seeing you at the event in subsequent days to follow, honor that. Say "Yes," to being seen and that "it was great to see them there as well." Don't hide from being human but also don't give your students something to gossip about because of your behavior choices.

2. What do you do when your students develop leadership roles in school and take on addressing policies?

   **Suggested Response 2:** Your goal as a teacher is to not take sides between your students and the school. Your goal is to help your students develop critical consciousness and learn to question and seek out ways to empower their communities. As students learn how to do this through your curriculum, teach them how to discern short-term goals from long-term goals. Have them evaluate how their concerns might build coalitions or breakdown leadership and voice. Build a relationship with students to model leadership so that you serve in an advisory role, not an adversarial one.

3. How do you encourage families to build and connect with what you are doing in your classrooms?

   **Suggested Response 3:** Make an effort to contact families so you can learn from them about their students. For example, if your first contact with parents is connected to parent-teacher conferences, then the point of contact was missed. Within the first weeks of school, establish a routine to call your families on the phone so you can ask them to tell you about their students and things you, as the teacher, should know. Create a space where you are studying your students and their families are teaching you about them. Do more asking than telling. These "informed communications" can happen through phone calls, home visits, attending events, etc. Have students create and post flyers about new or upcoming events and post them in your room. You should have a regular schedule for how to connect with families. In turn, when it is time for families to "show up" at school, they are eager because you have shown up for them.

# Appendix B

*Culturally Relevant Pedagogy Teacher Self-Assessment Tool*

| CRP Teacher Behaviors | Rate Yourself<br>1—No<br>2—Need help<br>3—Attempting<br>4—Experienced<br>5—Excellent | Reflection<br>What do you think you need to move up one level on the rating scale? |
|---|---|---|
| 1. Uses students' cultures to help them create meaning for content and learning. | | |
| 2. Emphasizes social and cultural success. | | |
| 3. Attempts creative approaches to teaching and learning. | | |
| 4. Sees themselves as a part of the communities in which they teach. | | |
| 5. Helps students make connections between their identities and the world. | | |
| 6. Develops scaffolding for students, constantly increasing student skills through more difficult ideas, etc. | | |
| 7. Develops a process where students set short-term and long-term learning goals that students can revisit. | | |
| 8. Encourages students to take a critical view of ideas and express their perspectives. | | |
| 9. Models and creates opportunities for students to read texts taking both a sociocultural and a critical view of ideas, themes, positioning, etc. | | |
| 10. Empowers students to explore their own funds of knowledge in various ways and use those knowledges as forms of evidence for their learning. | | |
| 11. Plans learning experiences for students to use their content knowledge to study local, regional, national, or global issues. | | |
| 12. Communicates to students how their content area learning specifically responds to local, regional, national, or global issues. | | |

# References

Aguirre, J. M., & Zavala, M. R. (2013). Making culturally responsive mathematics teaching explicit: A lesson analysis tool. *Pedagogies: An International Journal, 8*(2), 163–190.

Brown, A. F. (2010). "Just because I am a Black male doesn't mean I am a rapper!": Sociocultural dilemmas in using "rap" music as an educational tool in classrooms. In D. Alridge, J. B. Stewart, & V. P. Franklin (Eds.), *Message in the music: Hip hop history and pedagogy* (pp. 281–300). Washington, DC: The ASALH Press.

Brown, A. F., Bloome, D., Morris, M., Power-Carter, S., & Willis, A. I. (2017). Classroom conversations in the study of race and the disruption of social and educational inequalities. In M. T. Fisher & M. Souto-Manning (Eds.), *Disrupting inequality through education research: Review of research in education, 41*(1), 453–476.

Brown, A. F. (2013). We will understand it better by and by: Sojourning through racial literacy. In L. William-White, D. Muccular, G. Muccular, & A. F. Brown (Eds.), *Critical consciousness in curricular research: Evidence from the field* (pp. 146–160). New York, NY: Peter Lang.

Gay, G. (2013). Cultural diversity and multicultural education. *Curriculum Inquiry, 43*(1), 48–70.

Harding-DeKam, J. L. (2014). Defining culturally responsive teaching: The case of mathematics. *Cognitive Education, 1*(1).

Howard, T. (2003). Culturally relevant pedagogy: Ingredients for critical teacher reflection. *Theory into Practice, 42*(3), 195–202.

Kim, S., & Slapac, A. (2015). Culturally responsive, transformative pedagogy in the transnational era. *Educational Studies, 51*, 27–51.

Kumar, R., & Hamer, L. (2013). Preservice teachers' attitudes and beliefs toward student diversity and proposed instructional practices: A sequential design study. *Journal of Teacher Education, 64*(2), 162–177. https://doi.org/10.1177/0022487112466899

Ladson-Billings, G. (1995). But that is just good teaching! The case for culturally relevant prdagogy. *Theory into Practice, 34*(3), 159–165.

Ladson-Billings, G. (2017). The (R)Evolution will not be standardized: Teacher education, hip hop pedagogy, and culturally relevant pedagogy 2.0. In D. Paris & H. S. Alim (Eds.), *Culturally sustaining pedagogies: Teaching and learning for justice in a changing world* (pp. 141–156). New York, NY: Teachers College Press.

McCarty, T. L., & Lee, T. S. (2014). Critical cultural sustaining/revitalizing pedagogy and indigenous education sovereignty. *Harvard Educational Review, 84*(1), 101–124.

Milner, H. R. (2010). Reflection, racial competence, and critical pedagogy: How do we prepare preservice teachers to pose tough questions. *Race Ethnicity and Education, 6*(2), 193–208.

Morris, J. E. (2015). *Troubling the waters: Fulfilling the promise of quality public schooling for Black Children.* New York, NY: Teachers College Press.

Nieto, S. (2013). *Finding joy in teaching students of diverse backgrounds: Culturally responsive and socially just practices in U.S. classroom.* Portsmouth, NH: Heinemann.

Paris, D., & Alim, H. S. (2017). *Culturally sustaining pedagogies: Teaching and learning for justice in a changing world* (pp. 141–156). New York, NY: Teachers College Press.

Sleeter, C. (2012). Confronting the marginalization of culturally responsive pedagogy. *Urban Education, 47*(3), 562–584.

Souto-Manning, M., & Martell, J. (2017, March). Committing to culturally relevant literacy teaching as an everyday practice: It's critical! *Language Arts, 94*(4), 252–256.

Vavrus, M. (2015). *Diversity education: A critical multicultural approach.* New York, NY: Teacher College Press.

# PART II
## *Discovering the Context*

# MODULE 4

## Knowledge of Students

Theresa Y. Robinson

*Elmhurst College*

*Do not train a child to learn by force or harshness; but direct them to it by what amuses their minds, so that you may be better able to discover with accuracy the peculiar bent of the genius of each.*

—Plato

### MODULE DESCRIPTION

Planning for personalized instruction to meet individual learning needs is essential. Teaching teams or pairs should be able to answer three fundamental questions: 1) What do my students know and what are they able to do? 2) What do I know about my students linguistically, socially, and culturally? and, 3) How will I use my students' experiences and interests to inform my teaching? The ability to answer these questions can help guide the process of planning for instruction with the whole child in mind. This module focuses on the importance of knowing your students academically as well as the experiences and context in which they live outside of the school walls.

Most teaching teams or pairs know their students in the context of classrooms and typically use efforts to know their students academically. The purpose of this module is to support the pair or team to understand the importance of knowing each student as a whole person which is an essential element in planning for instruction and eventual teaching. There is much to know about students that can be helpful in the classroom. This module is designed to provide resources and ideas to help the teaching team understand how to take advantage of social, cultural, and economic funds of knowledge that can be integrated into teaching.

## Theory/Conceptual Framework

This module is conceptualized on the social cognitive theory work of John Dewey, Albert Bandura, and Lev Vygotsky. John Dewey philosophized that curriculum should arise from a student's interest; Bandura suggested that learning is a social process, and Vygotsky believed that student learning is a derivative of the culture surrounding each learner.

Culture is a very broad term, whose connotation is typically around race and ethnicity. However, the expression of culture in a student's life extends far beyond who the student is both ethnically and racially. Culture describes a way of knowing and doing things like art, music, dance, and writing. Culture can also be used to describe the social groups to which one belongs, like religious organizations and sports teams. Bourdieu (1986) introduced the term "cultural capital" in sociology to describe the benefit that dominant groups like Whites, males, and Christians have in the expression of their culture in major institutions like schools. Cultural capital in its objectified state, is in the form of cultural goods like pictures, books, dictionaries, and musical instruments (Bourdieu, 1986). Students from underrepresented groups, however, did not have capital that was used in schools, because books, images and materials reflected the majority culture. This lack of cultural capital reflected in classroom materials is a component of a deficit theory used to explain lack of achievement. Deficit theories assume that some children because of genetic, cultural, or experiential differences are inferior to other children—that is, they have deficits that must be overcome in order to learn (Nieto & Bode, 2012). A teacher with a deficit perspective attributes poor achievement to variables such as language, social development, and intelligence. The problem with this perspective is that it places all responsibility for children's failure on their families and communities and positions the teacher as having little to no influence on student learning.

To counter this deficit perspective Moll, Amanti, Neff, and Gonzales (1992) ethnographically studied the home lives and classrooms of working class Mexican families in Tucson, Arizona. What they found was that when teachers began to get to know their students' lives outside of schools, there was a "fund of knowledge" that could be drawn from that study that could, and did, support curriculum and instruction. In classrooms, however, teaching teams rarely draw on these funds of knowledge; of the child's world outside the context of the classroom (Moll et al., 1992). This research introduced the term funds of knowledge in educational settings to describe strategic knowledge and related activities essential in how a household functions and develops. Understanding the home and family cultural assets that bring well-being can further be used to affirm students in their classrooms. Rios-Aguilar, Marquez-Kiyama and Gravitt (2011) went on to describe what students bring to the classroom that a teacher can use as an asset to be used in selecting instructional materials and strategies for teaching and assessment. They challenged teachers and researchers to view funds of knowledge as a source of capital for poor students, and to use the funds of knowledge approach for understanding educational opportunity.

Knowing one's students in a meaningful way that can influence instructional planning can be challenging because the process is personal, requires cultural competence, and takes

**Figure 4.1** Why doesn't Mr. X know?

time and effort. In order to do this work, teachers must first reflect on their own personal assets and then explore and utilize what students bring to the teaching and learning experience. Howard (2003) posits that teachers need to understand that racially diverse students frequently bring cultural capital to the classroom that is often drastically different from mainstream norms and worldviews. Yet, in most cases, what these students bring to school is not identified or treated as beneficial to academic achievement. Sadly, they often are framed as deficiencies. If a child's first language is not English it is often seen as a deficiency to overcome rather than an asset to incorporate.

Understanding funds of knowledge as social capital can counter deficit perspectives of children from underrepresented groups. In this way a student's experiences with language can be used as an asset in teaching and learning. Teaching teams or pairs are held accountable for providing evidence of their use of knowledge of students to impact student learning. One such teacher preparation requirement that has been adopted by approximately 41 U.S. States is the Education Teacher Performance Assessment (edTPA) (SCALE, 2014). One rubric of this assessment of teacher candidates is entitled "Using Knowledge of Students to Inform Teaching and Learning." The criteria requires teacher candidates to be able to justify learning tasks and show examples of how they have used student personal, cultural, and community assets in planning, instruction, and assessment. Likewise, the widely used teacher-evaluation tool, the Danielson Framework for Teaching (Danielson, 2007), asks teachers to demonstrate knowledge of students. The elements of the planning rubric include, but are not limited to, knowledge of students' language proficiency, interests, and cultural heritage. Fortunately, to be licensed in many states, teacher candidates must now demonstrate that they know their students socially, culturally, and academically.

The foundation of effective teaching is content knowledge, pedagogical content knowledge, and knowledge of assessment. However, the culturally competent teacher is further able to build trusting relationships via a deep understanding of each student's interests, learning preferences, language experiences, and funds of knowledge to impact student learning. Knowledge of students to inform teaching means affirming each student's identities not only academically but socially and culturally in teaching. Knowing your students means knowing and understanding the whole child. The Association of Supervision and Curriculum Development (ASCD, 2018) defines the whole child approach as an effort to change the conversation about education from a focus on narrowly defined academic achievement to one that promotes the long-term development and success of all children. One of the five tenets of the whole child approach to teaching and learning is that each student has access to personalized learning and is supported by qualified, caring adults. Personalized learning may be achieved by a deep understanding of the lives and experiences of the students beyond their academic needs.

The complexity of teaching for new teachers, including understanding multiple sources of learning standards and professional evaluation criteria for teachers requires formal support. Situational guidance and mentoring from an experienced educator, like an instructional coach, school administrator, or student teaching supervisor, may make the process of understanding the importance of using student funds of knowledge to impact student learning less complex.

## Specific Questions to Guide Discussion

1. As a teacher, what cultural assets do you bring to the learning experience? (e.g., member of a sports team, sing in a choir, highly organized, traveled abroad, Italian grandparents)

2. How have you identified the cultural assets that your students bring to the learning experience?

3. Describe strategies you use to deepen your understanding of each student's interests and everyday experiences.

4. Identify family and community assets you can use to contribute to each student's learning experience.

5. Describe your students academically. What are their learning preferences, academic strengths, and areas for improvement?

6. Describe what you know about each student's language use and experiences out-of-school and in-school (e.g., African American Vernacular English, talk story, Spanglish, Patois speakers).

## Productive Practices

1. *Learn student names quickly.*
   a. Learning student names is an act of caring and allows you as teacher to build positive relationships with students and to develop a community of learners.
   b. Knowing and using student names support classroom management.
   c. Create a seating chart with student names for each of your classes or periods/blocks. Use word associations and visual clues to remember each student's name (i.e., Talkative Theresa or Debbie with long, brown hair).
   d. Check and rehearse the pronunciations of each student's first and last name. Ask the students if there is a special nickname they would like for you to use in class.
2. *Explore your own personal and family histories and interests.*
   a. This reflection allows you to understand how you have developed your own values and beliefs.
   b. This self-exploration helps you to better understand yourself including biases, stereotypes, and or prejudices.
3. *Share your cultural histories and interests with your students.*
   a. This helps you to relate on a personal level with your students.
   b. Model expectations for developing relationships that are built on communication.
4. *Visit and participate in student extracurricular activities.*
   a. Attend student sporting events, club meetings, and extracurricular activities of students.
   b. Demonstrate that you are interested in each student's life outside of the classroom as well as in the classroom.
5. *Acknowledge and validate each student's differences as well as commonalities with others.*
   a. Culture and language may contribute to attitudes and behaviors exhibited by students.
   b. Be careful not to make assumptions that can lead to stereotyping students. Each student is unique and wants to be treated as an individual with membership in a cultural group(s).
   c. Use multicultural literature, bilingual texts, and materials that affirm each student's identity and can help to develop cultural competence among all students.

## What Would You Do?

Ask your team or pair the following questions. For suggested responses to questions, see Appendix A.

1. What would you do if a student accused you of being racist?

2. A student says they will be absent and miss one week of school because their family is traveling to their original home country or other part of the U.S. (i.e., "down south," Belize, Jamaica, or Mexico). What would be your response?

3. What would you do if a student does not speak academic English during discussions in class?

## Reflective Professional Growth Activities

Consider these ideas or activities to facilitate and foster teacher growth and reflection. Select one or two ideas to help facilitate this reflection process that will help the teacher, pair, or team to understand the importance of knowing their students. Be sure to choose an activity that would be the most effective.

### Idea 1: Select Multicultural Literature That Reflects the Identities and Experiences of Your Students

Select literature and media that represent varied racial and ethnic backgrounds, family structure, language backgrounds, and perspectives. Integrate multicultural non-fiction reading to support conceptual understanding and the development of critical and historical thinking. Use multicultural literature to help students think critically about big transferable ideas like healthy lifestyles, democracy, change, and science technology and society. For bilingual students, locate books and materials that are written in the home (primary) language and the new language.

**Evidence:** Identify and provide a multicultural text set (e.g., literature, vocabulary list, music, poetry, cartoons). Provide a rationale for how the multicultural literature will be used to support student learning.

### Idea 2: I Am From *Poem*

Have students create *I Am From* poems. Each line of the poem should start with *I Am From*. Each line should express something that makes the student unique as a person (e.g., family, ethnic heritage, favorite things, interests, language, character traits, talents). Take a picture of each student. Mount the picture with the *I Am From* poem and create a class display highlighting what makes each student unique (*K–12 Classroom Teaching*, Guillaume, 2016, p. 38).

**Evidence:** Provide a photograph of the class display.

### Idea 3: Student Interest Survey

Complete a *Getting to Know You* inventory (Appendix B) with your students to learn their interests, cultural heritage, and funds of knowledge. Share your own cultural heritage and interests with your students. Have students share their personal interests to build a community of learners. Determine what assets students bring to the classroom that may be incorporated into instruction and assessment. Form small groups to review the survey. Use information gathered from the survey as you plan for instruction and teach.

**Evidence:** Provide a summary of the information gathered from the interest surveys using a master copy of the interest survey. Identify themes in order to group responses.

### Idea 4: Student Learning Profile Summary

Create a chart (see Figure 4.2 as an example) to describe any required special supports (i.e., students whose first language is not English, students who are gifted and talented, students with Individualized Education Plans, developing readers/writers, students not experiencing academic success). Briefly describe any required accommodations or modifications that will affect your instruction in this teaching experience.

**Evidence:** Provide a copy of one class's learning profile summary table (see Appendix C for a blank template of the chart).

| Student's First Name | Academic Strengths and Needs | Funds of Knowledge | Social and Personal Qualities |
|---|---|---|---|
| Anna | Above grade level in reading comprehension | White family; traveled to Ireland and the UK on several occasions; Irish ancestry | Loves to communicate with peers |
| Rebecca | Striving learner in reading comprehension | White, large family—she is the oldest of five children. | Needs constant positive feedback |
| Cameron | Above grade level in reading comprehension | African American, is very knowledgeable about African American history; Lived in New York until first grade | Must challenge him at a higher level. Loves science and history |

**Figure 4.2** Example of a student learning profile chart.

## Follow-Up, Monitoring, and Goal Setting

Complete the follow-up questions for the selected reflective professional growth activity.

### *Idea 1: Multicultural Literature*
- Explain what big ideas were taught using a particular text set.
- Describe how and why certain texts were selected according to your knowledge of students.

### *Idea 2:* I Am From *Poem*
- What interesting things did you learn about your students?
- What new information did you learn about your students?
- How has your perspective changed or stayed the same since reading the *I Am From* poems?

### *Idea 3: Student Interest Survey*
- What themes relating to interests did you recognize from the whole class?
- How will you use student interests while planning for instruction and teaching?
- What did you learn about your students academically?
- What are some ways you might apply the funds of knowledge of children and families into teaching and learning?

## Idea 4: Student Learning Profile Summary

- Discuss the learning needs of the students in a class/block or period by category.
- Discuss what plans for supports will be provided for individuals and groups of students.
- Discuss the chart that has been prepared.

## Resources

### Videos

**Film:** *Stand and Deliver*

This film tells the story of Jaime Escalante, a Los Angeles mathematics teacher, who was able to teach Mexican-American students calculus when others had given up on them. This feature movie provides an excellent example of culturally responsive teaching. Starring Lou Diamond Phillips.

Musca, T., & Menendez, R. (1988). *Stand and deliver*. United States: Warner Bros.

**3 Types of Language**

In this TED talk, Jamila Lysicot discusses three different types of language: home language, social language, and academic language. Understanding these different forms of language can help educators understand the complicated history of English and its importance in the lives of students.

Lysicot, J. (2014). *TED talk: Three ways to speak English*. Retrieved from https://www.ted.com/talks/jamila_lyiscott_3_ways_to_speak_english

### Web Resources

**Teaching for Tolerance: A Project of the Southern Poverty Law Center**

This is a website where educators who care about diversity, equity, and justice can find news, suggestions, free classroom materials, and support.

Teaching Tolerance. (1991–2018). *Educating for a diverse democracy*. Retrieved from http://www.tolerance.org/

**The Algebra Project (AP)**

The AP's mission is to reform mathematics education including high school as well as middle grade initiatives. AP's work seeks a national response to establish a fundamental right: the right of every child to a quality, public school education. AP's unique approach to school reform includes developing sustainable, student-centered models by building coalitions of stakeholders within the local communities, particularly historically underserved populations.

The Algebra Project. (2018). Retrieved from www.algebra.org

### The Zinn Education Project: A Collaboration Between Rethinking Schools and Teaching for Change

This website offers free, downloadable lessons and articles organized by theme, time period, and reading level for middle and high school classrooms. Its goal is to introduce students to a more accurate, complex, and engaging understanding of United States history than is found in traditional textbooks and curricula.

The Zinn Education Project. (2018). *Teaching a people's history*. Retrieved from www.Zinnedproject.org

### LibriVox: Free Public Domain Audiobooks

This website offers audiobooks read by volunteers from all over the world. The books are offered in many different languages including English, French, Spanish, and German. The website provides access to free public domain audiobooks that can be listened to on a computer, iPod, or other device. LibriVox is a great resource for teachers to support multiple learning preferences.

LibriVox. (2018). *Free public domain for audio books*. Retrieved from https://librivox.org/

## Key Terms and Definitions

**Asian:** Asian is a broad term used to describe people from the continents of Asia. The term is also a misnomer because it often leaves out groups of people from the country of India, although it is on the continent of Asia.

**Black:** Black is a broad term used to refer to people of African descent from the African Diaspora including America, South America, and the Caribbean islands.

**Culture:** Culture is a broad concept that encompasses everything used to describe a people (e.g., their shared ways of knowing, thinking, perceiving, creating, evaluating, interaction, and doing).

**Cultural Capital:** Cultural capital is the transmission of values, tastes, languages, dialects, and cultures of a group that are hidden forms of hereditary transmission of capital.

**Cultural Competence:** Cultural competence is a process of learning that leads to an ability to effectively respond to the opportunities posed by the presence of racial and cultural diversity in a defined social system.

**Deficit Perspective:** Deficit perspective is an assumption that some students because of genetic, cultural, or experiential differences are inferior to other students. The assumption is that these students have deficits that must be overcome before they are to learn.

**Diversity:** Diversity is a broad term referring to the variety of points of view, of experience, and of making meaning that encompasses complex differences in groups and individuals. Racial, ethnic, gender, and ability are sources of diversity.

**English Language Learner (ELL):** ELL is a term that identifies students who are developing English language proficiency. The term is a misnomer because it assumes that children whose first language IS English are not English language learners.

**Ethnicity:** Ethnicity refers to cultural characteristics such as language, religion, geography/national origin, food, dress, music, etc.

**Funds of Knowledge:** Funds of knowledge are life experiences, strategic knowledge, and skills that learners bring from their homes, established relationships, social activities, and communities that can be used to develop concepts and skills in the classroom setting (i.e., home language, family occupations, family traditions, household chores, international travel).

**Hispanic:** Hispanic refers to people whose heritage is from Mexico, Central and South America, and Spanish speaking Caribbean islands and Spain.

**Latinx:** Latino refers to people whose heritage is from Mexico, Central and South America, and Spanish speaking Caribbean islands. Used interchangeably with Hispanic and the preference to use one or the other is a personal choice. Latino is frequently used to identify people of Latin American origin or ancestry that includes Brazil.

**LEP:** Limited English Proficient (LEP) is a largely abandoned term to refer to students whose first language is not English. It is still in use in some governmental documents.

**Minority:** Minority is any group that has less power than the majority as evidenced by lower pay, restricted opportunities, limited political access, and other forms of discrimination. The term is often used as a misnomer. It is more apropos to identify the racial or ethnic group by label than to refer to groups of people as minorities.

**Race:** Race is a way of classifying people that was once believed to be genetic. It is a socially and legally constructed concept used to classify people on visible characteristics such as skin color and body type.

# Appendix A

## *What Would You Do? Questions with Suggested Responses*

1. What would you do if a student accused you of being racist?

   **Suggested Response 1:** Make a request to have a private conversation with your student. Make sure to actively listen during your meeting. During this conversation ask questions like, What does it mean to you for someone to be racist? What did I do that made you feel like I was being a racist? What could I have done differently? Affirm the student's concerns and offer clarification where needed. Take ownership of the perception and assure the student that you care and are concerned about them socially as well as academically.

2. A student says they will be absent and miss one week of school because their family is traveling to their original home country or other part of the U.S. (i.e., "down south," Belize, Jamaica, Mexico). What would be your response?

   **Suggested Response 2:** Show interest in your students' visits to family in another state or country. Affirm the culture of your students by asking that they share their experiences with you and the class upon their return if they would like. Often a visit to another country or state provides students with rich experiences with local flora and fauna, music, and language, etc. Draw upon these experiences during classroom discussions and when creating assignments.

3. What would you do if a student does not speak academic English during discussions in class?

   **Suggested Response 3:** Academic language takes 5–10 years to develop, therefore consider the cognitive demand of an activity before providing correctives and feedback. First, adjust the complexity of the language you are using as a teacher depending on the proficiency level of the students. For low cognitive demanding activities focus on corrective feedback of student language. For high cognitive demanding activities focus on ideas and meaning as opposed to providing corrections in language.

# Appendix B

*Getting to Know You Inventory*

**Part I: I would like to get to know you better as my student. Please answer all the prompts in the text boxes.**

| |
|---|
| My name is _____<br>I like to be called _____<br>My birthday is _____ |
| I live with _____<br>_____<br>_____ |
| Outside of school my favorite activity is _____<br>_____<br>_____ |
| The top three careers I am interested in are:<br>1. _____<br>2. _____<br>3. _____ |

**Part II: Complete each of the following stems using complete sentences.**

1. If I had a million dollars, I would…
2. If I could meet one person it would be…
3. I am really good at…
4. Sometimes I struggle with…
5. One thing I am concerned about in this class is…
6. One thing I am excited about in this class is…
7. After I graduate, I want to…

**Part III: Fill in your funds of knowledge in the chart below.**

| Fund of Knowledge | Examples |
|---|---|
| Home language | e.g., Arabic, Spanish, Polish, Italian |
| Favorite TV/YouTube show | e.g., *Sid the Science Kid*, *Dora the Explorer* |
| Family values and traditions | e.g., holiday celebrations, religious beliefs, work ethic |
| Family occupations | e.g., fishing, construction, lawn care, police, cashier |
| Household chores | e.g., sweeping, doing dishes, vacuuming |

# Appendix C
## *Student Learning Profile Chart*

| Student's First Name | Academic Strengths and Needs | Funds of Knowledge | Social and Personal Qualities |
|---|---|---|---|
| | | | |
| | | | |
| | | | |
| | | | |
| | | | |

# References

Association for Supervision and Curriculum Development. (2018, May). *The whole child approach*. Retrieved from http://www.ascd.org/whole-child.aspx

Bourdieu, P. (1986). The forms of capital. In J. Richardson (Ed.), *Handbook of theory and research for the sociology of education*. New York, NY: Greenwood.

Danielson, C. (2007). *Enhancing professional practice: A framework for teaching* (2nd ed.). Alexandria, VA: ASCD.

Guillaume, A. (2016). *K–12 classroom teaching: A primer for new professionals* (5th ed.). Boston, MA: Pearson.

Howard, T. C. (2003). Culturally relevant pedagogy: Ingredients for critical teacher reflection. *Theory Into Practice, 42*(3), 195–202.

Moll, L., Amanti, C., Neff, D., & Gonzales, N. (1992). Funds of knowledge for teaching: Using a qualitative approach to connect homes and classrooms. *Theory into Practice, 31*(2), 132–141.

Nieto, S., & Bode, P. (2012). *Affirming diversity: The sociopolitical context of multicultural education* (6th ed.). Boston, MA: Pearson.

Rios-Aguilar, C., Marquez-Kiyama, J., & Gravitt, M. (2011). Funds of knowledge for the poor and forms of capital for the rich? A capital approach to examining funds of knowledge. *Theory and Research in Education, 9*(2), 163–184.

SCALE: Stanford Center for Assessment and Equity. (2014). *About edTPA*. Retrieved from https://scale.stanford.edu/teaching/edtpa

# MODULE 5

# Partnering With Families

Linda Dauksas
*Elmhurst College*

*My teachers did their best to teach me, but how could I care about math and integers when my family life was full of fractures and frictions? How could I care about helping verbs at school when words never seemed to help me at home? How could I focus on schoolwork when defending my mother from her crack-addicted, alcoholic boyfriend who became a regular part of my home routine? And how could I care about going to school when I wasn't even sure I would have a home to go to at night?*

—Manny Scott

## MODULE DESCRIPTION

Families are ever present in schools today, and families come in many forms with a variety of members, values, norms, and beliefs. Understanding the changing definition of families is essential for today's teachers. Accepting all families and building partnerships with them is critical to the success of the student, the teacher, the teaching team, and the entire learning community. Engaging families in our learning communities should be transformative for schools, students, and families. This module will support the development of family/school partnerships that positively impact the students and stakeholders in the learning community.

## Theory/Conceptual Framework

The U.S. Census Bureau defines family as a group of two people or more related by birth, marriage, adoption, and residing together (Grant & Ray, 2016). This legal definition is challenged in schools today, where family is more accurately defined as a group of people who are collectively raising a child, including influencing and providing for the child's needs to the best of the group members' abilities. One should acknowledge that over time the members of the group, known as family, may change as may the intensity of their involvement.

Family involvement has always had a presence in schools and learning communities, yet families weren't always seen as partners in their learning communities. Families were often the visitors. When families did attend schools, their involvement was tangential, consisting of dropping in for Back to School night and/or meeting for a parent–teacher conference. Thiers (2016) called these "random acts of parent involvement" (p. 41). Schools today are working to replace the random acts of parent involvement with the highly desired and positively impactful family engagement. Family engagement occurs when there is an on-going, reciprocal, strengths-based partnership between families and schools (Grant & Ray, 2016). These ongoing partnerships are co-constructed, characterized by trust, shared values, bidirectional communication, mutual respect, and attention to each party's needs (Lopez, Kreider, & Caspe, 2004). As Zacarian and Silverstone (2016) indicated, when families are invited to share something of value, their status (in the school) is transformed into an asset and a source of strength.

Past educational practices placed parents as the schools' audience. Today, students' families are the paradigm for the partnership, and the purpose of cultivating this partnership is student academic growth. Families can be defined as a group of people that may or may not be related to the student, providing care as well as resources to nurture the student's development. "In some cultures, multi-generational households are common, and extended family members and fictive kin have important roles in caring for and raising children (McAdoo, 2000). Henderson and Mapp (2002) highlighted the importance of family by recognizing that "all family members—siblings, grandparents, aunts, uncles, and fictive kin—who may be friends or neighbors, often contribute in significant ways to children's education and development."

According to the *Russell Sage Foundation Journal of the Social Sciences*, Harris and Robinson (2016) concluded that the past or traditional model for involving families failed to capture family support for each student's academic progress. Today, the primary purpose for embedded family engagement in schools is to build a family partnership and improve learning outcomes for students (Thiers, 2016).

From a review of the literature, Halgunseth and Peterson (2009) delineated six factors that are present when families engage with schools.

1. Families act as advocates for their students by actively taking part in decision-making opportunities.
2. Consistent and timely, two-way communication is facilitated through multiple forms, remaining responsive to the families' linguistic preferences.
3. Families share their knowledge and skills by volunteering. Teachers integrate information about their students' lives, families, and communities into their curriculum.
4. Schools emphasize the design of learning activities that extend beyond the classroom, into the community.
5. Families value education.

6. Schools allocate resources to provide professional development to enhance building partnerships and fostering responsiveness with families.

Family and community engagement in schools correlate with higher academic performance and school improvement. When stakeholders work together to support learning, students tend to earn higher grades, attend school more regularly, stay in school longer, and enroll in higher-level programs (National Education Association, 2008).

## Specific Questions to Guide the Discussion

1. Have you established an inclusive definition of family? How have you been able to embrace a strengths-based definition? Give some examples that exemplify this inclusive definition while communicating with families, speaking with students, and describing your students' families.

2. Describe the cultural, linguistic, and community assets that your students' families possess. If you are unsure, complete asset mapping for the school catchment area. How do these family assets support your curriculum? What community resources can your families share to support student learning?

3. Describe your students' interests. How can these interests be used to motivate your students? How have you embedded these interests into your instruction?

4. How do you determine family needs and remain respectfully responsive to these needs? Have you considered a family-to-family network to cultivate autonomy among families? What does this network look like?

5. Are you continually modeling respectful and responsive interactions with families across the entire learning community? Do you continually speak of families' assets and strengths? How do you engage with families in the community?

## Productive Practices

Principles of Family Support (Grant & Ray, 2016) with implementation activities.

1. *Schools work together to build positive relationships with families.*
   a. Routinely invite families into your classroom.
   b. Include students' family photos or selfies in your classroom.
   c. Create a website or blog to share daily classroom events.
   d. Supply textbook copies to the local library for family lending and homework support.

  e. Create a menu of options for families to join the life of your classroom, include activities that can be completed at home (preparing materials).
  f. Consider hosting a school-based family event (e.g., book fair, cultural fair, fun-fair, yard sale). Be sure that supports for the family are available (e.g., child care, dinner, transportation).
2. *Schools recognize the capacity of families and honor their role in supporting the development of all families' members.*
  a. Foster a family-to-family network.
  b. Establish a family advisory board to support shared decision-making.
  c. Contact cultural brokers in the community to assist new families who may be learning English or may be new to the country or region.
  d. Create a family board on your webpage. Share information/photos received from families related to student learning.
3. *Schools understand that families are an important resource.*
  a. Partner with families to create family workshop topics. Have family members lead workshops, sharing their skills and expertise (e.g., cooking, wood-working, gardening) with other families and staff.
4. *Schools engage families and strengthen their cultural, racial, and linguistic identities.*
  a. Be prepared to learn from your families.
  b. Send surveys to families to learn about their customs and celebrations, including families' funds of knowledge.
  c. Attend a community event sponsored by a culture other than your own.
  d. Invite families into the classroom to share their traditions, customs, and/or literature as it relates to your curriculum.
5. *Schools embed programs in the communities.*
  a. Offer/teach a class or program in the community.
  b. Display student work in one of the public community buildings (e.g., city hall, library, restaurant).
  c. Host a community-based school campaign/walk/fair/rally to raise awareness of your school or classroom with community stakeholders. Ask vendors with resources to attend, providing take-aways to stakeholders.
  d. Foster a partnership or service project with members from another community entity (park district, assisted living, shelter or school).
6. *Schools advocate for families and supply resources when needed.*
  a. Create an asset map, or have your students create an asset map, to define a variety of resources including: infrastructure, human, political, natural, social, financial, and cultural. Post the map and key as a resource on your class website.
  b. Have your class undertake an advocacy project, providing necessary resources for specific community members.
7. *Schools model principles of family support demonstrated in their interactions, activities, and policies.*
  a. Seek daily opportunities to talk face-to-face with families.
  b. Highlight families' strengths in your interactions with families and faculty.
  c. Plan to attend events or meetings sponsored by family groups (e.g., PTO, PTA).

## What Would You Do?

Ask your team or pair the following questions. For suggested responses to questions, see Appendix A.

1. What would you do if the conversations in the staff lounge continually center on families, their lack of involvement, and perceived lack of gratitude regarding the educational services provided to their children. Do you engage in these conversations that cast doubt and dispersions about families or do you stand up for families and help your colleagues develop perspective and understanding regarding family engagement in schools?

2. What would you do if it is apparent that the number of families that participated in your parent–teacher conferences was significantly lower than the number of families that participated in the past. Do you take ownership for the low numbers of families that attended and improve the rate of participation for your classroom or do you cite other factors for the low attendance numbers?

3. What would you do if there are over a dozen languages spoken by your students' families. Most families are English learners and have indicated the desire to communicate in their first language. Where do you go to seek the resources needed to communicate respectfully and effectively with all of the families of your students?

## Reflective Professional Growth Activities

Consider these ideas or activities to facilitate and foster teacher growth and reflection. Select one or two ideas to help facilitate this reflection process that will help the teacher, pair, or team to understand family partnerships and how they enhance students' learning. Remember that you know the individuals best so be sure to choose an activity that would be the most effective.

### *Idea 1: Family Visits*

Conduct family visits or virtual family visits at mutually agreed upon locations. Family visits can provide an essential link to students' lives, cultures, and lifestyles. These visits may be in the home or in community buildings (e.g., libraries, parks, restaurants) or completed virtually. Reflect on the information gathered from the family in the non-educational settings. Are families more comfortable and confident outside the classroom? Continue to reflect on the barriers some families experience when coming to schools. Lightfoot (2003) called these barriers "ghosts in the classroom." We must acknowledge these ghosts in order to build partnerships.

**Evidence:** Document your visits and keep the documentation in a temporary student file (secured). Summarize the visit and record any action needed or follow-up responsibilities on the part of both parties.

### *Idea 2: Survey*

Send a short survey to families. Ask about their preference for communicating. What style of communication do they prefer? What time of day is best for them to communicate? Create a framework for communicating. Are you using a website, blog, or newsletter? Is the information translated into the family's language? Reflect on the communication you receive from families. Do your messages foster two-way reciprocal communication? Or, is your communication one-way, providing only directions or expectations? (see Appendix B)

**Evidence:** Compile the data by creating a visual display. This will help to determine which style of communication is most desired. Be sure to delineate one-way and two-way communication on the visual display. Adhere to family preferences and share these data with your administrator to help demonstrate your responsiveness to a variety of communication styles.

### *Idea 3: Reflection on Family Engagement*

Reflect on the absence or presence of family members in your school and in your classroom. What factors impact the families' abilities to join your classroom? Identify the visible and invisible factors that shape families' engagement in schools. How does each family positively impact their student's learning?

**Evidence:** Ask families to sign in when they visit your classroom or revisit data in the school office visitor's log. These data should help direct your attempts at reaching and establishing relationships with students' families that have not yet visited. The data will also yield times and days when visits occur and can be disaggregated to reveal patterns of participation.

### *Idea 4: Personal Reflection & Impacts*

Identify your own family norms and personal biases. Don't allow your biases to interfere with your family interactions and partnerships. What information and knowledge do you need to better understand your students and their families? Have you identified cultural brokers (Lightfoot, 2003) in the community who can help you understand the variety of cultures and customs in your classroom? (see Figure 5.1; Appendix C).

**Evidence:** Create a t-chart. On one side, list your own family practices related to becoming involved with and engaging in schools. On the other side of the chart, list the practices of the families in your class today. Identify differences and target behaviors that impact building relationships. Pledge to learn more about these behaviors. View these behaviors as an opportunity to learn, not obstacles to overcome.

| My Family's | Students' Families | Implications |
|---|---|---|
| My mom did not work outside our home. | Both caregivers are working multiple jobs. | Learn more about how families balance work and parenting responsibilities. |
| I lived in a nuclear family. | Many of my students live with extended family members. | Get to know as many family members as possible, not just parents. |
| My family lived in the same neighborhood for 12 years. | Many of my students move from neighborhood to neighborhood frequently. | Assist families arriving and leaving the school with supports for students, and review information that is sent or received from another school. Help acclimate new families to the community. |
| My family lived in a single family home. | A few of my students live in urban areas, within a subsidized housing development. | Learn more about community housing options. |
| My parents spoke English as their first language. They spoke Italian with my grandparents. | Families speak several languages and English is not their first language. | Translate materials. |
| My Mom went to my parent–teacher conferences by herself because my Dad worked 12 hours a day. | Several families do not attend conferences because they do not have transportation. | Offer flexible meeting times and places (including home visits). |
| My Mom did not volunteer in my class. | Some families frequently come into the classroom. | Offer families opportunities to volunteer from home. |
| My Mom did not complain or make special requests of my teachers/school. | Families express dissatisfaction and make several requests regarding placements and teachers. | Listen carefully! |

**Figure 5.1** Family Engagement Behavior Audit T-Chart (Norms and Personal Bias).

## Follow Up, Monitoring, and Goal Setting

Complete the follow-up questions for the selected reflective professional growth activity.

### Idea 1: Reflecting on a Home Visit

- How has the home visit changed your relationship with the student and the family?
- How has the home visit influenced the student's performance?
- Has the home visit provided the family with more autonomy in the classroom or school? What behaviors evidence this autonomy?

## Idea 2: View Family Communication as Data

- Which form of communication provides the most reciprocity (e.g., face-to-face, email, newsletter, phone call)?
- Are you respecting the families' preferences for communication (e.g., time of day, form, message content)? How have these exchanges of information fortified your relationships with families?
- Have you remained responsive to each family's communication style? How can you encourage the silent family to become more participatory?

## Idea 3: Collect Data on Family Attendance

- What does your data reveal about families' attendance and/or engagement in learning-related activities inside and outside of school?
- Is family engagement, or the lack thereof, congruent with the depth of your relationships or the lack of a relationship?
- What factors impact families' absence from the classroom or school?
- What resources do families need in order to engage in the classroom, school, and/or student learning? How can you supply these resources?

## Idea 4: Assessing Yourself

- When you think of your own schooling, what type of relationship did your family have with the school?
- What values and beliefs grew out of your own experiences?
- Do you think your own teachers accepted your family's structure?
- How did your family's experiences with teachers and schools impact your expectations for the families of your students?
- Are you able and willing to accept the diversity of family roles and family engagement in your classroom?

# Resources

## Web Resources

### Taking a Closer Look: A Guide to Online Resources on Family Involvement

This resource guide provides annotated Web links from 2000 and after about a variety of sources about family involvement. This guide is a compilation of 126 national organizations, most of which are from the field of education.

> Weiss, H. B., Faughnan, K., Caspe, M., Wolos, C., Lopez, M. E., Kreider, H. (2005, September). *Taking a closer look: A guide to online resources on family involvement.* Retrieved from https://rhyclearinghouse.acf.hhs.gov/sites/default/files/docs/13868-Taking_A_Closer_Look.pdf

### Center on School, Family, and Community Partnerships

Johns Hopkins University conducts and disseminates research, programs, and policy analyses that produce new and useful knowledge and practices that help parents, educators, and members of communities work together to improve schools, strengthen families, and enhance student learning and development.

Johns Hopkins University (n.d.). *Center for social organization of schools*. Retrieved from http://web.jhu.edu/CSOS/about.html

**Communities in Schools**

Communities in Schools has connected community resources with schools to help students succeed in school and in life. During its 30-year history, the organization has coordinated the delivery of resources into schools in a way that is responsive, cost-efficient, and results-oriented.

Communities in Schools (n.d.). *Triple your impact*. Retrieved from www.communitiesinschools.org

**Especially for Parents**

Information from the U.S. Department of Education that provides numerous resources educators can share with families, including a tool kit for Hispanic families.

U.S. Department of Education (n.d.). *Parents*. Retrieved from https://www2.ed.gov/parents/landing.jhtml

**Global Family Research Project**

The key component of this project is complimentary learning. The concept focuses on linking school and non-school learning supports to foster student learning and academic progress.

TSNE Mission Works (n.d.). *Welcome to the global family research project*. Retrieved from https://globalfrp.org/

**Parent Involvement in Children's Education: Efforts by Public Elementary Schools**

This document is a report relating the findings from the *Survey on Family and School Partnerships in Public Schools*, K-8, conducted by the National Center for Educational Statistics (NCES). The findings address a number of parent involvement topics.

National Center for Educational Statistics. (1998, January). *Parent involvement in children's education: Efforts by public elementary schools*. Retrieved from http://nces.ed.gov/surveys/frss/publications/98032

## Key Terms and Definitions

**Advocacy:** The case of arguing in favor of something, such as a cause, idea or policy. Case advocacy benefits individual students. Class advocacy benefits groups of students and families.

**Asset mapping:** Representation of a community's strengths and resources depicted on a community map. Strengths and resources can be related to basic needs, education, recreation, health care, community services, international services, etc.

**Cultural brokers:** Para-educators, family advocates or school liaisons that are able to cross boundaries into differing cultural milieus and promote open communication between groups of teachers and parents.

**Cultural deficit model:** The belief that values, as transmitted through the family, are dysfunctional and the cause of poverty and lack of education.

**Family centered partnerships:** Relationships that are respectful, flexible, culturally sensitive, and involve the family both as decision-makers and active participants.

**Family engagement:** A mutually collaborative, working relationship with the family that serves the best interest of the student, in either the school or home. The purpose of family engagement is to increase student achievement and active engagement by the home, school, and community in order to help students learn and develop to their full potential.

**Funds of knowledge:** Life experiences, knowledge, and skills that learners bring from their homes and communities that can be used to develop concepts and skills in the classroom setting (e.g., home language, family occupations, family traditions, family responsibilities).

**Kinship care:** Grandparents or other relatives who raise children when parents are unable to do so; the arrangement may be temporary or a permanent legal guardianship.

**Multigenerational family:** A household that contains three or more generations of a family.

**Nuclear family:** Family type in which the parents are first time married; the children living with them are their biological or adopted children; and no other adults or children live in the home.

**Reciprocal communication:** Two-way communication where teachers and families equally share information, ask questions and express opinions.

**Sub-family:** Family type where a parent and child(ren) live with the child(ren)'s grandparents, with the grandparents remaining the head of the household but the parent raising the chlld(ren).

# Appendix A

## *What Would You Do? Questions with Suggested Responses*

1. What would you do if the conversations in the staff lounge continually center on families, their lack of involvement, and perceived lack of gratitude regarding the educational services provided to their children? Do you engage in these conversations that cast doubt and dispersions about families or do you stand up for families and help your colleagues develop perspective and understanding regarding families' engagement in schools?

    **Suggested Response 1:** You stand for families. You share respect for families. You help colleagues understand families' strengths by sharing families' assets. For example, instead of complaining about families' lack of engagement or attendance, you highlight the families' work ethic and ability to work multiple jobs to provide for their families.

2. What would you do if it is apparent that the number of families that participated in your parent–teacher conferences was significantly lower than the number of families that participated in the past? Do you take ownership for the low numbers of families that attended and improve the rate of participation for your classroom or do you cite other factors for the low attendance numbers?

    **Suggested Response 2:** You take ownership and revisit all of your contacts with each family. You contact each family that attended conferences and thank them. You also contact each family that did not attend and invite them to your classroom for another opportunity to establish a partnership focusing on their student's strengths. If they still don't attend you continue to communicate regarding their students' strengths. You continue to keep data on the numbers of the families that you communicate with and work toward communicating with 100% of your families.

3. What would you do if there are over a dozen languages spoken by your students' families? Most families are English learners and have indicated the desire to communicate in their first language. Where do you go to seek the resources needed to communicate respectfully and effectively with all of the families of your students?

    **Suggested Response 3:** You seek multi-lingual speakers within your district and cultural brokers (i.e., community members that speak the languages of your families), who are willing to volunteer to support the learning of students and their families. Create efficient communication strategies *with* these stakeholders. Strategies should foster a sense of community and include reciprocal electronic and face-to-face communication. For example, with permission include the lingual support volunteer during conferences or when sending electronic communication.

# Appendix B

## *Parent Survey on Preferred Communication*

Sample questions to ask families:

- Who are your student's family members?
- What are some important dates or events for your family?
- What traditions or customs does your family practice?
- What are some typical weekly routines in your household?
- What do you want to know about what your student will learn in my class?

Sample questions to ask students:

- Who's in your family?
- What's your favorite thing to do with your family?
- What's your favorite family meal?
- What's your favorite holiday and how do you celebrate it?
- What's the most relaxed time of day for your family? What goes on then?
- What's the most hectic time of day for your family? What goes on then?

*Source:* Wicht, S. (2015, May 26). *Families have much to share: Use these ideas to include the religious and nonreligious diversity of students' home lives in your practice.* Retrieved from https://www.tolerance.org/magazine/families-have-much-to-share

# Appendix C

*Family Engagement Behavior Audit T-Chart*

**Norms and Personal Bias**

| My Family's | Students' Families | Implications |
|---|---|---|
| | | |
| | | |
| | | |
| | | |
| | | |
| | | |
| | | |
| | | |

## References

Grant, K., & Ray, J. (2016). *Home, school and community collaboration: Culturally responsive family engagement.* Los Angeles, CA: SAGE.

Halgunseth, L., & Peterson, A. (2009). *Family engagement, diverse families, and early childhood education programs: An integrated review of the literature.* Washington, DC: NAEYC.

Harris, A., & Robinson, K. (2016). RSF: The Russell Sage Foundation. *Journal of the Social Sciences, 2*(5), 186–201.

Henderson, A., & Mapp, K. (2002). *A new wave of evidence: The impact of schools, community, and families on student achievement.* Austin, TX: Southwest Educational Development Laboratory.

Lightfoot, S. L. (2003). *The essential conversation: What parents and teachers can learn from each other.* New York, NY: Random House.

Lopez, M. E., Kreider, H., & Caspe, M. (2004). Co-constructing family involvement. *Evaluation Exchange, 2*(4), 2–3.

McAdoo, H. P. (2000). *Black children second edition: Social emotional and parental environments.* Thousand Oaks, CA: SAGE.

National Education Association. (2008). Parent, community and family involvement in education. Washington, DC.

Scott, M. (2017). *Even on your worst day you can be a student's best hope.* Alexandria, VA: ASCD.

Thiers, N. (2016). Unlocking families' potential: A conversation with Karen L. Mapp. *Educational Leadership, 75*(1), 40–44.

Wicht, S. (2015, May 26). *Families have much to share: Use these ideas to include the religious and nonreligious diversity of students' home lives in your practice.* Retrieved from https://www.tolerance.org/magazine/families-have-much-to-share

Zacarian, D., & Silverstone, M. (2016). Building partnerships through classroom-based events. *Educational Leadership, 75*(1), 12–18.

# MODULE 6

# Knowing the Community and Utilizing Its Resources

Theresa Y. Robinson
*Elmhurst College*

*True community is based upon equality, mutuality, and reciprocity. It affirms the richness of individual diversity as well as the common human ties that bind us together.*
—Pauli Murray

*I am a reflection of the community.*
—Tupac Shakur

## MODULE DESCRIPTION

This module is designed to support the teaching team in gaining a perspective on the social, political, economic, and cultural context of the community in which teaching and learning occur. Additionally, the module provides support to the pair and/or team to understand the community outside of the school in order to support building a community of learners inside the school and classroom. This understanding, including the availability of resources and services, can be used to support families, students, and instruction. The module also describes the importance of using strategies for getting to know the community and using its resources to promote learning. This is especially important for educators who are not members of the school community. Knowing and honoring the community promotes an ethic of care for the school and the learners in the classroom.

## Theory/Conceptual Framework

Students bring cultural capital in the form of personal or family assets to the classroom. Similarly, the school community offers assets that teachers may use to support teaching and learning. Burns, Paul & Paz (2012) define a community as a group of people living in the same locality, a group of people sharing common interests or similar identity, or the district or locality in which such groups live. Dorfman (1998) extended the idea of community to include services and resources. Access to services and resources play an important role in student success both socially and academically. Payne (1998) lists six types of resources students may need: financial, emotional, mental, spiritual, physical, and relationship/role models (Figure 6.1). These resource areas help teachers identify areas of needs for students. Furthermore, knowing the community and its resources will support teachers in providing access to needed services in an area of need for students.

> **Financial**—Having the money to purchase goods and services.
> 
> **Emotional**—An internal resource that shows itself through stamina, perseverance, and choices that avoid negative behaviors; the most important of all resources.
> 
> **Mental**—Mental abilities and acquired skills like reading, writing, and computing.
> 
> **Spiritual**—Believing in divine purpose and guidance. A powerful resource by providing students a sense of capability worth, and value.
> 
> **Physical**—Having physical health and mobility.
> 
> **Relationships/Role Model**—An external resource; Having access to friends, family, knowledge bases, and adults which are appropriate and can help nurture the child.

**Figure 6.1** Types of resources. Adapted from *A Framework for Understanding Poverty Modules 1–9 Workbook*, by Ruby K. Payne, PhD. All rights reserved. Published by aha! Process, Inc. www.ahaprocess.com

Current teacher and student demographics suggest that the majority of teachers are White females and the student population in K–12 schools is increasingly racially, ethnically, and linguistically diverse. According to the National Center for Education Statistics (2011), White teachers accounted for 82% of the teaching force and collectively Black, Hispanic, Asian, Pacific Islander, American Indian, and Alaskan natives comprised 18% of the teaching force. This trend points to the need to ensure that teachers understand the communities in which their students are members and how to engage their families. It is imperative that teachers who do not share similar cultural experiences as their students get to know the students and communities in which they are teaching.

Perceptions of poor and ethnically diverse students often represent a deficit perspective. A deficit perspective assumes that students have deficits like language, culture, and/or social experiences that must be overcome if they are to learn (Nieto & Bode, 2012). Stoddard, Braun, & Koorland (2011) cited research that found that the White preservice teachers they studied perceived ethnic minority children in underserved communities as lacking intelligence, unmotivated, difficult to work with, and apt to cause discipline problems. These attitudes toward families from culturally diverse communities can significantly impede efforts for successful collaboration between home and school (Amatea, Cholewa, & Mixon, 2012). To counter deficit perspective attitudes, Ferguson (2008) recommends that teachers use communication styles called "high help" and "high perfectionism."

> High help is when the teacher communicates convincingly that h/she likes when students ask questions and that she loves to help them when they are confused or making mistakes. High perfectionism is when the teacher consistently and continually presses students to strive for both understanding and accuracy in their assignments which communicate high expectations. (Ferguson, 2008)

Amatea et al., (2012) studied the impact of coursework and field experiences to explore the change in perspective of preservice teachers about working with low-income and/or ethnic minority families. The authors concluded that the teachers' greatest gains were in implementing family centric practices such as engaging in a home visit, attending community events or shopping at neighborhood stores. With experience and action, teachers are more likely to understand their pupils and local school neighborhoods. This understanding will help teachers to provide a more relevant curriculum and a level of caring that stems from what the community communicates as needs (Fife-Demski, 2016). Seminal research conducted by Moll, Amanti, Neff, and Gonzalez (1992) gave voice to the perspective that students' lives outside of school were rich and could be used as a source for the development of good teaching or a 'fund of knowledge.'

Teachers must be able to care at a critical level within the local community to better understand and connect with their pupils (Fife-Demski, 2016). There are two main purposes for knowing the community in which educators serve: 1) to better understand pupils and their needs, and 2) to use community resources to support student learning. Knowledge and use of community resources can be categorized into two areas. Teachers can use community resources to support the well-being of students or the resources can be used to support what is taught and how it is taught. See Figure 6.1 for a list of types of resources that can be used for curriculum and instruction.

Connecting students and families to community resources may meet financial, emotional, physical, or mental needs of the student and/or family. Meeting these needs maximize opportunities for student learning. A school community may have a public library that provides after-school programming, tutoring, or reading programs including places of worship like temples, churches, synagogues, and mosques. Parks, museums, zoos, community centers, and recreational facilities can also be sources for curriculum materials and experts. All of these community assets can be used to bring authentic learning experiences into the classroom and lessons. These community assets can be sources of authentic learning experiences for teaching and learning. Knowing the school community even when the students are not members of the community is important and will assist teachers to provide a more relevant curriculum (Fife- Demski, 2016).

## Specific Questions to Guide Discussion

1. In what ways have you connected with the community and its members?

2. What organizations are present in the school community that support students' social, emotional, and health and wellness needs?

3. In what ways have you encouraged students and families to use resources to support learning outside of the classroom?

4. How can you use community resources to support student learning?

5. What have you learned about the community in which you teach? What have you identified about the community's historical, cultural, and economic demographics.

## Productive Practices

Immerse yourself in the physical context of the learners that you teach (e.g., community of the school, summer camp, after-school programs) in order to best understand them. Network with community members to find opportunities for collaboration in order to support curriculum and instruction.

1. *Tour the community.*
    a. Tour the community in which the school or classroom is located. Take note of grocery stores, restaurants, places of worship, shops, parks, museums, and community centers.
    b. Build your background knowledge about the presence and absence of resources in the community.
2. *Shop and eat locally.*
    a. Shop at local grocery and convenience stores. Eat at local restaurants to increase your visibility and connection to the local community.
    b. Visit and shop in these establishments because it helps us to learn about where our students live.
3. *Volunteer for extracurricular activities.*
    a. Volunteer to serve as an after-school club sponsor.
    b. Support and attend student sporting and academic events.
4. *Create effective communication models.*
    a. Establish effective school-to-home and home-to-school communication systems with families. (e.g., a newsletter, website or blog).
    b. Connect families to community resources that strengthen and support student learning and well-being.

5. *Community Service*
    a. Volunteer for community service events. Volunteering for community service events builds upon your knowledge of community needs and ways to support student needs.
    b. Make a list of community services in the neighborhood that includes contact names, phone numbers, and emails.

## What Would You Do?

Ask your team or pair the following questions. For suggested responses to questions, see Appendix A.

1. What would you do if you were stopped by police and questioned about your presence in the community?

2. What would you do if there was an event in the school community and you did not feel comfortable attending it?

3. What would you do if your school community lacked technology resources to address the needs of the 21st century learner?

## Reflective Professional Growth Activities

Consider these ideas or activities to facilitate and foster teacher growth and reflection. Select one or two ideas to help facilitate this reflection process that will help the teacher, pair, or team to understand the connection of knowing the community and utilizing its resources to impact student learning. Remember that you know the individuals best so be sure to choose an activity that would be the most effective.

### *Idea 1: Community Member Interview*

Interview a community member involved in supporting education (e.g., minister, school board member, community liaison or activist). In preparation for the meeting, choose and contact a community member to interview, schedule the interview, ask for permission to record the interview if needed, and write a list of questions to ask. You may want to use the following questions to begin your interview:

1. What value does the community and its members place on education?
2. In what ways are you involved with the school district?

The interview may be conducted face-to-face, by telephone, or virtually. Take notes on salient points from the interview.

**Evidence:** Written reflection on the impact of the interview on your knowledge of the community and its resources; Include responses to your questions and a list of possible student learning activities that integrate community resources.

## *Idea 2: Community Service Activity*

Target your volunteer efforts. Identify and work with an agency so that your efforts are responsive and address a need. The organization or agency may not need books, but may need socks or other items of clothing (e.g., a PADS shelter). Be sure to highlight this work within the school district community (e.g., website, board meeting, social media).

Before beginning a community service activity to benefit the community, reflect on the following questions: 1) What fear, if any, do you have about working with the agency and the population it serves? and 2) What do you hope to learn from the experience? Find a cause that you care about, fits your schedule, and an organization that supports the cause. Examples of organizations include shelters, parent organizations, hospitals, and police or fire departments. Some examples of community service activities include but are not limited to:

1. Collecting children's books for shelters, libraries, and schools.
2. Volunteering for community clean-up projects (e.g., Clean and Green).
3. Teaching computer skills at a senior center or assisted living center.
4. Offering to teach a class or program in the community.
5. Supporting a local animal shelter.

You may involve your students and their families in volunteerism (e.g., asking for donations for drives, creating and distributing flyers). After participating in a community service event, you may want to include an educational component for your class by integrating a service learning project into your curriculum.

**Evidence:** Written description of the volunteer activity, response to pre-volunteer questions, and the outcomes of the community service activity.

### Idea 3: Community Asset Mapping: Doc the Block (adapted from Dorfman (1998), and Burns (2012)

It is important to focus on community assets that are in or near the school's attendance boundaries. Use a community walk or drive with online research to determine the resources available for teaching and learning. Get a local map and locate the school district's boundaries. Drive through the community in which you teach. What restaurants, libraries, stores, museums, and places of worship are in the community and frequented by the students and their families? What kind of housing do you see? Note the signage as you explore the community. Do you see any signs that are written in other languages?

**Evidence:** Choose one of the items below as evidence for idea number 3.
*Choice A:* Create a newsletter, website, or blog for parents with local resources including website addresses to support their students' learning.
*Choice B:* Create a map of the community including markers that identify useful resources (e.g., landmarks, parks, libraries).

## Idea 4: Our Neighborhood: Media Project

Invite students and families to send in photos and videos from around the neighborhood/community of the school. Create a visual presentation (i.e., Imovie, Prezi, PowerPoint, Google photo album, Slide Share or bulletin board of photos). Show the video at a school Open House or during parent teacher conferences. When students see themselves in books, photo displays, etc. they will be far more engaged in the text and material.

**Evidence:** Provide evidence of the completed media project. This may be a photo of the bulletin board or electronic access for viewers to the presentation.

## Idea 5: Resource Analysis

What resources do your students have access to? Choose one class, period, or block of students where you will complete a resource analysis chart. Using the Resource Analysis Chart, write in information that you know about your students from informal observations, student interest inventories, or parent teacher conferences. Use a question mark (?) where the resources are uncertain.

**Evidence:** Provide a completed chart (see Figure 6.2 for an example, see Appendix B for a blank template).

| Student Name | Financial Resources | Emotional Resources | Mental Resources | Spiritual Resources | Physical Resources | Relationships Role Models |
|---|---|---|---|---|---|---|
| Tyla | Family has access to financial resources, mother is a teacher and her father is a union machinist. | Tyla tends to give up easily when faced with challenging tasks if she isn't successful on the first try. | She is an avid reader but is striving to improve her writing skills. | Her family members are active in their local church and she participates in the youth choir. | She runs on the school's track team and dances with an African dance troupe. | – Mother<br>– Father<br>– Family members<br>– Pastor<br>– Church members<br>– Choir director<br>– Youth choir members<br>– Track team members<br>– Track coach<br>– Dance teacher<br>– Dance troupe members |

**Figure 6.2** Example of Resource Analysis Chart. *A Framework for Understanding Poverty. Modules 1–9 Workbook*, by Ruby K. Payne, PhD. All rights reserved. Published by aha! Process, Inc.

# Follow-Up, Monitoring, and Goal Setting

Depending on the idea chosen from the reflective professional growth activities, complete the following before you begin your next observation.

## *Idea 1: Community Member Interview*

- Who did you interview, and why did you choose this community member? What did you learn about the value the community and its members place on education?
- What interesting facts about the community did you learn from the interview? How did the information impact your thinking about your curriculum and instruction?
- How does the organization/agency support the school district and how can you use these resources in teaching and learning?
- How are the values of the community similar or different from your own?

## *Idea 2: Community Service Activity*

- What organization did you volunteer for? What did you learn about the needs of the community?
- How did the event help support the local community?
- What was the identified challenge/community need? What did you learn from the experience?
- What did you learn about yourself as a result of the community service activity? Compare and contrast the needs of the school community to your own community's needs.
- Describe how what you learned about the community will be integrated into your instruction and assessment.

## *Idea 3: Cultural Asset Mapping: Doc the Block*

- Provide a list of community assets that you found that can be used for planning and instruction.
- Describe how you plan to use the museum or park district for examples as a community asset in planning for instruction and assessment.
- Name something interesting that you found about the school community. How will you use this knowledge to support teaching and student learning?

## *Idea 4: Our Neighborhood: Media Project*

- How did the students respond when creating and viewing the "Our Neighborhood" media project?
- How will you extend the project in order to impact student learning (i.e., launch a unit, generate writing a paper, participate in a service learning project)?
- What did you learn about the community from this project? How will you use this information in your teaching and learning?

## Idea 5: Resource Analysis

- What patterns in resources did you discover were needed for the whole class, period, or block?
- How will you use community resources to support students' needs based on the analysis? What will you do to transform students' experiences while in school?
- How will you connect individual students to resources they may need?

## Resources

### Web Resources

**A Community Resource Toolkit**

This website promotes family engagement in the State of Illinois for improving child outcomes in the early years at the systems level. The organization uses policy advocacy, data research, and power building to advance the needs of marginalized communities.

Burns, J. C., Paul, D. P., & Paz, S. R. (2012, April). *Participatory asset mapping: A community research lab toolkit.* Retrieved from www.advancementprojectca.org

**Doc Ur Block**

This website provides a syllabus and PowerPoint for a 10th grade sociology class where students learn to do sociological research on their own communities.

Education for Liberation Network. (2009–2012). *Doc Ur Block.* K. Wand Yange and Jeff Duncan-Andrade. Retrieved from http://www.edliberation.org/resources/lab/records/doc-ur-block

**Parent Engagement Toolkit**

This online pdf provides access to the Parent Engagement Toolkit for Educators. The documents include assessment tools educators can use to assess their level of family and community engagement in their school(s).

Boston Public Schools. (n.d.). *Be reflective: Engagement mindset & impact.* Retrieved from https://www.bostonpublicschools.org/cms/lib/MA01906464/Centricity/Domain/112/Pages%20from%20ParentEngagement%20ToolkitForEducatorsPart2FINALpdf.pdf

## Key Terms and Definitions

**Authentic learning:** An instructional approach that allows students to construct knowledge in a meaningful way using real-world problems, issues, and projects. It is a learning by doing approach to learning.

**Community asset mapping:** Representation of a community's strengths and resources depicted on a community map. Strengths and resources can be related to basic needs, education, recreation, health care, community services, international services, etc.

**Community service**: Volunteer work intended to support the community and its members in a particular area of need in an effort to improve the quality of life for community residents.

**Cultural capital:** Transmission of values, tastes, languages, dialects, and cultures of a group that are hidden forms of hereditary transmissions of capital. Cultural capital includes the power, knowledge, and resources located in the norms of cultures and languages.

**Deficit perspective:** The assumption that some students because of genetic, cultural, or experiential differences are inferior to other students. The assumption is that these students have deficits that must be overcome before they can learn (e.g., race, ability, non-native English speakers).

**Funds of knowledge:** Life experiences, strategic knowledge, and skills that learners bring from their homes, established relationships, social activities, and communities that can be used to develop concepts and skills in the classroom setting (i.e., home language, family occupations, family traditions, household chores, international travel).

**Service learning**: A teaching and learning strategy integrating community service with instruction and reflection designed to strengthen communities and teach civic responsibility. Service learning is more than community service, it must have a learning component.

# Appendix A

## *What Would You Do? Questions with Suggested Responses*

1. What would you do if you were stopped by police and questioned about your presence in the community?

   **Suggested Response 1:** Always comply with law enforcement and answer all questions. Make sure to keep your hands visible and do not motion to reach for anything unless instructed.

2. What would you do if there was an event in the school community and you did not feel comfortable attending?

   **Suggested Response 2:** It is important to show interest in students' lives outside of the school. Explore reasons why you might feel uncomfortable attending. Possible reasons may include being racially or ethnically in the minority, or a safety concern. Some school communities may have perceived or realistic perceptions about safety. Make plans to attend the function and take a friend to ease any concerns you may have.

3. What would you do if your school community lacked technology resources to address the needs of the 21st century learner?

   **Suggested Response 3:** Apply for locally funded grants for teachers. Provide suggestions for student use of technology outside of the classroom (i.e., using a public library, scheduling lab time during class time for projects). Find creative ways for students to use cellular devices for activities outside of class.

# Appendix B
## *Resource Analysis Chart Template*

| Student Name | Financial Resources | Emotional Resources | Mental Resources | Spiritual Resources | Physical Resources | Relationships Role Models |
|---|---|---|---|---|---|---|
|  |  |  |  |  |  |  |
|  |  |  |  |  |  |  |
|  |  |  |  |  |  |  |

*A Framework for Understanding Poverty Modules 1–9 Workbook*, by Ruby K. Payne, PhD. All rights reserved. Published by aha! Process, Inc.

# References

Amatea, E. S., Cholewa, B., & Mixon, K. A. (2012). Influencing preservice teachers' attitudes about working with low income and/or ethnic minority families. *Urban Education, 47*(4) 801–834.

Burns, J. C., Paul, D. P., & Paz, S. R. (2012, April). *Participatory asset mapping: A community research lab toolkit.* Retrieved from www.advancementprojectca.org

Dorfman, D. (1998). *Mapping community assets workbook.* Portland, OR: Northwest Regional Educational Laboratory. (n.d.). Retrieved from http://www.nwrel.org/ruraled/

Ferguson, R. F. (2008). *Helping students of color meet high standards.* In M. Pollock (Ed.), *Everyday antiracism: Getting real about race in school.* pp. 78–81. New York, NY: New Press.

Fife-Demski, V. (2016). Crossing borders with a level of caring. *Curriculum & Teaching Dialogue, 18*(1/2), 71–83.

Moll, L., Amanti, C., Neff, D., & Gonzalez, N. (1992, November 2). Funds of knowledge for teaching: Using a qualitative approach to connect homes and classrooms. *Theory into Practice, 31,* 132–140.

National Center for Education Statistics. (2011). Retrieved from https://nces.ed.gov/

Nieto, S., & Bode, P. (2012). *Affirming diversity: The sociopolitical context of multicultural education* (6th ed.). Boston, MA: Pearson.

Payne, R. K. (2001). *Framework for Understanding Poverty.* Highland, TX: Aha! Process, Inc.

Payne, R. K. (1998). *Framework for Understanding Poverty: Modules 1–9 Workbook.* Highland, Texas: Aha! Process.

Stoddard, K., Braun, B., & Koorland, M. (2011). Beyond the school house. Understanding families through preservices experiences in the community. *Preventing School Failure, 55*(3), 158–163.

# PART III
*Putting It All Together*

MODULE 7

# Creating a Positive Climate in the Classroom

Wendy A. Harriott

*Monmouth University*

*I have come to the frightening conclusion that I am the decisive element in the classroom. It's my personal approach that creates the climate. It's my daily mood that makes the weather. As a teacher, I possess a tremendous power to make a child's life miserable or joyous. I can be a tool of torture or an instrument of inspiration. I can humiliate or humor, hurt or heal. In all situations, it is my response that decides whether a crisis will be escalated or de-escalated and a child humanized or de-humanized.*

—Haim Ginott

## MODULE DESCRIPTION

One of the most important areas for a teacher to understand and implement is how to create a positive classroom climate and culture for all learners. Provided within this module are multiple suggestions and resources to help facilitate an understanding of how to think about creating a positive classroom environment. Within the scope of this module, the following areas will be introduced: creating positive expectations and a welcoming environment, setting the stage for a collaborative classroom among students and with other professionals, planning and organizing prior to the school year and during the first week, setting up a structured, predictable

> classroom setting, and creating useful rules, routines, and cues for transition times. Ultimately, the classroom climate that a teacher creates will set the stage for positive student behaviors, student learning, and engagement throughout the school year.

## Theory/Conceptual Framework

Creating a positive classroom climate is one of the most important first steps for teachers to consider as they prepare for the school year. A positive classroom climate is a prerequisite condition in establishing an environment where students are able to learn and, at the same time, feel a sense of belongingness. Teachers create this climate in a variety of ways, including how they present themselves as professionals, how they arrange classroom furniture and materials, how they decorate the room, and how they greet and interact with students on a daily basis. Creating a welcoming classroom for students takes a great deal of prior planning and preparation. Specifically, teachers need to plan for establishing clear behavioral expectations, strategies for welcoming students, organizing the classroom, and developing motivating lesson plans. Jones (2001) considers classroom arrangement as the keystone for classroom management. He suggests that the way the teacher sets up the classroom arrangement will prevent most classroom disruptions. Additionally, teachers must display respect and warmth for every student. Each student needs to feel valued in order to be successful. Student learning may also be enhanced when teachers provide a high rate of positive statements and praise for engaging in behavioral expectations as posted in the classroom (Simonsen, Fairbanks, Briesch, Myers, & Sugai, 2008).

Within today's classrooms, various professionals come together and work collaboratively to meet the needs of the diverse students in their classrooms. This ability to work cooperatively in planning and teaching affects student learning, behaviors, and the classroom climate (Winter, 2007). Collaboration is defined as two or more professionals implementing shared teaching, decision-making, goal setting, and accountability for a diverse group of students (Friend & Cook, 2009). Teachers have to work on their collaborative relationships in order to learn how to function together as a successful team. Teachers must make specific plans on how they will communicate, finding common times to work together, and developing shared roles and responsibilities for their classrooms (Conderman, 2011). It is important for teachers to make it a priority at the beginning of the year and on an ongoing basis to work on establishing and nurturing collaborative relationships with other professionals.

Another important area for consideration in creating and setting up a classroom environment is the overall structure and predictability of the classroom. Creating a class that is highly structured and predictable can help prevent behavior problems because students are aware of the expectations, feel more safe and comfortable when they know what to expect, and ultimately, are more engaged in instructional time (Conroy, Sutherland, Snyder, & Marsh, 2008; Kerr & Nelson, 2010). When students are aware of expectations and are provided with clear directions and procedures to follow, student engagement increases while off-task behavior decreases (Kerr & Nelson, 2010).

Establishing rules and routines is another important area related to classroom climate. Classroom rules create explicit expectations for student behaviors (Jones & Jones, 2012). Rules are most effective when they are positively stated, concrete, and observable (Simonsen et al., 2008). Implementing routines in a classroom environment is considered the "backbone of daily classroom life," (Murry, 2002). Routines (also called procedures), should be established at the beginning of the school year. They must be modeled, taught, and practiced so that students begin to use them automatically during daily classroom life. Establishing routines serves many purposes in the classroom, including helping to maintain a safe and academic-focused environment, spending time getting to know one another, facilitating mutual respect, and establishing cooperative learning groups. Further, Pedota (2007) reports that developing classroom routines is a major goal in setting up a positive classroom climate. As students learn the routines and follow them on a daily basis, the time for learning increases, while the time for transitions decreases. The goal is to attempt to decrease transition times. If there are long delays between activities, this can result in inappropriate behaviors for some students (Emmer & Evertson, 2013). Providing cues for transitions and teaching routines to make transitions seamless, greatly reduces the probability of student misbehavior.

Overall, how teachers plan and organize their classrooms prior to the school year (including classroom arrangement, establishing collaborative relationships, planning lessons, and planning routines) is crucial to creating a positive classroom climate for the year. Additionally, how teachers plan activities and lessons for the beginning of the school year set the tone for the year. All professionals must devote time to developing and creating the best possible learning setting for their students.

## Specific Questions to Guide Discussion

1. Describe how you modeled a positive, welcoming, professional teacher presence during the past week. What specific things did you do or say to demonstrate positive expectations? What ideas do you have to add to the classroom environment to make it more welcoming and accepting for individuals from various cultures?

2. Describe activities you use or plan to use to help establish positive relationships among students at the beginning of the year. What ideas do you have to make your future classroom welcoming for both students and other professionals?

3. Describe how you will plan to create a positive classroom climate prior to the start of the school year. Describe how you will plan your classroom arrangement, first day/week activities, record keeping, etc., in order to promote a positive environment. What resources/information do you think you will need to properly prepare your classroom?

4. Describe how you collaborate and plan for class on a weekly and daily basis. Reflect on a lesson you were involved in during the past week. How did your planning affect the lesson? What additional steps should be added to your planning/preparation to enhance student behaviors and learning?

5. Examine the established classroom rules. Describe how you might modify the rules based on your observations and interactions with students. Describe ideas you have for teaching and implementing the rules on a daily basis. Describe various ways to improve students' abilities to follow the rules using positive expectations and opportunities to practice following the rules.

6. Describe various classroom routines and transition cues used. Analyze why specific routines are implemented. Describe how you plan to assist students with various transitions during the school day.

## Productive Practices

1. *Create and maintain a positive, professional presence and classroom.*
    a. Dress professionally. Observe others in the building, including the principal and other teachers, and make sure your dress is similar. It is always better to be overdressed than underdressed.
    b. Remember to relax and smile when appropriate (e.g., greetings, daily interactions).
    c. Greet and address students by name using the correct pronunciation.
    d. Create a plan and activities to establish positive relationships with your students.
    e. Organize your classroom to be informative, inviting, and inclusive of individuals from various cultures. Ensure that all posters, photographs, and books displayed in your classroom include people from various ethnicities, races, genders, etc.
    f. Model a demeanor of "positive expectations." Expect and guide all students to succeed in academics and behaviors.
    g. Use specific praise to reinforce positive behaviors that students exhibit to demonstrate how they follow classroom rules or routines.
2. *Establish a collaborative classroom culture among students and with other professionals.*
    a. Prepare "Getting to Know You" activities for the first few days of class. These activities are important to allow students to get to know each other and feel comfortable learning and sharing the classroom space for the school year. Sample activities are listed below.
        - Have pairs of students conduct interviews with each other to learn classmates' names and a few facts about each other (i.e., hobbies, family members). Students can then introduce each other to the class.
        - Ask students to complete a brief questionnaire identifying their favorite subjects, interests, etc. The results can then be shared class-wide or in small groups (e.g., "The thing I do best is...").
        - Ask students from last year's class to write letters to your students, telling them what to expect, suggestions for maintaining a high grade, etc. Share these letters with your students.
    b. Prepare your students and classroom to be inviting to other professionals who may spend part of the day with you and your class (e.g., speech language pathologists, co-teachers, paraprofessionals, other related services personnel).

- Allow time for each professional to share who they are and how they will work with the class for the year. Ask each professional to prepare a short activity or lesson to become engaged with the whole class so students can become familiar and comfortable with all who work within your classroom setting.
- Allocate time to meet with each professional on a regular basis to coordinate lesson planning and/or consult regarding a student or group of students. Make sure you find a time to meet that is workable for each partner. It is important to establish roles and responsibilities for each professional early in the school year to minimize misunderstandings.
- Spend time communicating with the various professionals with whom you work. Take the time to learn more about how each professional prefers to communicate (e.g., email, in person meetings, phone, Skype). Establishing good working relationships/partnerships will lead to better communication and better outcomes for the students in your class.

3. *Allocate time for planning/organizing prior to the school year.*
   a. Prepare your classroom so that all desks and other work areas are arranged to maximize class time and space. Consider student and teacher movement, a clear visual path, and organization. Your room should be arranged to be consistent with your instructional goals (e.g., clearly designated work spaces, flexible spaces for individual and cooperative group work).
   b. Prepare the classroom so all students have appropriately labeled personal spaces to store their belongings. Ensure that you provide an appropriate work space for your co-teacher and other professionals who work within your classroom setting.
   c. Prepare all needed instructional materials (e.g., pens, paper, reference materials, pencil sharpener) to be easily accessible to you and your students.
   d. Use classroom wall spaces primarily for educational purposes (e.g., the alphabet, word walls, steps for Writer's Workshop, multiplication tables, a map of the world).

4. *Establish and maintain a highly structured and predictable classroom setting.*
   a. Allocate time for planning/organizing prior to each school week and on a daily basis.
   b. Prepare lessons at least one week in advance.
   c. Ensure you are fully planned for the whole school day. Create a detailed lesson plan for each subject/class, prepare materials making sure they are ready for all activities, and have several "Back up" plans for lessons/activities that you might need to change at the last minute. Always plan more material than you think you will need. (*Note:* It is always better to over plan rather than have extra time at the end of a class with no planned activities.)
   d. Post a "Do Now" (or "Bell Ringer") for students to become engaged immediately when they enter your classroom.
   e. Provide an agenda/schedule at the beginning of each day/lesson so students know what is coming up throughout the day. If there will be last minute changes in the schedule (e.g., a special assembly), provide students with a "heads up" as soon as possible. When advance notice is not possible (e.g., emergency drills), have clear specified routines in place for students to follow.
   f. Reorganize classroom arrangements and materials based on the instructional activities for the day/week.

5. *Create, post, and use classroom rules.*
   a. Create 5–7 rules with your students to use on a daily basis.

b. State rules in terms of behaviors you want to see (i.e., use "Keep hands to yourself" instead of "Do not hit").
c. Post the rules in a visible location in your classroom.
d. Teach/model how to follow the rules. Provide opportunities for students to practice adherence to the rules. Teach the consequences for not following the rules.
e. Review and reteach the rules as needed throughout the school year.
6. *Create and establish daily classroom routines and procedures for transitions.*
   a. The routines you establish depend on your individual students' ages and ability levels (For example, routines for sharpening pencils might be needed at the elementary level but are not necessary in secondary classrooms).
   b. Plan cues to signal that transitions are approaching. Plan routines for transitions into and out of the classroom: beginning the school day or period, moving from one activity to another, leaving the classroom, and ending the day. Common transition cues include playing music, ringing a bell, hand-claps, and a visual countdown.
   c. Consider establishing routines for room use: accessing and storing materials, using the pencil sharpener, use of special areas in the classroom (e.g., centers), etc.
   d. Consider including routines for individual work and teacher-led instructional time (e.g., how to ask and answer questions, when students may talk to each other, how to request additional assistance, what to do when work is completed).
   e. Establish routines for general classroom procedures (e.g., collecting homework, distributing materials, handling interruptions, using the restroom, eating in the cafeteria, preparing for fire and other disaster drills, using student helpers).
   f. Model, teach, practice, and reteach classroom transitions and routines during the first weeks of class and as needed throughout the school year. Remember, students need to learn and practice routines and transitions until they can perform them automatically.

*Note:* Please remember to include your co-teacher or team in planning and implementing all of the above Productive Practices.

## What Would You Do?

Ask your team or pair the following questions. For suggested responses to questions, see Appendix A.

1. What would you do if a student didn't follow an established classroom rule or routine?

2. What would you do if a student made an inappropriate comment about a poster that displayed a person of a different race, ethnicity, or gender?

3. What would you do if students refused to participate or share information about themselves during "getting to know you" activities during the first days of school?

# Reflective Professional Growth Activities

Consider these ideas or activities to facilitate and foster teacher growth and reflection. Select one or two ideas to help facilitate this reflection process that will help the teacher, pair or team to create a positive climate in the classroom. Remember that supervisors are instructional leaders and should know the person(s) well, so be sure to choose a growth activity that would be the most effective for them.

## *Idea 1: Creating a Positive Classroom Climate*

Reflect on the ways a positive climate and expectations for all students in your classroom are established. What do you do to create and nurture relationships with your students? Additionally, what phrases do you say to create positive expectations for all? Reflect on the ways that collaborative relationships with other professionals associated with your students and the classroom are developed and maintained. Describe new strategies to enhance your classroom climate. Implement a few new strategies and reflect on how well they worked. Describe how you might revise your strategies in the future.

**Evidence:** A written list of strategies to enhance a positive classroom climate for all students. A reflection on new strategies implemented with data to demonstrate the effectiveness of each strategy.

## *Idea 2: Planning for Class*

Interview 4–5 teachers in the school building or district where you are placed. Create questions prior to the interview to learn about how they plan before the school year, the first week of school, and on a daily basis. What tips can they share with you to improve your own classroom planning strategies? Locate resources to assist you in improving your planning strategies.

**Evidence:** Written reflection based on evidence gained during teacher interviews. The reflection must include ideas for improving planning strategies.

## *Idea 3: Reflecting on Classroom Arrangements*

Visit several other classrooms in your school or district. Take notes on how you might use or modify the room arrangement for your classroom. Draw a map of the classroom arrangement for one class that you visited. Include student movement patterns on your diagram. Which arrangements are consistent with the instructional goals/activities that you observed? Can all students and teachers easily access all needed materials? Can all professionals see and access all students easily from all areas of the room? Do the visuals/activities in the room reflect individuals from various cultures? What suggestions do you have to improve the classroom environments you observed?

**Evidence:** Notes and a diagram on observed classroom environments with suggestions for improvement.

## Idea 4: Analyze Classroom Rules, Routines, and Transitions

Reflect on the classroom rules, routines, and transition times used in your classroom. Does each rule and routine serve a purpose? Were they effective or not? Describe a plan for modifying each as needed. Collect data on how long various transitions take within your classroom. Do you have ideas to make transitions easier and flow more quickly? Which routines/rules need to be modified for a specific student or group of students? Why do you think each routine/rule should be modified? Provide data to support your ideas.

**Evidence:** Written reflection on how the rules/routines are working with suggestions for improvement. Include a list of effective/appropriate rules/routines you have used or observed. Report on data collected of various transition times.

# Follow-Up, Monitoring, and Goal Setting

Complete the follow-up questions for the selected reflective professional growth activity.

## Idea 1: Creating a Positive Classroom Climate

- Describe three new strategies you plan to implement to improve classroom climate overall and to enhance a relationship with a target student or a small group of students.
- Additionally, describe three new strategies you plan to use to improve the collaborative relationship with other professionals with whom you work.
- What data will be collected to determine the effectiveness of the strategies you used to relate with students and other professionals?
- What are some specific steps that you are going to take to ensure that this continues?
- Do you have anything else you want to discuss in the area of a positive classroom climate before we move on to the next topic?
- Do you have any further questions?

## Idea 2: Planning for Class

- What did you learn about planning prior to and during the school year from your interviews?
- What strategies/ideas do you plan to use in your daily preparation for the class?
- What resources have you found to help with planning prior to the school year?
- Do you have anything else you want to discuss related to preparation before we move on to the next topic?
- Do you have any further questions?

## Idea 3: Reflecting on Classroom Arrangements

- What did you learn about classroom arrangements from your visits?
- What new ideas do you have to improve classroom settings?
- What types of classroom arrangements did you find to be effective?
- What suggestions do you have to make your classroom more inclusive of all cultures/races?

- What are some specific steps that you are going to take to implement your ideas now or in the future?
- Do you have anything else that you want to discuss in the area of positive classroom arrangements before we move on to the next topic?
- Do you have any further questions?

## *Idea 4: Analyze Classroom Rules, Routines, and Transitions*

- Share the daily routines used in your classroom.
- Describe how you can embed opportunities to practice routines in your classroom.
- Describe how you might modify each routine for a different grade level or classroom setting.
- Share the various procedures used during transition times in your classroom.
- Describe how you might modify each for a different grade level or classroom setting.
- Describe the rules (posted and unwritten) used in your classroom.
- Do you think any should be revised? How and why do you suggest these changes?
- Describe methods used to teach rules.
- Do you have anything else you want to discuss related to rules, routines, and/or transitions before we move on to the next topic?
- Do you have any further questions?

# Resources

## *Articles*

**Online Support in Classroom Management**

This study examines feedback from beginning teachers who attended a classroom management workshop, followed by eight weeks of online support. It describes techniques that were used by teachers and found to be effective.

Baker, C., Gentry, J., & Larmer, W. (2016). A model for online support in classroom management: Perceptions of beginning teachers. *Administrative Issues Journal: Education, Practice, & Research, 6*(1), 22–37. doi:10.5929/2016.6.1.3

**Lessons From Beginning Teachers**

This article examines reflections from beginning teachers in order to determine seven strategies for improving classroom management.

Eckert, J. (2014). Teach like a novice: Lessons from beginning teachers. *Phi Delta Kappan, 96*(2), 13–18.

**Motivation Through Routine Documentation**

This article offers a classroom management strategy using documentation to motivate students academically and behaviorally. It aligns with self-determination theory.

Koth, L. J. (2016). Motivation through routine documentation. *American Secondary Education, 45*(1), 59–69.

### Cracking the Behavior Code

This article discusses student management strategies in the classroom. It examines how teacher–student relationships can reinforce or correct undesirable behaviors.

Rappaport, N., & Minahan, J. (2012). Cracking the behavior code. *Educational Leadership, 70*(2), 18.

### Routines of Classroom Management

This article discusses the importance of routines and structure in terms of classroom management. It is divided into three sections: structures, routines, and maintaining behavior.

Lester, R. R., Allanson, P. B., & Notar, C. E. (2017). Routines are the foundation of classroom management. *Education, 137*(4), 398–412.

### Teaching Social Curriculum

This article identifies climate building as a key classroom management strategy. It details specific climate building techniques to maximize learning and minimize disruptions.

Skiba, R., Ormiston, H., Martinez, S., & Cummings, J. (2016) Teaching the social curriculum: Classroom management as behavioral instruction. *Theory into Practice, 55*(2), 120–128.

## *Books*

### Developing a Learning Classroom

This book explores three ways to create a learner-centered classroom environment through relationships, relevance, and rigor. It highlights creating a safe learning environment and establishing rules and procedures.

Cooper, N., & Garner, B. K. (2012). *Developing a learning classroom: Moving beyond management through relationships, relevance, and rigor*. Thousand Oaks, CA: Corwin.

### Proactive Classroom Management

This book includes a wealth of teacher created and approved strategies for classroom management. It has ready-to-use tools that promote positive behavior and student responsibility.

Denti, L. G. (2012). *Proactive classroom management, K–8: A practical guide to empower students and teachers*. Thousand Oaks, CA: Corwin.

### Classroom Management for Elementary Teachers

This book is a guide for classroom teachers to create and maintain a classroom management plan. The author emphasizes the need to put in the initial time and effort in order to have more engaged and cooperative students.

Evertson, C. M., & Emmer, E. T. (2013). *Classroom management for elementary teachers* (9th ed.). Boston, MA: Pearson.

### Handbook of Classroom Management

This book provides an overarching perspective on classroom management. It is divided into ten chapters discussing various aspects of classroom management including theories, research, and areas in need of further research.

Evertson, C. M., & Weinstein, C. S. (2006). *Handbook of classroom management: Research, practice, and contemporary issues*. Mahwah, NJ: Erlbaum.

## Class-Wide Positive Behavior Interventions and Supports

This book includes how to implement positive behavior interventions and supports (PBIS) in K–12 classrooms. Practical guidelines are included for creating the classroom environment, teaching using positive expectations, and establishing strategies to reinforce behaviors.

Simonsen, B., & Myers, D. (2015). *Classwide positive behavior interventions and supports*. New York, NY: Guilford Press.

## The Classroom Management Book

This book provides 50 ways to organize and structure a classroom to create a safe and positive environment for student learning.

Wong, H. K., Wong, R. T., Jondahl, S. F., & Ferguson, O. F. (2014). *The classroom management book*. Mountain View, CA: Harry K. Wong.

## The First Days of School: How to be an Effective Teacher

This book helps teachers to be effective teachers on the first days of school by highlighting three essential characteristics of effectiveness. The three characteristics are positive expectations, classroom management, and lesson mastery.

Wong, H. K., Wong, R. T., & Seroyer, C. (2009). *The first days of school: How to be an effective teacher*. Mountain View, CA: Harry K. Wong.

# *Modules*

## Early Childhood Behavior Management

This module teaches the importance of establishing rules for young children aligned with school behavior expectations, developing and displaying established rules in learning environments, identifying strategies for teaching and enforcing rules, and communicating with families about rules. The estimated length of this module is 1.5 hours.

The IRIS Center (2016). *Early childhood behavior management: Developing and teaching rules*. Retrieved from https://iris.peabody.vanderbilt.edu/pd-hours/school-district-platform/available-modules/

## Classroom Management 101

This set of six modules deals with various components of classroom management. Each module consists of ten, 5–10 minute long lessons. Included is the option to download the lessons, and link to additional resources.

- Module 1: Having the right mindset
- Module 2: How to prepare your plans
- Module 3: How to prevent problems from happening
- Module 4: Strategies to deal with problems that come up
- Module 5: Nine techniques to inspire, engage, and motivate students to learn
- Module 6: Thirteen classroom problems and how to troubleshoot

Teach 4 the Heart (2017). *Classroom management 101*. Retrieved from http://academy.teach4theheart.com/p/classroom-management-101

## Classroom Management for Student Engagement

This set of four modules deals with different aspects of classroom management. Each module includes a PowerPoint version available for download and a self-reflection checklist. Activities have been designed for both individual teachers and school teams. It also includes a classroom management survey to take prior to completing the course.

Module 1: Rules and Routines
Module 2: Acknowledgement Systems
Module 3: Consequence Systems
Module 4: Room Arrangement

Wisconsin Positive Behavioral Interventions and Supports Network (2016). *Classroom management for student engagement*. Retrieved from https://www.wisconsinpbisnetwork.org/educators/pbis-in-action/classroom-management.html

## *Videos*

### Practical Classroom Management

This video discusses the importance of practical strategies for classroom management addressing both individual and whole class management. It discusses different scenarios and strategies for effective classroom management. (Time: 72:00)

American Psychological Association (2017). *Practical classroom management*. Retrieved from http://www.apa.org/education/k12/classroom-management.aspx

### Build Relationships

This video focuses on establishing student-teacher relationships. It also includes teaching character through good relationships. (Time: 2:00)

The Teaching Channel (2017). *Build relationships: More than teaching math*. Retrieved from https://www.teachingchannel.org/videos/building-relationships-through-gestures

### Caring and Control Create a Safe, Positive Classroom

This video provides strategies to maximize student engagement through classroom culture and procedures. It emphasizes the sense of community within the classroom, and using the first 20 days to establish procedures and set expectations. (Time: 14:00)

The Teaching Channel (2017). *Caring and control create a safe, positive classroom*. Retrieved from https://www.teachingchannel.org/videos/create-a-safe-classroom

### New Teacher Survival Guide

This video is aimed at new teachers to help them with classroom management and setting up an orderly, safe space for students to learn. It shadows a teacher in the Bronx, New York who uses seven classroom management strategies to change her classroom. The strategies include establishing routines, using physical proximity, developing individual strategies for students, using non-verbal cues, using games and competition, and others. (Time: 11:00)

The Teaching Channel (2017). *New teacher survival guide: Classroom management*. Retrieved from https://www.teachingchannel.org/videos/new-teacher-classroom-management

## Web Resources

**American Psychological Association: Classroom Management**

This website provides teacher modules on classroom management and includes Response to Intervention (RTI).

Kratochwill, T. R., DeRoos, R., & Blair, S. (2018). *American Psychological Association: Classroom management.* Retrieved from http://www.apa.org/education/k12/classroom-mgmt.aspx

**Improving Students' Relationships With Teachers**

This website includes information about building positive student-teacher relationships, the do's and don'ts, ways to improve the relationships, an FAQ section, and where to find more information.

Rimm-Kaufman, S., & Sandilos, L. (2018). *American Psychological Association: Improving students' relationships with teachers to provide essential supports for learning.* Retrieved from http://www.apa.org/education/k12/relationships.aspx

**Helping Schools Build Systems of Support**

New Jersey Positive Behavior Support in Schools (NJ PBSIS) is a collaboration between the New Jersey Department of Education Offices of Special Education and The Boggs Center, Rutgers Robert Wood Johnson Medical School. This website has information on universal intervention planning resources, function-based problem solving resources, classroom environment resources, resources for parents, and upcoming events.

Rutgers, The State University of New Jersey (2015). *NJ PBSIS: Helping schools build systems of support.* Retrieved from www.njpbs.org

## Key Terms and Definitions

**Positive expectations**: Believing that your students can achieve and complete the tasks you assign.
**Classroom climate**: The feeling your students have when they are in a learning environment.
**Rules**: A list of important guidelines that are needed to help the classroom function smoothly.
**Routines**: A set of procedures to use in daily classroom life.
**Professional presence**: The "aura" of a teacher, how teachers carry themselves. How teachers project to the class, "I am in control and I know what I am doing."
**Transition**: The time between any two activities.

# Appendix A

## *What Would You Do? Questions with Suggested Responses*

1. What would you do if a student didn't follow an established classroom rule or routine?

   **Suggested Response 1:** It is important to ensure the student is aware that the rule or routine exists. The teacher should do this by referring the student to the Classroom Rules poster, created by students and the teacher on the first day of school. Also, the teacher could model and demonstrate some examples and non-examples of how to follow the rule/routine. Further, it is important to also review the rule or routine one-on-one with the student, helping them to practice it, if necessary. Finally, provide multiple opportunities for the student to practice the rule/routine and make sure to acknowledge the student when he/she displays the rule/routine using positive, specific feedback.

2. What would you do if a student made an inappropriate comment about a poster that displayed a person of a different race, ethnicity, or gender than himself or herself?

   **Suggested Response 2:** It is important to let the class know that the comment was inappropriate and that you will address it later with the student. (Depending on the age level of the class, this could be a "teachable moment." For example, in a secondary classroom, the teacher could talk about acceptance and social justice issues). Further, it is important to talk with the student privately and inform him/her that the comment was inappropriate and unacceptable. You could give the student a related outside reading assignment (to enhance his/her knowledge not as a punishment). This could also be used as an opportunity to teach the whole class about diversity through a discussion or mini-lessons. Finally, depending on your school's policies, it may be recommended to report this to the school guidance counselor and/or an administrator to ensure that it is documented in case the student is also involved in making inappropriate comments to peers.

3. What would you do if students refused to participate or share information about themselves during "getting to know you" activities during the first days of school?

   **Suggested Response 3:** The teacher should talk with the student(s) individually at the next available opportunity and try to determine the reason behind the student's hesitation. Another possible solution would be to also talk to the student(s)' previous teachers to gather additional information. Finally, the teacher could provide differentiated "getting to know you" activities designed to match the student(s)' strengths and comfort levels.

## References

Conderman, C. (2011). Methods for addressing conflict in cotaught classrooms. *Intervention in School and Clinic, 46*, 221–229.

Conroy, M. A., Sutherland, K. S., Snyder, A. L., & Marsh, S. (2008). Classwide interventions: Effective instruction makes a difference. *Teaching Exceptional Children, 40*(6), 24–30.

Emmer, E. T., & Evertson, C. M. (2013). *Classroom management for middle and high school teachers.* Upper Saddle River, NJ: Pearson.

Friend, M., & Cook, L. (2009). *Interactions: Collaboration skills for school professionals* (5th ed.). Boston, MA: Pearson.

Jones, F. (2001). *Tools for teaching.* Santa Cruz, CA: Fredric H. Jones & Associates.

Jones, V., & Jones, L. (2012). *Comprehensive classroom management: Creating communities of support and solving problems.* Boston, MA: Pearson.

Kerr, M. M., & Nelson, C. M. (2010). *Strategies for managing behavior problems in the classroom.* Upper Saddle River, NJ: Prentice Hall.

Murry, B. P. (2002). *The new teacher's complete sourcebook: Grades K–4.* New York, NY: Scholastic.

Pedota, P. (2007). Strategies for effective classroom management in the secondary setting. *Clearing House: A Journal of Educational Strategies, Issues, and Ideas, 80*(4), 163–166.

Simonsen, B., Fairbanks, S., Briesch, A., Myers, D., & Sugai, G. (2008). Evidence-based practices in classroom management: Considerations for research to practice. *Education and Treatment of Children, 31*, 351–380.

Winter, S. M. (2007). *Inclusive early childhood education: A collaborative approach.* Upper Saddle River, NJ: Pearson.

# MODULE 8

# Using the Co-Teaching Models

David Hoppey
*University of North Florida*

Keri Haley
*University of West Florida*

Megan Robinson
*University of North Florida*

*The most valuable resource that all teachers have is each other. Without collaboration our growth is limited to our own perspectives.*
—Robert John Meehan (2010)

## MODULE DESCRIPTION

This module provides a definition of what co-teaching is and presents an overview of the various co-teaching models that teaching pairs or teams can use during instruction. Additionally, this module provides support for wrestling with the challenges associated with co-teaching including setting appropriate expectations, communicating between partners and among teams, and designing co-planned or collaborative instruction.

## Theory/Conceptual Framework

Cooperative teaching or co-teaching has been around for years. A widely held definition of co-teaching is two or more teachers working side-by-side to deliver instruction in the same physical space to improve student outcomes (Friend & Cook, 2017). Initially, co-teaching was used as an inclusive service delivery option for students with disabilities and paired a general education teacher and special education teacher together to deliver instruction. The use of co-teaching in schools today, however, is not limited to teaching between general education and special education teachers. Today, one sees the use of co-teaching strategies in collaborative teaching teams, paraprofessional support models, and most recently in teacher preparation programs as a way to combat challenges with traditional student teaching placements (e.g., cooperating teacher's reluctance to handoff responsibility).

The six specific models listed of co-teaching come from the work of Friend and Cook (2017). The first three (One teach, one observe, One teach, one assist, and Team teaching) are whole group models of instruction. The last three (Station teaching, Parallel teaching and Alternative teaching) are suitable for small group instruction.

1. *One teach, One observe:* In this model, one teacher delivers instruction while the other observes. The goal can be to assess student learning and assess student understanding or to provide teacher feedback on instruction. This model has also been called mentor modeling (Badiali & Titus, 2010). Mentor modeling occurs when one teacher observes the other teacher in action with the goal of understanding the children, content, or teaching strategy, and reflects on the teaching observation collaboratively after the lesson. One teach, one observe can also be used to provide a format for peer teachers to observe and reflect on individual and peer instructional practice.

2. *One teach, One assist:* This model centers on one teacher leading instruction while the other teacher circulates around the classroom to monitor individual progress and provide individual assistance as needed. One alternative strategy when using this model is *teaching on purpose* (Vaughn, Schumm, & Arguelles, 1997). *Teaching on purpose* involves one co-teacher providing mini-lessons (1–2 minutes) to targeted students based on previous lessons. These mini-lessons serve as a check for understanding or an extension and formalized process for the teacher who is assisting during whole group instruction.

3. *Team Teaching:* In team teaching, both teachers cooperatively and actively teach together and share responsibility and all instructional duties. This model can be challenging because it requires the greatest amount of trust and planning between the partners or team. On the other hand, it also allows for innovation and creativity to emerge. For example, co-teachers can interject thoughts about the content, provide a divergent point of view, purposefully ask questions, or read different character roles in a story (Badiali & Titus, 2010; Friend & Cook, 2017; Heck & Bacharach, 2015/2016).

4. *Station Teaching:* While station teaching, the teaching pair or team are actively involved in instruction. Each plans and leads instruction for a station. The students rotate from one station to the next, learning and engaging with new material. This co-teaching method requires in-depth co-planning before instruction to decide what content to teach and what student groupings to use (Badiali & Titus, 2010; Friend & Cook, 2017; Heck & Bacharach, 2015/2016). Challenges of this model include pacing and noise levels as teachers must end their stations at the same time and the voice levels in the room can become quite high.

5. *Parallel Teaching:* In parallel teaching, the class is divided in half and both teachers present the same material at the same time. Similar to station teaching, this model requires extensive co-planning and grouping decisions must be predetermined so the content can be differentiated to meet student learning needs (Badiali & Titus, 2010; Friend & Cook, 2017; Heck & Bacharach, 2015/2016). An additional benefit is that parallel teaching reduces the student to teacher ratio but drawbacks include pacing, and noise levels.
6. *Alternative Teaching:* When using alternative teaching, one teacher takes a small group of students and provides instruction that is different than what the large group is receiving. Alternative teaching supports differentiation while co-teaching as each teacher delivers different content to their groups. Most often this model is used for remediation but it also can be used for enrichment. Student groups should be flexible allowing all students to work with either co-teacher depending on the purpose of the lesson (Badiali & Titus, 2010; Friend & Cook, 2017; Heck & Bacharach, 2015/2016).

Co-teaching is used differently in schools at all grade levels depending on the purpose of learning and the needs of the learners. The co-teaching models or strategies are also taught to pre-service educators in teacher preparation programs. The co-teaching model is based on the belief that cooperating teachers are more than hosts of the student teacher. Cooperating teachers are school-based teacher educators that play a critical mentoring role in teacher candidate development (Clarke, Triggs, & Nielsen, 2014). First, cooperating teachers provide induction to the profession for the student teacher (Friend, Embury, & Clarke, 2015). Second, they assume the role of educative mentors who are co-learners that create opportunities for student teacher learning (Feiman-Neimser, 1998; Langdon & Ward, 2015). Educative mentoring requires both partners to continually make their thinking public by sharing thoughts, insights, ideas, and questions (Bradbury, 2010; Feiman-Neimser, 1998, 2001; Langdon & Ward, 2015). Three practices, which can be naturally embedded into co-teaching student teaching models, are critical to improving teaching practice: (1) planning/co-planning, (2) observing and debriefing teaching, and (3) analyzing student work (Heck & Bacharach, 2015/2016; Hudson, 2013; Kang, 2017; Langdon & Ward, 2015). In all, the co-teaching models described above shift the discussion to collaborating on authentic teaching tasks and using data-based decision-making to improve student outcomes while simultaneously focusing on teacher learning.

## Specific Questions to Guide Discussion

1. Considering the opportunity to have two teachers in the classroom, how can you both maximize the potential outcomes for K–12 learners?

2. How would (do) each of you view your role within each of the six co-teaching models?

3. Describe how you envision a gradual release of responsibility to promote a shared decision-making process within your co-teaching partnership. What factors are necessary to assist co-teacher(s) as they attempt to increase their responsibilities in

the collaborative classroom? This question is helpful to use with teacher candidates, novice teachers or teachers with limited experience in co-teaching.

4. What types of collaborative qualities does each of you have to offer? What do you foresee as your biggest personal challenge in working within a collaborative unit? How can you overcome your challenges for the benefit of working collaboratively within a co-teaching experience?

## Productive Practices

1. *Plan collaboratively.* One of the most effective and well-researched ways to work together in a collaborative teaching arrangement is to plan with your co-teacher (Gallo-Fox & Scantlebury, 2015; Shin, Lee, & McKenna, 2016). Effective mentor and preservice co-teachers use shared planning time to discuss both lesson plans and ways to respond to other classroom needs (Pettit, 2017). Although finding time to lesson plan together can be difficult, dedicated planning time with your co-teacher should occur at least once every week. This planning time is beneficial to both teachers and students (Gallo-Fox & Scantlebury, 2016; Pratt, 2014; Strieker, Gillis, & Zong, 2013). It not only capitalizes on the expertise of multiple professionals, allowing a teaching team to learn from one another, but it enhances the metacognitive process, improves teacher self-efficacy, and student success (Gallo-Fox & Scantlebury, 2015; Guise, Habib, Thiessen, & Robbins, 2017; Parker, Alvarez McHatton, Allen, 2012; Pellegrino, Weiss, & Regan, 2015; Pettit, 2017; Shin et al., 2016).
2. *Utilize many collaborative teaching styles.* There are several styles of collaborative teaching and all can be useful depending upon the needs of the students in your classroom setting. Common among these methods are one teach/one assist, one teach/one observe, station teaching, parallel teaching, alternative/supplemental teaching, and team teaching (Baeten & Simons, 2014; Friend, 2014; Parker et al., 2012). Mentor and pre-service teachers can maximize these models by selecting the best method of teaching for each lesson based on the lesson's purpose while taking into consideration the needs of the students. Effective and responsive co-teachers are flexible (Pratt, 2014). They teach *together* and apply or interchange these teaching styles with fluidity as necessitated by students' needs (Gallo-Fox & Scantlebury, 2015; Pellegrino et al., 2015; Pettit, 2017; Pratt, 2014; Shin et al., 2016; Strieker et al., 2013).
3. *Analyze data.* Great mentor/preservice collaborative teachers work together to meet students' learning needs (Gallo-Fox & Scantlebury, 2016; Pettit, 2017). Collaborative teams analyze formal and informal student data together to identify gaps in learning and make instructional decisions. Using data to establish student need is a common educational practice at all levels of instruction and a task in which co-teachers should engage together to ensure shared understanding of instructional goals (Farley-Ripple & Buttram, 2014). Teachers who analyze data collaboratively share knowledge of their students' strengths and weaknesses and are better able to attack gaps in instruction (Gallo-Fox & Scantlebury, 2015; Tschida, Smith, & Fogarty, 2015). In the shared practice of data analysis, co-teachers engage in reciprocal learning that broadens their understanding of both the data and the students.
4. *Share responsibility.* Finding balance in a collaborative teaching relationship can be tricky. Members of a collaborative team often report feelings of inequality in

the co-teaching relationship with one teacher assuming a dominant role, and the other, submissive (Bennett & Fisch, 2013; Guise et al., 2017; Pellegrino et al., 2015; Shin et al., 2016). This dynamic can be even further exacerbated by the natural hierarchy created by the preservice/supervising teacher relationship (Strieker et al., 2013). To alleviate this imbalance and encourage self-efficacy of collaborative teachers, practice shared responsibility (Gallo-Fox & Scantlebury, 2016). Sharing classroom responsibility can manifest itself through gradual release of teaching duties, co-planning, using a checklist for shared duties, or in any other manner that divides the workload equitably between the collaborative teaching pair (Gallo-Fox & Scantlebury, 2015). In any form, shared responsibility provides learning experiences for preservice teachers, leads to improved preservice teacher self-efficacy, and removes the burden of complete task responsibility for planning, management, and instruction within the co-teaching classroom from the supervising teacher (Baeten & Simons, 2014; Parker et al., 2012; Strieker et al., 2013).

5. *Reflect on the process and communicate.* Communication is a critical, if not the most important, element of collaborative teaching, and a vital part of reflection between co-teachers (Bennett & Fisch, 2013; Gallo-Fox & Scantlebury, 2015; Shin et al., 2016; Strieker et al., 2013). Working together to identify strengths and weaknesses in lessons, management styles, or any number of other factors that influence teaching and learning will inform practice of both the preservice and mentor teacher (Pratt, 2014; Weiss, Pellegrino, & Brigham, 2017). Collaborative teaching pairs who respond most effectively to student needs are clear about what does and does not work in the classroom and in their professional technique (Baeten & Simons, 2014; Pettit, 2017). They take time to reflect on the collaborative process and have the necessary, albeit potentially uncomfortable, conversations about their shared practice. Great collaborative preservice and mentor teaching pairs regularly assess the strength of a lesson plan, effectiveness of a behavior management system, and any other element of their classroom that needs to be addressed. Having an open dialogue with one another about what is going well and what needs to be adjusted benefits both the teachers and the students within the collaborative classroom (Gallo-Fox & Scantlebury, 2016; Pellegrino et al., 2015).

## What Would You Do?

Ask your team or pair the following questions. For suggested responses to questions, see Appendix A.

1. What would you do if you and your co-teaching partner could not agree on how to share teaching responsibilities?

2. What would you do if your co-teacher treated you like an assistant, rather than a co-teaching partner?

3. What would you do if your co-teacher did not like to use data to inform instruction?

## Reflective Professional Growth Activities

Consider these ideas or activities to facilitate and foster teacher growth and reflection. Select one or two ideas to help facilitate this reflection process that will help the teacher, pair, or team to understand the co-teaching strategies. Remember that you know the individuals best so be sure to choose an activity that would be the most effective.

### *Idea 1: Who Are You as a Collaborative Teacher?*

Consider your own personal strengths and weaknesses with respect to working collaboratively with other individuals. List those strengths and weaknesses on the organizer below. Share with each other the resources and expertise you offer your collaborative teaching pair or team. Now ask yourselves, what is collaborative teaching? What do you believe constitutes a collaborative teaching environment? In your opinion, what does learning look like? What would learning look like in a collaborative teaching classroom? Write down on the organizer below what you believe collaborative teaching looks like. Now consider the same for what you believe collaborative teaching does not look like and write your thoughts in Figure 8.1. Now that you have considered some of the elements that create a collaborative teaching pair, what do you each envision to be your roles and responsibilities within that partnership? Lastly, consider the non-negotiables. What are your "pet peeves" in relation to working collaboratively? What are your "pet peeves" in relation to instruction and classroom management? Share these with each other and discuss how you can, as a unit, create a well-balanced partnership in the classroom.

**Evidence:** Completed Figure 8.1.

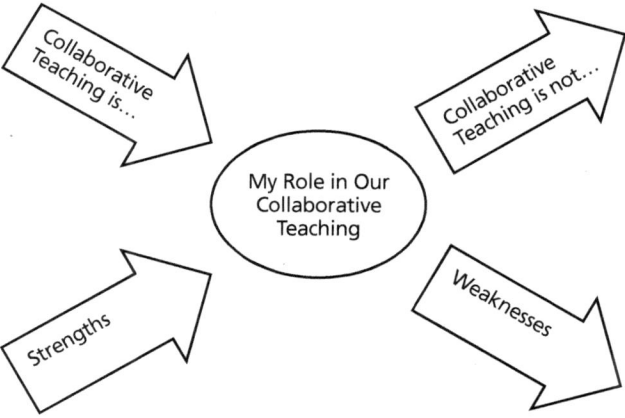

**Figure 8.1** Advanced organizer for reflecting on role in collaborative teaching.

## Idea 2: Lesson Planning for Two, Constructing the Collaborative Teaching Pair

Collaborative teaching requires a combined effort from beginning to end. Therefore, ask yourselves what content and teaching expertise do you have to offer your collaborative teaching pair. Knowing this, how can you share the lesson planning duties? Decide when you will plan together and how often. How can you approach lesson planning that begins with the content teacher (or classroom teacher) taking the lead, then gradually releasing more responsibility to the other teacher? How can this same release of responsibility be accomplished as you utilize the six collaborative teaching models in your lessons? Design three lesson plans together and discuss the roles you will each share and the rate at which responsibilities will shift as the teacher's presence increases.

**Evidence:** Lesson plans incorporating the teacher into the collaborative teaching experience with the other teacher. Include lessons that demonstrate three of the six collaborative teaching models (one lesson from one teach, one observe or one teach, one assist; two lessons from the remaining models).

## Idea 3: Agreeing on Alternative Methods of Assessment

Individually, consider your views on formative and summative assessments. Now ask yourselves how alternative methods of assessment enter the picture you created in your mind? Together, discuss what formative and summative assessments can look like in your collaborative teaching pair. How will you know your students are learning? How can you use your collaborative teaching pair to include alternative methods of assessment?

**Evidence:** In a lesson plan designed together, outline means of both informal and formal formative assessments. Develop a rubric together to use for an alternative method of assessment within one of your previously designed lesson plans.

## Idea 4: The Data Duo

Together as the collaborative teaching pair (the two assigned teachers), gather formative assessment data from three content areas or three separate classes. Together, analyze the data, looking for strengths, weaknesses, and patterns among the students. Once you've done this individually, discuss your findings and graph the data together. Then group your students into the top 25%, the middle 50%, and the bottom 25%. Determine what collaborative teaching models will best address meeting the varying needs of these students.

**Evidence:** Graph of assessment data. Subsequent lesson plans to address the differentiated needs of students.

## Idea 5: Reflection

Video record a collaboratively taught lesson. Together with the video, corresponding lesson plan, and supporting assessments, analyze and reflect on the effectiveness of the lesson, your communication, and the manner in which you taught together using one of the collaborative teaching models. Decide what to teach in subsequent lessons and how you would change what or how you taught if you taught the same lesson again.

**Evidence:** Video of a collaboratively taught lesson, corresponding lesson plan, and formative assessment data.

## Follow-Up, Monitoring, and Goal Setting

Complete the follow-up questions for the selected reflective professional growth activity.

### *Idea 1: Who Are You as a Collaborative Teacher?*

Share your organizer on what you determined collaborative teaching is and is not along with your strengths and weaknesses with each other.

- Discuss where and how your strengths can enhance each of the co-teaching models.
- Considering each other's strengths, how can each of you provide balance among the roles and responsibilities?
- What have you learned about each other?
- Do you have any questions about working collaboratively?

### *Idea 2: Lesson Planning for Two, Constructing the Collaborative Teaching Pair*

Let us take a look at the lesson plans you developed together.

- Do your lessons represent a gradual release of responsibility with the content teacher taking a less active role and the other teacher(s) taking on more?
- What did you find difficult in the release of responsibility within the planning process?
- What did you find easy?
- How do you both feel you will share the responsibilities going forward?
- Do you have any questions about planning collaboratively?

### *Idea 3: Agreeing on Alternative Methods of Assessment*

- When creating your rubric for an alternative method of assessment, what did you learn about each other's understanding of assessment?
- Did you agree that the rubric you designed assessed the appropriate skills and objectives?
- Did you disagree on any concepts, and if so, how did you negotiate your differences?
- Do you have any questions going forward about collaboratively designing assessments?

### *Idea 4: The Data Duo*

- Considering the data on your student outcomes, what learning patterns have you both identified?
- Can you share your data and explain your reasoning?

- How can you maximize your co-teaching pair to address the needs you identified?
- What alterations may be needed within your co-teaching pair?
- How will you determine whether your alterations are having a positive effect?
- Do you have questions related to your student outcome data before we move to the next topic?

## *Idea 5: Reflection*

We are going to reflect on the video of your selected lesson and the corresponding data.
- Do you feel that the lesson went as planned?
- If you were to grade yourselves, what letter grade would you give yourselves given the collaborative teaching model you used and the cohesiveness of your collaborative pair?
- In your lesson, what did you see that went well?
- What did you see that you believe can be improved?
- What adjustments within your collaborative teaching plans do you feel you need to make, and by when do you aim to accomplish any adjustments?
- Do you have any questions about effective collaborative teaching?

## Resources

### *Articles*

**Enhancing Student Learning Through Mentor-Intern Partnerships**

The authors present a definition and six models of co-teaching for teachers to use. They argue that co-teaching has the potential to be an effective arrangement for attending to student learning, preparing a teacher candidate to enter the profession, and eliminating some of the snags and pitfalls associated with traditional student teaching.

Badiali, B., & Titus, N. E. (2010). Co-teaching: Enhancing student learning through mentor-intern partnerships. *School-University Partnerships, 4*(2), 74–80.

**Co-Teaching Versus Apprentice Teaching**

The authors analyze co-teaching and apprentice teaching for teacher preparation.

Friend, M., Embury, D. C., & Clarke, L. (2015). Co-teaching versus apprentice teaching: An analysis of similarities and differences. *Teacher Education and Special Education, 38*(2), 79–87.

**A Better Model for Student Teaching**

This article outlines how to transform your teacher education program to utilize a co-teaching model. Examples are provided.

Heck, T. W., & Bacharach, N. (2015/2016) A better model for student teaching. *Educational Leadership, 73*(4), 24–29.

**Co-Teaching Strategies**

Article provides an overview of strategies to use before, during, and after co-teaching with your partner.

Murawski, W., & Dieker, L. (2018). 50 ways to keep your co-teacher: Strategies for before, during, and after co-teaching. *Teaching Exceptional Children 40*(4), 40–48.

## Web Resources

### Co-Teaching in the Real World

Marilyn Friend discusses co-teaching and how to make the collaborative relationship work in practice.

Council for Exceptional Children. (n.d.). *Co-teaching in the real world*. Retrieved from http://pubs.cec.sped.org/teaching-exceptionally-1-2/

### Preparing to Use the Co-Teaching Models

Materials to support the collaborative team in using the co-teaching models.

*Co-Teaching: What it is and what it is not.* (n.d.) Retrieved from https://www3.bucksiu.org/cms/lib/PA09000729/Centricity/Domain/64/AllHandouts%20Coteaching.pdf

### Begin With Co-Planning

Savannah Flakes discusses the importance of planning and assessment in a collaborative classroom.

Flakes, S. (2014, October 14). *Inclusion Corner: Begin with co-planning*. Retrieved from http://exclusive.multibriefs.com/content/inclusion-corner-begin-with-co-planning/education

### The Art of Co-Teaching

Savannah Flakes describes co-teaching and how to use co-teaching models.

Flakes, S. (2014, December 1). *Inclusion Corner: The art of co-teaching*. Retrieved from http://exclusive.multibriefs.com/content/inclusion-corner-the-art-of-co-teaching/education

### Council for Exceptional Children Parity Tool

This is a helpful tool to assess shared responsibility in the classroom.

Friend, M. (2013). *Co-Teach! Building and sustaining effective classroom partnerships in inclusive schools*. Retrieved from https://tooloftheweek.org/wp-content/uploads/2017/09/TOW-9-25-17-CoTeach.pdf

### Strategies and Innovations for Implementing Collaborative Teaching

This website provides a lesson planning tool for teachers in a collaborative setting.

Lewis, J. (2014). Pre-service teacher learning collaborative. *Next Gen Tools: Strategies and Innovations for Implementing Breakthrough Models*. Retrieved from https://library.educause.edu/~/media/files/library/2014/8/ngb1409-pdf.pdf

### 6 Steps for Successful Co-Teaching

The National Education Association provides steps used by teachers to make co-teaching work.

Marston, N. (n.d). *6 steps for successful co-teaching*. Retrieved from http://www.nea.org/tools/6-steps-to-successful-co-teaching.html

## Co-Teaching Observation Checklist

A simple tool for personal reflection of the co-teaching models as well as a tool for supervisors observing teachers using the co-teaching models.

Murawski, W. (2005). *Co-teaching observation checklist.* Retrieved from https://wvde.state.wv.us/federal-programs/resources/documents/Co-TeachingChecklist.pdf

## Successful Co-Teaching

A "how-to" article from the Council for Exceptional Children on how to successfully co-teach.

Murawski, W. (n.d.). *Successful co-teaching.* Retrieved from http://www.cec.sped.org/News/Special-Education-Today/Need-to-Know/Need-to-Know-CoTeaching

## Co-Teaching Tools

Co-teaching tools from the Oklahoma Department of Education including the Sharing Hopes, Attitudes, Responsibilities, and Expectations (S.H.A.R.E.) protocol.

Oklahoma Department of Education. (n.d.). *General education curriculum snapshots.* Retrieved from sde.ok.gov/sde/sites/ok.gov.sde/files/Coteaching%20Tools.pdf

## Eight Tips for Making the Most of Co-Teaching

Education Weekly introduces eight behavioral changes and instructional tips that can improve co-teaching.

Sacks, A. (2014, October 15). Eight tips for making the most of co-teaching. Retrieved from http://www.edweek.org/tm/articles/2014/10/15/ctq_sacks_coteaching.html

## Six Approaches to Co-Teaching

A quick reference guide to six styles of co-teaching.

State Education Resource Center. (2004). *Six approaches to co-teaching.* Retrieved from http://ctserc.org/component/k2/item/50-six-approaches-to-co-teaching

## Cooperative Teaching

Definitions and examples of cooperative teaching practice in K–12 schools.

The University of Kansas. (n.d.). *Cooperative teaching.* Retrieved from http://www.specialconnections.ku.edu/?q=collaboration/cooperative_teaching

## Effective Co-Teaching Strategies

The article provides information about the models for co-teaching and how to share classroom responsibility.

Villa, R. (n.d.). *Effective co-teaching strategies.* Retrieved from http://www.teachhub.com/effective-co-teaching-strategies

## Modules

### Co-Teaching Modules 201

The Georgia Department of Education's toolkit of instructional content for co-teachers to use as they support students in general education classrooms. The materials include research articles, tools, and videos.

Georgia Department of Education. (n.d.). *Co-Teaching models 201: Introduction.* Retrieved from http://www.gadoe.org/Curriculum-Instruction-and-Assessment/Special-Education-Services/Pages/Co-Teaching-Modules-201—Introduction.aspx

### Instructional Accommodations & Co-Teaching

This module provides a case study that discusses issues surrounding instructional accommodations and modifications and co-teaching.

The IRIS Center. (2014, December 15). *Instructional accommodations & co-teaching: A broken arm.* Retrieved from https://iris.peabody.vanderbilt.edu/wp-content/uploads/pdf_activities/case_based/IA_Broken_Arm.pdf

### Communication for Collaboration

An interactive online module focused on communication for collaboration that describes effective practices for communicating with professionals and uses a decision-making process to select effective communication practices.

U.S. Office of Special Education Programs. (n.d.). *Module 3: Communication for collaboration.* Retrieved from http://community.fpg.unc.edu/connect-modules/learners/module-3

## Videos

### Co-Teaching: Mentoring in a Collaborative School Setting

Salisbury University provides examples of co-teaching between pre-service teachers and cooperating teachers in action. Additionally, the site provides tools to use in the field for cooperating teachers, field supervisors, and teacher candidates.

Salisbury University. (n.d.). *Salisbury University co-teaching videos.* Retrieved from http://www.salisbury.edu/pds/Collaborative_Materials/videos.html

### The Academy for Co-Teaching and Collaboration at St. Cloud State University

Materials include a 75 minute DVD, *Changing Student Teaching through Co-Teaching: Collaboration That Makes A Difference,* that includes footage from co-taught classrooms, interviews with teacher candidates, cooperating teachers, and school and university administrators.

St. Cloud State University. (n.d.). *The academy for co-teaching and collaboration.* Retrieved from https://www.stcloudstate.edu/soe/coteaching/default.aspx

### Co-Planning and Co-Teaching

An informational video that describes co-teaching and how to plan as a co-teacher.

Sweeney, D. (2014, October 22). *Co-planning and co-teaching* [YouTube Channel]. Retrieved from https://www.youtube.com/watch?v=4a8em_wVPo8

**Five Co-Teaching Formats**

Curry School of Education at the University of Virginia provides five definitions of the co-teaching models and accompanying video examples.

University of Virginia. (2014, August 6). *5 co-teaching formats* [YouTube Channel]. Retrieved from http://faculty.virginia.edu/coteachUVA/5formats.html

**Co-Teaching at Its Best**

An informational video on the basics of co-teaching.

Wisconsin DPI. (2016, January 15). *Co-Teaching at its best* [YouTube Channel]. Retrieved from https://www.youtube.com/watch?v=Xurgvdq3J8s

## Key Terms and Definitions

**Alternative teaching**: Alternative teaching is when one teacher takes a small group of students and provides instruction that is different than what the larger group is receiving.

**Co-teaching:** Co-teaching is when two or more teachers work side-by-side to deliver instruction in the same physical space to improve student outcomes.

**Gradual release of responsibility**: A framework used in teacher mentoring that purposefully transfers responsibilities from one teacher, who provides initial teaching, to additional teachers who have shared responsibility in a collaborative teaching setting.

**One teach, One observe:** In this model, one teacher delivers instruction while the other observes. The goal can be to assess student learning and assess student understanding or to provide feedback to the teacher on their instruction.

**One teach, One assist**: This model centers on one teacher leading instruction while the other teacher circulates around the classroom to monitor individual progress and provide individuals assistance as needed.

**Parallel Teaching:** Parallel teaching is when the class is divided in half and both teachers present the same material at the same time.

**Station Teaching:** During station teaching, both teachers are actively involved in instruction. Each plans and leads instruction for a station and the students rotate from one station to the next.

**Team Teaching:** Both teachers cooperatively and actively teach together and share responsibility and all instructional duties.

# Appendix A

## *What Would You Do? Questions with Suggested Responses*

1. What would you do if you and your co-teaching partner could not agree on how to share teaching responsibilities?

    **Suggested Response 1:** I would develop a time to meet and use a protocol to openly and honestly discuss the ongoing benefits and persistent challenges evident in the partnership. Some readings that could be useful to guide these discussions include Sileo (2011) Getting to Know Your Co-Teacher or Murawski and Dieker (2004) Tips and Strategies for Co-Teaching at the Secondary Level.

2. What would you do if your co-teacher treated you like an assistant, rather than a co-teaching partner?

    **Suggested Response 2:** I would move beyond using protocols as mentioned above, by discussing how each partner brings different strengths and weaknesses to the partnership. Recognize that in most cases where cooperating teachers and teacher candidates co-teach, there is a power dynamic that needs to be unpacked. This can occur by finding ways to apply the tenets of the gradual release of responsibility model where over time the teacher candidate assumes more responsibilities. This will allow the teacher candidate and mentor to find a way to move towards a shared understanding on their roles.

3. What would you do if your co-teacher did not like to use data to inform instruction?

    **Suggested Response 3:** I would first ask questions and learn about how my partner uses data to understand their perspective. Next, share your ideas about how to collaboratively move the partnership forward by gathering, analyzing, and interpreting student data around persistent problems of practice. Developing a professional relationship based on inquiry into student learning allows co-teachers to plan and provide differentiated instruction to meet all students' needs. Only by raising questions, implementing evidence-based practices, and examining student data together can co-teachers achieve the desired student learning outcomes.

# References

Badiali, B., & Titus, N. E. (2010). Co-teaching: Enhancing student learning through mentor-intern partnerships. *School-University Partnerships, 4*(2), 74–80.

Baeten, M., & Simons, M. (2014). Student teachers' team teaching: Models, effects, and conditions for implementation. *Teaching and Teacher Education, 41*, 92–110.

Bennett, D. J., & Fisch, A. A. (2013). Infusing co-teaching into the general education field experience. *Interdisciplinary Journal of Teaching and Learning, 3*(1), 18–37.

Bradbury, L. U. (2010). Educative mentoring: Promoting reform-based science teaching through mentoring relationships. *Teaching as the learning profession: Handbook of policy and practice, 1*, 3–22.

Clarke, A., Tiggs, V., & Nielsen, W. (2014). Cooperating teachers' participation in teacher education. A review of the literature. *Review of Educational Research, 84*(2), 163–202.

Council for Exceptional Children. (2016, Feb 2). Co-teaching in the real world. *Teaching Exceptionally Podcast.* Podcast retrieved from http://pubs.cec.sped.org/teaching-exceptionally-1-2/

Farley-Ripple, E. N., & Buttram, J. L. (2014). Developing collaborative data use through professional learning communities: Early lessons from Delaware. *Studies in Educational Evaluation, 42*, 41–53.

Feiman-Neimser, S. (2001). From preparation to practice: Designing a continuum to strengthen and sustain teaching. *The Teachers College Record, 103*(6), 1013–1055.

Feiman-Neimser, S. (1998). Teachers as teacher educators. *European Journal of Teacher Education, 21*(1), 63–74.

Flakes, S. (2014, October 14). *Inclusion corner: Begin with co-planning.* Retrieved from http://exclusive.multibriefs.com/content/inclusion-corner-begin-with-co-planning/education

Flakes, S. (2014, December 1). *Inclusion corner: The art of co-teaching.* Retrieved from http://exclusive.multibriefs.com/content/inclusion-corner-the-art-of-co-teaching/education

Friend, M. (2013). Parity, Parity, Parity. In *Co-teach! Building and sustaining effective classroom partnerships in inclusive schools.* Retrieved from https://tooloftheweek.org/wp-content/uploads/2017/09/TOW-9-25-17-CoTeach.pdf

Friend, M. (2014). *Co-teach! Building and sustaining effective classroom partnerships in inclusive schools* (2nd ed.). Greensboro, NC: Marilyn Friend.

Friend, M., & Cook, L. (2017). *Interactions: Collaboration skills for school professionals.* Boston, MA: Pearson Education.

Friend, M., Embury, D. C., & Clarke, L. (2015). Co-teaching versus apprentice teaching: An analysis of similarities and differences. *Teacher Education and Special Education, 38*(2), 79–87.

Gallo-Fox, J., & Scantlebury, K. (2015). "It isn't necessarily sunshine and daisies every time": Coplanning opportunities and challenges when student teaching. *Asia-Pacific Journal of Teacher Education, 43*(4), 324–337.

Gallo-Fox, J., & Scantlebury, K. (2016). Co-teaching as professional development for cooperating teachers. *Teaching and Teacher Education, 60*, 191–202.

Georgia Department of Education. (n.d.). *Co-teaching Modules 201.* Retrieved from http://www.gadoe.org/Curriculum-Instruction-and-Assessment/Special-Education-Services/Pages/Co-Teaching-Modules-201—Introduction.aspx

Guise, M., Habib, M., Thiessen, K., & Robbins, A. (2017). Continuum of co-teaching implementation: Moving from traditional student teaching to co-teaching. *Teaching and Teacher Education, 66*, 370–382.

Heck, T. W., & Bacharach, N. (2015/2016) A better model for student teaching. *Educational Leadership, 73*(4), 24–29.

Hudson, P. (2013). Strategies for mentoring pedagogical knowledge. *Teachers and Teaching, 19*(4), 363–381.

Kang, H. (2017). Preservice teachers' learning to plan intellectually challenging tasks. *Journal of Teacher Education, 68*(1), 55–68.

Langdon, F. J., & Ward, L. (2015). Educative mentoring: A way forward, *International Journal of Mentoring and Coaching in Education, 4*(4), 240–254.

Lewis, J. (2014). Pre-service teacher learning collaborative. *Next Gen Tools: Strategies and Innovations for Implementing Breakthrough Models*. Retrieved from https://library.educause.edu/~/media/files/library/2014/8/ngb1409-pdf.pdf

Marston, N. (n.d.). *6 steps to successful co-teaching*. Retrieved from http://www.nea.org/tools/6-steps-to-successful-co-teaching.html

Meehan, R. J. (2010). *A teacher's treasures: Bounty for all (2nd ed.)*. Mustang, OK: Tate.

Murawski, W. (2005). *Co-teaching observation checklist*. Retrieved from https://wvde.state.wv.us/federal-programs/resources/documents/Co-TeachingChecklist.pdf

Murawski, W. (n.d.) *Successful co-teaching*. Retrieved from https://www.cec.sped.org/News/Special-Education-Today/Need-to-Know/Need-to-Know-CoTeaching

Murawski, W., & Dieker, L. (2004). Tips and strategies for co-teaching at the secondary level. *Teaching Exceptional Children, 36*(5), 52–58.

Murawski, W. W., & Dieker, L. (2008). 50 Ways to keep your co-teacher: Strategies for before, during, and after co-teaching. *Teaching Exceptional Children, 40*(4), 40–48.

Oklahoma Department of Education. (n.d.). Co-teaching tools. Retrieved from sde.ok.gov/sde/sites/ok.gov.sde/files/Coteaching%20Tools.pdf

Parker, A., Alvarez McHatton, P. A., & Allen, D. D. (2012). Elementary and special education pre-service teachers' understandings of collaboration and co-teaching. *Journal of Research in Education, 22*(1), 164–195.

Pellegrino, A., Weiss, M., & Regan, K. (2015). Learning to collaborate: General and special educators in teacher education. *The Teacher Educator, 50,* 187–202.

Pettit, S. L. (2017). Preparing teaching candidates for co-teaching. *The Delta Kappa Gamma Bulletin: International Journal for Professional Educators, 83*(3), 15–23.

Pratt, S. (2014). Achieving symbiosis: Working through challenges found in co-teaching to achieve effective co-teaching relationships. *Teaching and Teacher Education, 41,* 1–12.

Sacks, A. (2014, October 15). *Eight tips for making the most of co-teaching*. Retrieved from http://www.edweek.org/tm/articles/2014/10/15/ctq_sacks_coteaching.html

Salisbury University. (n.d.) *Salisbury University co-teaching videos*. Retrieved from http://www.salisbury.edu/pds/Collaborative_Materials/videos.html

Shin, M., Lee, H., & McKenna, J. W. (2016). Special education and general education preservice teachers' co-teaching experiences: A comparative synthesis of qualitative research. *International Journal of Inclusive Education, 20*(1), 91–107.

Sileo, J. M. (2011). Co-teaching: Getting to know your partner. *Teaching Exceptional Children, 43*(5), 32–38.

St. Cloud State University. (n.d.). *Academy for co-teaching and collaboration*. Retrieved from https://www.stcloudstate.edu/soe/coteaching/default.aspx

Strieker, T., Gillis, B., & Zong, G. (2013). Improving pre-service middle school teachers' confidence, competence, and commitment to co-teaching in inclusive classrooms. *Teacher Education Quarterly, 40*(4), 159–180.

State Education Resource Center. (2004). *Six approaches to co-teaching*. Retrieved from http://ctserc.org/component/k2/item/50-six-approaches-to-co-teaching

Sweeney, D. (2014, October 2014). *Co-planning and co-teaching* [YouTube Channel]. Retrieved from https://www.youtube.com/watch?v=4a8em_wVPo8

Tschida, C. M., Smith, J. J., & Fogarty, E. A. (2015). "It just works better": Introducing the 2:1 model of co-teaching in teacher preparation. *The Rural Educator, 36*(2), 11–26.

University of Kansas. (n.d.). *Cooperative teaching*. Retrieved from http://www.specialconnections.ku.edu/?q=collaboration/cooperative_teaching

University of North Carolina. (n.d.). *CONNECT module 3: Communication for collaboration*. Retrieved from *http://community.fpg.unc.edu/connect-modules/learners/module-3*

University of Virginia. (2014, August 6). *5 co-teaching formats* [YouTube Channel]. Retrieved from http://faculty.virginia.edu/coteachUVA/5formats.html

Vanderbilt University. (n.d.) *Instructional accommodations & co-teaching: A broken arm*. Retrieved from https://iris.peabody.vanderbilt.edu/wp-content/uploads/pdf_activities/case_based/IA_Broken_Arm.pdf

Vaughn, S., Schumm, J., & Arguelles, M. (1997). The ABCDEs of co-teaching. *Teaching Exceptional Children, 30*(2), 4–10.

Villa, R. (n.d.) *Effective co-teaching strategies.* Retrieved from http://www.teachhub.com/effective-co-teaching-strategies

Weiss, M. P., Pellegrino, A., & Brigham, F. J. (2017). Practicing collaboration in teacher preparation: Effects of learning by doing together. *Teacher Education and Special Education, 40*(1), 65–76.

Wisconsin DPI. (2016, January 15). *Co-teaching at its best* [YouTube Channel]. Retrieved from https://www.youtube.com/watch?v=Xurgvdq3J8s

# MODULE 9

# Promoting Engagement and Positive Behavior

Jaime L. Zurheide
*Elmhurst College*

*An effective teacher manages a classroom. An ineffective teacher disciplines a classroom."*
—Harry Wong

### MODULE DESCRIPTION

When handling challenging behaviors in the classroom, it is always easier to prevent behaviors from occurring instead of having to respond to those behaviors after they happen. This module will provide you with information about ways to encourage positive behavior in your class, keep students engaged in instruction, and discourage negative behavior. Guided questions, activities, and resources will help you choose appropriate strategies to use in your own practice.

## Theory/Conceptual Framework

Student behavior is influenced by a number of variables. While some students require specific individualized interventions for their behavior, the majority of behavior problems in the classroom can be prevented through teacher-level strategies (Lane, Menzies, Ennis, & Oakes, 2015). These include using instructional strategies that lead to a high level of student engagement, reinforcing positive behavior, using proactive strategies to prevent potential negative behaviors, and redirecting minor misbehavior.

One way to improve student engagement is to increase the number of opportunities students have to participate in the classroom. An Opportunity to Respond (OTR) is defined as any teacher action that requires an active response from students (Haydon, Borders, Embury, & Clarke, 2009; Lane et al., 2015). Research suggests that students should have the opportunity to respond multiple times per minute in order to be fully engaged in the lesson (Haydon et al., 2009; Sutherland, Adler, & Gunder, 2003). Examples of OTRs include calling on students' raised hands, choral responding, and the use of response cards. When using response cards, a teacher provides some sort of academic prompt (e.g., asks a question, gives a math problem to solve) and the students write the answer on a piece of paper or individual dry erase board. They then share their responses by holding up the paper/board for the teacher to see (Haydon et al., 2009). Electronic versions of response cards can also be used with responses projected onto the board. In addition to teacher-directed strategies used in whole class instruction, having students respond to peers and work in small groups can be other effective ways to increase OTRs in the classroom (Haydon, MacSuga-Gage, Simonson, & Hawkins, 2012). Peer grouping strategies such as Think-Pair-Share, Numbered Heads Together, Cooperative Learning, and Classwide Peer Tutoring have been shown to be effective ways to increase engagement and reduce off task behavior (Greenwood, 1997; Haydon et al., 2012; Hunter & Haydon, 2013; Lane, Menzies, Bruhn, & Crnobori, 2011).

Incorporating student choice into instruction is also an effective way to increase engagement in the classroom. Allowing students choices about their learning has been shown to increase intrinsic motivation and effort on tasks (Patall, Cooper, & Robinson, 2008) and reduce problem behavior (Shogren, Faggella-Luby, Bae, & Wehmeyer, 2004). Choice can be incorporated into academic instruction in a variety of ways, including allowing students to select topics for areas of study or assignments, to choose where and with whom they will work, or to determine the order in which they complete activities and the medium they will use for assignments (e.g., paper or electronic submissions). When allowing choice, teachers should be sure to provide clear options for students to choose from and set expectations as to how students can appropriately exercise their choices.

Along with improving engagement in the class, teachers need to use specific reinforcement strategies to encourage positive behavior and reduce negative behavior. Behavior-specific praise or contingent praise as opposed to more general praise provides a clear connection between the praise and the behavior exhibited by the student in order to encourage the student to continue using the positive behavior (Conroy, Sutherland, Snyder, & Marsh, 2008; Lane, et al., 2015). Teachers should also be sure to utilize praise frequently and at a higher frequency than more negative forms of feedback such as reprimands or behavior correction. In fact, for students with behavioral difficulties and disabilities, it is recommended that the ratio should be at least 4 to 1 (i.e., four instances of praise for each correction/reprimand; Myers, Simonsen, & Sugai, 2011).

Active supervision or close monitoring of students is one strategy to help discourage negative behavior in students (Conroy et al., 2008; Colvin, Sugai, Good, & Lee, 1997; DePry & Sugai, 2002; Lane et al., 2015). According to DePry & Sugai (2002), active supervision involves three components: (a) teachers continuously scan the classroom and circulate among students making sure to visit areas of the class where problems are more likely to occur;

(b) teachers have frequent interactions with students as they are circulating, talking to students and providing reminders for behavior (e.g., precorrection); and (c) teachers give positive feedback to students who are engaging in appropriate behavior. Precorrection, a component of active supervision, is also a helpful strategy for preventing negative behaviors (Colvin, Sugai, & Patching, 1993; DePry & Sugai, 2002; Walker, Ramsey, & Gresham, 2004). When teachers use precorrection, they provide reminders, either verbal or a gesture, about appropriate behavior before students have a chance to display negative behavior. For example, if a teacher knows that students struggle with transitioning quietly to lunch, the teacher might remind the students about the expectations for walking in a line in the hallway before the students line up. Then as the students are walking to lunch, the teacher could provide additional reinforcement of appropriate behavior that is observed.

When students engage in minor negative behaviors (e.g., calling out, not following directions) a teacher may need to provide correction or redirection in order to address the behavior. Redirection involves providing a cue for students to remind them of the behavior they should be demonstrating. For example, if students are not on task, the teacher could provide a verbal reminder to the entire class about the current expectations, or the teacher could walk over to an individual student's desk and provide a physical cue to remind them of the behavioral expectation (e.g., pointing to section in their book they should be reading). Often just moving in closer proximity to a student who is engaging in negative behavior can be enough of a reminder for students to stop minor misbehaviors. While it is sometimes necessary, teachers should be careful about using reprimands, or negative feedback on behavior, as that could lead to increased behavioral problems (Kerr & Nelson, 2009). Additionally, before providing any redirection or reprimand, the teacher should determine if the behavior would best be addressed by ignoring; this is often helpful for minor attention-seeking behaviors where the correction provided by the teacher would only serve to further reinforce the behavior (Kerr & Nelson, 2009).

## Specific Questions to Guide Discussion

1. Describe strategies you used this week in order to elicit responses from students. Think about times when students are responding to you and to their peers. How did these strategies help to get all students engaged in the learning? What is the level of OTRs in your class? Do all students have the opportunity to respond multiple times within a lesson? How do you incorporate peer learning and grouping strategies into your instruction in order to increase OTRs? What lessons this week provided the most opportunities for students to respond? What specific strategies did you use in those lessons?

2. How have you incorporated student choice into your instruction this week? How did students respond to having choices in their learning? Are there other ways you can incorporate student choice into your lessons? What lessons this week had the most student engagement? What set those lessons apart from others?

3. What specific strategies have you used this week to encourage positive student behavior and discourage negative behavior? How do you use praise in your class? What are some examples of what you would say to praise students? Do you provide students with praise that is specific to their behavior or more general? How do you provide students with reminders/prompting about behavioral expectations?

4. How do you provide active supervision of students in your class? Are there ever times when students are not supervised fully? Do you focus on specific students or areas of the class for more intensive supervision? If so, how did you pick those students/areas? As you are supervising the class, what do you do in order to reinforce positive behavior and prevent negative behavior? Do you see any differences in how you supervise students and how your co-teacher or team supervises?

5. What types of minor misbehaviors did you respond to this week? Could these behaviors have been prevented if you utilized strategies prior to the behavior (e.g., active supervision, precorrection)? What strategies did you use to respond to minor misbehaviors this week? How did you redirect students who were engaging in off-task or disruptive behaviors? Did you feel that the strategies you used were effective or do you need additional strategies to address the behavior of some students? Do you see any differences in how you supervise students and how your co-teacher or team supervises?

## Productive Practices

1. *Use multiple types of OTRs including both teacher and peer-directed strategies.*
    a. Reduce your use of raised hands and calling on individual students. This only allows a select few students to respond and decreases the engagement in the class. Furthermore, students who struggle with the material can become anxious if called on to respond in front of the class.
    b. In whole-class lessons, utilize choral responding strategies by either having all students verbally respond or respond using a gesture (e.g., thumbs-up/thumbs-down, fist-to-five; see "Key Terms" for more details). Teach students a signal for when you want all students to respond (e.g., saying "everyone" and holding out your hand to the class).
    c. Give students the opportunity to respond to a peer (e.g., Think-Pair-Share, Turn-and-Talk; see "Key Terms" for more details) in order to allow everyone to express their thoughts. Incorporate cooperative learning and peer tutoring strategies into your instruction.
    d. Utilize response cards as a method of increasing OTRs. For example, instead of having individual students come up to the board to solve math problems, have individu-

al marker boards so all students can complete the problem, and then hold them up to show their response. Check out specific apps/computer programs that can serve as response cards (e.g., Plicker, Kahoot; see "Resources" for more information).
2. *Provide opportunities for students to have choice in the classroom.*
   a. Find simple ways to incorporate choice into classroom activities. For example, allow students to choose what color they want to use to write or what type of paper they will use. Be sure to give students clear directions and options for their choices (e.g., a choice among three colors of paper).
   b. Think about ways you can give students more of a say in their learning such as providing flexible seating for some activities or a choice of the medium they will use in an assignment. For options that require more work on your part (e.g., providing new seating options in the class such as standing desks and bean bag chairs), be sure you come up with a plan for how the options will be implemented and specific procedures students will follow.
   c. Teach students how to make wise choices that enhance their learning. For example, if you are going to allow students to choose where they will sit for an activity, teach them how to reflect on their own learning and determine what works best for them.
3. *Use active supervision of the class at all times.*
   a. Don't always remain at the front of the class. Circulate so you are able to supervise and interact with all students. While you circulate, be sure to reinforce positive behavior and provide precorrection for potential negative behaviors.
   b. For students who have difficulties maintaining focus or exhibiting positive behavior, seat them in an area of the class where they will have the least number of distractions or opportunities to misbehave. For some students, this is the front of the room, but for others the side or back may be most effective. It is important to ensure they are in an area where they can be observed at all times and you have frequent contact with them to reinforce behavior.
4. *Maximize the engaged time in your class.*
   a. Make sure students have something to do at all times. Down time can lead to behavior problems if students are bored or unsure of the expectations. This does not mean that you cannot have unstructured time in the class but be sure students are clear about the expectations and have a list of options for things they can do during that time. For example, if you have indoor recess one day, give students a list of activities that they may choose from (e.g., use a computer, play a game with a peer, read, or draw).
   b. Minimize the time lost when transitioning from one activity to another. Give students a warning before the transition so they can be prepared, provide clear directions for the transition, and teach students specific routines to follow to ensure an efficient transition.
   c. When transitioning from one activity/subject to another, be sure to give students advance warning so they know what they need to do in order to wrap up one activity and move on to the next. Provide precorrection/reminders as needed to encourage positive behavior during transition times.
5. *Give students frequent reminders and feedback on their behavior.*
   a. Utilize precorrection. If there is an activity or situation where you anticipate potential behavioral problems (e.g., lining up for recess) provide students with ad-

vanced reminders about the behavioral expectations (e.g., "Remember when we line up, our hands should remain at our sides and we should be facing forward.").
   b. Utilize frequent behavior-specific praise. Praise should directly state the specific behavior the student exhibited (e.g., "You did a great job remembering to walk quietly in the hallway.") instead of just providing a general statement (e.g., "Excellent work!"). It is also helpful to connect praise directly to positive outcomes (e.g., "Great job staying focused on your assignment. Because you were focused, you were able to complete your assignment and earn free time."). It is also important to praise students at a higher rate than issuing reprimands/corrections (i.e., a ratio of 4 to 1 is suggested).
6. *Respond to minor misbehavior in a way that encourages positive behavior without drawing attention to the misbehavior.*
   a. When addressing minor misbehavior problems in the class, try to focus on preventative and positive strategies (e.g., active supervision, precorrection, praising positive behaviors) first. Preventing a behavior before it happens is more effective than correcting the behavior after it occurs.
   b. If a student needs to be redirected, begin by providing a simple prompt to remind the student of the behavioral expectations (e.g., moving in closer proximity to students, or giving a gentle verbal reminder).
   c. If students need a more formal reprimand for their behavior, be sure to talk to them in private so as not to embarrass them or draw additional attention to the behavior. Speak to students in a calm voice, focusing on the behavioral expectations and not specific qualities of the student (e.g., "It is important to stay quiet during reading time so all students can concentrate on their work." as opposed to "You are always making noises and bothering other students.").

## What Would You Do?

Ask your team or pair the following questions. For suggested responses to questions, see Appendix A.

1. What would you do if a student refuses to work with another student?

2. What would you do if a student seems to be excessively demanding of your attention (e.g., calling your name repeatedly, raising their hand constantly, engaging in negative behaviors in order to get your attention)?

3. What would you do if you are having classwide behavioral difficulties (e.g., many students off task, disruptive behavior) and preventative strategies have not been effective?

## Reflective Professional Growth Activities

Consider these ideas or activities to facilitate and foster teacher growth and reflection. Select one or two ideas to help facilitate this reflection process that will help the teacher, pair, or team to understand promoting engagement and positive behavior. Remember that you know the individuals best so be sure to choose an activity that would be the most effective for them.

### Idea 1: Increasing Opportunities to Respond

Try out new methods for increasing OTRs in your lessons over a couple of days. Write these methods into your lesson plans and make sure to include direct teaching of the methods to your students (e.g., for choral responding, teach students a signal you will use when you want them to respond). After you teach the lessons, reflect on the use of the OTRs and your perception of the engagement in the class.

**Evidence:** Inclusion of methods in lesson plans with teacher reflection.

### Idea 2: Analyzing Student Responses and Teacher Reinforcement

Collaborate with a teacher or your team to record a lesson. This professional growth activity works well when working in a co-teaching context and using the One Teach, One Observe model to record teacher actions. Watch the video and note the number of OTRs, reinforcement (behavior-specific praise and general praise), and reprimands/corrections per student. Use Figure 9.1 below to record your data. Include OTRs provided to the entire class (e.g., choral responding) and general praise given to the class. Add notes on the types of OTRs you use (e.g., choral responding, peer responding) and any observations you have about your use of praise.

Analyze your data to reflect on your use of OTRs and praise overall. Are you providing students with multiple opportunities to respond during the lesson? Are you using a variety of OTR strategies? Also, identify patterns in your use of OTRs and praise/reprimands across students (e.g., do certain students get more or less opportunities to respond or praise compared to others?).

**Evidence:** Complete Figure 9.1 displaying OTR, praise, and reprimand data.

| Student | Opportunity to Respond | Behavior-Specific Praise | General Praise | Reprimand/Correction |
|---|---|---|---|---|
| Ex: Manuel | Provided three opportunities for Manuel to respond using the whiteboard. | "Manuel, you are doing well with following multi-task directions." | "Excellent job everyone!" | "Manuel, do not play with your scissors! This can be harmful to you and others." |

**Figure 9.1** Reflective data chart to analyze OTRs and praise.

## Idea 3: Increasing Engagement During Instruction

Come up with some ideas for increasing engagement in your lessons and write specific strategies into your lesson plans for the week. Plan for different grouping strategies that give students increased opportunities to respond to peers and determine ways to give students choice in the lesson. During the lesson, provide active supervision to ensure students are on task and behavior problems are minimized. After the lesson, reflect on the different strategies you used and the effect they had on the engagement of students in the lesson. This reflection-on-practice is helpful for co-teachers or teams to do as they plan and/or teach collaboratively.

**Evidence:** Completed lesson plan with highlighted strategies to increase student engagement; Reflection-on-action notes.

## Idea 4: Increasing the Use of Precorrection and Redirection

Identify areas in your class where students are struggling to meet behavioral expectations (e.g., transitioning to a new activity, working in peer groups). Target specific areas where precorrection would be helpful. Come up with a specific plan for how you will implement precorrection including when, where, and how you will use it. For example, do you need to have students rehearse the behavior (e.g., have them practice walking in a quiet line)? Determine what type of prompting you will use for precorrection (e.g., come up with a specific script for what you will say to students or a specific signal/gesture you will use). Also include plans for how you will redirect students who engage in negative behavior. Take anecdotal notes about your use of precorrection/redirection and the resulting effect on the behavior of interest.

**Evidence:** Planning documents for precorrection/redirection (e.g., script and plan for using); Notes reflecting on outcome.

# Follow-Up, Monitoring, and Goal Setting

Complete the follow-up questions for the selected reflective professional growth activity.

## Idea 1: Increasing Opportunities to Respond

- Which OTR methods did you choose to implement and why did you choose those methods?
- Did you have to teach your students any specific procedures for using the OTR methods?
- Were the OTR methods used effectively or do you think students needed more instruction in the procedures?
- What might you do differently next time?
- Do you think utilizing these OTR strategies helped to improve engagement in your class, and if so, what makes you say that?
- Going forward, what are you going to do to continue to improve the opportunities students have to respond in your class?
- Are you going to continue using these new strategies or are there other ones you want to try?

## Idea 2: Analyzing Student Responses and Teacher Reinforcement

- Based on your data, do you feel that you are providing students with multiple OTRs during the lesson?
- What patterns do you notice in your use of OTRs and praise/reprimands across students?
- Do you feel that you were fairly equitable in your use of praise with students or are there certain students you praise more than others? Is your ratio of praise to redirection/reprimands at least 4 to 1?
- What goals do you have for increasing your use of OTRs and behavior-specific praise in your future lessons?
- What strategies will you use to help you reach these goals?
- How will you monitor your progress?

## Idea 3: Increasing Engagement During Instruction

- What did you choose to focus on to improve the level of engagement in your class?
- How did you incorporate peer grouping strategies and student choice into your lesson?
- How did you provide active supervision during the lesson to ensure all students were engaged in the instruction?
- Do you feel the strategies you used were effective in improving student engagement?
- Moving forward, what are you going to do to ensure your students are engaged in instruction?

## Idea 4: Increasing the Use of Precorrection and Redirection

- What areas in your class did you identify for this activity and why did you choose these specific areas?
- How did you plan to implement precorrection with your students?
- Did you need to have students rehearse the behavior, and if so, how did you do this?
- What type of prompting did you use for precorrection?
- How effective was your use of precorrection in reducing the behavioral difficulties you identified?
- Did you need to provide any redirection to address any minor misbehavior, and if so, how did you redirect students in a way that focused on positive behavioral expectations and avoid drawing attention to the negative behavior?
- How else might you incorporate precorrection/redirection into your class?

# Resources

## *Articles*

### Classwide Interventions

This article provides information on preventative strategies such as contingent praise, OTR, close supervision, and providing feedback. It is written specifically for special education teachers but the techniques can be applied to all classrooms.

Conroy, M. A., Sutherland, K. S., Snyder, A. L., & Marsh, S. (2008). Classwide interventions: Effective instruction makes a difference. *Teaching Exceptional Children, 40*(6), 24–30.

### Low-Intensity Strategies

This special issue of the journal, *Beyond Behavior*, has articles detailing several strategies described in this chapter including behavior-specific praise, precorrection, and instructional choice.

Mooney, P. & Ryan, J. B. (2018). Low intensity strategies to enhance school success [special issue]. *Beyond Behavior, 27*(3).

## *Books*

### Supporting Behavior for School Success

This book details several strategies discussed in this chapter (e.g., OTRs, behavior-specific praise) in addition to many others. Complete descriptions of each strategy are provided along with steps for implementation.

Lane, K. L., Menzies, H. M., Ennis, R. P., & Oakes, W. P. (2015). *Supporting behavior for school success: A step-by-step guide to key strategies.* New York, NY: Guilford Press.

### Classwide Positive Behavior Interventions and Supports

This book provides information about common behavioral interventions and supports including ways to improve engagement, reinforce appropriate behavior, and prevent negative behavior.

Simonsen, B., & Myers, D. (2014). *Classwide positive behavior interventions and supports: A guide to proactive classroom management.* New York, NY: Guilford Press.

## *Videos*

### Teaching Channel: Behavior

This collection of videos provides strategies for student behavior including many of the strategies discussed in this module.

The Teaching Channel. (2018). *Behavior.* Retrieved from https://www.teachingchannel.org/videos?page=1&categories=topics_behavior&load=1

### Teaching Channel: Engagement

This collection of videos provides strategies for maximizing student engagement.

The Teaching Channel. (2018). *Engagement.* Retrieved from https://www.teachingchannel.org/videos?page=1&categories=topics_engagement&load=1

## Web Resources

**IRIS Center**

The IRIS Center contains modules, case studies, skill sheets, and other resources related to special education. If you visit their resource locator and click "fundamental skill sheets" you will find descriptions of several strategies discussed in this chapter.

IRIS Center. (2011). IRIS resource locator. Retrieved from https://iris.peabody.vanderbilt.edu/resources/iris-resource-locator

**Kahoot!**

This website has a method for response cards where students use an electronic device (e.g., phone, computer, tablet) to respond to questions. *Kahoot!* can be played as a competitive game to increase student engagement and test their knowledge of topics.

*Kahoot!* (n.d.). Retrieved from https://kahoot.com

**Plickers**

Plickers is a type of response card where students have an individual code on a paper that they turn for different responses. The teacher is able to scan the class using a phone or tablet to record student responses.

Plickers. (2018). *Tailor instruction with instant feedback.* Retrieved from https://www.plickers.com/

**Evidence-Based Intervention Network**

The EBI is a website with comprehensive information about academic and behavioral interventions. Interventions are organized based on the type of student difficulty. Intervention summaries are provided for teachers to use when implementing the intervention.

University of Missouri. (2011). *Evidence-based intervention network.* Retrieved from http://ebi.missouri.edu/

**National Center on Intensive Intervention**

Through this website you can learn the basics about intensive intervention. They also explain the process, provide tools for assessment and intervention, implementation support, and resources in literacy, math, and behavior.

National Center on Intensive Intervention at American Institutes for Research. (n.d.). Retrieved from http://www.intensiveintervention.org/

**Specific Behavioral Interventions**

This site contains overviews of common behavioral interventions. The site offers descriptions of interventions along with sample handouts to use.

National Center on Intensive Intervention at American Institutes for Research. (n.d.). *Specific behavioral interventions.* Retrieved from http://www.intensiveintervention.org/behavior-strategies-and-sample-resources

**Intervention Central**

The site details specific information on using the *Numbered Heads Together* strategy.

Intervention Central. (n.d.). *How to: Improve group responding: Numbered heads together.* Retrieved from http://www.interventioncentral.org/node/992122

## Key Terms and Definitions

**Active Supervision**: Active supervision involves scanning of the classroom and frequent interactions with students where they are provided reminders for their behavior and praise for exhibiting positive behavior.

**Behavior-Specific Praise**: Praise that clearly describes the behavior the student exhibited (e.g., "You did a great job using a quiet voice in the hallway.").

**Choral responding**: A strategy for increasing OTRs. In choral responding, all students respond in unison either verbally or through a gesture (e.g., thumbs up).

**Classwide Peer Tutoring**: A strategy where the teacher pairs students of similar academic levels into tutoring teams. The teams take turns tutoring each other on academic content (i.e., reciprocal peer tutoring) and the teams earn points for working together.

**Contingent praise**: This type of praise, similar to behavior-specific praise, is contingent on the student demonstrating a specific behavior.

**Cooperative learning**: An instructional strategy that involves students working together on a learning task. Cooperative learning often involves using different student roles in the group (e.g., recorder, reporter, time-keeper) to ensure all students are contributing to the group's efforts.

**Fist-to-five**: A choral responding strategy where students hold up their hand with fingers displaying a number that corresponds to a teacher question (and a fist for zero). For example, students rate their level of understanding of a concept (5 = fully understand, 3 = somewhat understand, 0 = don't understand at all).

**Numbered Heads Together**: A peer learning strategy where the teacher places students in groups of 4 and assigns each student in the group a number. The teacher poses a question or prompt for groups to discuss. Then the teacher randomly calls on a number to respond (e.g., any 2s who know the answer).

**Opportunity to Respond (OTR)**: Any strategy where the teacher provides a prompt, such as asking a question, and the student provides a response.

**Precorrection**: Providing reminders or prompts about expected behavior prior to behavior occurring. Usually used to target specific behaviors that have been problematic in the past.

**Redirection**: Providing reminders or prompts about expected behavior after negative behavior has occurred.

**Reinforcement**: Anything provided to a student as a reward for positive behavior.

**Reprimand**: Providing negative feedback on behavior. Reprimands should generally be avoided in favor of more positive strategies.

**Response Card**: A type of OTR where students record their response on a physical object (e.g., individual marker board, piece of paper, electronic device) and hold it up to show to the teacher.

**Think-Pair-Share**: A peer learning technique where students first think about their own response to a prompt or question, then pair up with a partner to discuss. The teacher then calls on individual pairs to share ideas from their discussion.

**Thumbs-up/Thumbs-down**: A choral responding technique where students hold up a thumbs-up if they agree with a question and a thumbs-down if they disagree. A thumbs to the side can also be used to indicate if students are not sure.

**Transition**: A time when students are moving from one activity or subject to another.

# Appendix A

## *What Would You Do? Questions with Suggested Responses*

1. What would you do if a student refuses to work with another student?

   **Suggested Response 1:** As with all behavioral related concerns, it is always best to try to prevent this from happening instead of having to deal with it afterwards. Prior to assigning groups, some teachers have students privately list several students they would like to work with for group activities and several that they would not like to work with. This is also a good way to get a feel for the social dynamics of a classroom and identify students who may potentially be excluded. You can also directly teach students how to work with other students and how to be a good partner during group activities. Remind students that we have to work with all sorts of different people and sometimes we may not be friends with someone (or even get along with them) but we need to be able to work with them. Students should change partners/groups frequently so they get a chance to work with a variety of students in the class. If you continue to have difficulties, I would privately ask the student why they don't want to work with the other student. There may be a very good reason (e.g., the other student is being a bully). You should never force a student to work with someone who is being mean to them in any way. You may need to work with some pairs/groups to resolve potential conflicts or you just may need to reassign groups.

2. What would you do if a student seems to be excessively demanding of your attention (e.g., calling your name repeatedly, raising their hand constantly, engaging in negative behaviors in order to get your attention)?

   **Suggested Response 2:** First, it is helpful to try to understand why the student seeks attention. Are they not confident with their academic skills so they keep asking for help? Do they need some instruction in social skills to learn specific ways to ask for attention? Maybe there is something going on outside of school that is causing them to seek out additional adult attention. Understanding why the student seeks attention will help you figure out what to do in order to address the behavior. It may help to provide the student with positive attention more frequently in order to decrease their need to engage in behavior to gain negative attention. If a student is frequently requesting help with work, first determine if the work is at the correct academic level for the student. Then, begin by giving them frequent attention as they begin their work but gradually decrease attention and praise them for attempting to work on their own. Some teachers also use the rule "ask three before me" where students must ask three peers for help before talking to the teacher. Sometimes you need to clearly state the behavioral expectation to a student and then ignore their attempts to get your attention. This is known as extinction. However, note that when using this technique, student behavior may increase first prior to decreasing (e.g., they may become even more demanding of your attention before gradually decreasing their behavior).

3. What would you do if you are having classwide behavioral difficulties (e.g., many students off task, disruptive behavior) and preventative strategies have not been effective?

   **Suggested Response 3:** First, I would make sure you have fully utilized all preventative strategies. Do you have clear rules, procedures, and consequences? Are your lessons well-structured and engaging? Do students know what is expected of them at all times? Are you using active supervision and precorrection effectively? It may help to have another teacher observe you to be sure you are doing everything you can to prevent the behavioral difficulties. If these strategies are still not effective, you may need to use a specific classwide intervention or incentive to address the behavior. See the Evidence Based Intervention Network for ideas: http://ebi.missouri.edu/?cat=22

# References

Colvin, G., Sugai, G., Good, R. H., III, & Lee, Y. Y. (1997). Using active supervision and precorrection to improve transition behaviors in an elementary school. *School Psychology Quarterly, 12*(4), 344–363.

Colvin, G., Sugai, G., & Patching, B. (1993). Precorrection: An instructional approach for managing predictable problem behaviors. *Intervention in School and Clinic, 28*(3), 143–150.

Conroy, M. A., Sutherland, K. S., Snyder, A. L., & Marsh, S. (2008). Classwide interventions: Effective instruction makes a difference. *Teaching Exceptional Children, 40*(6), 24–30.

DePry, R. L., & Sugai, G. (2002). The effect of active supervision and pre-correction on minor behavioral incidents in a sixth grade general education classroom. *Journal of Behavioral Education, 11*(4), 255–267.

Greenwood, C. (1997). Classwide peer tutoring. *Behavior and Social Issues, 7*(1), 53–57.

Haydon, T., Borders, C., Embury, D., & Clark, L. (2009). Using effective instructional delivery as a classwide management tool. *Beyond Behavior, 18*(2), 12–17.

Haydon, T., MacSuga-Gage, A. S., Simonsen, B., & Hawkins, R. (2012). Opportunities to respond: A key component of effective instruction. *Beyond Behavior, 22*(1), 23–31.

Hunter, W., & Haydon, T. (2013). Examining the effectiveness of numbered heads together for students with emotional and behavioral disorders. *Beyond Behavior, 22*(3), 40–45.

Kerr, M. M., & Nelson, C. M. (2009). *Strategies for addressing behavior problems in the classroom* (6th ed.). New York, NY: Pearson.

Lane, K. L., Menzies, H. M., Bruhn, A. L., & Crnobori, M. (2011). *Managing challenging behaviors in schools: Research-based strategies that work*. New York, NY: Guilford Press.

Lane, K. L., Menzies, H. M., Ennis, R. P., & Oakes, W. P. (2015). *Supporting behavior for school success: A step-by-step guide to key strategies*. New York, NY: Guilford Press.

Myers, D. M., Simonsen, B., & Sugai, G. (2011). Increasing teachers' use of praise with a response-to-intervention approach. *Education and Treatment of Children, 34*(1), 35–59.

Putall, E. A., Cooper, H., & Robinson, J. C. (2008). The effects of choice on intrinsic motivation and related outcomes: A meta-analysis of research findings. *Psychological Bulletin, 134*(2), 270–300.

Shogren, K. A., Faggella-Luby, M. N., Bae, S. J., & Wehmeyer, M. L. (2004). The effect of choice-making as an intervention for problem behavior: A meta-analysis. *Journal of Positive Behavior Interventions, 6*(4), 228–237.

Sutherland, K. S., Alder, N., & Gunter, P. L. (2003). The effect of varying rates of opportunities to respond to academic requests on the classroom behavior of students with EBD. *Journal of Emotional and Behavioral Disorders, 11*(4), 239–248.

Walker, H. M., Ramsey, E., & Gresham, F. M. (2004). *Antisocial behavior in school: Evidence-based practices*. Belmont, CA: Wadsworth.

# MODULE 10

# Using Individualized Interventions for Challenging Behaviors

Mary B. Haspel
*Monmouth University*

*If a child doesn't know how to read, we teach. If a child doesn't know how to swim, we teach.*
*If a child doesn't know how to multiply, we teach. If a child doesn't know how to drive, we teach.*
*If a child doesn't know how to behave, we ... teach? ... punish?*
—Herner

## MODULE DESCRIPTION

Behaviors can present obstacles to individual learning as well as disrupt instruction within the classroom. It is important to understand the variables that affect student behavior as well as the strategies that are used to effectively intervene and address these issues in school. This module will provide a framework for understanding the functions of behavior as well as a systematic approach for developing individualized interventions in the classroom.

## Theory/Conceptual Framework

Managing student behavior can be one of the most significant obstacles a new teacher will encounter. There is a general tendency to label students with challenging behaviors with adjectives such as, "lazy," "unfocused," "problematic," or "bad." An important first step is to determine if a behavioral intervention is necessary. Factors that warrant intervention in school include the following: if it impedes the learning of the individual, if it impacts the learning of others within the environment, or if it is potentially harmful to the student, peers or staff (Steege, Watson, & Gresham, 2009). While these types of behaviors can be stressful for a teacher, it is important to understand that it is not an inherent attribute of the individual (O'Neill et al., 2015). In a school setting, there are numerous variables that affect a student's behavior, such as work demands, attention from peers, difficulties with learning or even events occurring at home.

The scientific approach to understanding human behavior is generally known as applied behavior analysis or ABA. The foundation of ABA is based upon the premise that there are three variables within a behavioral event: the antecedent (A) or "what came before," the behavior (B) or "what is observed," and the consequence (C) or "what came after." Simply stated, if a behavior is followed by a desired consequence, it is more likely to happen again (Cooper, Heron, & Heward, 2007). Similarly, if a behavior is followed by an undesired consequence, then it is less likely to happen again. As a result, behavior serves one of two essential functions: to access/obtain pleasant consequences or to escape/avoid unpleasant consequences (O'Neill et al., 2015). These functions, which are respectively maintained by positive and negative reinforcement, are highly predictable and applicable to all individuals (see Figure 10.1). In addition, they serve as the essential components of functional assessment. See the graphic representation in Figure 10.1.

There are three approaches to conducting functional assessment, however, this module will focus on implementing indirect and direct assessment. Within indirect assessment, interviews, rating scales, and record reviews are conducted with school staff, caregivers and when appropriate, the student. This allows for the teacher to develop a well-rounded operational

| Positive Reinforcement **+** | Negative Reinforcement **−** | Behavior is Increased |
|---|---|---|
| Occurs when you **access or obtain** something preferred or pleasant | Occurs when you **avoid or escape** something non-preferred or unpleasant | |
| **Example for Positive Reinforcement**<br>A: Teacher says, "What letter is this?"<br>B: Student states correct answer<br>C: Teacher says, "Great job!" and gives student a high five. | **Example for Negative Reinforcement**<br>A: Teacher says, "It's time for work."<br>B: Student complains<br>C: Teacher says, "OK, five more minutes of play time." | |
| **Anticipated Results** | | |
| Behavior of answering questions is likely to increase in the future because it was successful in accessing attention and praise. | Behavior of complaining is likely to increase in the future because it was successful in avoiding work. | |

**Figure 10.1** Explanation of reinforcement.

definition of the behavior and ensure that the behavior has been adequately described in measurable terms. However, indirect assessment is highly subjective and it is important to incorporate objective measures, such as direct observation and data collection (O'Neill et al., 2015). The direct assessment portion incorporates those components and captures the function of the behavior by examining the impact of the behavior in relation to the student's ability to learn.

While indirect and direct assessment should be present in a formal evaluation, each piece can be used separately to understand and address challenging behavior. Because it is a process, either approach can be conducted over time or as needed. Unlike other types of assessment, there are no federal or state laws that dictate what functional assessment *must* look like, only best practice. Furthermore, there are no federal or state laws that stipulate *who* can conduct a functional assessment. If teachers have the tools and knowledge to conduct a functional assessment, they can more quickly identify potential functions of the behavior and develop an effective intervention strategy.

## Specific Questions to Guide Discussion

1. Describe the existing behavioral management system in the classroom. Are there any specific supports that are effective for the student with challenging behaviors? If so, which ones?

2. Describe the student with challenging behavior. How is the behavior impacting the student's learning or the learning of others? Is the behavior potentially harmful in any way?

3. Describe this student's strengths. What are the student's challenges? How do these strengths and challenges relate to the behavior?

4. Describe a scenario (or scenarios) where the student with challenging behaviors *does not* exhibit any behaviors. What are the environmental conditions of this scenario? Who is present in this scenario? What is the learning context/expectations? Are there any patterns amongst environmental conditions (e.g., people, learning context, time) that relate to this student's success?

5. Describe learning abilities as they relate to behavioral challenges. If a student's academic needs are not being met within the current instructional practices, how would you address those needs first? What aspects of instructional design, curriculum, and teaching are critical for this student?

## Productive Practices

1. *Reflect upon specific academic and behavioral needs.*
   a. What is the student accessing or avoiding as a result of the student's behavior? Carefully consider each of the following in order to identify potential reinforcing variables:
      - Does the student *access or obtain attention* from staff or students as a result of the behavior?
      - Does the student *access or obtain preferred items or activities?*
      - Does the student *avoid or escape non-preferred tasks or activities?*
   b. Examine the behavior within the current system of behavioral supports. If there are any supports that are actively working for the student within the classroom, identify how those could be modified or individualized before conducting a much more intensive intervention.
   c. If it appears that a formal assessment needs to be conducted, consult with the appropriate district personnel in regard to obtaining consent from the student's parents, as well as following district procedure for conducting a functional assessment in a classroom.

2. *Examine variables within the environment.*
   a. An important aspect of the functional assessment process is the identification of variables that relate to the behavior, which can be actions and/or reactions of others. So it is important to be mindful that an outcome of the assessment will more than likely require a behavioral change of others as well as yourself.
   b. Not every student is equal, some need more time and attention. Be mindful of giving individual students what they need rather than having all students receive the exact same attention and support.
   c. Focus on what you would like the student to exhibit behaviorally versus making the challenging behavior 'go away'. The most valuable part of behavior assessment is the identification of ways to *correct* the behavior. Focus on what to teach and how the student can learn a more appropriate behavior.

3. *Be thorough and collect sufficient information.*
   a. Functional assessment is the only type of assessment that takes time and involves many other individuals. Take your time to collect your information on how often the behavior occurs as well as identify variables that relate to the behavior (e.g., work, attention). Do not feel pressured to arrive at a solution before you have adequate data to support your recommendations.
   b. Consider all sources. For example, interview people such as special area teachers, security guards, lunchroom personnel, and paraprofessionals. These personnel can be easily overlooked and typically have valuable insights into student behaviors.

4. *Let data guide decisions.*
   a. Consult data prior to making any changes or adjustments in the plan. It typically takes at least two full weeks for an intervention to have an effect on behavior (if the intervention is being implemented with fidelity or the way in which it has been written). Be cautious in making rapid changes, unless there are risk factors to be considered, such as potential harm to the student or others.
   b. Analyze success and challenges via the data rather than personal modalities (e.g., "Behaviors have decreased by 25% in the school environment and 50% at

home" versus, "The plan is working better at home than in school"). This will avoid any defensiveness or personal inquiries.

5. *Create communication channels.*
   a. Ensure that all personnel involved in the student's daily activities are informed about the intervention or plan and are clear on its implementation.
   b. Establish a clear modality for communicating successes and challenges with the student. It is important that the student is actively involved in the process and is aware of personal growth. It is also important for the student to voice possible solutions for behavioral challenges.
   c. Ensure that there is a clear home-school connection. Considerations should include: How will data be shared with the family? How will changes/modifications to the intervention or plan be communicated? What are the student's goals for behavioral change and how will progress be monitored? What is the family's preferred communication modality?

## What Would You Do?

Ask your team or pair the following questions. For suggested responses to questions, see Appendix A.

1. What would you do if you have no time to collect data?

2. What would you do if the data did not indicate a clear pattern or function?

3. What would you do if another staff member refused to implement the plan?

## Reflective Professional Growth Activities

Use these activities to facilitate reflection for the pair or team. While these activities are designed to systematically guide the team through the functional assessment process, feel free to choose one or a few activities to help facilitate the process. In collecting ABC (i.e., Antecedent, Behavior, Consequence) data, it might be helpful if one member of the team teaches while one observes. Remember that you know your team the best so be sure to choose an activity that would be the most effective.

### *Idea 1: Create an Operational Definition and Collect ABC (Antecedent, Behavior, Consequence) Data*

Working as a team, describe a challenging behavior in clear, measurable terms. Use the sample below to guide the development of your operational definition:

*Noncompliant (unclear):* "Any time Johnny doesn't listen"

*Noncompliant (clear):* "Any occurrence of Johnny verbally refusing to follow teacher directions, complying with staff instructions, and/or adhering to classroom rules that are followed by a correlating action (e.g., He states, "No" and does not complete the work)."

Then, collect an ABC sample of the behavior together (see Figure 10.2).

Were you able to capture a sample of the behavior using your operational definition? If not, is your operational definition clear enough? Is the type of data collection appropriate? Once agreement has been reached between you, your teaching partner or team, collect additional ABC data. While research supports direct observation of approximately 15–20 occurrences of behavior (O'Neill et al., 2015), it may not be feasible in your setting, so focus on collecting enough data to establish a sufficient pattern.

**Evidence:** Creation of an operational definition with clear descriptors and measurable criteria with a hypothesis statement identifying the perceived function of the behavior based upon the completed ABC data (Example: *During group instruction, Johnny will engage in noncompliant behavior in order to avoid doing work.*).

## *Idea 2: Conduct Interviews/Rating Scales*

Consider all of the individuals who work closely with this student. While there are a multitude of commercially available rating scales and interview forms, the most significant questions typically resemble the following:

- What does the behavior look like (operational definition)?
- How often does the behavior occur?
- When does it occur? When does it not occur?
- Where does it occur? Where does it not occur?
- With whom does it occur? With whom does it not occur?
- How would you trigger/avoid the occurrence of the behavior?
- What typically happens in reaction to the behavior?
- How does the student communicate?

| Antecedent (What happened immediately before?) | Behavior (What was the student's response?) | Consequence (What happened immediately after?) | What is being accessed or avoided? |
|---|---|---|---|
| Johnny's teacher said, "It's time for work." | Johnny slumped in his chair and said, "NO!" | Teacher says, "Johnny, come on now, I know you can do it!" but Johnny does not respond. | Work is avoided and Johnny receives teacher attention after he engages in behavior (e.g., he is negatively reinforced when he avoids the work and positively reinforced when the teacher comes over and talks to him). |

**Figure 10.2** Example of Antecedent, Behavior, Consequence (ABC) data.

- What does the student seem to like/dislike?
- What are the student's strengths/challenges?
- What choices are available to the student throughout daily activities?
- How often are preferred items or activities made accessible to the student?
- Are there any health or medical issues that may be affecting the behavior?

**Evidence:** A completed interview and/or rating scale conducted with two or more people regarding a challenging behavior including clear, identified variables that relate to the behavior.

## *Idea 3: Establish a Baseline Measure*

Practice collecting baseline data. It might be helpful for the teacher candidate or novice teacher to observe someone collecting the data beforehand to ensure understanding of the process prior to doing it independently.

In order to establish a baseline measure, more than one instance of the behavior needs to be captured. While 15–20 occurrences over 2–5 days is ideal (O'Neill et al., 2015), identify a reasonable baseline period with your pair or team. In collecting baseline data, it might be helpful if one member of the team teaches while one collects the data.

Baseline measure: Identify a type of data that would best capture the current rate of a challenging behavior. Consider the following:

- What am I observing? Write down the behavior exactly as you plan to measure it.
- How am I observing? How often do I plan to observe and for how long?
- What type of data am I gathering? Use the chart below (see Figure 10.3) to guide you in selecting the most appropriate data collection method:

**Evidence:** A baseline measure is calculated that demonstrates the overall occurrence or impact of the behavior (Example: *The behavior is occurring on average for 12 minutes of every 40 minute instructional period.*)

| Type of data | Description | Rationale | Example |
|---|---|---|---|
| **Frequency or Event Recording** | A calculation of the exact number of times a behavior occurs; can also be converted to a rate-based calculation | Use when the behavior has a clear beginning and ending and does not occur at extremely high rates | Leaving the classroom; Johnny darted from the classroom 3x today. |
| **Interval Recording** | An approximation of the rate of behavior occurring within a specific time period | Use when the behavior does not have a clear beginning and ending and occurs frequently | Noncompliance; Johnny exhibited noncompliant behavior for 3 out of 4 (10) minute intervals within a 40 minute math period. |
| **Duration Recording** | A measure of how long a behavior occurs | Use when a behavior has a clear onset and occurs for longer periods of time | Tantrums; Johnny had a tantrum that lasted for 17 minutes |
| **Latency Recording** | A measure of how long until a behavior occurs | Use when it is important to determine how long until a behavior begins | Off task; Johnny was off task for the first 5 minutes of morning meeting. |

**Figure 10.3** Baseline Measures.

| | **Terminology Reference Guide for Creating a Behavior Plan** | | | |
|---|---|---|---|---|
| **Assessment Variables** | **Antecedent Events** What events are occurring before the problem behavior? | **Problem Behavior** What is the behavior that is negatively impacting the student and/or others? | **Maintaining Consequences** What is the student accessing or avoiding as a result of the behavior? | **Function** Is the student's problem behavior maintained by positive or negative reinforcement? |
| **Behavior Plan Components** | **Preventative Strategies** What strategies can you use to decrease the problem behavior from occurring? | **Replacement Skills** What behavior would you like to see the student perform instead? | **Consequence Strategies** How will you re-direct or avoid reinforcing the problem behavior? | **Reinforcement System** How will you reinforce replacement skills or desired behaviors so that it serves the function of problem behavior? |

**Figure 10.4** Terminology reference guide for behavior plans.

## *Idea 4: Create a Behavior Support Plan*

A behavior plan must address all of the variables identified within the functional assessment. In creating a behavior plan it might be helpful if one member of the team teaches while one assists in the implementation of the plan. Identify antecedent or prevention strategies based upon your observations that would decrease the likelihood of the behavior occurring. Identify replacement behaviors that you would like to see instead as well as a method for providing immediate feedback and reinforcement (e.g., praise, token system, rewards) for these behaviors. Identify a strategy for withholding reinforcement for the target behavior or redirecting the target behavior to the replacement behavior. Utilize the chart (see Figure 10.4) to guide you in creating a behavior plan using the data you have already collected.

**Behavior Planning Chart**

The following chart is used to systematically create a behavior plan (see Figure 10.5). The variables identified through the functional assessment should be aligned for each component of the behavior plan (see Figure 10.6).

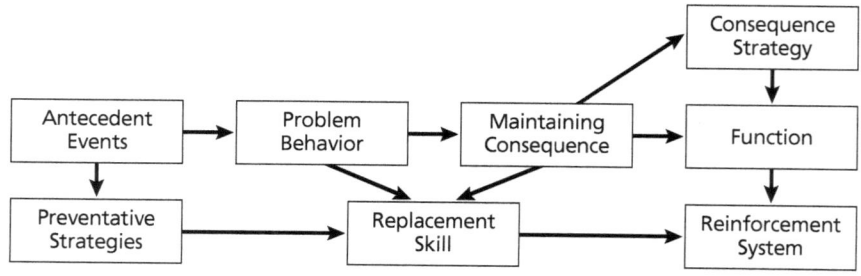

**Figure 10.5** Behavior planning chart.

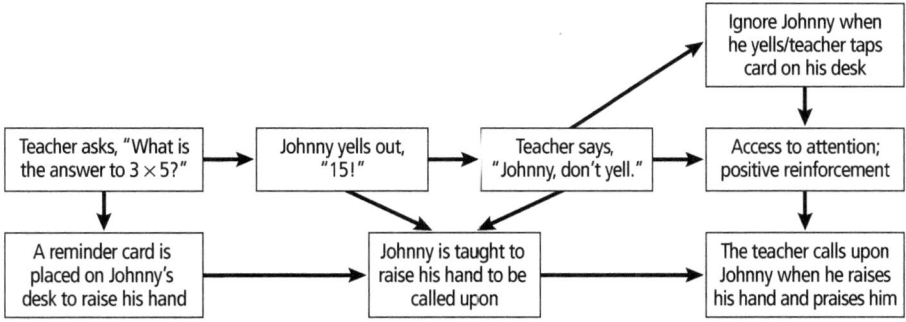

**Figure 10.6** Example of completed behavior planning chart.

*Evidence:* Complete the template (Figure 10.6) using the chart (Figure 10.7) to help guide identification of appropriate strategies. Strategies should collectively result in making the challenging behavior ineffective, inefficient, and irrelevant (O'Neill, et al, 2015). There are additional resources that are helpful in intervention planning available in the *Web Resources* section of this module.

*Note:* The chart in Figure 10.7 is intended to provide examples or suggestions of strategies; it is not intended to be an exhaustive list of strategies to address behavior.

| | Antecedent or Preventative Strategies | Replacement Skills | Consequence Strategies | Reinforcement System |
|---|---|---|---|---|
| **Access or Obtain (Attention)** | Proximal seating<br>Peer buddy<br>Call on student frequently<br>Give praise for correct behaviors<br>Place reminder card on desk for expected behavior | Raising hand<br>Initiating play<br>Greeting others<br>Reciprocal conversation<br>Gaining attention | Ignore behavior<br>Redirect to visual cues<br>Praise peers for ignoring behavior<br>Remind student of appropriate attention-seeking behavior (model it if necessary) | Provide praise and immediate attention every time the student exhibits appropriate attention-seeking behavior<br>Prompt peers to respond to play initiations or conversation initiations |
| **Access or Obtain (Preferred Activities or Objects)** | Provide predictable opportunities to access item/activity<br>Use predictable schedules<br>Use visual cues to indicate turns<br>Role play waiting or teaching to accept "no" as a response | Request appropriately<br>Wait appropriately<br>Turn-taking<br>Accept no (e.g., the item or activity if it is unavailable)<br>Request alternate item | Avoid providing access to item and/or activity<br>Take away item if obtained inappropriately<br>Remind student of when the student can access item<br>Remind student to take turns<br>Remind student to request alternate item | Immediately reinforce appropriate requests for the item or activity by allowing access for specific periods of time (a timer is recommended)<br>Immediately reinforce appropriate turn taking<br>Provide high levels of praise |
| **Avoidance or Escape (Non-preferred Activities)** | Mix easy tasks with difficult tasks<br>Offer choices with tasks<br>Use visual cues<br>Incorporate breaks into the daily schedule or routine | Request a break<br>Request help<br>Verbalize frustration<br>Ask peer for assistance | Do not allow a learner to leave the instructional area<br>Reduce the level of demand (e.g., instead of writing, say it out loud)<br>Decrease the intensity of the demand (e.g., instead of five problems, assist learner in completing two successfully) | If a learner requests, help appropriately, immediately respond to this request<br>If a learner requests for a break, then provide a break for a short period (use a timer)<br>Praise student and peer if assistance is provided through peer |

**Figure 10.7** Example of Strategies by Function.

## Idea 5: Evaluate the Plan

Analyze the success of a behavior support plan by reviewing the data with your partner or team and answering the following questions:

1. Is the target behavior decreasing?
2. Is the replacement behavior increasing?
3. Are all aspects of the plan being implemented consistently?
4. Are the data being collected appropriately and accurately?
5. Has the plan been communicated to all those who are expected to implement it?
6. Is there a communication plan for home?
7. Are there any aspects of this plan that will result in possible crisis? If so, have the appropriate personnel consulted with the school administration to determine how to address it?
8. Has a goal for success been identified?
9. What is the plan for reduction in supports once the goal has been met?
10. What generalization or self-regulation measures can be incorporated into a long-term plan for this student?

**Evidence:** Based off of these questions, make adaptations to the behavior support plan; data should be used to guide all decisions to change and/or modify the plan. A plan should have two full weeks of implementation with fidelity prior to making any changes. A target behavior should have a clear reduction from baseline data prior to reducing supports or thinning reinforcement schedules.

# Follow Up, Monitoring, and Goal Setting

Complete the follow-up questions for the selected reflective professional growth activity.

## Idea 1: Create an Operational Definition and Collect ABC Data

- Let's examine your operational definition and the sample you collected.
  - Did you have to make any revisions to your original definition? If so, what were they?
- Let's look at your ABC and baseline data.
  - What was the function of the behavior based upon your ABC data?
  - Based upon these data, what will you do to address the behavior and ensure that it is no longer reinforced?
  - Do these data allow you to understand the behavior in a clearer, more objective manner?
  - Do you have any further questions?

## Idea 2: Conduct Interviews/Rating Scales

- What information did you gather from conducting your interviews?
- Were you able to establish correlating variables across environments and settings?
- What were the similarities across different settings and what were the differences?
- Based upon these data, were there any changes to the environment that can be made?
- Were there any preventative strategies that can be implemented? If so, how would you make these changes?
- Do you have any further questions?

## Idea 3: Collect Baseline Data and Establish a Baseline Measure

- What was the result of your baseline measure?
- What was the most challenging aspect of collecting the data and how would you troubleshoot it in the future?
- Are there any additional changes or recommendations that you want to make based upon your analysis of the data?
- Do you have any further questions?

## Idea 4: Create a Behavior Support Plan

- How well were you able to identify antecedent, replacement, and consequence strategies based upon your data?
- Do you feel that you have adequate means to prevent and address the challenging behavior?
- Are there any outstanding concerns that you have with implementing either the antecedent or consequence strategies?
- In regard to the replacement behavior, have you identified opportunities to teach this behavior? What about a reinforcement system to strengthen this behavior?
- Do you feel that you will be able to consistently gather data on your plan once it is in effect? If not, who can you use to support you in your data collection?
- Do you have any further questions?

## Idea 5: Evaluate the Plan

- Let's look at your data and systematically go through each of the questions from the previous section.
    - How well were you able to answer each question?
    - Based upon your answers, do you feel that you have a successful plan?
    - What impact did you see on the student?
    - What impact did you see on your classroom?
    - Do you feel that you successfully communicated it to other staff as well as the student's family/caregivers?
    - What would you do differently in the future?
    - Do you have any questions?

# Resources

## Articles

**Thirty Years of Research on the Functional Analysis of Problem Behavior**

This article validates the efficacy of using functional assessment to address challenging behavior as well as the importance of matching function to intervention strategies.

Beavers, G. A., Iwata, B. A., & Lerman, D. C. (2013). Thirty years of research on the functional analysis of problem behavior. *Journal of Applied Behavior Analysis, 46*, 1–21.

**FBAs and BIPs**

This article identifies four common challenge areas for practitioners in conducting functional behavior assessment and implementing behavior intervention plans. Specific focus is given to issues regarding precision, accuracy, and consistency across settings and personnel.

Hirsch, S. E., Bruhn, A. L., Lloyd, J. W., & Katsiyannis, A. (2017). FBAs and BIPs: Avoiding and addressing four common challenges related to fidelity. *Teaching Exceptional Children, 49*(6), 369–379.

**Function-Based Intervention Plans**

This article addresses strategies to support implementation of behavior plans. In addition, the authors offer insight and guidance on how to teach the plan to the staff as well as the target student.

Liaupsin, C. J., & Cooper, J. T. (2017). Function-based intervention plans: What and how to teach. *Beyond Behavior, 26*(3), 135–140.

**Functional Assessment-Based Interventions**

This article offers practical guidance to educators in identifying functions of behavior within the classroom setting and matching intervention to function. Each section of the article is organized in relation to a function of behavior, enabling readers to locate specific and pertinent information quickly.

Oakes, W. P., Lane, K. L., & Hirsch, S. E. (2017). Functional assessment-based interventions: Focusing on the environment and considering function. *Preventing School Failure: Alternative Education for Children and Youth*, 1–12.

**An Example of a Teacher's Experience Using a Functional Behavior Assessment and Function-Based Intervention**

This article explores the feasibility of teachers implementing functional behavior assessment in the classroom and provides a detailed overview of one teacher's experience with the assessment process.

Young, A., & Bauer-Yur, A. (2013). Making the case for teacher use of functional behavior assessment and function-based intervention in the classroom: An example of one teacher's experience. *National Teacher Education Journal, 6*(3), 23–28.

## Modules

**Functional Behavior Assessment**

This module provides step-by-step video-based instruction on conducting and completing functional behavior assessment.

AFIRM Team. (2015). *Functional Behavior Assessment*. Chapel Hill, NC: National Professional Development Center on Autism Spectrum Disorders, FPG Child Development Center, University of North Carolina. Retrieved from http://afirm.fpg.unc.edu/functional-behavior-assessment

**Using a Functional Behavior Assessment for Students With Autism**

This module provides comprehensive, text-based instruction on the implementation of functional behavior assessment.

Autism Internet Modules. (2014). *Functional Behavioral Assessment*. Columbus, OH: Ohio Center for Autism and Low Incidence Disabilities. Retrieved from www.autisminternetmodules.org

**Basic FBA to BIP Learning Modules**

This module provides school-based personnel with an interactive overview of the basics of functional behavior assessment as well as the development of behavior support plans.

Portland State University. (2017). *Basic FBA to BIP Learning Modules.* Portland, OR: TASN and Portland State University. Retrieved from https://sites.google.com/a/pdx.edu/basicfba/e-learning-modules

## Web Resources

**Evidence-Based Intervention Network**

The EBI is a website with comprehensive information about academic and behavioral interventions. Interventions are organized based on the type of student difficulty. Intervention summaries are provided for teachers to use when implementing the intervention.

University of Missouri. (2011). *Evidence-based intervention network*. Retrieved from http://ebi.missouri.edu/

**National Center on Intensive Intervention**

Through this website, you can learn the basics about intensive intervention. The website also explains the process, provides tools for assessment and intervention, and implementation support, and provides resources in literacy, math, and behavior.

National Center on Intensive Intervention at American Institutes for Research. (n.d.). Retrieved from http://www.intensiveintervention.org/

**Positive Behavioral Interventions and Supports**

This organization provides support to schools, districts, and states to build and implement systems using a multi-tiered approach to social, emotional, and behavior support.

U.S. Office of Special Education Programs. (2018). *Positive behavioral interventions and supports.* Retrieved from http://www.pbis.org/default.aspx

**PBIS World**

This website includes a variety of behaviors that a teacher may find in the classroom. It provides the characteristics and symptoms of behaviors, and then goes through the tiers of *Response to Intervention* and provides ideas to implement based on each individual student.

PBIS World. (2018). *Welcome to PBIS World: Click on a behavior to start.* Retrieved from http://www.pbisworld.com/

## Key Terms and Definitions

**Antecedent**: An antecedent is the event that happens directly prior to the occurrence of a behavior.

**Behavior**: The behavior is the response of the individual to the antecedent and consequence conditions; in functional assessment, this can also be referred to as the target behavior or the maladaptive behavior.

**Behavior Intervention Plan (BIP)**: A Behavior Intervention Plan is developed as a result of a functional behavior assessment that identifies preventative strategies, replacement behaviors, consequence strategies as well as reinforcement strategies.

**Consequence**: The consequence is the event that occurs directly after a behavior occurs.

**Direct assessment**: A direct assessment is a functional assessment strategy involving direct observation and gathering of data on a behavior; typically used in conjunction with indirect assessment.

**Extinction**: Extinction is a consequence strategy that requires reinforcement to be withheld in order to decrease a behavior.

**Functional analysis**: A functional analysis is a functional assessment strategy that involves the manipulation of variables relating to behavior; can be conducted through controlled, contrived situations or through systematic presentation of different antecedent and consequence conditions to test a behavioral hypothesis.

**Functional behavior assessment**: A functional behavior assessment is the systematic process of identifying variables relating to a behavior in order to determine function and baseline rate; also referred to as functional assessment.

**Indirect assessment**: An indirect assessment is a functional assessment strategy that involves conducting record reviews, rating scales, and interviews to identify variables that relate to behavior; typically used in conjunction with direct assessment.

**Punishment**: A punishment is the presentation or withdrawal of a stimulus as a consequence that results in a decrease in behavior.

**Reinforcement**: A reinforcement is the presentation or withdrawal of a stimulus that results in an increase in behavior.

**Setting event**: A setting event is the factors in the environment that relate to the occurrence of a behavior.

# Appendix A

## *What Would You Do? Questions with Suggested Responses*

1. What would you do if you have no time to collect data?

    **Suggested Response 1:** Use an indirect assessment tool that can help understand the behavior, such as the Functional Assessment Screening Tool (March et al., 2000) or Functional Assessment Interview (O'Neill, Albin, Storey, Horner, & Sprague, 2015). Both of these tools can be completed fairly quickly and are a great way to understand the behavior better and guide your selection of support strategies.

2. What would you do if the data did not indicate a clear pattern or function?

    **Suggested Response 2:** Identify what behavior you would like to see, then create a plan to teach that skill and reinforce the specific behavior you want to see. Do not implement any consequence strategies unless you have a clear understanding of the function of the behavior.

3. What would you do if another staff member did not implement the plan correctly or refused to follow it? Likewise, what would you do if peers felt that the student with the behavior plan was receiving special treatment?

    **Suggested Response 3:** In both of these scenarios, it is important to understand the perspective of the other person. Let the staff member or peers know that you empathize with their position, but that it is important to provide the individualized support that this student needs. Explain that just as you would provide a reading intervention to a student with a learning disability, you would provide a behavior plan for a student with behavioral challenges.

## References

Beavers, G. A., Iwata, B. A., & Lerman, D. C. (2013). Thirty years of research on the functional analysis of problem behavior. *Journal of Applied Behavior Analysis, 46*(1), 1–21.

Cooper, J. O., Heron, T. E., & Heward, W. L. (2007). *Applied behavior analysis* (2nd ed.). Upper Saddle River, NJ: Prentice-Hall.

Hirsch, S. E., Bruhn, A. L., Lloyd, J. W., & Katsiyannis, A. (2017). FBAs and BIPs: Avoiding and addressing four common challenges related to fidelity. *Teaching Exceptional Children, 49*(6), 369–379.

Liaupsin, C. J., & Cooper, J. T. (2017). Function-based intervention plans: What and how to teach. *Beyond Behavior, 26*(3), 135–140.

March, R. E., Horner, R. H., Lewis-Palmer, T., Brown, D., Crone, D., Todd, A. W., & Carr, E. (2000). *Functional Assessment Checklist: Teachers and Staff (FACTS)*. Eugene, OR: Educational and Community Supports.

O'Neill, R. E., Horner, R. H., Albin, R. W., Sprague, J. R., Storey, K., & Newton, J. S. (2015). *Functional assessment and program development for problem behavior: A practical handbook* (3rd ed). Pacific Grove, CA: Brooks.

Young, A., & Bauer-Yur, A. (2013). Making the case for teacher use of functional behavior assessment and function-based intervention in the classroom: An example of one teacher's experience. *National Teacher Education Journal, 6*(3), 23–28.

# MODULE 11

## Collecting Student Data and Assessment

Kathryn L. Lubniewski

*Monmouth University*

*When teachers do formative assessments effectively, students learn at roughly double the rate than they do without it.*

—Dylan Wiliam

### MODULE DESCRIPTION

It is critical that teachers, pairs, and teaching teams understand the variety of assessment tools, procedures, and limitations to make the most informed decisions. This module will provide support so that you can facilitate an understanding of assessment, along with guided questions and resources to support the pair or team's success.

## Theory/Conceptual Framework

Assessment in the classroom is complex to say the least. The complexity stems from the manner in which teachers and administrators use the term "assessment" interchangeably to refer to evaluation and grading (Salvia, Ysseldyke, & Bolt, 2010). Assessment is a general term used to refer to "the wide variety of methods or tools that educators use to evaluate, measure, and document the academic readiness, learning progress, skill acquisition, or educational needs of students" (Great Schools Partnership, 2015). Assessments can be further categorized as either diagnostic, formative, or summative. Like instructional strategies, teams need to understand when to use each form of assessment to maximize student learning (McLane, 2015). A diagnostic assessment is used to assess student prior learning and determine teaching priorities. Formative assessment is generally a low stakes measurement, used to monitor student learning throughout the lesson or unit (Dexter & Hughes, n.d.; Land, Hirsh, & Wagner, 2010). The teacher provides ongoing feedback that is used to improve student learning and also the teacher's understanding of student need (Teaching Excellence & Educational Innovation, 2015). Summative assessment is used after instruction and can be used to evaluate student learning as well as instructional effectiveness. Standards are mandated and assessments are required for a quality education, but both require constant attention due to the ever-changing assessment requirements in schools (Snyder, 2010). The development of appropriate and useful assessments for student learning ensure that students are meeting instructional objectives, and that unit goals are aligned to local, state, and national standards for learning (Bourke & Mentis, 2014).

A three-part framework for assessment helps to guide an understanding of the complexity of formative and summative assessment within specific content areas (Black, 2015). The first component of the framework is a review of the standards and objectives (including the state standards, IEP goals, and language and communication goals) for the students. The second component considers specific practices in which the teacher provides assessment feedback to help deepen student knowledge and independence (Black, 2015; Dann, 2014) and to focus on how learners are interpreting and understanding the feedback provided by the team (Blount & Rodriguez, 2015; Dann, 2014). To determine the effectiveness of instructional strategies, there needs to be "continual monitoring and operationalization of the standards and assessment in the context of good teaching" (Snyder, 2010, p. 543). The third component addresses continual reflection about assessment and instructional practices. To continue their professional development, teaching pairs or teams need to reflect on the data collection process to help understand the learning gap (Dann, 2014; Layton & Robin, 2007), collaborate across content areas (e.g., ensure exploration of vocabularies, multiple modalities of assessments), and use research-based strategies, as well as review instructional approaches based on the data (DeLuca, Chavez, & Cao, 2013; Mahdavi & Haager, 2007).

Boykin (2014) states, "More focus should be put on assessment for learning (formative assessment) rather than assessment of learning (summative assessment); and on assessment of the learning context and not just assessment of students. Moreover, educational assessments should be coupled with a schooling purpose that emphasizes more human capacity building rather than sorting and selecting" (p. 499). It is crucial for teaching partners and teams to understand the complexity of assessment within the content area, determine specific strategies of assessment and feedback, and evaluate and reflect upon their teaching to ensure that assessments focus on a deeper understanding of learning and not just rote memory of facts (Emberger, 2006; Stefanakis, 2002).

## Specific Questions to Guide Discussion

1. Describe the instructional objectives from a learning experience this past week. What evidence did you collect to make sense of what the students have learned? What did you do once you collected and analyzed these data?

2. Describe a lesson where you used formative assessments. What did you learn from analyzing the data? How did this understanding alter your continuing instruction?

3. Describe a lesson where you used summative assessment. How did you alter your instruction after the lesson/unit based on these data? What did the data show at the end of the lesson?

4. What does meaningful feedback look like? Describe how you provide meaningful feedback to the students?

5. How do you assess student use of academic language prior to a lesson? During a lesson? After a lesson?

## Productive Practices

1. *Always remember the objective.*
   a. Pre-assessment, during assessment, and post-assessment should be incorporated in the lesson. Assessments should focus on the lesson objectives and connect to the outcomes that you want the students to demonstrate after their learning.
2. *Evaluate your assessments.*
   a. What is your objective(s)? What parts of the assessment connect to those specific objectives? How are students going to show that they met each specific objective? What parts of the assignment or product are going to be evaluated?
   b. What is the readability of the assessment? Make sure the assessment has a readability at the appropriate level. If you need help determining readability levels, see the *Resources* section of this module, under web resources.
   c. What is the academic language content-specific vocabulary (i.e., vocabulary specific to the content area) that needs to be taught? What is the academic language general-instructional vocabulary (i.e., vocabulary that crosses content areas) that needs to be taught? Be sure that you have taught both types of academic vocabulary prior to assessing them. Use synonyms for words that may be difficult to understand.
   d. What kinds of assessment will you use? Formative or summative?
   e. Is the assessment going to be graded? If it is, then be sure to have students practice (and apply the feedback you have provided to them) prior to grading. How are you going to grade the assessment? What weight will it hold compared to other grades that you collect in class?
3. *Adapt your assessment for specific learning needs.*
   a. Use *Universal Design for Learning* (see web resources below for more information) strategies to design the assessment to be accessible to all learners.
   b. Consider using differentiated instruction to design different products for the students to show what they learned.
   c. Make sure to provide accommodations for specific students.
   d. As documented by the Individualized Education Plan (IEP), modify assessments for students with disabilities.

4. *Provide meaningful feedback.*
   a. Address each student's individual strengths and needs relative to the measured learning objectives. What do you expect each student to KNOW and be able to DO?
   b. Provide specific oral and/or written feedback to learners that can be concretely applied and measured.
   c. Check for student understanding regarding the written and oral feedback that you give. Ask students to repeat your feedback in their own words.
   d. Provide individual feedback that challenges students to perform at a level that may exceed the learning objective.
   e. How are you supporting each student to understand and use your feedback to further their own learning related to the learning objectives?
5. *Collect data.*
   a. It is important to assess along the way but be sure that you collect *evidence* of student learning.
   b. Collect student data by using a formalized method that works for you (i.e., documenting your observations by recording student behaviors on a clipboard that includes a roster of the class).
   c. Record the behaviors and the date/time that you observed them.
6. *Use qualitative and quantitative measures.*
   a. Qualitative measures are used to describe student qualities and are subjective from the teacher's perspective. The data can be observed but not measured numerically (e.g., student observations, rating scales, checklists, performance-based tasks, or anecdotal notes).
   b. Quantitative data is usually collected at a single point of time and represented numerically (e.g., tests, forced answer, multiple choice, state, and district assessments).
   c. Document all measures of assessment with reliable methods. Continue to ask yourself, "Is this information an accurate representation of student achievement?" and "Do I have any reasons or factors that cause me to doubt the accuracy of this information?"
7. *Have a specific plan.*
   a. Now that you have the data, what are you going to do with it? Be sure to use the data to improve your teaching and to determine your next steps in planning instruction.
   b. Make sure your practices are supported from the research and/or theory.
   c. Reflect on your plan. How do you know it is working? What are some areas of improvement?

## What Would You Do?

Ask your team or pair the following questions. For suggested responses to questions, see Appendix A.

1. Carin is not doing well in social studies. You assign the class homework to complete. What would you do if you begin to notice that every time she turns in her work it looks like it's been completed by someone else, and she receives 100%?

2. You assigned a research paper, as part of your summative assessment, at the end of the grading period. The students work on this individually during your class time. What would you do if the assignments have been turned in and you identify that Christopher has plagiarized and lifted an entire paper from the internet?

3. What would you do if you notice that whenever you provide Giselle with positive or constructive feedback she becomes more introverted, closes down, and stops completing the activity?

## Reflective Professional Growth Activities

Consider these ideas or activities to facilitate and foster teacher growth and reflection. Select one or two ideas to help facilitate this reflection process. Each activity is designed to help the teacher, pair, or team to understand how to assess and collect student data in order to make instructional changes to increase student achievement. Remember that you know the individuals best so be sure to choose an activity that would be the most effective.

### Idea 1: Collecting Student Data

Collect (formative or summative) data from a lesson or unit. What evidence did you collect to make sense of what the students have learned? How did this connect to your objective? What did you do once you had these data? What would you do differently?

**Evidence:** Data for each individual student in class and a written reflection answering the questions above.

### Idea 2: Assessing Academic Language Across the Content Areas

When planning for the following week, choose a lesson where you will collect quantitative and qualitative pre- and post-assessment data on the key vocabulary in the upcoming lesson (not specifically a Language Arts/English lesson). Remember the data that you collect should focus on identifying patterns of learning across the class. Note any changes of instruction needed based on the pre-assessment data. Chart both sets (pre-, post-) of data for each student. Discuss next steps for instruction of specific students based off of the post-data (this may be *individual work* from a group task).

**Evidence:** Complete Figure 11.1 of pre- and post-test data and a list of next steps for specific students. For a blank template, see Appendix B.

| | Example of Quantitative Data Chart Pre-Test/Post-Test | | | | | | |
|---|---|---|---|---|---|---|---|
| **Name of Student** | solubility | diffraction | permeability | neutron | proton | isotope | **Next Steps** |
| Sasha V. | | | | X | X | X | Use direct instruction to teach missing vocabulary word. Then have Sasha practice with vocabulary through experiments and lab reports where she has to show use of the specific word. |

**Figure 11.1** Pre- and post-test data chart. *Note:* **X** = was able to verbally identify the vocabulary word

## Idea 3: Assessing Students With Specific Learning Needs

Prior to the lesson and discussion with your supervisor, select students with specific learning needs (e.g., a student with an IEP, a student with a 504 plan, an English Language Learner, a striving learner, a student who is gifted or needing greater challenge). Schedule an interview with one key stakeholder (i.e., special education teacher, reading/math specialist, ELL teacher) to discuss assessment strategies to support each student in the classroom. Prior to the interview, create specific questions about assessment strategies and your target students.

**Evidence:** List of stakeholder interview questions (at least 5) with responses that are specific to the targeted students.

## Idea 4: Providing Student Feedback

Collaborate with your teaching partner or team to video a 30 minute part of your lesson. Watch the video and focus on the feedback that you provide to the students. Your teaching partner can complete this while observing you and/or you can complete this as you self-reflect and watch the video.

**Evidence:** Complete the *Student Feedback Record* chart (Figure 11.2). For a blank version see Appendix C.

## Idea 5: Evaluating the Assessment

Choose or create a formal assessment that you are going to use to assess the students on a future upcoming unit or lesson. Answer the following questions:

1. What is the purpose of the assessment (e.g., test)? Connect it to your objectives.
2. What are the specific questions on the assessment that are going to show student achievement for that objective?
3. What is the readability of the assessment? Does the test read "on-grade level" or "below-grade level"?
4. What are some ways that you can adapt the assessment to make it more accessible to students (e.g., *Universal Design for Learning*, differentiated, accommodations, format)?

Based on these questions, make adaptations to the original test.

**Evidence:** Show changes between the original assessment and the updated assessment.

| Name of Student | Direct Quote of Teacher Feedback | Student Response | Any Additional Teacher Response | Reflection (Be specific for each individual's feedback. How did your feedback support the student's strengths *and* needs?) |
|---|---|---|---|---|
| Livi | Great job following the directions of the word problem, Livi! | smile | n/a | This supported Livi's strengths in _____ and helped build her confidence in math. |

**Figure 11.2** Student feedback record.

# Follow Up, Monitoring, and Goal Setting

Complete the follow-up questions for the selected reflective professional growth activity.

## *Idea 1: Collecting Student Data*

Share with me the data that you collected.
- What was your objective? Can you show me the evidence for meeting objective #1? (continue with this question until you go through all of the objectives).
- What did you do with the data? How did this alter your instruction?
- What did you then do differently?
- What are some specific steps that you are going to take to ensure that this change in practice continues?
- Do you have anything else you want to share in the area of assessment before we move on to the next topic? Do you have any further questions?

## *Idea 2: Assessing Vocabulary Across the Content Areas*

- What did you learn about assessing content-specific and general instructional vocabulary?
- Can you share your list of next steps?
- Which steps have you already begun to implement?
- What are some specific steps that you are going to take to ensure that this continues?
- Do you have anything else you want to share in the area of assessment before we move on to the next topic? Do you have any further questions?

## *Idea 3: Assessing Students with Specific Learning Needs*

- What did you learn from your interview?
- How have your assessments changed now that you know this information (be specific and ask about target students)?
- What are some specific steps that you are going to take to ensure that this continues?
- What are some professional or community resources you can use to help support you?
- Do you have anything else you want to share in the area of assessment before we move on to the next topic? Do you have any further questions?

## *Idea 4: Providing Student Feedback*

- What did you learn from watching the instructional video that you recorded?
- What did you notice about yourself when you provided feedback?
- What are some strengths that you observed regarding your student feedback?
- Did you have any biases when you provided feedback (if so, have the pair or team name them)?
- What are some ways that you can improve your feedback?
- What are some specific steps that you are going to take to ensure that you continue to work on your identified areas of improvement? Do you have any further questions?

## Idea 5: Evaluating the Assessment

Please share your two assessments.
- Why did you make these changes? Was there research to support each change?
- What have you learned from this activity?
- What are some specific steps that you are going to take to ensure that you continue to evaluate your assessments?
- Do you have anything else you want to share in the area of assessment before we move on to the next topic? Do you have any further questions?

# Resources

## Articles

### Understanding Student Errors

This article discusses the importance of evaluating student error to help "deepen and refine students' partial understandings." The authors provide middle school math examples with rationales and tips for teachers.

McNamara, J., & Shaughnessy, M. M. (2011). *Student Errors: What can they tell us about what students DO understand?* Retrieved from http://www.mathsolutions.com/documents/studenterrors_jm_ms_article.pdf

### Interactive Teaching and Learning Activities

This PDF provides multiple activities a teacher can use to have students interact with the classroom content. Many of the activities take less than 5 minutes to complete.

Teaching Effectiveness Program. (2014, Fall). *Interactive Teaching and Learning Activities.* Retrieved from http://tep.uoregon.edu/pdf/assessment/Student-Engagement-Techniques.pdf

## Modules

### Assessing the General Education Curriculum

This module highlights classroom considerations that promote access to the general education curriculum for students with disabilities.

The IRIS Center. (2016). *Assessing the General Education Curriculum: Inclusion Considerations for Students with Disabilities.* Retrieved from http://iris.peabody.vanderbilt.edu/module/agc/

### Evidence-Based Practices in Assessment

This module, the first in a series of three, discusses the importance of identifying and selecting evidence-based practices. When you have completed the module, be sure to visit parts two and three:
  Part 2: Implementing a Practice or Program With Fidelity
   http://iris.peabody.vanderbilt.edu/module/ebp_02/#content
  Part 3: Evaluating Learner Outcomes and Fidelity
   http://iris.peabody.vanderbilt.edu/module/ebp_03/

The IRIS Center. (2016). *Evidence-Based Practices (Part 1): Identifying and Selecting a Practice or Program.* Retrieved from http://iris.peabody.vanderbilt.edu/module/ebp_01/#content

## *Videos*

**Assessing Young Dual Language Learners**

Professor Carol Hammer presents on current research about dual language learners at the 2008 Dual Language Learners Institute General Session. (Time: 33:05)

Head Start (2015, December 22). *Assessing Young Dual Language Learners: What You Need to Know and Why*. Retrieved from http://eclkc.ohs.acf.hhs.gov/hslc/tta-system/cultural-linguistic/Dual%20 Language%20Learners/prof_dev/conferences/CarolHammer.htm

**Assess and Plan With Exit Tickets**

This video demonstrates the use of exit tickets to assess learning and plan future lessons. (Time: 2:17)

The Teaching Network. *Assess and Plan with Exit Tickets*. Retrieved from https://www.teachingchannel. org/videos/teacher-assessment-strategy

**Daily Assessment With Tiered Exit Cards**

A teacher demonstrates how to provide quick and effective reteaching with daily tiered assessments. (Time: 4:35)

The Teaching Network. *Daily Assessment with Tiered Exit Cards*. Retrieved from https://www.teachingchannel.org/videos/student-daily-assessment

**Formative Assessment and Progress Monitoring**

This video outlines the ways that ongoing and varied assessments inform instruction. (Time: 13:56)

The Teaching Network. *Formative Assessment and Progress Monitoring*. Retrieved from https://www.teachingchannel.org/videos/formative-assessment-monitoring-1

**Monitoring Progress and Using Formative Assessment**

One school monitors student progress on a daily basis both formally and informally. (Time: 13:51)

The Teaching Network. *Formative Assessment and Progress Monitoring*. Retrieved from https://www.teachingchannel.org/videos/formative-assessment-monitoring-2

## *Web Resources*

**The UDL Guidelines**

The UDL Guidelines are a tool used in the implementation of Universal Design for Learning, a framework to improve and optimize teaching and learning for all people based on scientific insights into how humans learn. This web resource provides concrete suggestions that can be used in any discipline to provide accessibility to all learners.

CAST (2018). *Universal Design for Learning Guidelines* (v. 2.2). Retrieved from http://udlguidelines .cast.org

## Determining Readability

A factor that impacts assessment is the readability of the assessment tool. With this tool, educators can assess the readability of their assignments and assessments.

Readable.io (2018). *How readable is your content writing.* Retrieved from https://readability-score.com/

## Doing What Works

The goal of this website is to help educators understand and use research-based practices through interviews, multimedia examples, and sample materials from real schools and classrooms. The idea is that these tools can help educators take action.

WestEd (1995–2018). Improving education through research, development, and service. Retrieved from http://www.wested.org/project/doing-what-works/

## National Center on Educational Outcomes (NCEO)

The National Center on Educational Outcomes (NCEO) offers materials and services for individuals concerned with educational assessments and the outcomes of all students. Some of the materials and services they provide are publications about assessment, principles to guide inclusive assessment systems, recommendations for developing assessment policies and guidelines, and current research that is being conducted in the area of assessment by their organization.

National Center on Educational Outcomes. (2016). Retrieved from http://www.nceo.info/

## National Center on Intensive Intervention

Through this website you can learn the basics about intensive intervention. The website also explains the process, provides tools for assessment and intervention, offers implementation support, and includes resources in literacy, math, and behavior.

National Center on Intensive Intervention at American Institutes for Research. (n.d.). Retrieved from http://www.intensiveintervention.org/

## National Center on Standards and Assessments Implementation (CSAI)

The CSAI's goal is to provide research-based materials and support to build state capacity and productivity, college and career readiness and success, enhance early learning outcomes, help create great teachers and leaders, have innovative ideas in learning, help to decrease the school turnaround, and evaluate standards and assessment implementation.

The Center on Standards and Assessment Implementation. (n.d.). *Selective alternatives for assessing college and career readiness.* Retrieved from http://www.csai-online.org/#3

# Key Terms and Definitions

**Adaptations**: Adaptations are any alteration to instruction. This includes accommodations and modifications.

**Academic language**: Academic language is any language that is needed by students to be successful in schools (e.g., discipline or content-specific vocabulary, general instructional language, grammar, and punctuation).

**Accommodations**: Accommodations are when one changes the process used for how students learn, not what they learn. The objective remains the same.

**Assessment**: Assessment refers to a wide variety of methods or tools that educators use to evaluate, measure, and document the academic readiness, learning progress, skill acquisition, or educational needs of students.

**Diagnostic assessment**: Diagnostic assessment is a measurement used to assess a student's prior learning and determine teaching priorities.

**Differentiated instruction**: Differentiated instruction is a way to alter instruction to meet the needs of all learners. The process begins by knowing your student, then adapting the content of the curriculum, the process of the teaching, and the product or how students show what they learned. Differentiated instruction also applies to the type of learning environment used during instruction (e.g., large group, skill groups, stations) to address student needs.

**Evidence**: Evidence is student work, discourse (written, oral, discussion), performance (fine arts or presentation, conducting an experiment) that supports or demonstrates one's level of thinking and/or knowledge of a topic or objective. Evidence can be qualitative or quantitative. Examples of qualitative evidences are teacher observational notes, checklists of student discourse, and observed student performance indicators. In contrast, quantitative evidences are tests, quizzes, local or state assessments, or class assignments with a specific numerical value or points to demonstrate one's level of thinking and/or knowledge of a topic or objective.

**Formative assessment**: Formative assessment is a measurement used to monitor student learning through the lesson or unit. The teacher provides ongoing feedback that can be used to improve their teaching and for the students to improve their learning

**Quantitative research method assessments**: Quantitative research method assessments are usually collected at a single point of time and represented numerically (e.g., tests, forced answer, multiple choice, state and district assessments).

**Qualitative research method assessments**: Qualitative research method assessments are used to describe student qualities and are subjective from the teacher's perspective. The data can be observed but not measured numerically. Some examples might include (e.g., student observations or "kid watching," rating scales, checklists, performance-based tasks, or anecdotal notes).

**Summative assessment**: Summative assessment is a measurement used after instruction that should be used to evaluate student learning as well as teacher effectiveness.

**Universal Design for Learning**: Universal Design for Learning (UDL) is a specific framework that reduces barriers to instruction to guide teacher practice that includes using a variety of formats when presenting information and having students respond and demonstrate their skills.

# Appendix A

## *What Would You Do? Questions with Suggested Responses*

1. Carin is not doing well in social studies. You assign the class homework to complete. What would you do if you begin to notice that every time she turns in her work it looks like it's been completed by someone else, and she receives 100%?

   **Suggested Response 1:** First of all, do not collect data from homework assignments. It is hard to determine who has completed the homework and it is not an accurate assessment. Second, reach out to Carin to ask if she has support at home to complete her homework and gather more details. Finally, reach out to her family and work with them on the best ways to practice what is going on inside the classroom and how it can be worked on at home.

2. You assigned a research paper, as part of your summative assessment at the end of the grading period. The students work on this individually during your class time. What would you do if the assignments have been turned in and you identify that Christopher has plagiarized and lifted an entire paper from the Internet?

   **Suggested Response 2:** You first want to identify if there is a school policy in place that you need to follow. Secondly, you want to meet with Christopher to discuss the severity of plagiarizing. Finally, depending on the age of the student, you want to facilitate a conversation with Christopher's family about what has occurred. Ideally, this conversation should come from the student and you have more of a facilitative role.

3. What would you do if you notice that whenever you provide Giselle with positive or constructive feedback she becomes more introverted, closes down, and stops completing the activity?

   **Suggested Response 3:** Meet with Giselle and have an open discussion about how things are going in class and at home. Then share your concerns in the classroom with her. See if you can make a plan so that she's comfortable in the class and that you are able to provide feedback as well.

Module 11: Collecting Student Data and Assessment ■ 175

# Appendix B
*Blank Template for Pre-Post Data Collection*

| | \multicolumn{7}{c}{Quantitative Data Chart Pre-Test/Post-Test} |
|---|---|---|---|---|---|---|---|
| Name of Student | Insert vocabulary word #1 | Insert vocabulary word #2 | Insert vocabulary word #3 | Insert vocabulary word #4 | Insert vocabulary word #5 | Insert vocabulary word #6 | Next Steps |
| | | | | | | | |
| | | | | | | | |
| | | | | | | | |
| | | | | | | | |
| | | | | | | | |

# Appendix C
*Blank Template for Student Feedback Record*

| Name of Student | Direct Quote of Teacher Feedback | Student Response | Any Additional Teacher Response | Reflection (Be specific for each individual's feedback. How did your feedback support the student's strengths *and* needs?) |
|---|---|---|---|---|
| | | | | |
| | | | | |
| | | | | |
| | | | | |
| | | | | |

# References

Black, P. (2015). Formative assessment—An optimistic but incomplete vision. *Assessment in Education: Principles, Policy & Practice, 22*(1), 161.

Blount, G. P., & Rodriguez, R. G. (2015, May). Hispanics in Texas higher education: An assessment of the state "closing the gaps" initiative. *European Scientific Journal, 1*(special ed.), 191–211.

Boykin, A. W. (2014). Human diversity, assessment in education and the achievement of excellence and equity. *The Journal of Negro Education, 83*(4), 499–521.

Bourke, R., & Mentis, M. (2014). An assessment framework for inclusive education: Integrating assessment approaches. *Assessment in Education: Principles, Policy & Practice, 21*(4), 384.

Dann, R. (2014). Assessment "as" learning: Blurring the boundaries of assessment and learning for theory, policy and practice. *Assessment in Education: Principles, Policy & Practice, 21*(2), 149.

DeLuca, C., Chavez, T., & Cao, C. (2013). Establishing a foundation for valid teacher judgement on student learning: The role of pre-service assessment education. *Assessment in Education: Principles, Policy & Practice, 20*(1), 107.

Dexter, D. D., & Hughes, C. (n.d.). *Progress Monitoring within a Response-to-Intervention Model.* Retrieved from http://www.rtinetwork.org/learn/research/progress-monitoring-within-a-rti-model

Emberger, M. (2006, March/April). Helping teachers think like assessors. *Principal,* 38–39.

Great Schools Partnership. (2015, November 10). *The glossary of education reform: Assessment.* Retrieved from http://edglossary.org/assessment/

Laud, L., Hirsh, S., & Wagner, M. (2010). Maximize student achievement with formative assessment. *ASCD Express, 6*(1).

Layton, C. A., & Robin, H. L. (2007, January). Use authentic assessment techniques to fulfill the promise of No Child Left Behind. *Intervention and School Clinic, 42*(3), 169–173.

Mahdavi, J. N., & Haager, D. (2007, Spring). Linking progress monitoring results to interventions. *Perspectives on Language and Literacy, 33*(2), 25–29.

McLane, K. (2015). *Getting Started: How Do I Implement Progress Monitoring in My School?* Retrieved from http://www.rti4success.org/sites/default/files/howdoiimplementpminmyschool.pdf

Salvia, J., Ysseldyke, J. E., & Bolt, S. (2010). *Assessment in Special and Inclusive Education (11th ed.).* Belmont, CA: Wadsworth Cengage Learning.

Snyder, C. W. (2010). Standards and assessment in education. *Development, 53*(4), 540–546.

Stefanakis, E. H. (2002). *Assessment for learning.* Retrieved from https://sites.google.com/site/assess4learning/assessment-defined

Teaching Excellence and Educational Innovation. (2015). *What is the difference between formative vs. summative assessment.* Retrieved from https://www.cmu.edu/teaching/assessment/basics/formative-summative.html

# MODULE 12

## Collaborative Planning for Instruction

Debbie F. Cosgrove
*Elmhurst College*

*Alone we can do so little, together we can do so much.*
—Helen Keller

*If your plan is for one year, plant rice; if your plan is for ten years, plant trees; if your plan is for one hundred years, educate children.*
—Confucius

### MODULE DESCRIPTION

This module focuses on the elements of planning for instruction within the context of collaborative teaching. Several key principles inform the structure of the module, its suggested productive practices, and professional development activities. First, strong lesson planning provides the foundation for successful teaching practice. Second, teacher collaboration is important to the instruction and the culture of effective schools (Friend & Cook, 2017). Third, when teachers choose to teach collaboratively, they should also ask questions and use shared tools to help them to plan, implement, and evaluate their collaborative effort. The module addresses five major areas: (a) preparation steps for collaborative planning, (b) alignment of educational standard(s) to the instructional learning objective(s), (c) selection of educational experiences supported by best practices and educational theory and/or research, (d) organization of the instructional experience(s) using collaborative teaching practices, and (e) teacher reflection-on-action and/or reflection-in-action (Schön, 1983) to determine the effectiveness of the collaboratively-designed instructional process (planning, instruction, and evaluation).

## Theory/Conceptual Framework

There are many factors to consider when planning for instruction. Ralph Tyler, one of the most prominent names in American educational studies and author of the bestselling book, *Basic Principles of Curriculum and Instruction* (Tyler, 1949), suggests four key questions to ask when planning for instruction: (a) "What educational purpose and objective(s) should the teacher identify?"; (b) "What educational experiences can be selected that address the attainment of the purpose or objective?"; (c) "How can these educational experiences be effectively organized?"; and (d) "How can teachers assess whether the educational purpose was achieved?" These questions written nearly seven decades ago are still relevant for teachers today. The importance of teacher collaboration is yet another important factor to consider when planning for instruction (Friend & Cook, 2017). Effective collaborative plans used within a co-teaching context must incorporate clear goals and learning objectives, as well as selected co-teaching strategies that best address individual student learning needs.

Education is undergoing reform at both national and local levels. Multiple revisionary initiatives have had a significant impact on public schools (P–12) and institutions of higher education. As schools grapple with meeting recent legislative demands that often require changes in practice, teacher collaboration has emerged as a solution to meeting diverse student learning needs and providing equitable services to all students. The one-teacher classroom is no longer the norm. Moreover, many educators believe that teacher collaboration can improve learner outcomes in the inclusive classroom (Brownell, Adams, Sindelar, Waldron, & Vanhover, 2006; Scruggs, Mastropieri, & McDuffie, 2007). Collaborative planning is necessary if collaborative teaching is to succeed (Friend, Reising, & Cook, 1993; Walther-Thomas, Bryant, & Land, 1996). Today, collaborative teams plan, teach, assess, and problem-solve to address individual student learning needs. The changing structures in schools for how children receive instruction and intervention call for increased teacher collaboration and the sharing of educator expertise. One questions whether the one-teacher/one-classroom model can still be effective.

The effectiveness of collaborative teaching depends on the knowledge and communication skills that the teachers contribute to the collaborative planning process. Effective planning is grounded in a knowledge of individual students and their academic, behavioral, social, and cultural needs. Beginning with the end pedagogical goal in mind, teachers ask what they want their students to *know* and be able to *do* during the learning activities. Teachers determine the conditions or contexts in which students will demonstrate their learning. They also identify the criteria that they will use to assess whether students have met the objectives (Burden & Byrd, 2016).

According to Zemelman, Daniels, and Hyde (2012), planning for instruction should consider learning activities and strategies that are research-based, student-centered, cognitive, and interactive for students. Student-centered teachers affirm and use each student's cultural background and language as assets for culturally responsive teaching. Thanks to this responsiveness, instructional materials and activities are sensitive to the identities of linguistically, academically, ethnically, and racially diverse students.

Teachers who implement best practice standards in instruction know supporting research and keep current with changes in technology, procedures, and expanding knowledge in the contents that they teach. Best practices in teaching are informed largely by shared recommendations offered by curriculum reports from professional educational associations that is, National Council for the Social Studies, National Council of Teachers of English, International Reading Association, National Council of Teachers of Mathematics, National Research Council, Partnership for 21st Century Skills, and American Association for the Advancement of Science (Price & Nelson, 2014). Some best practice principles include experiential, hands-on learning; emphasis on higher-order thinking; attention to affective needs and the varying cognitive styles of students; use of cooperative or collaborative activities; use of formative assessments and effective feedback to guide student learning; increased opportunities for students to set goals, share learning, and evaluate personal progress; reading of real texts, primary sources, and non-fictional texts; and active learning that includes critical thinking, problem-solving, and communication among peers (Zemelman, Daniels, & Hyde, 2012; Marzano, 2007). The selection of teaching best practices to address diverse student needs, together with the selection of co-teaching strategies, are essential elements of effective collaborative planning.

Successful collaborative planning requires more than content understanding, familiarity with standards and assessments, and writing clear objectives that guide instruction. Teachers must also be in relationship with each other through direct communication, active questioning, and intent listening. Martin (2009) tells us that "participation in the planning process is critical because a shared understanding of the intended plan of action provides each person with a 'sense of the game'" (p. 581). Lack of shared planning time poses a definite obstacle to collaborative planning and its success (Davis, Dieker, Pearl, & Kirkpatrick, 2012; Murawski, 2006). A consistent shared planning time should be non-negotiable among teachers and supported by school and district administration. Without a protected time for sharing expertise between co-teachers, "teachers will often teach a class the way they have always taught it and there is not value added by the second professional educator" (Murawski, 2012, p. 8). Researchers found that without a consistent co-planning agenda, co-teachers often relied on using the *one teach-one assist* or *one teach-one observe* co-teaching strategies, which provided minimal opportunities for differentiation in practice (Magierra & Zigmund, 2005; Murawski, 2010; Weiss & Lloyd, 2003).

In 2017, I questioned teacher candidates in a student teaching seminar about planning while co-teaching. The teacher candidates were expected to co-teach daily with their experienced mentor or cooperating teacher. At week five of a 15-week student teaching experience, the students shared some of the behaviors that helped them be successful in collaborative planning with their cooperating teacher. These behaviors included (a) flexibility: showing a willingness to change course during a lesson; (b) consistency in planning: setting a consistent time for planning together; (c) modeling: observation and discussion of behaviors of other teacher pairs or teams as they planned together—conscious modeling of these behaviors; (d) accountability: holding each member of the pair responsible for contributing and revising lesson elements; (e) two-way communication: providing for direct communication about lesson expectations, lesson elements, and planning tools; and (f) pair/team reflection: regular reflection on lesson planning and student performance data to set new goals for learning (students and teachers).

Some challenges that the teacher candidates identified regarding collaborative planning included:

1. Lesson planning was often seen as an outcome and not as a process. This understanding interfered with on-going reflection on connected lessons and student performance.
2. Face-to-face planning was not always possible.
3. Grade level pre-planned units made it more difficult for the teacher candidate to share new ideas when planning with others.
4. Classroom management issues often threatened the progression and pacing of lesson(s).
5. The pair often had differing views about the use of assessment strategies and the analysis of student data.

The success of any collaborative planning effort depends on the quality of communication used to discuss these challenges among all who collaborate. Supervisors need to acknowledge each teacher's potential to contribute to this conversation.

## Specific Questions to Guide Discussion

1. What talents and expertise does each member bring to the planning process? How can these talents and areas of expertise be used to strengthen the learning experience of the students?

2. How do you incorporate others in the instructional planning process? (e.g., cooperating teacher, team member, ESL specialist, gifted/talented teacher, special education teacher, interventionists, or other professionals).

3. What strategies do you use to reach a shared understanding of student identities, selected content standards, learning objectives, student learning targets, and learning activities?

4. What theory and/or research-based and culturally responsive best practices will you use in your instruction? Why?

5. What co-teaching strategies will you use to engage learners? Provide an instructional rationale for each choice.

6. What planning resources, including technology, do you use to facilitate the collaborative planning process?

## Productive Practices

1. *Set a specific time and place to plan. Send written reminders before each meeting.* Always set a time and place to collaborate and plan for instruction. Issue a written reminder to team members regarding the time, place, and purpose of each meeting. It is difficult to comprehensively plan in short segments of time, through email or texts, or passing in the hallways between class periods. Meet regularly with the pair or team and keep detailed notes of the instructional decisions that are made.
2. *Acknowledge each teacher's potential for contribution. Ask questions to clarify.* When planning collaboratively, it is important that team members feel comfortable contributing their ideas. Affirm the voice of each team member. Encourage each person to share their thinking. Reach a shared understanding among planners about the meanings of content standards, learning objectives, and student targets. Ask clarifying questions to understand content and procedures. Learn to speak and understand the same instructional language!
3. *Encourage specialists to incorporate program goals into the planning process.* Invite teacher specialists who support individual student needs to attend collaborative planning meetings. These educators (e.g., ESL specialist, special education teacher, interventionists) can contribute helpful information regarding instructional goals for students who receive additional supports (e.g., language goals for English language learners, IEP/504 goals for special education students, Tier II and III goals for RtI students).
4. *Develop and follow communication procedures for collaborative meetings.* Decide how you will communicate during and after planning sessions. Appoint a team leader to facilitate meetings of more than two people. Keep written records of your planning meetings that include who was there, the date/time, details about what was discussed, and action items that clearly record who is responsible for completing them. Consider using technology tools so that all members of the pair or team can access and revise written plans in person and virtually.
5. *Establish a process to engage in shared reflection on the instructional process.* Reflect on the planning process before and after instruction. Key questions to ask the team include: Which students achieved the instructional learning objective(s)? Which students did not achieve the instructional learning objective(s)? What student performance evidence support these claims? How well did the co-teaching strategies work with the selected learning activities? How does the achievement data inform our continued shared planning and instruction? What goals can we set to improve our effectiveness as co-teachers?

## What Would You Do?

Ask your pair or team the following questions. For suggested responses to the questions, see Appendix E.

1. What would you do if you do not have a protected time for collaborative planning in your weekly schedule?

2. What would you do if your pair or team member does not want to spend quality time engaged in the collaborative planning process and would rather plan informally or "on the fly?"

3. What would you do if you hear several students talking about their perception that one of the teachers on the collaborative teaching pair or team "is not a real teacher?"

## Reflective Professional Growth Activities

Consider these ideas or activities to facilitate and foster teacher growth and reflection. Select one or two ideas to help facilitate the teacher reflection process to help the pair or team to understand the collaborative planning process. Remember that supervisors as instructional leaders should know their pairs or teams well, so be sure to choose a growth activity that will be the most effective for them.

### *Idea 1: How to Unpack a Standard*

When teaching collaboratively, it is important that the co-teaching pair or team understands the selected content standard(s) by identifying the student thinking skills or verbs (underline these) and concepts/nouns (circle these) that the standard specifies. A shared understanding of the standard is necessary before teachers can write the learning objective(s) that will be targeted during instruction. Use the following template to help you to unpack the standards that will anchor your instruction (see Appendix A). Also visit https://www.isbe.net/Pages/Unpacking-the-Common-Core-Activity.aspx to learn more about the unpacking process.

**Evidence:** The teaching pair or team will select several priority standards to "unpack" before designing the lesson or lesson segment. The pair will agree on the skills (verbs) and concepts (nouns) of the lesson and also the cognitive level of each skill according to Bloom's *Revised Taxonomy* or Webb's *Depth of Knowledge* (DOK; see Appendix A).

### *Idea 2: Design a Collaborative Teaching Planning Board or Lesson*

Consider using a collaborative online planning tool to increase communication within your team. Here are some suggestions that are helpful for any collaborative planning context. The first to visit is Trello at www.trello.com to view a free productivity system that allows its users to create boards in order to plan and organize products. Another free site for planning is Planboard by chalk.com. Experience this online lesson planner tool for the ipad at https://www.planboardapp.com. You may also want to review other resources for online planning and grading at www.chalkboard.com and www.planbook.com.

Another popular format to use for collaborative planning is the Google Doc. Open a Google account and try it out at https://www.google.com. These web-based planning tools will help provide a format for collaborative planning, editing, and sharing of ideas when designing lessons and units. Other online tools to explore for collaborative planning include:

Skype at www.Skype.com, Edmodo at www.Edmodo.com, and Dropbox at www.dropbox.com (sharing of large files). *The Co-Planner* by Lisa Dieker (4th edition, 2015; ISBN 918-1-941171-00-4) is a co-teaching lesson plan book that may also be helpful for any pair or team. You can access this tool at www.knowledge-by-design.com/planbook.html.

> **Evidence:** The teaching pair will choose and utilize an online planning tool to use for collaborative planning. The selected planning tool should be presented by the pair or team to the supervisor for review after several weeks of use.

## *Idea 3: Pairs Check: Complete the* Planning Protocol for Collaborative Teaching

Use the *Planning Protocol for Collaborative Teaching* (Appendix B) to help the pair or team to assess whether they have included the essential elements of planning in their lessons. The protocol should be completed *before* the pair or team presents the lesson segment or three to five lessons. At the end of the protocol, the pair should reflect collaboratively on their lesson(s) and identify changes they will make as they move forward in their teaching.

> **Evidence:** The teacher pair or team will complete the *Planning Protocol for Collaborative Teaching* as an audit of the essential elements of planning that will guide in the development of their co-taught or team-taught lesson segments and units.

## *Idea 4: Lesson Planning for Collaborative Teaching/Reflection-in-Action (Weekly)*

Use the *Lesson Planning for Collaborative Teaching* (weekly) template to plan with your pair or team (see Appendix C). This organizer includes essential planning elements and helps the planners to approach daily planning based on student performance data. The template is organized in a 5 day plan that bases the planning process on formative student assessment data. (At mid-week, the pair or team proceeds cautiously with the learning sequence taking into consideration student misconceptions or enrichment needs which may alter the choice of instructional strategies). The weekly lesson plan template ends with a *Collaborative Reflection on Lesson Planning and Learning* that provides an opportunity for the pair or team to reflect on their collaborative teaching. The pair or team sets personal and shared goals that meet the SMART goal criteria (**S**pecific, **M**easurable, **A**chievable, **R**esults-based and **T**ime-sensitive; see Appendix D).

> **Evidence:** Completion of the *Lesson Planning for Collaborative Teaching* template on a weekly basis; Completion of the *Collaborative Reflection on Lesson Planning and Learning* including SMART goals in written form.

# Follow-Up, Monitoring, and Goal Setting

Complete the follow-up questions for the selected reflective professional growth activity.

## *Idea 1: How to Unpack a Standard*

- What content standards did you choose to "unpack" together?
- How did the "unpacking" activity help you to better understand the meaning of selected content standard(s) and the alignment of the standard(s) to the learning objective(s)?
- What level of thinking did your learning objectives address according to Bloom's *Revised Taxonomy* or Webb's *Depth of Knowledge?* (Many districts also use these acronyms: HOTS [Higher Order Thinking Skills] or LOTS [Lower Order Thinking Skills])
- What goals can you set for your pair or team as you continue to align content standards and student learning objectives?

## *Idea 2: Design a Collaborative Teaching Planning Board or Lesson*

- What online collaborative planning tool did you jointly agree to use?
- What were the benefits of using the online collaborative planning tool to plan your lesson(s)?
- Did you experience any drawbacks or concerns when you used the online collaborative planning tool to design your lesson(s)?
- What goals can you set for your pair or team as you move forward with the use of online collaborative planning tools to design your lesson(s) (e.g., refine use with the tool we chose, try another tool)?

## *Idea 3: Pairs/Team Check: Complete the* **Planning Protocol for Collaborative Teaching**

- How did you use the *Planning Protocol for Collaborative Teaching* to guide your lesson planning and co-teaching practice?
- Were there any lesson planning elements that were difficult for your pair or team to address? If "yes," why do you think this occurred?
- How did you reflect collaboratively on your lesson(s)?
- Can you identify what planning elements went well?
- Can you agree on things that you would like to change as you progress with your collaborative planning?
- What planning goals did you set as a pair/team as you continue to refine your collaborative planning efforts?

## *Idea 4:* **Lesson Planning for Collaborative Teaching/***Reflection-in-Action (Weekly)*

- How did you use the *Lesson Planning for Collaborative Teaching* template to guide your lesson planning?

- How did your original learning plans change as you analyzed student achievement data throughout the week?
- What rationale did you use for selecting particular co-teaching strategies?
- In your weekly shared reflection on the learning plans, what did you do well? What could you have done differently?
- What shared goals have you selected from your work together this week? How will you measure these goals using the SMART criteria?

## Resources

### *Articles*

**Tips for Effective Co-Planning**

This article contains many useful ideas for collaborative planning including a *What/How/Who Co-Planning Form* (p. 13) and a sample *Co-Planned Lesson* (p. 14).

Murawski, W. W. (2012). 10 tips for using co-planning time more efficiently. *Teaching Exceptional Children, 44*(4), 8–15.

### *Books*

**Co-Teach! Building and Sustaining Effective Classroom Partnerships in Inclusive Schools (3rd Edition)**

This updated edition (2018) is a helpful source for co-teaching for teachers and supervisors at all grade levels. It includes relevant research and applicable strategies to use in co-teaching contexts. The book specifically addresses shared planning and scheduling priorities.

Friend, M. (2018). *Co-Teach! Building and sustaining effective classroom partnerships in inclusive schools (3rd edition)*. Greensboro, NC: Marilyn Friend, Inc.

**Planning for the Dance**

Chapter 5 in this book addresses planning for co-teaching and includes numerous planning resources (e.g., lesson plan templates, scheduling forms, co-teaching models) that are simple to use with pairs or teams.

Murawski, W., & Dieker, L. (2013). *Leading the co-teaching dance: Leadership strategies to enhance team outcomes*. Arlington, VA: Council for Exceptional Children.

**The Reflective Practitioner**

Schön discusses the process of reflection-in-action (during practice) and reflection-on action (looking back at practice). Both of these reflection types are used in professional growth activity #4 in this module.

Schön, D. A. (1983). *The reflective practitioner: How professionals think in action*. New York, NY: Basic Books.

## Web Resources

### Changing Student Teaching Through Co-Teaching: Collaboration That Makes a Difference

This 75 minute DVD includes footage from co-taught classrooms, interviews with teacher candidates, cooperating teachers, and school and university administrators, all of whom have participated in the co-teaching initiative.

St. Cloud State University. (2018). *The academy for co-teaching and collaboration.* Retrieved from https://www.stcloudstate.edu/soe/coteaching/default.aspx

### Co-Mentoring Student Teachers' Handbook

This is a helpful tool to use with student teachers who are co-teaching with their cooperating teacher. The handbook can be downloaded from the Hope College Education Department website and incorporates ideas from *Launch Into Teaching* from Michigan State University, and *The Academy for Co-Teaching and Collaboration* at St. Cloud State University and TWH Consulting. Original Research is funded by a U.S. Department of Education, Teacher Quality Enhancement Partnership Grant.

Hope College. (n.d.). *Search results for "co-teaching."* Retrieved from https://hope.edu/search-results.html?keywords=coteaching

Bacharach, N., Heck, T., & Dahlberg, K. (2013). Researching the use of co-teaching in the student teaching experience. In C. Murphy & K. Scantlebury (Eds), *Moving forward and broadening perspectives: Coteaching in international contexts.* New York, NY: Springer.

### Common Core State Standards

This website includes the Common Core State Standards in English Language Arts (ELA) and Mathematics for teachers to access when lesson planning. The standards can also be viewed on a convenient free app.

National Governors Association Center for Best Practices, Council of Chief State School Officers. (2010). *Common Core State Standards.* Retrieved from http://www.corestandards.org

### Co-Teaching Core Competency Framework

This framework provides the supervisor or administrator with a tool to evaluate twenty-two core competencies of co-teaching as distributed among four different domains (a) the learner and learning, (b) the task at hand, (c) instructional practice, and (d) professional responsibility. The competencies under Domain 3 describe planning that apply to Module 12: Collaborative Planning for Instruction. The *Co-Teaching Core Competency Framework* can be downloaded from the www.coteachsolutions.com or 2teachllc.com websites.

Murawski, E., & Lochner, W. (2014). *Co-teaching core competency framework.* Retrieved from https://2teachllc.com/ and www.coteachsolutions.com

### Co-Teaching Core Competency Observation Checklist

This is an easy to use evaluation tool to help co-teaching pairs or teams assess their work together. The tool includes three checklists: (a) Look for Items, (b) Listen for Items, and (c) Ask for Items. Co-planning is addressed in the third checklist: Ask for Items.

Murawski, E., & Lochner, W. (2015). *The co-teaching core competencies observation checklist.* Retrieved from www.coteachsolutions.com

**Mentoring Teacher Candidates Through Co-Teaching: Collaboration That Makes a Difference**

This helpful mentoring handbook includes many resource activities from the Academy for Co-Teaching and Collaboration at St. Cloud State University in Minnesota. It is an excellent resource to use with student-teaching pairs or teams as they co-teach. Original research for this book was funded by the U.S. Department of Education, Teacher Quality Enhancement Partnership Grant. St. Cloud, Minnesota.

Heck, T., & Bacharach, N. (2010). *Mentoring teacher candidates through co-teaching: Collaboration that makes a difference.* St. Cloud, MN: St. Cloud State University. Retrieved from https://twhcoteaching.com/product/mentoring-teacher-candidates-co-teaching-handbook/

**National Professional Resources, Inc.**

This website hosts free and purchased resources for educators on a wide variety of educational topics including co teaching and planning. The site also includes helpful links to state and national organizations.

National Professional Resources. (2018). *The educator's choice for classroom and professional development resources.* Retrieved from https://www.nprinc.com

**Unpacking the Common Core Activity**

The Illinois State Board website (www.isbe.net) includes numerous resources to use with teachers to unpack learning standards for lesson planning. You will also find a facilitator's guide and sample templates that show the unpacking process.

Illinois State Board of Education. (n.d.). *Unpacking the Common Core activity.* Retrieved from https://www.isbe.net/Pages/Unpacking-the-Common-Core-Activity.aspx

# Key Terms and Definitions

**Academic vocabulary**: Academic vocabulary refers to words and phrases used within a content discipline. Two different categories of words and phrases are used during instruction. The first category is called content-specific vocabulary and includes words and phrases that students must know from the content area to be able to comprehend a lesson (e.g., science vocabulary: photosynthesis, mineral, igneous). The second category refers to instructional vocabulary that includes words that cross content areas and are essential to the understanding of the particular lesson (e.g., compare, contrast, evaluate).

**Bloom's taxonomy of learning (Revised)**: Anderson et al. (2001) present a revised version of Benjamin Bloom's (1956) taxonomy or categorization of thinking that students demonstrate during learning experiences. The revised taxonomy expands on Bloom's original taxonomy by naming four different types and levels of knowledge: (a) factual, (b) conceptual, (c) procedural, and (d) metacognitive. Additionally, the revised taxonomy includes six levels of thinking or functions of thought that are organized from lower-order to higher-order thinking. These are expressed in verb form: (a) remember, (b) understand, (c) apply, (d) analyze, (e) evaluate, and (f) create.

**Collaborative student teaching**: A collaborative teaching process where the cooperating teacher and the teacher candidate build a strong teaching relationship through the development and use of communication, collaboration, planning, and reflection in order to provide shared instruction for all learners. The cooperating teacher and the teacher candidate utilize the co-teaching models (i.e., One teach/One observe, One teach/One assist, Station Teaching, Parallel Teaching, Alternative Teaching, and Team Teaching) and are actively involved and engaged in all aspects of the instructional cycle (i.e., planning, instruction and assessment).

**Depth of Knowledge (DOK) model**: Norman Webb (1997/2006) presents four different levels of cognitive expectation or depth of knowledge: (a) knowledge acquisition (recall and reproduction), (b) knowledge application (working with skills/concepts), (c) knowledge analysis (short-term strategic thinking), and (d) knowledge augmentation (extended strategic thinking). Webb focuses on the context or setting in which students will demonstrate their depth of thinking.

**Learning standard**: Student academic content standards that are the target of student learning. When referring to specific standards, always include the *number and text* of each standard on the lesson plan. If only a portion of a standard is being addressed, then list only the part or parts that are relevant to the lesson(s).

**Instructional learning objective**: The instructional learning objective defines what students should know, understand and/or be able to do during the course of a lesson. The learning objective should be clearly written, measurable, and based on a selected learning standard(s). The student objective or outcome should include concrete, observable student actions, describe the condition or context for where or how the action occurs, and also include the criteria or level of performance expected of the student. The learning objective includes three parts: observable action, condition, and criteria.

**Reflection-on-action**: This term, created by researcher Donald Schön (1983), refers to the process used to reflect and evaluate teaching. The process is most effective by analyzing a video tape of teaching or more commonly through a planned discussion of the lesson(s) with a colleague(s). Reflection-*on*-action typically occurs after the teaching event but can also be strategically addressed during the course of an extended lesson sequence. Teachers begin this reflective process by asking questions such as (a) What did we do well in the lesson? and (b) What needs to be changed before we move forward? Schön also speaks about reflection-*in*-action which refers to a teacher or pair's ability to "think on one's feet" or to make conscious changes to instructional practice while engaged in teaching.

**Student learning target**: The student learning target is a restatement of the instructional learning objective in student-friendly language. The student learning target describes what the student should be able to do during the course of a lesson. Often student learning targets begin with an I CAN... statement. Students are also frequently asked to self-assess at the end of the lesson about whether they have achieved the learning target.

# Appendix A

## *Unpacking Template for Standards-Based Instruction*

1. Choose the standards you want to unpack that will be a part of your lesson(s) or unit.
2. Circle the verbs (functions, skills, or actions) and categorize these verbs by thinking level (see Bloom's *Revised Taxonomy* or Webb's *Depth of Knowledge*). Underline the nouns (concepts or ideas).
3. Determine the "big idea" of the standard and write it in your own words.
4. Re-write the "big idea" into a learning target that uses child-friendly vocabulary and starts with I CAN . . .
5. Compose essential questions that will engage students in the lesson(s).
6. Suggest a progression of learning activities and assessments to address each learning standard.

**Unpacking a Learning Standard**

| Write the Common Core Standard(s) or Content Standard(s): |||
|---|---|---|
| **What are the Skills? (verbs)** What students need to be able to do | **What are the Concepts? (nouns or noun phrases)** What students need to know | **What is the Thinking Level?** (Bloom's Taxonomy or Webb's Depth of Knowledge) |
| **What is the Big Idea of the Standard(s)?** |||
| **What are some Essential Questions to engage the learner?** |||
| **What learning progression of activities will occur during the lesson(s)?** |||
| **What pre-requisite skills must be taught and considered before the lesson(s) begins?** |||
| **What formative assessments will be used during the lesson to demonstrate understanding?** |||
| **What summative assessments are planned after the completion of the lesson(s)?** |||

*Source:* Adapted from Berchard, V. (2015, May). Unpacking Template from Teaching and Learning Network. Retrieved from www.teachingandlearningnetwork.com

# Appendix B

## *A Planning Protocol for Collaborative Teaching*

Debbie F. Cosgrove

Use the following protocol to guide the development of your collaboratively planned lessons.

| Teacher 1 _____ Date _____ |
| --- |
| Teacher 2 _____ |
| **A. Collaborative Planning:** Has the pair or team identified the essential elements of planning and alignment in the lesson or lesson segment? |

| Planning Elements | Check your progress | Yes | No |
| --- | --- | --- | --- |
| | | **Please detail.** | |
| **Content Learning Standard(s)** (Common Core ELA and Math standards, Next Generation Science standards, etc.) | Did you jointly select learning standards for this lesson or lesson segment? Remember that learning standards are written to be achieved by the *end of a year of study.*<br>List Standards: | | |
| **Language Learning Standards** (English language development standards/Spanish language development standards) | Have you identified language standards for English Language Learners (ELLs)? (see the ESL specialist for further support)<br>List Standards: | | |
| **Learning Objectives** | Did you write instructional learning objectives that align directly from the selected content or language standards? Remember that learning objectives are written to be achieved by the *end of the lesson.*<br>List learning objectives: | | |
| **Academic Language: Vocabulary** | Have you identified priority subject-specific vocabulary that students need to know in order to understand the lesson(s)?<br>List subject-specific vocabulary:<br><br>Have you identified general academic vocabulary that students need to know in order to understand the lesson(s)?<br>List general academic vocabulary: | | |

| Planning Elements | Check your progress | Yes | No |
|---|---|---|---|
| | | **Please detail.** | |
| **Assessment** | Have you planned to pre-assess your students regarding the pre-requisite skills that they need in order to successfully accomplish the learning objective(s) (pre-assessment)? | | |
| | Have you planned to provide your students with opportunities to demonstrate their understanding of the learning objective(s) during your instruction (formative)? | | |
| | Have you planned to provide your students with opportunities to demonstrate their understanding or achievement of the learning objective(s) after instruction (summative)? | | |
| **B. Instructional Practice: Has the pair or team decided which learning activities and co-teaching strategies to use during collaborative instruction?** | | | |
| **Research-based best practices** | Have you selected learning activities that are grounded in research-based best practice and informed by theory and/or research?<br>List activities: | | |
| **Learning Preferences (Visual, auditory, kinesthetic)** | Have you addressed student learning preferences through a variety of instructional strategies and teaching resources? | | |
| **Diverse Student Needs** | Have you identified individual student learning needs and developed activities that address these special needs including assistive and adaptive resources and learning supports?<br>Identify special student needs: | | |
| **Affirmation of Multicultural Assets** | Have you designed activities that are culturally relevant to your students and affirm the language, cultural backgrounds, and interests that each student brings to the learning process? | | |

| Planning Elements | Check your progress | Yes | No |
|---|---|---|---|
| | | Please detail. | |
| **Use of co-teaching models/strategies** | Have you identified what co-teaching models/strategies you will utilize throughout the lesson(s) to address student needs and performance as determined by the learning objective(s)?<br><br>Describe your co-teaching plan:<br><br>One teach/One assist:<br>One teach/One observe:<br>Parallel Teaching:<br>Alternative Teaching:<br>Team Teaching:<br>Station Teaching: | | |
| **C. Reflection-in-Action: Has the pair or team met to discuss the collaborative teaching of the lesson(s)?** | | | |
| **Reflect and Refine the Collaborative Teaching Practice** | Have you allowed time to share teaching observations, evaluate student learning, and reflect collaboratively on the teaching process?<br><br>What changes will you make as you move forward as a teaching pair or team? | | |
| **D. Resources: Has the pair or team identified and located materials and other resources to use to differentiate instruction for learner needs?** | | | |
| **Resources and Materials** | Have you identified a list of all resources and materials, including technology, to meet your content standards, learning objectives, culturally relevant materials, etc? | | |

… 193

# Appendix C
## *Lesson Planning for Collaborative Teaching (One Week)*
### Debbie F. Cosgrove

Team Members: _____

Monday, (Date) _____

**Move Forward With Data-Driven Plans**

| Learning Standard(s): | Co-Teaching Strategies: |
|---|---|
| Learning Objective: | Student Learning Target: I will … |
| Activities: | Materials/Resources/Tech: |

| T1 will: | T2 will: | T3 will: |
|---|---|---|

| Assessments: | Notes/Differentiation/Accommodations: |
|---|---|

Academic Vocabulary (instructional & content specific):

Tuesday, (Date) _____

| Learning Standard(s): | Co-Teaching Strategies: |
|---|---|
| Learning Objective: | Student Learning Target: I will … |
| Activities: | Materials/Resources/Tech: |

| T1 will: | T2 will: | T3 will: |
|---|---|---|

| Assessments: | Notes/Differentiation/Accommodations: |
|---|---|

Academic Vocabulary (instructional & content specific):

**Wednesday, (Date) _____**

**Proceed With Caution**
**Reteaching? Misconceptions? Enrichments?**

| Learning Standard(s): | Co-Teaching Strategies: |
|---|---|
| Learning Objective: | Student Learning Target: I will ... |
| Activities: | Materials/Resources/Tech: |

| T1 will: | T2 will: | T3 will: |
|---|---|---|

| Assessments: | Notes/Differentiation/Accommodations: |
|---|---|

Academic Vocabulary (instructional & content specific):

---

**Thursday, (Date) _____**

| Learning Standard(s): | Co-Teaching Strategies: |
|---|---|
| Learning Objective: | Student Learning Target: I will ... |
| Activities: | Materials/Resources/Tech: |

| T1 will: | T2 will: | T3 will: |
|---|---|---|

| Assessments: | Notes/Differentiation/Accommodations: |
|---|---|

Academic Vocabulary (instructional & content specific):

| Friday, (Date) _____ | **Stop and Reflect**<br>**Chart a New Course** | |
|---|---|---|
| Learning Standard(s): | Co-Teaching Strategies: | |
| Learning Objective: | Student Learning Target: I will . . . | |
| Activities: | Materials/Resources/Tech: | |
| T1 will: | T2 will: | T3 will: |
| Assessments: | Notes/Differentiation/Accommodations: | |
| Academic Vocabulary (instructional & content specific): | | |

# Appendix D

## *Collaborative Reflection on Lesson Planning and Learning (Use after one week or 3–5 lessons)*

### Debbie F. Cosgrove

| Collaborative Reflection on Lesson Planning and Learning for the Week of _____ |
| :---: |
| (Reflection-on-Action) |

| What did we do well? | What could we have done better? |
| --- | --- |
|  |  |

What did the assessments (formative and summative) tell us about student understanding and misconceptions?

Personal Goal Setting: After reflecting on the learning plans and student achievement for this week:

T1 will:

T2 will:

T3 will:

**Collaborative Goal Setting**

After reflecting on the learning plans and student achievement for this week, we will commit to the following as we prepare learning plans for the following week.
WE WILL…

Goal 1:

Goal 2:

Goal 3:

**QUICK CHECK**
**How SMART are your shared goals?**
**Record your thinking.**

Are they SPECIFIC?

Are they MEASURABLE?

Are they ACHIEVABLE?

Are they RESULTS-BASED?

Are they TIME-SENSITIVE?

# Appendix E

*What Would You Do? Questions with Suggested Responses*

1. What would you do if you do **not** have a protected time for collaborative planning in your weekly schedule?

   **Suggested Response 1:** First, review the time releases that the pair or team has that include times before and after school. Next, look for opportunities when the pair or team can plan during times when students are engaged in special classes (e.g., the fine arts, physical education). Some pairs or teams may choose to meet during a shared lunch/recess period. It is important that the administrator knows that you are engaged in collaborative teaching and that joint planning is critical to your teaching success. Many schools will arrange for a substitute teacher to cover classes during a prearranged time so that pairs or teams can plan together. Typically, the substitute will teach a class for an hour or two to support this effort.

2. What would you do if your pair or team member does not want to spend quality time engaged in the collaborative planning process and would rather plan informally or "on the fly?"

   **Suggested Response 2:** There is no doubt that collaborative planning with two or more teachers requires extra time on everyone's part. It is important to remember that for collaborative teaching to be successful, there needs to be a dedicated effort from each practitioner to engage in collaborative planning. The supervisor or administrator should spend time with the pair and/or team to discuss the important prerequisites for successful collaborative planning. In a guided supervisory context, the supervisor should ask the pair and/or team to commit to collaborative planning expectations before they actually engage in collaborative teaching. Utilize the Planning Protocol for Collaborative Teaching in this module to help the pair and/or team to recognize the complexity of collaborative teaching and the importance of planning for its implementation. The pair or team should be held accountable for keeping detailed notes or plans that document this planning process.

3. What would you do if you hear several students talking about their perception that one of the teachers on the collaborative teaching pair or team "is not a real teacher?"

   **Suggested Response 3:** One of the essential understandings about collaborative teaching is that it requires parity among pair or team members. When teachers teach collaboratively, they need to be cognizant of making equal contributions during planning, teaching, and assessment practices. Do the teachers balance their instruction during class so that one is not perceived as the "lead" for all of the lessons? Have the teachers discussed grading and behavioral expectations so that one teacher is not the only person making decisions in these areas? Are the teachers' names clearly posted in the classroom, on newsletters, and on report cards? Do teachers affirm the positions/roles of each other in front of their students as "teachers" and not "assistants?" Do parents know that the teachers are engaged in a collaborative teaching model? Reference the checklist entitled Parity, Parity, Parity from Co-Teach! Building and sustaining effective classroom partnerships in inclusive schools, by M. Friend (2017).

## References

Anderson, L. W., Krathwohl, D. R., Airasian, P. W., Cruikshank, K. A., Mayer, R. E., Pintrich, P. R., ... Wittrock, M. C. (2001). *A taxonomy for learning, teaching, and assessing: A revision of Bloom's taxonomy of educational objectives.* Boston, MA: Allyn & Bacon.

Brownell, M. T., Adams, A., Sindelar, P., Waldron, N., & Vanhover, S. (2006). Learning from collaboration: The role of teacher qualities. *Exceptional Children, 72*(2), 169–185.

Burden, P., & Byrd, D. (2016). *Methods for effective teaching: Meeting the needs of all students.* Enhanced Pearson eText, 7th Edition. Boston, MA: Pearson.

Davis, K., Dieker, L., Pearl, C., & Kirkpatrick, R. (2012). Planning in the middle: Co-planning between general and special education. *Journal of Educational and Psychological Consultation, 22,* 208–226.

Friend, M., & Cook, L. (2017). *Interactions: Collaboration skills for school professionals.* Boston, MA: Pearson Education.

Friend, M., Reising, M., & Cook, L. (1993). Co-teaching: An overview of the past, a glimpse of the present, and considerations for the future. *Preventing School Failure: Alternative Education for Children and Youth, 37*(4), 6–10.

Martin, S. (2009). Learning to teach science. In W. M. Roth & K. Tobin (Eds), *The world of science education: Handbook of research in North America* (pp. 569–586). Rotterdam, Netherlands: Sense.

Marzano, R. (2007). *The art and science of teaching.* Alexandria, VA: Association for Supervision and Curriculum Development.

Murawski, W. W. (2006). Student outcomes in co-taught secondary English classes: How can we improve? *Reading and Writing Quarterly, 22,* 227–247.

Murawski, W. W. (2010). *Collaborative teaching in elementary schools: Making the co-teaching marriage work!* Thousand Oaks, CA: Corwin Press.

Murawski, W. W. (2012). 10 tips for using co-planning time more efficiently. *Teaching Exceptional Children, 44*(4), 8–15.

Price, K. M. & Nelson, K. L. (2014). *Planning effective instruction.* Belmont, CA: Wadsworth, Cengage Learning.

Schön, D. A. (1983). *The reflective practitioner: How professionals think in action.* New York, NY: Basic Books.

Scruggs, T. E., Mastropieri, M. A., & McDuffie, K. A. (2007, July 1). Co-Teaching in inclusive classrooms: A metasynthesis of qualitative research. *Exceptional Children, 73*(4), 392–416.

Tyler, R. W. (1949). *Basic principles of curriculum and instruction.* Chicago, IL: The University of Chicago Press.

Walther-Thomas, C., Bryant, M., & Land, S. (1996, July 1). Planning for effective co-teaching. *Remedial and Special Education, 17*(4), 255–264.

Webb, N. (1997/2006). *Research monograph number 6: Criteria for alignment of expectations and assessments on mathematics and science education.* Washington, DC: CCSSO.

Weiss, M. P., & Lloyd, J. (2003, Jan 1). Conditions for co-teaching: Lessons from a case study. *Teacher Education and Special Education, 26*(1), 27–41.

Zemelman, S., Daniels, H., & Hyde, A. (2012). *Best practice: Bringing standards to life in America's classrooms.* Portsmouth, NH: Heinemann.

# MODULE 13

---

# Differentiating Your Instruction

Lisa Burke
*Elmhurst College*

*One size does NOT fit all.*
—Carol Tomlinson

### MODULE DESCRIPTION

Teachers should have a good understanding of the strengths and needs of the K–12 students in their classrooms. An important skill for teachers to develop is the ability to differentiate their instruction to meet each student's needs and to provide challenge and accessibility to all learners. This module will provide foundational information about differentiated instruction as well as guided questions, activities, and resources to support teachers, pairs, and teams as they work to differentiate their instruction.

## Theory/Conceptual Framework

Students in classrooms today represent a diverse group of individuals. They represent differing interests, learning abilities, knowledge of general content and concepts, and cultural backgrounds and experiences. Given these differences, K–12 teachers need to be responsive for meeting the needs of all their students through tasks and activities that both challenge and provide accessibility for those students that need it (Anderson, 2007). Tomlinson (2014) notes the importance of teacher understanding that all students do not learn the same way but all deserve engaging and purposeful activities that are developed with the positive expectation for student success. A teacher who applies the elements of differentiated instruction is one who can embrace student differences and utilize classroom frameworks that include flexible groupings, respectful activities for all, ongoing assessment, and collaborative processes between teacher and student (Tomlinson, 2014; Logan, 2011).

One of the most essential aspects of differentiated instruction is the idea that assessment is an ongoing process and should not be thought of as separate from instruction (Tomlinson, 2014). A key element of the differentiation process is for teachers to have an excellent understanding of the entry points for each student related to a given concept or skill that is taught (Logan, 2011). In addition, teachers should be able to identify how each of their students learns and then uses formative assessments to continually reflect on the success or failure of the activities that have been planned (Parsons, Dodman, & Burrowbridge, 2013). Teachers who can flexibly adapt their instruction, rearrange instructional groupings, and use a student's learning profile and their interests to design meaningful instruction are those that will be more effective with their teaching (Tomlinson, 2014; Parsons, Dodman, & Burrowbridge, 2013).

Successful differentiation requires careful consideration of assessment data that the teacher continuously collects (Tomlinson, 2014). It will be much easier for teachers to differentiate the content, process, product or learning environment if they have carefully assessed their students in relation to content understandings, interests the students have, and how students like to learn. Differentiating the content means a teacher adapts what the students are learning about. Differentiating the process means a teacher provides different activities for the students to engage in to learn the content. Differentiating the product means a teacher creates multiple ways for the students to demonstrate their learning. Differentiating the learning environment means that a teacher creates an environment that is safe, positive, and a comfortable place to learn for all students regardless of their learning preferences, strengths, and needs. The aforementioned curricular elements should be differentiated based on a student's readiness level with identified concepts or skills, a student's interest toward a particular skill or concept, and a student's learning profile or way of learning the skill or concept (Tomlinson, 2014). Classrooms and learning tasks and activities should be multifaceted so that students of all ability levels and with different backgrounds and experiences are challenged and have supports provided for them (Logan, 2011).

In summary, differentiating instruction is a way for K–12 teachers to be responsive to varying needs, backgrounds, interests, and learning profiles for their students (Stanford & Reeves, 2009). Teachers need to realize that one way of teaching a given concept or skill may not accommodate all of the students in a classroom. Creating learner options for engaging with the content taught and the skills assessed will provide more meaningful educational experiences. Teaching students with the philosophy that "one size does *not* fit all" can transform a student's experience from mundane to impactful learning. This is something that every teacher should strive to accomplish.

## Specific Questions to Guide Discussion

1. What do you know about your students' learning profiles, interests, and background knowledge? How did you use this information in the planning of your activities?

2. Did you create a pre-assessment tool to use for gauging student understanding of what you were going to teach? If so, what was the pre-assessment? Describe what you found out about the student's knowledge and skill levels. How did you use this information to plan your lesson?

3. Share the outcome of your lesson(s). What do you want your students to know, understand, and be able to do? Given what you know about your students and their learning needs, will *all* students be able to meet your outcome(s) for the lesson(s)? Describe ways you can alter or modify the outcome(s) so that all students have the opportunity to meet the outcome(s) or objective(s) of your lesson.

4. Describe the activities, tasks, and assessments in your lesson(s). Are they appropriately challenging and equally engaging for all learners based on their learning profiles and interests? How will you alter the tasks/activities (content, process, product, or environment) to meet the needs of all your learners yet keep all tasks equally respectful and appealing regardless of a student's needs?

5. Describe the flexible grouping options you have considered for your students? Have you considered a variety of grouping configurations (e.g., individual, small group, whole group)? How can you group students in a variety of ways so that students are working in heterogeneous groups and homogeneous groups? How can you incorporate ways for students to make choices about tasks or groups with whom they will work?

## Productive Practices
(Nunley, 2006; Stickland, 2009; Tomlinson, 2003)

1. *Determine learning profiles and interests of your students.*
   a. Administer a student profile survey or a student interest survey which will help you and your students identify learning preferences and interests. A student profile survey should focus on describing how students learn (i.e., working alone or with partners/groups, sharing information learned by writing or drawing, being musically or artistically inclined). A student interest survey should focus on identifying cultural assets, topics students want to learn about, favorite things to do, subjects students feel good about or like in school and those they feel are hard for them, etc.
2. *Identify what you want students to be able to know, understand, and do.*
   a. Create outcomes/objectives that are observable, measurable and standards-based.

b. Evaluate your outcome(s) to ensure that it is challenging and provides accessibility for all learners. If it doesn't, adapt or alter it so that it will!
c. Align your outcomes/objectives with the tasks, activities, and assessment choices throughout your lesson.
3. *Develop pre-assessment tools and ongoing assessment procedures that provide you with information about the backgrounds, prerequisite knowledge, and developing knowledge of all your students.*
   a. Look carefully at the pre-assessment results and determine the strengths and needs of your learners.
   b. Reevaluate your outcomes/objectives and learning tasks to ensure that students will be able to access the lesson content based on the pre-assessment information.
   c. Adjust outcomes/objectives and learning tasks by differentiating content, process, product, and learning environment to challenge or provide support for those students that need it.
   d. Infuse assessments throughout your lesson(s) in a variety of formats (not just pre- and post-assessments).
4. *Create learning tasks, activities, and assessments that differentiate content, process, product, and learning environment.*
   a. Identify clearly what (content) students should know, understand, and be able to do. Provide different levels of the content or topics for students to study and learn about based on pre-requisite knowledge and interests.
   b. Identify the activities (process) that the students will engage in so that they can develop understandings about the content. Provide activities that are multi-modal for students who have differing learning profiles. Consider using learning stations or centers, personal agendas or learning contracts, cooperative learning groups, choice boards, tiered activities, and problem-based or inquiry-learning projects.
   c. Identify how students will demonstrate what they have learned or what they have come to know (product). Develop specific measurable criteria, evaluation checklists, or task specific rubrics that you systematically share with your students so they know the learning outcome and have a clear understanding of what the final product should be (assessment).
5. *Develop flexible grouping procedures.*
   a. Create multiple working formats for your students. These should include individual, small group, and whole group learning opportunities.
   b. When creating small group formats, include groups that are both heterogeneous and homogeneous for your students.
   c. Allow your students to work with independent study formats. Provide them with agendas or learning contracts so they have a way of tracking what needs to be done.

## What Would You Do?

Ask your team or pair the following questions. For suggested responses to questions, see Appendix A.

1. What would you do if a student wanted to move to another group, activity, or task but you thought that it would be too hard for the student?

2. What would you do if a parent questioned why you have multiple learning tasks/options for a particular unit/concept you are teaching?

3. What would you do if other teachers on your team do not think differentiating instruction is a worthwhile teaching method?

## Reflective Professional Growth Activities
(Nunley, 2006; Stickland, 2009; Tomlinson, 2003)

Consider these ideas or activities to facilitate and foster teacher growth and reflection. Select one or two ideas to help facilitate this reflection process that will help the teacher, pair, or team to understand the process of differentiating instruction. Remember that supervisors are instructional leaders who should know their teachers, pairs, or teams well, so be sure to choose a growth activity that would be the most effective for them.

### *Idea 1: Identify Student Learning Profiles, Interests, Cultural Assets, Strengths, and Needs*

What did you find out about your students that you didn't know before? How can you use this information to plan and/or adapt your lesson or make your lesson more challenging or accessible for your students?

**Evidence:** Completed student profile surveys, interest surveys, or pre-assessment data.

### *Idea 2: Design a Differentiated Activity for a Learning Unit*

What do you want students to know (facts/vocabulary), understand (big ideas or essential understandings), and be able to do (skills)? This sequence of learning (know, understand, do) is often referred to as the KUD. Based on your students' profiles, what are different versions of the learning task that are differentiated based on readiness, interest, or learning preference/profiles? Is there a good match between the versions of the task and each student's needs?

**Evidence:** Completed chart (see Figure 13.1) or graphic organizer of differentiated or different versions of the tasks.

> **Student Outcomes Based on KUD Categories**
> Identify what students should KNOW (facts/vocabulary), UNDERSTAND (big ideas), and DO (skills)
> **KNOW:** Identify the characters, setting, and theme of a story.
> **UNDERSTAND:** An author has a purpose for writing narrative text (to entertain) and all narrative text has a structure which includes characters, setting, and a theme of the story.
> **DO:** Explain the author's purpose of a particular text citing the characters, setting, and theme of the story. Include in the explanation, connections to self, other texts, and the world.
>
> **TASK VERSION 1:** Research (e.g., books from the library, searching appropriate online resources) a famous person in history whose personal characteristics, experiences, and life reflect a main character and central theme of the story you have read. Write an essay that compares and contrasts the story assigned by your teacher with the famous person that you researched.
>
> **TASK VERSION 2:** Write a poem about yourself and one of the main characters in the story assigned by your teacher. Your poem should reflect how you and the character are alike and different and how both you and the character relate to the theme of the story.
>
> **TASK VERSION 3:** Using a graphic organizer, compare and contrast yourself with one of the main characters in the story that you read.

**Figure 13.1**   Example chart on student outcomes based on KUD categories.

## *Idea 3: Create a Tiered Lesson or Learning Menu for Your Students*

For one lesson, the pair or team should collaborate to create alternate activities (i.e., tiered lesson, learning menu) for the students to complete. A tiered lesson (see Idea 2) allows students to work towards the same outcome but the activities are geared toward student abilities or learning preferences. A learning menu is organized around a certain topic or concept for students to choose an activity and then work independently to extend learning about a concept or topic. Activities that might appear on a learning menu about characterization include (a) creating an award for a favorite character in a story, (b) creating a comic strip conversation between characters in a story, and (c) surveying classmates about their favorite characters in a common story/book read. The roles of the teachers during the lessons/activities should be identified to facilitate student understanding. The teachers should debrief after the lesson to evaluate student work samples.

**Evidence:** Lesson plans and student work samples used to evaluate student outcomes for the activities/learning tasks.

## *Idea 4: Evaluate a Differentiated Activity for Your Classroom*

Carry out the activity that you have designed. After your students have completed the task/activity ask them to answer the following questions.

1. What was the point of this activity?
2. How did this activity match what you already knew about the topic?
3. How did this activity match your interests about this topic?
4. How did this activity match how you like to learn new topics?
5. What would have made this activity a better learning experience for you?

For young students, you can create a picture rating scale that aligns with the questions. This is also a helpful strategy for English language learners and striving readers. Analyze and reflect on your students' answers and revise/adapt the learning task or future tasks.

**Evidence:** Completed answers to the questions above.

## Follow-Up, Monitoring, and Goal Setting

(Nunley, 2006; Stickland, 2009; Tomlinson, 2003)

Depending on the idea chosen from the reflective professional growth activities, complete the following before you begin your next observation.

### *Idea 1: Identify Student Learning Profiles, Interests, Cultural Assets, Strengths, and Needs*

- What did you learn about your students?
- What are some specific steps you can take to collaborate with the general education teachers to enhance and accommodate your students' instruction?
- How will you use this information to differentiate the outcomes/objectives, the learning tasks/activities, and the assessment tool?
- How have you incorporated ongoing assessment into your lesson?
- What are some specific needs of your students that need to be addressed?
- How does identifying your students' profiles before you finish planning help the lesson planning process?
- Do you have any further questions about how you can use the information about your students?

### *Idea 2: Design a Differentiated Activity for a Learning Unit*

- Have you identified what you want your students to know, understand, and be able to do in an observable and measurable way?
- Is the KUD organizer (know, understand, do) aligned with standards, learning tasks, and the assessment?
- What are the different versions of the learning task that you developed?
- Are all the learning tasks equally appealing for your students and do they all offer differing levels of support, complexity, and challenge?
- Do the different versions of the tasks meet the needs of all learners?
- Are there any other versions of the task that can be created?
- Do you have any further questions about the versions of the task?

### *Idea 3: Create a Tiered Lesson, Learning Station/Center, or Learning Menu for Your Students*

- What differentiated instructional strategy did you decide to use?
- What are the elements of differentiated instruction that the activity incorporates (content, process, product, learning environment)?
- How does the strategy you chose meet the needs of your students?

- What do the work samples tell you about what your students learned and how they were able to access the content?
- Do you have any further questions about the differentiated instructional strategy you used?

## *Idea 4: Evaluate a Differentiated Activity for Your Classroom*

- What did the students say about the differentiated activity?
- How do their comments inform what you will do next time?
- Do you have any further questions?

# Resources

## *Articles*

### Examining Differentiated Instruction

This article shares the basic principles of differentiated instruction as well as ways to implement differentiated instruction in a classroom.

Logan, B. (2011). Examining differentiated instruction: Teachers respond. *Research in Higher Education Journal, 13,* 1–14.

### Broadening the View of Differentiated Instruction

This article reinforces the idea that differentiated instruction should occur at all stages of the learning cycle: planning, instruction, and assessment.

Parsons, S., Dodman, S. L., & Burrowbridge, S. C. (2013). Broadening the view of differentiated instruction. *Phi Delta Kappan, 95*(1), 38–42.

### Using Differentiated Instruction, Retrofit Framework, and Universal Design for Learning

This article shares ideas for differentiating instruction in diverse classrooms.

Stanford, B., & Reeves, S. (2009). Making it happen: Using differentiated instruction, retrofit framework, and universal design for learning. *Teaching Exceptional Children Plus, 5*(6), 2–7.

## *Books*

### 100 More Ways to Differentiate Instruction in Inclusive K–12 Classrooms

This book is filled with different activities that a teacher can use to differentiate instruction.

Kluth, P., & Danaher, S. (2013). *From text maps to memory caps: 100 more ways to differentiate instruction in inclusive K–12 classrooms.* Baltimore, MD: Brookes.

### How the Best Teachers Differentiate Instruction

This accessible and practical guide shows teachers how to provide their students with a variety of ways to strengthen their understanding of new material.

Magee, M., & Breaux, E. (2010). *How the best teachers differentiate instruction.* New York, NY: Routledge.

### Great Ways to Differentiate Mathematics

This book helps experienced and novice teachers to effectively and efficiently differentiate mathematics instruction in grades K–8.

Small, M. (2017). *Great ways to differentiate mathematics: Instruction in the standards-based classroom.* New York, NY: Teachers College Press.

### How to Differentiate Instruction in Academically Diverse Classrooms

This book is a practical guide for teachers that provides the fundamentals for differentiating instruction and shares strategies for doing so.

Tomlinson, C. A. (2017). *How to differentiate instruction in academically diverse classrooms* (3rd ed.). Alexandria, VA: ASCD.

### How to Differentiate to Improve Student Success at all Learning Levels

This book provides forms and tools to aid teachers in differentiating activities and assessments.

Zapata, Y. P., & Brooks, R. (2017). *Adapting unstoppable learning: How to differentiate instruction to improve student success at all learning levels.* Bloomington, IN: Solution Tree Press.

## *Modules*

### Differentiating Instruction

This module provides hands-on learning to experience the different ways for differentiating instruction. The module includes audio-interviews of experts, videos, and practical activities the viewer can complete.

The Iris Center. (2017). *Differentiating instruction: Maximizing instruction of all students.* Retrieved from https://iris.peabody.vanderbilt.edu/module/di/

### Universal Design for Learning

This module provides a hands-on learning experience on how to universally design instruction. The module includes audio-interviews of experts, videos, and practical activities the viewer can complete.

The Iris Center. (2017). *Universal Design for Learning: Creating a Learning Environment that Challenges and Engages All Students.* Retrieved from https://iris.peabody.vanderbilt.edu/module/udl/

## *Videos*

### New Teacher Survival Guide

This video series highlights teacher interviews and actual classroom activities that involve differentiated instruction.

The Teaching Channel. (2017). *New teacher survival guide: Differentiating instruction.* Retrieved from https://www.teachingchannel.org/videos/differentiating-instruction

### Differentiating With Learning Menus

This video series highlights teacher interviews and actual classroom activities that involve using learning menus to differentiate instruction.

The Teaching Channel. (2017). *Differentiating with learning menus.* Retrieved from https://www.teachingchannel.org/videos/differentiating-instruction-strategy

### Differentiating in Math Using Computer Games

This video series highlights teacher interviews and actual classroom activities that involve differentiating instruction for math class.

The Teaching Channel. (2017). *Differentiating in math using computer games.* Retrieved from https://www.teachingchannel.org/videos/differentiating-in-math

## Key Terms and Definitions

**Content:** Content refers to facts, concepts, theories, and principles that are taught and learned in a specific academic lesson.

**Differentiated instruction:** Differentiated instruction is a framework or philosophy for effective teaching that involves providing different students with different ways of learning.

**Heterogeneous:** Heterogenous grouping means that students of all levels are represented in the grouping structure of a class.

**Homogeneous:** Homogeneous grouping means that students of the same ability level are represented in the grouping structure of a class.

**Interest:** Interest refers to a student's affinity, curiosity, or passion for a topic or skill.

**KUD:** KUD is an advanced organizer that helps students identify what they should "know" (i.e., facts, vocabulary), "understand" (i.e., big ideas), and "do" (i.e., skills).

**Learning environment:** The learning environment refers to the diverse physical locations, contexts, and cultures in which students learn.

**Learning center:** A learning center is an area that is set aside in a classroom where educational materials are accessible to students.

**Learning menu:** The learning menu is a form of differentiated instruction where students are given a choice in how they learn.

**Learning profile:** The learning profile represents the complete picture of a student which includes learning preferences, strengths, and challenges. The learning profile is shaped by the individual's intelligence, preference of learning, culture and gender.

**Process:** Process describes the activities designed to ensure students use key skills to make sense of the essential ideas and information.

**Product:** Product refers to when a teacher creates multiple ways for the student to demonstrate what they know about the concept being taught.

**Readiness:** Readiness is a student's entry point for a particular skill or understanding.

**Tiered lesson:** A tiered lesson is a differentiation strategy that addresses a particular standard, key concept, and generalization, but allows several pathways for students to arrive at an understanding of these components based on their interests, readiness, or learning profiles (Adams & Pierce, 2004).

# Appendix A

## *What Would you Do? Suggested Responses*

1. What would you do if a student wanted to move to another group, activity, or task but you thought that it would be too hard for the student?

   **Suggested Response 1:** Speak with the student about their reasons for wanting to change. Explain why you thought the group, activity, or task would be good for the student. Create (with the student) a time-frame and some goals for the student to try another group, activity, or task.

2. What would you do if a parent questioned why you have multiple learning tasks/options for a particular unit/concept you are teaching?

   **Suggested Response 2:** Explain what differentiated instruction is and how it benefits ALL learners in the classroom. Explain to the parent about the different groups, activities, and tasks that you routinely use and why they benefit the child (be ready to share specific examples/data).

3. What would you do if other teachers on your team do not think differentiating instruction is a worthwhile teaching method?

   **Suggested Response 3:** Offer to share resources, units, and activities that you have used for differentiating your instruction. Offer to help the teacher(s) to get started differentiating their own instruction. Share your data or learning outcome results with the other teacher(s).

# References

Adams, C., & Pierce, R. (2004). *Tiered lessons: One way to differentiate mathematics instruction.* Retrieved from https://www.davidsongifted.org/Search-Database/entry/A10513

Anderson, K. M., (2007). Differentiating instruction to include all students. *Preventing School Failure, 51*(3), 49–54.

Logan, B. (2011). Examining differentiated instruction: Teachers respond. *Research in Higher Education Journal, 13,* 1–14.

Nunley, K. F. (2006). *Differentiating the high school classroom: Solution strategies for 18 common obstacles.* Thousand Oaks, CA: Corwin Press.

Parsons, S., Dodman, S. L., & Burrowbridge, S. C. (2013). Broadening the view of differentiated instruction. *Phi Delta Kappan, 95*(1), 38–42.

Stanford, B., & Reeves, S. (2009). Making it happen: Using differentiated instruction, retrofit framework, and universal design for learning. *Teaching Exceptional Children Plus, 5*(6), 2–7.

Strickland, C. (2009). *Exploring differentiated instruction.* Alexandria, VA: ASCD.

Strickland, C. (2009). *Professional development for differentiating instruction.* Alexandria, VA: ASCD.

Tomlinson, C. A. (2003). *Fulfilling the promise of the differentiated classroom: Strategies and tools for responsive teaching.* Alexandria, VA: ASCD.

Tomlinson, C. A. (2014). *The differentiated classroom: Responding to the needs of all learners* (2nd ed.). Alexandria, VA: ASCD.

# MODULE 14

# Responsible Digital Citizenship

Tracy Mulvaney
*Monmouth University*

*It is not enough to create rules and policy, we must teach everyone to become responsible digital citizens in this new society.*
—Mike Ribble

### MODULE DESCRIPTION

Globalization through technology has forced society to address citizenship through the lens of digital media. Technology affords us the ability to obtain immediate information. It further allows us to communicate with others and to share our lives through social media. All of these relatively recent innovations have created a need for digital citizenship standards. This module will provide a framework for understanding and teaching digital citizenship in today's collaboratively taught classrooms.

## Theory/Conceptual Framework

Today's P–12 students are exposed to multiple sources of digital technologies every day. Cell phones, iPads, electronic notebooks, laptop computers, and a multitude of other types of technologies have granted students unlimited access to online information. Although the World Wide Web (www) is a relatively new discovery that was introduced in the late 1980s, innovations in web-based technologies and programs continue to be developed at an incredibly swift rate (Couldry, 2012). Unlimited access to the Internet from the palm of one's hand leaves a student both empowered and vulnerable. As a result, the concept of digital citizenship must be defined, taught, and understood by P–12 students, teachers, administrators, families, and community members.

Digital citizenship is essential to teach technology users the norms of responsible and appropriate use of technology. Ribble (2017) identifies nine elements of digital citizenship: digital access, etiquette, law, literacy, communication, commerce, rights, and responsibilities, safety and security, and health and welfare (see Figure 14.1).

Each element is categorized into a simplistic framework for digital citizenship under the themes of: Respect for yourself and others, educate yourself/connect with others, and protect yourself and others. The Global Digital Citizenship Foundation paints a picture of a global digital citizen as a hero who follows the tenets of personal responsibility, global citizenship, digital citizenship, altruistic service, and environmental stewardship (Watanabe-Crockett, 2017). It is through following these five tenets and nine elements of digital citizenship, that teachers understand the skills and knowledge they must possess in order to navigate and teach in the world of digital citizenship.

Teaching digital citizenship is imperative for all teachers in a 21st century classroom environment. In fact, the International Society for Technology in Education (ISTE) has articulated a standard that addresses digital citizenship (see ISTE, Standard 3, Citizen, Figure 14.2). The Citizen standard requires that, "Educators inspire students to positively contribute and responsibly participate in the digital world" (ISTE, 2018).

The four components of the standard identify the need for teachers to create experiences for learners that result in digitally literate, compassionate, empathetic, ethical, and safe citizens. These standards help teachers achieve the newest form of citizenship, digital citizenship. The clearly articulated components of digital citizenship bridge the abstract concept of digital citizenship to practical behaviors. In an effort to achieve mastery of Standard 3, teachers should be compelled to ensure they exhibit appropriate digital behaviors. This could

| Theme | Element | Description |
| --- | --- | --- |
| Respect for yourself and others | Access | Full electronic participation and equality in society |
| | Etiquette | Appropriate and ethical conduct in the digital world |
| | Law | Electronic responsibility for digital behavior. |
| Educate yourself/ Connect with others | Literacy | Teaching and learning about the use of technology |
| | Communication | Exchange of information through a digital platform |
| | Commerce | Buying and selling of goods electronically |
| Protect yourself and others | Rights and Responsibilities | Digital freedoms extended to all (e.g., freedom of speech, privacy) |
| | Safety and security | Precautions to take to ensure safety |
| | Health and Welfare | Mental and physical well-being in the digital world. |

**Figure 14.1** Nine elements of digital citizenship. *Source:* Ribble (2014).

| International Society for Technology in Education (ISTE) Standard 3 Citizen ||| 
|---|---|---|
| Educators inspire students to positively contribute to and responsibly participate in the digital world | **Component** | |
| | 3a | Create experiences for learners to make positive, socially responsible contributions and exhibit empathetic behavior online that build relationships and community. |
| | 3b | Establish a learning culture that promotes curiosity and critical examination of online resources and fosters digital literacy and media fluency. |
| | 3c | Mentor students in safe, legal, and ethical practices with digital tools and the protection of intellectual rights and property. |
| | 3d | Model and promote management of personal data and digital identity and protect student privacy. |

**Figure 14.2** ISTE Standard 3 about Digital Citizenship. *Source:* ISTE Standards for Educators (2018).

be achieved by assessing their own online behavior by researching their digital *footprint* to determine whether they are modeling the behaviors prescribed in the standard.

## *Digital Footprint*

With the advent and widespread use of social media platforms (e.g., Facebook®, Instagram®, Snapchat®) classroom teachers are compelled to not only teach and monitor student digital behavior, but also to ensure that they themselves are also modeling behaviors that are characterized as good digital citizenship. To accomplish this, teachers are duty-bound to maintain a clean, online presence, a concept known as a digital footprint. Martin (2012) states, "Social Media is changing the way we communicate and the way we are perceived, both positively and negatively. Every time you post a photo, or update your status, you are contributing to your own digital footprint and personal brand." Your digital footprint can be a powerful networking tool but can conversely be a destructive force in one's career or personal life.

Teachers have an obligation to ensure that their digital footprints are free of inappropriate images, posts, writings, or other digital means that can present an unfavorable view to an employer or community. Joyce (2010) identifies six career-killing Facebook mistakes that individuals make, which is a strong reminder that a digital footprint can indeed affect one's employment. Mistakes include posting inappropriate pictures, complaining about employment, posting information that conflicts with a resume, being tagged in inappropriate texts or pictures from peers, not using or understanding security settings, and posting statuses that would present a negative image to an employer. This is only one of two dimensions of digital citizenship that teachers address. In addition to ensuring a clean digital footprint, teachers are asked to reflect upon their application of technology in the classroom. A widely known model called the substitution augmentation modification redefinition (SAMR) model, was developed to allow this reflection to take place (Ribble, 2014).

### The Substitution Augmentation Modification Redefinition Model

In an ongoing effort to improve digital citizenship, it is beneficial for teachers to reflect upon their application of technology integration in their classrooms. In 2006, Ruben Puentedura collaborated with the Maine Department of Education to create the SAMR model (Puentedura, 2014). The model identifies a continuum that measures the integration of technology into classroom settings (see Figure 14.3). The continuum starts with the *enhancement* levels of substitution and augmentation. On these levels, technology is a direct substitute.

The two levels are differentiated by the presence of a functional change, which occurs only in the augmentation level. The last two levels of modification and redefinition fall under *transformation.* Modification involves technology permitting a task redesign that can be significant. Redefinition allows previously inconceivable innovations to take place with technology in the classroom (Puentedura, 2014).

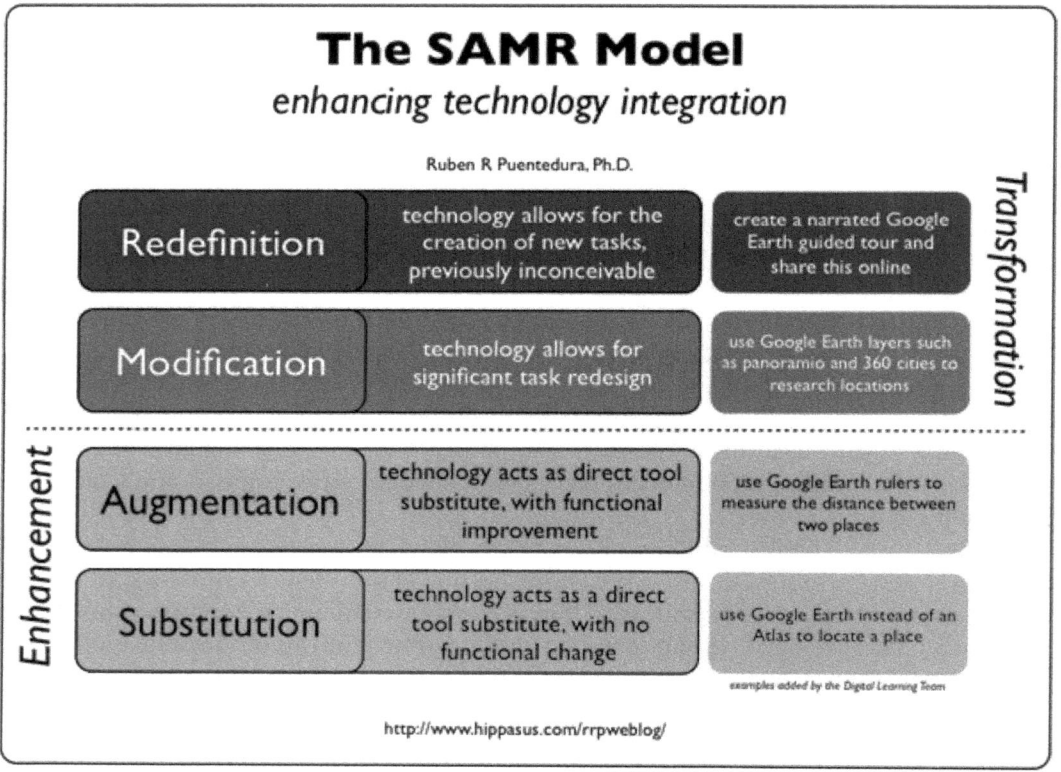

**Figure 14.3**   The SAMR Model. *Source:* Puentedura (2014).

## Specific Questions to Guide Discussion

1. What does digital citizenship mean in the context of a P–12 environment? How can the teacher, pair, or team model good digital citizenship? In what ways can a teacher monitor if students are practicing appropriate digital citizenship?

2. Review the school district policy on the acceptable use of technology. What does the policy include? Is there reference to social media and use of it as an instructional tool? Is there a district policy that addresses cyberbullying?

3. Using the SAMR Model, have the teacher, pair, or team pick a specific class and ask, what is the current level of technology integration? What is the rationale for that choice?

4. In what ways can the teacher, pair, or team use the Internet and social media as instructional tools? Discuss activities that can be part of a whole class, small group, or individual lesson. How can teachers use technology and online resources to meet the needs of a culturally and linguistically diverse class?

5. What is a digital footprint? How can an individual ensure that their digital footprint is appropriate? Can your digital footprint affect your ability to obtain or lose a teaching position?

## Productive Practices

1. *Model appropriate behaviors to your students.*
    a. Make good digital citizenship part of your classroom culture.
    b. Illustrate digital citizenship by showing social media posts that are supportive and appropriate.
    c. Use videoconferencing to connect with classrooms around the world.
    d. Incorporate the use of appropriate digital content and media in your classroom.
    e. Use digital media to support classroom social justice campaigns.
2. *Educate students about how to learn in a digital society.*
    a. Using the SAMR model, identify your own level of technology integration in the classroom. Set goals to improve how technology is integrated into the curriculum.
    b. Identify levels of student proficiency using digital media and content.
    c. Review appropriate netiquette (online etiquette) and social media behavior.
    d. Inform students of the nine elements of digital citizenship (https://www.sophia.org/tutorials/nine-elements-of-digital-citizenship).
    e. Engage students in the use of multiple types of digital media.
    f. Allow for the use of media presentation to demonstrate learning.

3. *Have students conduct data mines on themselves every 3–6 months. Data mines will allow students to examine their digital footprints.*
   a. Make certain students log out of browsers prior to searching for their digital footprint.
   b. Use quotation marks to search not only their legal names, but nicknames, usernames, and pseudonyms that may be tracked back to them.
   c. Continue to look through each page of results.
   d. Encourage students to check all major browsers such as Yahoo, Chrome, Safari, Firefox, and Bing.
4. *Demonstrate to students how to check privacy settings on all social media accounts that are not blocked by the school's firewall.*
   a. Show students how to access the privacy settings.
   b. Review each setting and explain the implications of not maintaining privacy.
   c. Encourage students to remove "friends" who they do not know.
   d. Teach the "grandma rule" and have students remove any posts their grandmother would not want to see.
   e. Have students look at images in which others have "tagged" them. If the images are not appropriate, remove the tag. If the picture is offensive, students should ask their friends to remove the picture.

## What Would You Do?

Ask your team or pair the following questions. For suggested responses to questions, see Appendix A.

1. What would you do if a teacher told you she was able to view your Facebook profile and you had content that may prohibit employment if searched by human resources?

2. What would you do if a student friended you on Facebook, Instagram, and Snapchat?

3. What would you do if a parent reported that their child was being cyberbullied by another child in your class?

4. What would you do if a friend tagged you in a picture in which an administrator may find offensive to the school community?

5. What would you do if you opened up a document on campus and discovered it contained a virus?

# Reflective Professional Growth Activities

Consider these ideas or activities to facilitate and foster teacher growth and reflection. Select one or two ideas to help facilitate this reflection process that will help the teacher, pair, or team to understand digital citizenship. Remember that you know the individuals best so be sure to choose an activity that would be the most effective.

## *Idea 1: Design and Implement a Robust Digital Citizenship Curriculum*

- Review district policy and procedures relating to technology, social media, cyberbullying, and digital resources.
- Review technology professional teaching standards and cross-reference them with content standards that delve into technology usage.
- Collaborate with other teachers to see how they integrate digital citizenship into their classes. Take a collaborative approach with a teacher, pair, or team to design the curriculum. Seek to collaborate with those in the district's instructional technology or curriculum department.
- Research best technology practices and identify 3–5 you want to build your curriculum around.
- Locate resources that will help you and your team to implement your curriculum with fidelity.
- Share your curriculum with school and district level administrators and teachers and ask for feedback for improvement.
- Implement an assessment plan to determine the effectiveness of your new curriculum.

**Evidence:** Select two collaboratively taught lesson plans to demonstrate evidence of digital citizenship.

## *Idea 2: Create a Guide for Students, Families, and Community Members About Online Citizenship.*

- With your pair or team, lead your class or grade level through the process of researching and preparing a guide about online citizenship, social media, and other digital media hints that families may not know about or understand.
- Survey stakeholders to determine what items should be included in the handbook.
- Inform stakeholders about their digital footprints. Encourage families, community members, and students to research their digital footprint and determine ways to "clean" it up.
- Include acceptable use policies for cell phones and digital media in the classroom and on campus.
- Advise students, parents, and school staff of new social media trends and how social media should be used responsibly.

**Evidence:** The online or hard copy of your guide about digital citizenship along with a written plan about how you intend to disseminate this plan to all stakeholders.

## Idea 3: Model Appropriate Digital Citizenship by Creating a Positive Online Presence for Your Classroom.

- Survey your class or grade level about the uses of common social media platforms.
- Collaborate with your co-teacher and students to create goals for creating an online class presence. What is the purpose? Who is the audience? How do we implement it? What are the guidelines?
- Create a classroom presence in each of the social media platforms discussed (e.g., Facebook page, Instagram). Be sure to review the district's policy for acceptable use.
- Work with students to plan, upload, and work within the social media platforms. Assign responsibilities to students such as: manager, editor, reporter, photographer, "tweeter," and other duties appropriate for the selected social media platform.

**Evidence:** Demonstration of social media class page on chosen application (e.g., Facebook page, Instagram).

# Follow-Up, Monitoring, and Goal Setting

Complete the follow-up questions for the selected reflective professional growth activity.

## Idea 1: Design and Implement a Robust Digital Citizenship Curriculum

- What did you learn about your district's policies relating to technology, social media, and other acceptable use of technology? Was there anything that surprised you? Are there any holes missing where policy was not comprehensive?
- Using the SAMR Model, assess your level of technology integration in your co-taught classroom and include it as a factor while developing your curriculum.
- Were you able to locate professional standards at the district, state, or national level that will help in guiding your curriculum? What were they?
- Describe two of the best practices for digital citizenship you were able to research, and why these two resonated with you, your pair or team, and your class?
- Were you able to design lessons using the curriculum? How did you incorporate the co-teaching models?

**Goal for Future Practice for Idea 1**

How can you ensure that you are keeping your curriculum current?

## Idea 2: Create a Guide for Students, Families, and Community Members About Online Citizenship.

- What did the stakeholder survey reveal that needs to be included in the handbook? Were there any items that surprised you?
- Did you receive any feedback from students, and/or families of community stakeholders about the digital footprint activity? What implications did your findings make?
- Have you considered ways in which you can use cell phones as instructional tools?

**Goal for Future Practice for Idea 2**

Think about ways you can disseminate the guide to stakeholders? Will you distribute it electronically? Will you host a class with your co-teacher for students, staff, and parents?

## Idea 3: Model Appropriate Digital Citizenship by Creating a Positive Online Presence for Your Classroom.

- What was your process for selecting responsibilities for students? Do these roles change?
- How can you further model your own appropriate digital citizenship while leading your class through this process?
- How will you meaningfully include students with special needs in this project?

**Goal for Future Practice for Idea 3**

How do you motivate students to continue to update the social media accounts on an ongoing basis? How can students measure the effectiveness of posting to social media?

# Resources

## Web Resources

### Nine Elements of Digital Citizenship

This website provides information about digital access, etiquette, law, literacy, communication, commerce, rights and responsibilities, safety and security, and health and welfare. This website presents the nine elements of digital citizenship in a concise and informative manner. It also includes ways in which professionals can advance digital citizenship education through ISTE. The author includes a link that allows readers to join his Digital Citizenship Network.

Ribble, M. (2017). *Digital citizenship: Using technology appropriately*. Retrieved from http://www.digitalcitizenship.net/nine-elements.html

### 5 Minute Film: Teaching Digital Citizenship

This site gives readers a list of eleven video resources on topics related to digital citizenship. These topics range from *Netiquette to What is Digital Citizenship*? Each film clip is approximately five minutes or less, with the exception of one titled *TEDxUIUC* which is approximately 20 minutes and focuses on surviving the era of connectivity.

Borovoy, A. E. (2014, October 24). *5 minute film festival: Teaching digital citizenship*. Retrieved from https://www.edutopia.org/blog/film-festival-digital-citizenship

### ISTE Standards for Students

The ISTE standards are articulated on this website. Standard 2, Digital Citizen, addresses students' rights and responsibilities while working and learning in a digital world. Safe, legal, and ethical behaviors are articulated within the standard.

ISTE Standards for Educators. (2018). Retrieved from https://www.iste.org/standards/for-educators

### Common Sense Education

The Common Sense Education website provides a plethora of resources for teachers to use to teach digital citizenship. The free site has a K–12 digital citizenship curriculum with a scope and sequence map. It also includes interactive games and activities that empower students to use technology in a responsible manner.

Common Sense Education. (n.d.). *Getting resources for teaching in the digital age.* Retrieved from https://www.commonsense.org/education/

### Our Space: Being a Responsible Citizen of the Digital World

The *Our Space* was developed by The GoodPlay Project (Harvard University Graduate School of Education) and Project New Media Literacies (University of Southern California Annenberg School for Communication and Journalism). The materials contained in the casebook encourage youth to reflect upon the risks and dangers related to working and learning using online resources. Students are asked to consider ethical responsibilities for themselves and others through role-play and reflective activities.

The GoodPlay Project, Harvard Graduate School of Education, Project New Media Literacies, and University of Southern California. (2011). *Our space: Being a responsible citizen of the digital world.* Retrieved from https://dmlcentral.net/wp-content/uploads/files/Our_Space_full_casebook_compressed.pdf

### iKeepSafe

Resources available to educators through iKeepSafe include Digital Citizenship, Privacy and Security, and Trainings & Education. The iKeepSafe mission is to help advance digital learning while providing a safe landscape for students, families, and school communities by supporting the protection of student privacy.

iKeepSafe. (2018). *Privacy compliance made simple.* Retrieved from https://ikeepsafe.org/

### Media Smarts

Created by Canada's Centre for Digital and Media Literacy, this website has resources to inform teachers, parents, and students about topics in digital and social media. The site has digital and media literacy topics that include topics such as digital citizenship, television and mobile media, body image in media, cyberbullying, and online ethics and privacy.

Media Smarts. (n.d.). *Canada's Centre for digital and media literacy.* Retrieved from http://mediasmarts.ca/

### Digizen.org

A Childnet International website that provides parents, teachers, and students with resources that teach digital citizenship, while teaching components of responsible and ethical online behavior.

Childnet International. (2005–2018). Retrieved from http://www.digizen.org/

### Digital Citizenship: Using Technology Appropriately

Mike Ribble, the creator of the ISTE, offers teachers and parents resources for teaching digital citizenship. Included in the website is a clear and concise definition of digital citizenship, along with a description of the nine elements of digital citizenship.

Ribble, M. (2017). *Digital citizenship: Using technology appropriately.* Retrieved from http://www.digitalcitizenship.net/

## Key Terms and Definitions

**Data mines:** Data mining is identifying trends in large sets of data using intelligent methods (statistics and data base systems).

**Digital citizenship:** Digital citizenship refers to the appropriate and socially acceptable behaviors and expectations of users of digital media.

**Digital footprint:** A digital footprint means the digital impression left on the Internet as a result of online activity.

**Firewall:** The firewall is a network or program that is designed to block unauthorized Internet access.

**Grandma rule:** The Grandma rule refers to a rule that encourages online users not to post things that their grandmother would not be proud of or allow.

**Hashtags (#):** Hashtags allow posts to be grouped with all other posts of that hashtag.

**Social media:** Social media includes online applications and websites that allow users to share content through social networking.

**Tagging (in respect to social media):** Tagging allows users to engage others by mentioning them in a post or comment on applications such as Facebook, Twitter, and Instagram.

# Appendix A

## *What Would You Do? Suggested Responses*

1. What would you do if a teacher told you she was able to view your Facebook profile and you had content that may prohibit employment if searched by human resources?

   **Suggested Response 1:** You should always follow the "grandmother rule." If it isn't content you would want your own grandmother to see, don't post it. If you have already posted content, then set your photo privacy setting for all pictures to "only me" as you go through your Facebook. Remove any content that is not appropriate. When you are done cleaning up your photos, you can change your settings back to allow your friends or the public to see your pictures. You should also contact your friends and let them know that you need to create a professionally appropriate presence on social media and ask that they not post inappropriate pictures of you or include you in posts that don't meet the "grandmother rule." Additionally, you should remove "tags" on any current photos that others tag you in and make sure that you set your tag settings to require you to approve any tags prior to having them automatically posted on your timeline.

2. What would you do if a student friended you on Facebook, Instagram, and Snapchat?

   **Suggested Response 2:** You can guarantee this will happen. First, check your school district policy to see if there is an articulated policy about social media. Ask a veteran teacher or an administrator about the school/district culture regarding social media. The general rule is to not accept friend requests from students on your personal pages on social media. You can tell your students up front that you do not accept friend requests from students. You may also want to create a classroom page so that students can be positively engaged in social media with you that models digital citizenship. You can use this classroom page as a communication and teaching tool. Many teachers do not use their full name as their profile name, so students and parents cannot search them.

3. What would you do if a parent reported that their child was being cyberbullied by another child in your class?

   **Suggested Response 3:** In 2014, the Department of Education and Center for Disease Control released the first definition of bullying. Since then, states have crafted laws and policies to address bullying. A website was launched to inform the public of bullying and cyberbullying (www.stopbullying.gov). An updated link to states with laws and policies can be found at https://www.stopbullying.gov/laws/index.html. Additionally, most state laws require that districts create policies on bullying and cyberbullying. You can locate that information in your district policy. Most laws require states to address bullying, retaliation, cyberbullying, and reporting. Check with your district policy, then with an administrator at your school to discuss how to address cyberbullying.

4. What would you do if a friend tagged you in a picture in which an administrator may find offensive to the school community?

   **Suggested Response 4:** Contact your friends and let them know that you need to create a professionally appropriate presence on social media and ask that they not post inappropriate pictures of you or include you in posts that do not meet the "grandmother rule." Additionally, you should remove "tags" on any current photos others tag you in and make sure you set your tag settings to require that you approve any tags prior to having them automatically posted on your timeline. Check your privacy settings regularly.

5. What would you do if you opened up a document on campus and discovered it contained a virus?

    **Suggested Response 5:** Contact your technology center and supervisor immediately. They will direct you based on the specific virus.

## References

Couldry, N. (2012). *Media, society, world: Social theory and digital media practice.* London, England: Polity Press.

ISTE Standards for Educators. (2018). Retrieved from https://www.iste.org/standards/for-educators

Joyce, E. (2010). *6 career-killing Facebook mistakes.* Retrieved from https://www.investopedia.com/financial-edge/0410/6-career-killing-facebook-mistakes.aspx.

Martin, A. J. (2012). *Brainy Quote.* Retrieved from https://www.brainyquote.com/quotes/amy_jo_martin_529757.

Puentedura, R. R. (2014). *SAMR in the classroom: Developing sustainable practice* [Web log post]. Retrieved from http://www.hippasus.com/rrpweblog/archives/2014/11/28/SAMRInTheClassroom_DevelopingSustainablePractice.pdf

Ribble, M. (2014). *Essential elements of digital citizenship.* Retrieved from https://www.iste.org/explore/ArticleDetail?articleid=101

Ribble, M. (2017). *Nine elements.* Retrieved from http://www.digitalcitizenship.net/nine-elements.html

Watanabe-Crockett, L. (2017, February 8). *Teaching global citizenship? Use these 10 essential questions.* Retrieved from https://globaldigitalcitizen.org/teaching-global-digital-citizenship-10-essential-questions?utm_source=hs_email&utm_medium=email&utm_content=42312298&_hsenc=p2ANqtz-80CjAHcfxg3V5W_CtSzM0QAuteuaSzMkfseAZ1c8uWNcmpG9e3ddo27OC67kqQyiIACsh1iZz7degE7036A_HjM_q_DQ&_hsmi=42312298

# MODULE 15

# Using Video to Facilitate Peer Coaching and Problem Solving With Pairs

*Excellence is the gradual result of always striving to do better.*
—Pat Riley

*The one great thing about a continuing collaboration is that they know you. And if you're really lucky, they really believe in you and think that your talent has some unending bounds to it.*
—Mark Ruffalo

A. Brooke Blanks
*Radford University*

## MODULE DESCRIPTION

Field experience provides opportunities for teachers to learn explicitly the art and science of effective collaboration. Peer coaching is a practice that provides teachers with increased support, discussions about teaching and learning, as well as personal and professional growth. This module describes how supervisors can facilitate and mentor peer coaching and collaborative problem solving for teachers, pairs, and teams during their teaching. In this module, videos of collaborative teaching are used throughout to further reflective practice in teaching.

## Theory/Conceptual Framework

The ability to reflect accurately on our own teaching practices is one of the most important elements of professional growth for classroom teachers (Lee, Nugent, & Kunz, 2014). Reflection can be particularly challenging for co-teachers who must explore and understand their use of effective content-based teaching practices as individuals and the implementation of effective co-teaching practices. Teachers benefit from experiences that include explicit instruction and support in reflecting on their own teaching. It is beneficial for pairs and teams to practice providing feedback to one another to develop effective peer coaching and problem solving skills under the guidance of their mentor teachers and supervisors (Joyce & Showers, 2002).

Video can be a powerful tool for teacher reflection and subsequent improvements in practice because it allows teachers to "see" what they are doing in the context of the classroom (Tripp & Rich, 2012). Video lends itself particularly well to collaborative peer coaching for field experiences because it allows teachers to: (a) see the mistakes other teachers make that they fail to recognize in themselves, and (b) notice substantial changes in practice over time as teachers gain more experience in the classroom over the course of a semester or academic year (Tripp & Rich, 2012). Opportunities to collaborate around peer feedback help teachers to explore, deconstruct, and analyze their teaching. And, frankly, most teachers, love to talk about teaching! But, talking alone is not enough. Video as a tool for peer coaching among teachers is most effective when used as part of a carefully constructed field experience that includes guided discussion, explicit expectations, and many opportunities for reflection.

Teachers benefit from tools that guide their understanding of their emerging practice. Co-teachers require significant opportunities for feedback and reflection in all areas of their general teaching practice in the larger context of a co-taught classroom and all the complexity that exists therein. Rubrics, explicit models, ongoing corrective feedback, and opportunities for repeated practice, help pairs to develop their shared "professional vision"; the hard and soft skills they need to understand the technical tools and strategies that effective teachers use to instruct and manage behavior, as well as, the communication and pragmatic skills that effective co-teachers need in order to be successful in inclusive classrooms (Seidel & Stürmer, 2014).

Teachers, especially those who may be novices, are easily overwhelmed by the complex interactions of content, behavior, and context within an entire standard lesson. Experiences using video as a pedagogical tool suggest that carefully articulated rubrics are helpful for self-evaluation and reflective practice. We have had success breaking down reflection and peer coaching activities among the following lesson components when using video with our pairs: lesson introduction and closure, classroom management, assessment, content delivery, and student engagement. Breaking down the complexity of the lesson plan allows teachers to focus on the parts and dig more deeply into instructional practice.

## Specific Questions to Guide Discussion

Video can be a useful tool for targeted coaching around specific challenges that a teacher experiences in the classroom that may be difficult to schedule for an in-person peer coaching session. It is helpful to consider what you want to get out of the video–observation–peer coaching cycle before you record your lesson. Examples may include things like: "Kid X always puts his head down during my full group instruction"; or "I am not really sure that I'm teaching this strategy the right way, I'd love some feedback and ideas on ways I could do it more effectively"; or "I only have half a class period to teach math today because of the pep rally. I don't normally rush through warm-ups but I need to get to the test review because I want feedback on the review activity I'm doing with the class." Thinking about these types of questions before you start recording your video helps you and your coach get the most out of the video sessions. The supervisor can guide a discussion with the "peer coaches" or teachers and ask the following reflective questions before they engage in any videotaping:

1. What is your pedagogical goal with the lesson you are about to record? In other words, what aspects of your teaching practice do you want to focus on when we talk about your video later?

2. Is there anything specific you want me to know about the students or the overall context of the classroom? For example, are there reasons for specific seating arrangements, use of paraeducators, unusual schedule changes, and so on, that will be useful to consider when implementing and reviewing your video? This question is more applicable for someone who is not in a collaborative teaching setting because the coach may not know the context of the classroom.

3. Are you experiencing any specific problems that you would like my help solving? For example, do you want me to focus on the behaviors within a specific small group rather than the entire class during your lesson?

## Productive Practices

1. *Explicitly teach the concept of critical friends and model the practice of giving constructive feedback.* Ask questions like: What went well in your lesson?; What would you do differently if you taught the lesson again?; or What strengths or areas of improvement can you identify from your lesson?
2. *Have teaching pairs annotate and provide feedback together using sample videos before evaluating each other's videos.* Use a tool (see Appendix C for an example) to guide their feedback and reflective comments about their individual teaching and co-teaching behaviors. Model a reflective conversation for your teacher, pair, or team (e.g., in person or on video chat) and request questions from them about the process.
3. *Share your personal experiences!* Asking for and receiving feedback from a colleague can be intimidating. Be prepared to be vulnerable in front of and with your pairs. This opens the door to honest, and sometimes challenging, discussions that can lead to shared understandings of co-teaching and feedback preferences. Your goal is to facilitate safe, productive, communication between the partners.

4. *Ask pairs to use videos to understand their co-teaching practice.* Ask them to create a tally of (a) which models they are using, (b) when are they using each model, and (c) what strengths and weaknesses they see in their implementations.
5. *Support your pairs as they get used to giving and receiving critical feedback.* Monitor the feedback that the pairs or teams give each other. Offer guidance, support, and tools they can use to enhance the quality of their feedback and their reflections. Praise instances of useful feedback. Call attention to errors or omissions of practice that neither person acknowledges in their feedback.

## What Would You Do?

Ask your team or pair the following questions. For suggested responses to questions, see Appendix A.

1. What would you do if you have never video-taped before?

2. What would you do if certain students in your class cannot be recorded?

3. How do you keep students from being distracted by the video (e.g., mugging for the camera)?

4. What would you do to make sure that you can record and store video without using up all of your data?

## Reflective Professional Growth Activities

Consider these ideas or activities to facilitate and foster teacher growth and reflection. Select one or two ideas to help facilitate this reflection process that will help the teacher, pair, or team to understand how to use video to support peer coaching. Remember that the goal of this module is for the "peer coaches" or teachers to eventually be supporting each other independently. As their supervisor, you also know the individuals best so be sure to choose an activity that would be the most effective for them.

### *Idea 1: Reflect on Personal Thoughts About Collaborative Teaching*

Define what each person thinks are important to collaborative teaching, what are essential elements of effective instruction, and what each person considers "constructive feedback." It is also important to help each person describe how they prefer critical feedback to be delivered. The S.H.A.R.E. worksheet (Appendix D) is a tool developed by co-teaching experts, Drs. Wendy Murawski and Lisa Dieker. This tool allows individual members of a pair or teaching team to articulate their hopes, attitudes, responsibilities, and expectations for multiple dimensions of teaching. It facilitates discussions about everything from discipline to grading to classroom logistics—many of the topics around which co-teachers struggle to communicate effectively. Teachers should complete the S.H.A.R.E worksheet individually and create a video of themselves discussing their individual responses. Teachers can review this video and their worksheet to determine if and how they have changed as a result of working together and identifying areas in which they still want to grow.

**Evidence:** Completed S.H.A.R.E. worksheet and notes from the conversation.

## Idea 2: Practice Co-Constructing Feedback and Annotations With Your Pairs by Using a Sample Third Party (Supervisor or Coach) Video and an Observation Tool

To prepare for this idea, first create an account with *Acclaim* (https://www.getacclaim.com/education/). Once you have an account, create a course by pressing the green tab in the right-hand corner that says "+New Course." Once you have created a new course, enter into the course by pressing the blue hyperlink that says the title of the course you created. Then select "+New Folder" and create a folder for the video annotation activity. For example, I created a course called, "Co-Teaching Reflective Videos," then I created a folder entitled, "Sarah & Roger's Reflections." In this folder, upload a selected video to use as a model for the teachers (Sarah & Roger).

The supervisor should select a video (e.g., www.edthena.com, www.teachingchannel.org, www.youtube.com) that shows a content area and grade level that is familiar to both teachers. Provide the pair with a verbal or written overview of what they can expect to see in the lesson, including the goals and objectives for the lesson. Before watching the video, discuss what kinds of evidence they think would demonstrate effective teaching. Watch the video together and have each person complete an observation protocol (see Appendix E) in which they take guided notes on what they have observed. Then, have the teachers upload their annotations on the video in *Acclaim*. To annotate the video each teacher should click on the link to the video, and then type in their responses in the textbox below the video. Be sure that each teacher submits their own annotation. Discuss the annotations and practice how each person should deliver the feedback.

**Evidence:** Annotated sample video and completed observation protocol.

## Idea 3: Model Receiving Feedback

To prepare for this idea, each pair or team needs to videotape a lesson of their collaborative teaching. Upload your video into *Acclaim* (see directions under Idea 2). Individually annotate the video with your feedback (use Appendix E, from the *Co-Teaching Core Competencies Observation Checklist* sections: *Look for Items* and *Listen for Items*). Be sure to remind your teaching pair or team to be open about the challenges and benefits of critical self-analysis, reflection, and processing feedback.

To prepare for the meeting with the pair or team, remind teachers to read over the submitted annotations. Engage in frank discussions about how you each interpreted the video tape: What do you agree with?; What do you disagree with?; What was difficult to accept?;

and What did you learn as a result of going through the process? Ask the teachers to discuss what annotations they would make, how they would word the feedback, and ask them to add these to the coach's video.

**Evidence:** Annotated pair or team video.

## *Idea 4: Identify a Difficult Co-Teaching Model for Repeated Practice and Reflection*

Ask the teacher, pair, or team to select a target co-teaching skill they want to focus on for improvement over a specific period of time. This should be an area of their practice in which they feel particularly challenged or even unsuccessful. For example, Pair A notices after several videos that they are stuck "tag teaming" rather than team teaching during whole group instruction. They are familiar with examples of effective team teaching from reading about it and observing exemplars, either in person or in video examples of experienced teachers. They co-plan their lessons with the intention of team teaching but realize after watching several videos that as a pair, their instructional delivery is not cohesive, and they are not using the model effectively. They decide to spend one month on an intensive self-study to problem-solve and improve their specific co-teaching practice. Encourage them to use a rubric to help evaluate the effectiveness of targeted components (see Appendix B).

**Evidence:** Annotated video conversations documenting growth in the implementation of the co-teaching model over time.

## *Idea 5: Practice With Rubrics*

The five rubrics in Appendix B are aligned with five critical components of a lesson. Ask the teachers to create five videos that demonstrate the target areas of each rubric. Ask the teacher or pair to use the rubrics separately to annotate the videos, make reflective statements, and provide feedback to each other. When these are completed, meet with them to discuss their annotations. Ask them to write individual reflections about what they learned from: (a) watching themselves and (b) reading the feedback their partner provided. When the teacher(s) have completed this process, review the materials and meet with them to give them feedback on their notes, suggestions, and verbal feedback on their co-teaching practices.

**Evidence:** Annotated videos, reflective writing, and discussion notes.

## *Idea 6: Professional Learning Community Video-Enhanced Book Study*

Book studies can be effective tools for building teacher expertise. An added benefit is that many people are familiar with book clubs around shared interests. Two books, *Difficult Conversations: How to Discuss What Matters Most* (Stone, Patton, & Heen, 2010) and *Crucial Conversations: Tools for Talking When the Stakes are High* (Patterson, Grenny, McMillan, & Switzler, 2012) are particularly useful for helping teachers develop "critical friendships."

Teachers benefit from using structured book studies as a tool for professional growth. Stone et al. (2010) provide practical tools for resolving conflicts. Provide the pairs with a structure for a Professional learning community (PLC) book study implementation. Tools for structuring book studies are provided in the *Resources* section of this module. As the semester progresses, ask the pairs to record their "difficult conversations" and to reflect on which strategies, from the book study, they see themselves using and which ones may be useful in subsequent conversations. Ask questions to scaffold their attention and thinking. Examples of useful questions are included in the next section.

**Evidence:** Book study materials and annotated video conversations.

## Follow-Up, Monitoring, and Goal Setting

Complete the follow-up questions for the selected reflective professional growth activity.

### Idea 1: S.H.A.R.E. Responsibility Video Conversations

Throughout the semester, conflicts and challenges that emerge in the classroom will likely be in the areas addressed by the S.H.A.R.E. worksheet (Appendix D). When this happens, ask pairs or teams to video themselves revisiting the worksheet to identify the specific area in which they are having difficulty. Questions to ask the pairs or teams to address may include:

- What are you doing or what is your partner doing that is problematic?
- Can you explain why it is problematic in terms of your students' learning or behavioral outcomes? Is this an area in which you can be flexible? Why or why not?
- Is this difference significant enough to be addressed or is it a minor situation that you can learn to live with and from which you can move forward?
- If you decide you want to change the situation because it is having a negative impact on your students, what do you need in terms of resources, ideas, and support to make that change happen?

### Idea 2: Practice Co-Constructing Feedback and Annotations

Share the *Peer Observation Protocol* (Appendix C). Ask each partner to use the *Peer Observation Protocol* while they are watching the video to take notes that will become the basis for their annotations. Ask the following questions:

- What parts did you annotate? Why?
- What did you find useful about using the *Peer Observation Protocol?*
- Were you comfortable having your peer observe your teaching? Uncomfortable?
- What Focus Question did you identify for your observer?
- Were you surprised about any observations and data that your observer shared with you?
- If you were to create your own observation protocol, would you include additional areas? Why?
- Are you interested in using the *Peer Observation Protocol* again with your team member?

Ask them to co-construct their own individualized protocol that they would like to use with each other in their own co-teaching practice.

## Idea 3: Be Explicit About Giving and Receiving Feedback

- How do you provide open dialogue when you give feedback? Please provide an example.
- How do you provide open dialogue when you receive feedback? Please provide an example.
- What do you believe is the "ideal" process for providing feedback?
- How did you use the rubrics when you provided feedback?

## Idea 4: Identify a Difficult Co-Teaching Model for Repeated Practice and Reflection

Once pairs or teams have identified a target co-teaching model to focus on intensely, provide resources they can use to learn more about the implementation. Articles and links to video exemplars are particularly helpful. Watch the videos and read the teachers' feedback to one another and their reflective comments. Share Murawski and Lochner's (2011) *Co-Teaching Core Competencies Observation Checklist* (Appendix E) and ask them to use it to evaluate their co-teaching strengths and needs. Each partner should complete their own checklist and then meet with the coach to discuss. During the discussion, ask guiding questions to encourage their emerging understanding of what they are doing well and where they continue to struggle. Questions may include:

- As a pair or team, what descriptors on the *Co-Teaching Competency Checklist* show little evidence and need to be strengthened?
- As a pair or team, what descriptors on the *Co-Teaching Competency Checklist* show substantial evidence?
- What do you see yourself doing in the video that is consistent with what we know is an effective use of this skill?
- I see you doing X here, what result were you expecting?
- What do you understand about the result as it relates to your practice?
- What questions do you have about where to go next?

## Idea 5: Talk About Rubrics

- What was useful about the five assigned rubrics?
- What did you learn when you watched one of your rubric videos?
- What changes will you make in future lessons from the feedback that was given to you?
- What was challenging about the five assigned rubrics?
- Describe how you would use a rubric to teach? To assess?
- Are all rubrics good rubrics? Why or why not?
- How do you provide feedback to support the use of rubrics?

## Idea 6: Professional Learning Community Video-Enhanced Book Study

Depending on the length of your book study, the following recommendations can be implemented throughout or once the book study is complete. The goal is to help pairs apply the tools from the book to work on resolving their differences rather than relying on help from the supervisor for the duration of the partnership. Initially, it can be helpful to meet with teachers individually to plan, brainstorm, or practice an upcoming conversation but we always want to push the teacher to initiate the conversations themselves. When teachers, pairs, or teams come to you for advice or help, the following questions may help guide your conversations:

- Can you please describe the big ideas from our book study that are most significant for you?
- Which strategies from the book study can you see yourself using to resolve conflicts?
- Can you show me some examples in the videos of your conversations with your partner?
- What do you recognize as strengths that you bring to your relationship?
- What do you recognize as needs in your relationship?
- What types of "difficult conversations" are most challenging for you?
- What does it mean to develop a "critical friendship" with a team member?
- When you watch your videos of these conversations, what tools are you using effectively and what would you like to continue to work on?

Resources grounded in the recommended books are widely available online for free and may be useful as your pairs begin to tackle more challenging conversations.

# Resources

## *Articles*

### Teaching With Rubrics: The Good, the Bad, and the Ugly

This article gives a brief overview of the structure and purposes of rubrics; reviews the benefits of using rubrics as both teaching and grading tools; warns against approaches that limit the effectiveness of rubrics; and urges instructors to take simple steps toward ensuring the validity, reliability, and fairness of their rubrics. Tips for using rubrics with undergraduate and graduate students are also included.

Andrade, H. G. (2005). Teaching with rubrics: The good, the bad, and the ugly. *College Teaching, 53*(1), 27–31.

### Tips and Strategies for Co-Teaching at the Secondary Level

This article begins with a case study and further identifies the different roles of individuals within the school and their impacts on co-teaching. The article gives insight into planning, instruction, and assessment and how to make these areas the most effective during co-teaching.

Murawski, W. W., & Dieker, L. A. (2004). Tips and strategies for co-teaching at the secondary level. *Teaching Exceptional Children, 36*(5), 52–58.

## Books

### How to Create and Use Rubrics for Formative Assessment and Grading

In this comprehensive guide, author Susan M. Brookhart identifies two essential components of effective rubrics: (a) criteria that relate to the learning (not the "tasks") that students are being asked to demonstrate and (b) clear descriptions of performance across a continuum of quality.

She outlines the difference between various kinds of rubrics (for example, general versus task-specific, and analytic versus holistic), explains when using each type of rubric is appropriate, and highlights examples from all grade levels and assorted content areas.

Brookhart, S. M. (2013). *How to create and use rubrics for formative assessment and grading.* Alexandria, VA: ASCD.

### Crucial Conversations

This book addresses how to communicate best when it matters most. *Crucial Conversations* gives you the tools you need to step up to life's most difficult and important conversations, say what's on your mind, and achieve the positive resolutions you want.

Patterson, K., Grenny, J., McMillan, R., & Switzler, A. (2012). *Crucial conversations: Tools for talking when stakes are high: 2nd edition.* New York, NY: McGraw-Hill.

Although this publisher website requires users to register, registration is free and provides access to many resources that are useful during a book study of *Crucial Conversations: Tools for Talking When the Stakes are High* (Patterson, Grenny, McMillan, & Switzler, 2012).

VitalSmarts. (2018). *Crucial conversations book.* Retrieved from https://www.vitalsmarts.com/resource/crucial-conversations-book/

### Difficult Conversations

This book provides a step-by-step approach to having those tough conversations with less stress and more success. You'll learn how to decipher the underlying structure of every difficult conversation, start a conversation without defensiveness, listen for the meaning of what is not said, stay balanced in the face of attacks and accusations, and move from emotion to productive problem solving.

Stone, D., Patton, B., & Heen, S. (2010). *Difficult conversations: How to discuss what matters most.* New York, NY: Penguin.

This PDF is available for free online as a resource from the publisher. It is a useful tool for a book study of *Difficult Conversations: How to Discuss What Matters Most* (Stone, Patton, & Heen, 2010, p. 233).

https://www.mainequalitycounts.org/image_upload/Difficult_Conversation_checklist.pdf

### Professional Learning Community Book Study Guide and Tools

This PDF provides explicit guidelines and specific suggestions for structuring an effective book study for teachers.

Florida Department of Education. (n.d.). *PLC book study guide.* Retrieved from http://www.broward.k12.fl.us/talentdevelopment/news/plc/PLC-Book-Study-Guidelines.pdf

## Video Annotation Tools

### Edthena

Contains a repository of sample videos; allows teachers to upload and annotate their own videos; allows coaches to structure guided learning activities and add materials related to videos.

R3 Collaboratives. (2018). *Edthena.* Retrieved from www.edthena.com

### IRISConnect

Allows teachers to upload and reflect on their own videos.

Iris Connect USA. (2018). *Improving teaching and learning with video.* Retrieved from http://www.iris-connect.com

### PD In Focus

Contains an extensive library of videos on a variety of instructional practices; provides PD assignments that allow coaches to structure user learning experiences; does not allow teachers to upload and annotate their own videos.

ASCD. (2018). *PD in focus.* Retrieved from http://pdinfocus.ascd.org

### Acclaim

Allows teachers to record, upload, and annotate videos.

Acclaim. (n.d.). *The #1 tool for video assignments.* Retrieved from https://www.getacclaim.com/education/

## Key Terms and Definitions

**Critical friend:** A trusted person who asks provocative questions, provides data to be examined through another lens, and offers critiques of a person's work as a friend. A critical friend takes the time to fully understand the context of the work presented and the outcomes that the person or group is working toward. The friend is an advocate for the success of that work (Costa & Kallick, 1993).

**Peer coaching:** A collaborative process in which two or more professionals work together to provide helpful feedback to one another on their teaching practices (Joyce & Showers, 2002).

**Professional learning community (PLC):** An ongoing process in which educators work collaboratively in recurring cycles of collective inquiry and action research to achieve better results for the students they serve. Professional learning communities operate under the assumption that the key to improved learning for students is continuous job-embedded learning for educators (Dufour & Eaker, 2009).

**Reflection:** The ability to observe and think critically about the events and practices that occurred in the classroom during an episode of teaching.

**Video annotation tools:** Software that allows viewers to link or embed notes to specific timestamps within a video.

# Appendix A

## *What Would You Do? Suggested Responses*

1. What would you do if you have never video-taped before?

   **Suggested Response 1:** If you have never video-taped before, become familiar with Edthena and Acclaim. Record yourself teaching using any devices that your students are likely to use. Upload your video to the annotation software you are using and practice all of the tools you will ask your students to use.

2. What would you do if certain students in your class cannot be recorded?

   **Suggested Response 2:** Focus the camera on the teacher exclusively and not the students or set up the camera to keep students who cannot be videoed out of the frame.

3. How do you keep students from being distracted by the video (e.g., mugging for the camera)?

   **Suggested Response 3:** Record early and often, even if you immediately delete most of the video. This helps the students to get used to being recorded and video-taping no longer becomes a distraction.

4. What would you do to make sure that you can record and store video without using up all of your data?

   **Suggested Response 4:** Use local wifi when recording with a cell phone or iPad rather than using cell phone data plans. Services like Edthena often have apps that you can put onto devices that allow direct-to-cloud secure storage so that videos are never actually stored on devices.

# Appendix B

## Video Assignment Rubrics

(Blanks, Daniel, & Minarik, 2015)

**Reflection Rubric for Video Submission:** *Lesson Introduction and Lesson Closure*

**Directions:**
1. Create a short video segment (no more than 15 minutes) that addresses lesson introduction and closure. Before you submit:
   a. Review your video and rate yourself using the sections of the rubric below.
   b. On the video, provide/embed *at least* four comments using the comment tools (questions, suggestions, strengths, and/or notes).
2. Although you will not be submitting video of the entire lesson, please provide a complete lesson plan so your coach has the context for the video submission.
3. Reflectively answer these questions about your co-taught lesson:
   a. In what ways did the lesson introduction affect the success of your complete lesson?
   b. How did the closure help cement the students' learning?

| Lesson Introduction Rubric | | | | | |
|---|---|---|---|---|---|
| **0** | **1** | **2** | **3** | **Comments** | |
| *The teacher...* | | | | | |
| delivered the lesson **without** establishing a purpose or creating interest. | **attempted** to establish a purpose and create interest with poor results. | established a **clear** purpose and created interest in what was to come by **linking to prior knowledge.** | *and...* **assessed prior knowledge.** | | |

| Lesson Closure Rubric | | | | | |
|---|---|---|---|---|---|
| **0** | **1** | **2** | **3** | **Comments** | |
| *The teacher...* | | | | | |
| **ended lesson abruptly** (ran out of time); **transitioned** to the next class or activity. | **reviewed big ideas/concepts** in lesson; **asked students if they had questions; assigned homework.** | **involved students in summarizing** key concepts/ideas in the lesson; **linked learning** to what was previously taught; **previewed** future learning. | *and...* **connected what was learned to larger ideas/concepts.** | | |

**Reflection Rubric for Video Submission:** *Classroom Management*

**Directions:**
1. Review the rubric below. Create a short video segment (~10 minutes) that addresses as many aspects of classroom management as you can capture (you might be editing a longer segment to just show this). Before you submit:
   a. Review your video and rate yourself using the rubric below (some may be rated as N/A).
   b. On the video, provide/embed *at least* five comments using the comment tools (questions, suggestions, strengths, and/or notes).
2. Although you will not be submitting video of the entire lesson, please provide a complete lesson plan so your coach has the context for the video submission.
3. Reflectively answer these questions based on your co-taught classroom:
   a. What worked well?
   b. What could have been better?
   c. What will you do differently next time?

| Classroom Management Rubric | | | | | |
|---|---|---|---|---|---|
| **Elements of the Rubric** | **0** | **1** | **2** | **3** | **Comments** |
| | *The teacher...* | | | | |
| **Behavioral and Academic Expectations** | created a classroom environment **primarily to control** student behavior; provided **no expectations** for student work and behavior. | created a classroom environment which is **teacher-directed;** reviewed behavioral **or** academic expectations established previously by the cooperating teacher. | **shared responsibility with students** for maintaining a respectful classroom environment; articulated explicit behavioral **and** academic expectations for a safe, positive learning environment. | **and...** encouraged **students and colleagues** to express expectations for openness, respect, and support; communicated high expectations by **expressing confidence** in students' abilities. | |
| **Student Rapport** | appeared to have **little to no positive relationships** with students; appeared **disinterested in and/or insensitive** to students' needs and interests; was **rude, negative, and/or disrespectful** toward students. | appeared to have a **formal relationship** with students; **seldom** appeared to take students' needs and interests into account; used a **respectful tone and mannerisms** toward students. | appeared to have **rapport with and respect for** the students; was **courteous and respectful** of students' needs and interests; modeled respect, **promoting positive peer relationships.** | **and...** appeared to **foster respectful relationships** among all members of the learning community; **practiced active listening** and encouraged students to independently resolve issues; created classroom interactions **showing appreciation and respect for** diverse cultures, differing perspectives, life experiences, values, and norms. | |

| Elements of the Rubric | Classroom Management Rubric (continued) | | | | Comments |
|---|---|---|---|---|---|
| | 0 | 1 | 2 | 3 | |
| | The teacher... | | | | |
| Rules, Routines, and Feedback | provided **no rules or routines** so the classroom was chaotic and disorganized; **permitted** distractions and misbehaviors to continue; expected or **waited for other adults** to assist with handling discipline problems. | provided **unclear** rules and/or routines or enforced them **inconsistently;** responded **inconsistently** to distractions and misbehaviors; **over-relied** on the use of punitive or negative discipline techniques. | provided **clear** rules and routines and enforced them **consistently;** used a **variety of non-punitive strategies** to address student behavior in a timely manner (e.g., nonverbal cues, proximity, seating); **logically applied appropriate consequences** for student behavior. | *and...* worked with students to **establish rules/routines** when appropriate; demonstrated an understanding of how **background and culture** influences behavior; offered **specific positive feedback, correction, and encouragement** throughout lesson. | |
| Directions | did not provide **any** directions. | provided **unclear directions;** released students to the next activity **before directions were given.** | provided **clear specific directions;** released students to the next activity **after directions were given.** | *and...* provided **directions in multiple formats** (e.g., oral, written); **checked in with students** to ensure that directions were understood. | |
| Awareness of Learning Environment | appeared **unaware** of students' behaviors and problems; was **unprepared** with materials; appeared **disorganized** throughout the lesson. | was aware of and **addressed** students' misbehaviors and problems **inconsistently;** was **underprepared.** | **monitored** the class for misbehavior/problems and **addressed** them quickly and positively; organized time **and** materials effectively. | *and...* demonstrated **With-it-ness** to address problems; actively **involved students** in managing the learning environment and making full use of instructional time. | |

**Reflection Rubric for Video Submission:** *Assessment*

**Directions:**
1. Create a short video segment (no more than 10 minutes) that addresses both formative and summative assessment. Before you submit:
   a. Review your video and rate yourself using the section of the rubric below.
   b. On the video, provide/embed *at least* three comments using the comment tools (questions, suggestions, strengths, and/or notes).
2. Although you will not be submitting video of the entire lesson, please share a complete lesson plan so your coach has the context for the video submission.
3. Reflectively answer this question based on your co-taught lesson: What did you learn from the assessment(s) that will guide your teaching the next time you meet with these students?

| Assessment Rubric | | | | | |
|---|---|---|---|---|---|
| **Elements of the Rubric** | **0** *The teacher...* | **1** | **2** | **3** | **Comments** |
| **Multiple Assessments** | taught the lesson **without providing opportunity** for students to express what they knew or are able to do; assessed **ALL** students **identically**, with no evidence of considering developmental needs, cultural, linguistic, social exceptionality, and/or background knowledge of students. | taught the lesson with **inconsistent** or **infrequent** opportunities to express what they knew **or** only **at the end of the lesson;** used only **one type** (either formative or summative) of assessment; used varying forms of assessments to accommodate *some* special needs of learners. | provided **consistent formal and informal** opportunities for students to demonstrate understanding; used **both formative and summative** forms of assessment; **modified classroom assessments and testing conditions** to accommodate learning differences (e.g., disabilities, gifts and talents). | *and...* utilized **multiple assessment** methods/modes to **scaffold** individual learner development and to offer appropriate levels of challenge to individual learners; used assessment tools and methods that encouraged students to apply **critical thinking and problem-solving skills;** ensured that **each individual learner** had a variety of opportunities to **demonstrate his or her learning.** | |
| **Data-Driven Instruction** | **ignored evidence** that adjustments needed to be made to the lesson to facilitate student learning. | responded to formative assessment **at times,** but at other times overlooked need for adjustment to facilitate student learning. | modified instruction as needed to facilitate student learning **throughout** the lesson based on formative assessment data. | *and...* adjusted instruction to **individual students' needs** (e.g., noticed Hans was unclear so paired with Mai to clarify). | |

| Assessment Rubric (continued) | | | | | |
|---|---|---|---|---|---|
| **Elements of the Rubric** | **0** | **1** | **2** | **3** | **Comments** |
| | *The teacher...* | | | | |
| **Feedback to Guide and Engage** | provided **very little** feedback; used primarily assessments that did not require interaction from or amongst students during the lesson (e.g., homework assignment, upcoming summative test). | provided feedback to students but **did not check that feedback was helpful** or understood, or the feedback provided may have been unclear; engaged students by **encouraging them to ask questions occasionally.** | provided students with **immediate and explicit** feedback about their work that guided them nearer to mastering the learning objectives associated with the lesson; engaged students **through dialogue frequently**; engaged students by **examining examples of quality work** that corresponded with assessments associated with this lesson. | *and...* engaged students in self and peer assessment in order to learn in a manner that developed students' metacognitive skills, guiding them to identify specific aspects of the performance that were effective as well as areas for improvement. | |

**Reflection Rubric for Video Submission:** *Content Delivery*

**Directions:**

1. Create a short video segment (~10 minutes) that addresses content delivery. Before you submit:
    a. Review your video and rate yourself using the section of the rubric below.
    b. On the video, provide/embed *at least* three comments using the comment tools (questions, suggestions, strengths, and/or notes).
2. Although you will not be submitting video of the entire lesson, please provide a complete lesson plan so your peer coach has the context for the video submission.
3. Reflectively answer this question about your co-taught lesson: Tell me three things you learned about yourself/your teaching when reviewing this video.

| Content Delivery Rubric | | | | | |
|---|---|---|---|---|---|
| **Elements of the Rubric** | **0** | **1** | **2** | **3** | **Comments** |
| | *The teacher...* | | | | |
| **Student Strengths and Needs** | ignored specific learner needs in the presentation of content. | presented main ideas and concepts to **meet the needs of one group** (teaching to the middle). | clearly and effectively presented main ideas and concepts using strategies to **meet diverse students' strengths and needs**. | *and...* used a variety of strategies to make concepts clear and engage students in content by **connecting it to interests, background knowledge, and real-world application.** | |

## Content Delivery Rubric (continued)

| Elements of the Rubric | 0<br>The teacher... | 1 | 2 | 3 | Comments |
|---|---|---|---|---|---|
| Content Representation | **represented content one way**, or the representations and explanations are **not appropriate** to the content. | provided **limited representations or explanations** of the key concepts in the content standards. | provided **multiple representations and explanations** of key concepts in the content standards being covered. Guided learners along a learning progression, and **encouraged learners to understand, questions, and/or analyze** ideas. | *and...* used representations and explanations reflective of learners' **cultures, linguistic backgrounds, interests, prior knowledge, and skill levels**. | |
| Content Area Knowledge | explained content **inaccurately;** made **no** attempt to link to important content or essential skills. | explained content accurately, but either was **too verbose or lacked examples/elaboration;** made **vague or superficial** links to important content and essential skills. | explained content **accurately** and clearly; made **clear** links to important content and essential skills. | *and...* demonstrated a **deep and flexible command of content area** knowledge; provided content information **beyond the Standards of Learning (SOL)** to enhance and extend student knowledge; extended students' understanding of the content by **going beyond SOL**. | |
| Instructional Role | assumed **only one instructional role** when **other approaches would have enhanced** content delivery. | assumed **more than one** instructional role but chose roles that were **not always appropriate** to the content or purposes of instruction. | **varied teacher role** in the instructional process, acting as instructor, facilitator, coach, and/or learner **in response to the content and purposes of instruction.** | *and...* served as an **advocate for learning** by consciously selecting or changing instructional roles to best meet the particular needs of individual and groups of learners. | |

**Reflection Rubric for Video Submission:** *Student Engagement*

**Directions:**
1. Create a short video segment (no more than 15 minutes) that addresses student engagement. Before you submit:
   a. Review your video and rate yourself using the sections of the rubric below.
   b. On the video, provide/embed *at least* five comments using the comment tools (questions, suggestions, strengths, and/or notes).
2. Please provide a complete lesson plan so your coach has the context for the video submission.
3. Reflectively answer these questions about your co-taught lesson:
   a. In what ways did the lesson go as you expected?
   b. In what ways were your expectations for the lesson not met?

| Student Engagement Rubric | | | | | |
|---|---|---|---|---|---|
| **Elements of the Rubric** | **0** | **1** | **2** | **3** | **Comments** |
| | *The teacher...* | | | | |
| **Student Interaction** | **did not facilitate** individual (guided practice) or group learning opportunities, when appropriate. | **ineffectively facilitated** individual **or** group learning opportunities (e.g., activities were disorganized; not enough scaffolding provided). | **effectively facilitated** individual **and** group learning opportunities. (e.g., students were engaged and had opportunities to practice concepts on their own and/or in groups). | *and...* provided multiple opportunities for **student-to-student interactions;** assigned **student roles** and responsibilities for group work; **interacted with students** during group tasks. | |
| **Activities & Resources** | disregarded students' **lack of engagement** in the lesson. | **addressed students who appeared disengaged but** did not adjust activities/ instruction. | **promoted student engagement** through whole group, small group, and/or individual activities, adjusting the lesson as needed. | *and...* provided **options and resources** to engage individual students in the lesson. | |
| **Instructional Time** | called on **few to no** individuals. | called **only** on individuals who drew attention to themselves (e.g., raising hands, calling out) and **did not use appropriate wait time**. | called on a **variety of individuals** and **often allowed wait time** for students to process thoughts. | *and...* **balanced instructional time** spent on questioning and discussion with other lesson activities (e.g., knew when to transition from student to student as well as into other planned activities); **strategically used wait time** when calling on individuals. | |

# Appendix C

## *Peer Observation Tool*

(based on Grimm, Kaufman & Doty, 2014)

**Before the Observation**
1. Discuss the context of the lesson and review the lesson plan.
2. Ask clarifying questions to ensure everyone understands the purpose and format for the observation.
3. Discuss what data will be collected and how it will be recorded.
4. Identify a *Focus Question* based on what the teacher is interested in learning about or problems the teacher is trying to solve in the classroom.
   Examples:
   - What is happening at the back table during full group instruction?
   - Am I implementing Check In/Check Out correctly?
   - Are my think-alouds effective? If not, how can I improve them?

**After the Observation**
1. Discuss overall impressions of the teaching and learning that were observed.
2. Describe specifically what the observer saw and heard during the observation from teacher(s) and students.
3. Ask clarifying questions about the instruction or the students to ensure the observer fully understands the context.
4. Discuss the data that were collected. Do these data answer the *Focus Question*?
5. Reflect on what has been learned through the data.
6. Brainstorm how instruction can be modified based on these data and identify resources needed to make these modifications.
7. Identify next steps and plan for follow-up.

# Appendix D

## SHARE Worksheet

(Murawski, 2003)

**S.H.A.R.E.**

**S**haring **H**opes, **A**ttitudes, **R**esponsibilities, and **E**xpectations

*Directions:* Take a few minutes to individually complete this worksheet. Be honest in your responses. After completing it individually, share the responses with your co-teaching partner by taking turns reading the responses. Do not use this time to comment on your partner's responses—merely read. After reading through the responses, take a moment or two to jot down any thoughts you have regarding what your partner has said. Then, come back together and begin to share reactions to the responses. Your goal is to either (a) Agree, (b) Compromise, or (c) Agree to Disagree.

1. Right now, the main *hope* I have regarding this co-teaching situation is:

2. My *attitude*/philosophy regarding teaching students with disabilities in a general education classroom is:

3. I would like to have the following *responsibilities* in a co-taught classroom:

4. I would like my co-teacher to have the following *responsibilities*:

5. I have the following *expectations* in a classroom:
   a. regarding discipline...
   b. regarding classwork...
   c. regarding materials...
   d. regarding homework...
   e. regarding planning...
   f. regarding modifications for individual students...
   g. regarding grading...
   h. regarding noise level...
   i. regarding cooperative learning...
   j. regarding giving/receiving feedback...
   k. other important expectations I have...

Also published in: Murawski, W. W., & Dieker, L. A. (2004). Tips and strategies for co-teaching at the secondary level. *Teaching Exceptional Children, 36*(5), 52–58.

# Appendix E

## *Co-Teaching Core Competencies Observation Checklist*
(Murawski & Lochner, 2011)

General Educator: _____ Special Service Provider: _____ Grade: _____
Observer: _____ Date/Time: _____

| | LOOK FOR ITEMS | ✓ 0 – Didn't See It<br>✓ 1 – Saw an Attempt<br>✓ 2- Saw It<br>✓ 3 – Saw It Done Well | | | | |
|---|---|---|---|---|---|---|
| | | 0 | 1 | 2 | 3 | DNOT |
| 4.5 Two or more professionals working together in the same physical space. | 0 = Only one adult; two adults not communicating at all; class always divided into two rooms<br>1 = Two adults in same room but very little communication or collaborative work<br>2 = Two adults in same room; both engaged in class and each other (even if not perfectly)<br>3 = Two adults collaborating together well in the same room | | | | | |
| 9.5 Class environment demonstrates parity and collaboration (both names on board, sharing materials, and space). | 0 = No demonstration of parity/collaboration; room appears to belong to one teacher only<br>1 = Some attempt at parity; both adults share a few materials and general space<br>2 = Parity exists; adults share classroom materials<br>3 = Clear parity; both names on board/report card; two desks or shared space; obvious feeling from teachers that it is "our room" | | | | | |
| 11.6 Both teachers begin and end class together and remain in the room the entire time. | 0 = One adult is absent or late; adults may leave room for times not related to this class<br>1 = One adult may be late or leave early or may leave for brief time<br>2 = One adult may be late or leave early but for remaining time, they work together<br>3 = Both adults begin and end together, and are with students the entire time<br>Note: if adults have planned to use a regrouping approach (e.g., "parallel") and one adult takes a group of students out of the room (e.g., to the library), that is perfectly acceptable | | | | | |
| 8.6 During instruction, both teachers assist students with and without disabilities. | 0 = Adults are not helping students or are only helping "their own" students<br>1 = There is some helping of various students but at least one adult primarily stays with a few of "their own"<br>2 = Both adults are willing to help all students but students seem to have one adult they prefer to work with<br>3 = It is clear that both adults are willing to help all students & that students are used to this | | | | | |
| 9.6 The class moves smoothly with evidence of co-planning and communication between co-teachers. | 0 = Little to no prior planning is evident<br>1 = All planning appears to have been done by one adult<br>2 = Minimal planning is evident; most appears to be done by one adult<br>3 = It is clear that both adults are comfortable with the lesson and know what is supposed to happen | | | | | |
| 8.8 Class instruction and activities proactively promote multiple modes of representation, engagement and expression (Universal Design for Learning-UDL) | 0 = There is no evidence of universal design; all students are expected to do the same thing<br>1 = There is minimal evidence of universal design; limited opportunities for choice in how students learn, engage & show what they've learned<br>2 = There is some evidence of universal design; some opportunities for choice in how students learn, engage & show what they've learned<br>3 = The class was universally designed; opportunities for choice in how students learn, engage & show what they've learned were well selected | | | | | |

*Note:* DNOT = Did Not Observe Teacher(s)

| | | 0 | 1 | 2 | 3 | DNOT |
|---|---|---|---|---|---|---|
| 3.7 Differentiated content and strategies, based on formative assessment are used to meet the range of learning needs. | 0 = There is no evidence of differentiation of instruction in the classroom<br>1 = There is minimal differentiation; most differentiation appears to be focused on groups rather than individuals<br>2 = Some differentiation is evident for individuals and/or groups<br>3 = It is clear that adults consider individual student needs and regular use of differentiation is evident | | | | | |
| 8.13 Technology (to include Assistive Technology) is used to enhance accessibility and learning. | 0 = There is no evidence of technology use<br>1 = Limited use of technology<br>2 = Technology provides students with access and is used intermittently or sporadically<br>3 = Multiple technologies are utilized to make materials and content accessible and are used regularly | | | | | |
| 5.7 A variety of instructional approaches (5 co-teaching approaches) are used, include regrouping students. | 0 = Students remain in large class setting and adults use One Teach-One Support with one adult primarily in lead<br>1 = Adults rely solely on One Teach/One Support or Team<br>2 = Adults regroup students (using Alternative, Parallel, or Station) at least once<br>3 = Adults use more than one of the 5 approaches (Friend & Cook's One Teach/One Support, Team, Parallel, Station & Alternative); at least one of the approaches involves regrouping students<br>* note – if teachers have been observed using other approaches in the past and only one approach is observed today (e.g., Stations), it is acceptable to recall previous observations and give a 2 for using a variety of approaches as adults have demonstrated competency | | | | | |
| 2.7 Both teachers engage in appropriate behavior management strategies as needed and are consistent in their approach to behavior management. | 0 = There is no obvious plan for behavior management, nor do adults appear to communicate about how they are approaching class management; possibly inappropriate class management<br>1 = Very little classroom management; mainly conducted by one teacher<br>2 = Behavior management strategies are utilized but there is very little clear evidence of how adults have communicated about their use<br>3 = It is evident that adults have discussed how they will approach classroom/behavior management and adults are consistent in their approach | | | | | |
| 11.3 It is difficult to tell the specialist from the general educator. | 0 = Observer could easily determine who was the general/specialist by their language/roles/ lack of parity<br>1 = Teachers kept traditional roles in the classroom but shared or switched roles once or twice<br>2 = Teachers worked at having parity in the class and shared most roles and responsibilities<br>3 = Adults shared the roles and responsibilities in the classroom and observer would not be able to tell who was the general/specialist | | | | | |
| 1.6 It is difficult to tell students with special needs from the general education students. | 0 = Observer could easily determine who were the general education or students with special needs by their lack of integration (e.g., students at back or separated from class)<br>1 = There was some inclusion of most students in most activities<br>2 = There was a clear attempt at inclusion of all students for most activities<br>3 = All students were included and integrated seamlessly into all activities, even when adaptations were needed | | | | | |
| Notes: | | **Look Fors Total:** | | | | |

| CO-TEACHING CHECKLIST: LISTEN FORs ||||||| 
| LISTEN FOR ITEMS || ✓ 0 - Didn't Hear It<br>✓ 1 - Heard it somewhat<br>✓ 2 - Heard it<br>✓ 3 - Heard it often |||||
| | | 0 | 1 | 2 | 3 | DNOT |
|---|---|---|---|---|---|---|
| 9.10 Co-Teachers use language ("we"; "our") that demonstrates true collaboration and shared responsibility | 0 = Adults do not communicate with one another.<br>1 = Adults use "I" language frequently (e.g., "I want you to…" or "In my class…"), lacking parity.<br>2 = Adults attempt to use "we" language and include each other, but it is clear that one adult is more used to "ruling" the class.<br>3 = Adults clearly use "we" language (e.g., "We would like you to…"), showing that they both share the responsibility and students know they are equally in charge. | | | | | |
| 5.9 Communication (both verbal and non-verbal) between co-teachers is clear and positive | 0 = Little to no communication is evident<br>1 = Communication is minimal, directive, or negative<br>2 = Limited communication but it is positive in nature<br>3 = Both adults communicate regularly as class progresses & are respectful and positive | | | | | |
| 1.8 Co-Teachers phrase questions and statements so that it is obvious that all students in the class are included | 0 = Class is very teacher-directed and little involvement by students<br>1 = Questions/statements are general and not inclusive of all students<br>2 = Most statements/questions are phrased to encourage participation from a variety of students.<br>3 = A clear attempt is made by both adults to engage all students through the use of a variety of types of questions and statements. | | | | | |
| 1.9 Students' conversations evidence a sense of community including peers with disabilities and from diverse backgrounds | 0 = Students do not talk to one another ever during class<br>1 = Specific students appear to be excluded from the majority of student interactions.<br>2 = Most students appear to be included in the majority of student interactions.<br>3 = It is evident from the students' actions and words that all students are considered an equal part of the class and are included in all student interactions. | | | | | |
| 8.16 Co-Teachers ask questions at a variety of levels to meet All students' needs (basic recall to higher order thinking) | 0 = Adults do not use questions and most instruction is directive.<br>1 = Questions are almost all geared just to one level (to the middle or "watered down")<br>2 = Teachers use closed and open questions at a variety of levels in a general manner.<br>3 = Closed and open questions are asked at a variety of levels in a way that demonstrates they are able to differentiate for specific students in order to ensure maximum (appropriate) levels of challenge. | | | | | |
| Notes: ||||| Listen Fors Total: | |

*Note:* DNOT = Did Not Observe Teacher(s)

## Co-Teaching Checklist: ASK FORs

| | ASK FOR ITEMS | ✓ 0 – No Evidence<br>✓ 1 – Little Evidence<br>✓ 2 – Some Evidence<br>✓ 3 – Substantial Evidence | |
|---|---|---|---|
| | | Rating | Circle Evidence |
| 7.2 Co-Planning | 0 = There is no evidence that this team co-plans. Most planning, if done at all, is done by one teacher.<br>1 = This team rarely co-plans and communicates primarily on the fly.<br>2 = This team co-plans at irregular times but does try to integrate both teachers' perspectives when possible.<br>3 = This team co-plans its lessons and integrates both teachers' areas of expertise to the maximum extent possible. | | Lesson Plans<br>Modified Materials<br>Letters Home/Syllabi<br>SHARE Worksheets<br>Problem Solving Worksheets<br>Other: |
| 8.5 Co-Instruction: Parity | 0 = There is no evidence that this team co-instructs. One teacher is clearly responsible as evidenced in documentation/plans etc..<br>1 = One teacher is clearly "lead" however the other does have intermittent areas of responsibility.<br>2 = Both teachers are provided turns in co-instruction.<br>3 = Teachers are comfortable in any role and roles are interchanging and fluid throughout the lesson plan. | | Lesson Plans<br>Behavior Documentation<br>Tiered Lessons<br>Class Notes<br>Other: |
| 8.1 Co-Instruction: Grouping | 0 = There is no evidence that this team regroups during instruction. Whole group instruction is the norm.<br>1 = At irregular times and for very specific activities, this class is regrouped into smaller groups.<br>2 = Cooperative learning is used in class regularly and small groups are used at least once a week.<br>3 = Whole group and regrouping approaches are used to match learning needs. Teachers clearly use regrouping regularly and are comfortable with a variety of the co-instructional approaches. | | Lesson Plans<br>Behavior Documentation<br>Tiered Lessons<br>Class Notes<br>Other: |
| 1.2 Co-Instruction: Differentiation | 0 = There is no evidence that this team differentiates for the class. All lessons appear created so that students are expected to do the same things.<br>1 = Minimal evidence demonstrates differentiation. What is available appears to focus on one or two specific students for limited activities or events (e.g., read test to Johnny).<br>2 = Teachers appear to integrate differentiated instruction, content and assessments into some lessons.<br>3 = Teachers regularly include differentiated instruction, content, and assessments into their lessons. They clearly consider the needs of all students. | | Lesson Plans<br>Behavior Documentation<br>Tiered Lessons<br>Class Notes<br>Other: |
| 6.1 Co-Assess | 0 = There is no evidence that this team co-assesses. One teacher is in charge of the grades and gradebook.<br>1 = Teachers talk about assessments at times but each teacher is primarily in charge of his/her "own" students.<br>2 = Teachers use differentiated assessments occasionally and are willing to share responsibility for grading.<br>3 = Teachers share responsibility for creating assessments, grading, and for students' overall success. Differentiated assessments are created when needed and both teachers are comfortable with adaptations. | | Grade Book<br>Modified Assignments<br>Individual Grading Reports<br>Other: |

Notes:

**Ask Fors Total:** [ ]

**Overall Total:** [ ]

0-29 Not Yet Co-Teaching   30-45 Emerging Co-Teaching   46-52 Developing Co-Teaching
53-59 Proficient Co-Teaching   60-66 Master Co-Teaching

# Appendix F

## *Peer Observation Protocol*

(from Killion, Harrison, Bryan, & Clifton, 2012)

Teacher: _____  Observer: _____

Date: _____

Grade/content: _____

I noticed that the students _____

_____

_____

_____

_____

I noticed that the teaching _____

_____

_____

_____

_____

I wonder _____

_____

_____

_____

_____

I learned _____

_____

_____

_____

_____

I plan to _____

_____

_____

_____

_____

## References

Blanks, B., Daniel, L., & Minarik, D. (2015). *Video assignment rubrics.* Radford University. School of Teacher Education and Leadership, Radford, VA.

Costa, A. L., & Kallick, B. (1993). Through the lens of a critical friend. *Educational leadership, 51,* 49–51.

DuFour, R., DuFour, R., & Eaker, R. (2008). *Revisiting professional learning communities at work: New insights for improving schools.* Bloomington, IN: Solution Tree Press.

Grimm, E. D., Kaufman, T., & Doty, D. (2014). Rethinking classroom observation. *Educational Leadership, 71*(8), 24–29.

Joyce, B., & Showers, B. (2002). Student achievement through professional development. In B. Joyce & B. Showers (Eds.), *Designing training and peer coaching: Our need for learning.* Alexandria, VA: Association for Supervision and Curriculum Development.

Killion, J. Harrison, C., Bryan, C., & Clifton, H. (2012). *Coaching matters.* Oxford, OH: Learning Forward.

Lee, S. C., Nugent, G., Kunz, G., & Houston, J. (2014). *Coaching for sustainability: Distance-based peer coaching science inquiry in rural schools* (No. 2014-11). R2Ed Working Paper.

Murawski, W. W. (2003). *Co-teaching in the inclusive classroom.* Bellevue, WA: Bureau of Education and Research.

Murawski, W. W., & Dieker, L. A. (2004). Tips and strategies for co-teaching at the secondary level. *Teaching Exceptional Children, 36*(5), 52–58.

Murawski, W. W., & Lochner, W. W. (2011). Observing co-teaching: What to ask for, look for, and listen for. *Intervention in School and Clinic, 46*(3), 174–183.

Patterson, K., Grenny, J., McMillan, R., & Switzler, A. (Eds.). (2012). *Crucial conversations: Tools for talking when stakes are high.* New York, NY: McGraw-Hill.

Seidel, T., & Stürmer, K. (2014). Modeling and measuring the structure of professional vision in preservice teachers. *American Educational Research Journal, 51*(4), 739–771.

Stone, D., Patton, B., & Heen, S. (2010). *Difficult conversations: How to discuss what matters most.* New York, NY: Penguin.

Tripp, T., & Rich, P. (2012). Using video to analyze one's own teaching. *British Journal of Educational Technology, 43*(4), 678–704.

# PART IV
## *Enhancing Professional Practice*

# MODULE 16

## Teachers and the Law

Paul R. Klenck
*Illinois Education Association-NEA*

Bernard F. Bragen Jr.
*Monmouth University*

Debbie F. Cosgrove
*Elmhurst College*

*We stand in the shadow of Jefferson who believed that a society founded upon the rule of law and liberty was dependent upon public education and the diffusion of knowledge.*
—Matt Blunt

### MODULE DESCRIPTION

Teacher preparatory programs graduate students with sufficient instructional and pedagogical knowledge to teach children effectively in their assigned licensed areas, and yet certain specific and practicable knowledge can only be learned via clinical practice and actual teaching. The pragmatic application of federal, state and local regulations along with the legal responsibilities of teaching children are areas often bereft of preservice teacher training. The goal of this module is to provide both supervisors and teachers with an overview of those legal parameters and some real-world applications that will enhance a teacher's expertise in this area. These skills will enable teachers to better meet their students' needs within the legal and ethical confines of appropriate instructional practice.

## Theory/Conceptual Framework

Teaching is a highly regulated profession. Federal, state and local governments enact laws and administrative rules affecting working conditions, teaching standards, student rights, parental responsibilities as well as a host of other areas. Public school employees are government employees, serve as role models, and are responsible for knowing and following these many regulations. For some laws, they will be evaluated on their compliance, and can be held liable for errors. Other laws directly affect their working conditions and rights. In all areas, they have a civic responsibility to influence the development and enactment of new laws and regulations.

These laws come from three sources: federal, state, and local. Indeed, the U.S. Constitution impacts classrooms, since school employees have constitutional due process rights before property (their paychecks) or liberty (their work reputation) may be taken from them by their government employer (*Cleveland Board of Education v. Loudermill,* 1985). Students have 4th amendment rights to be free from certain searches, and both teachers and students have 1st amendment rights to expression and assembly, though the school board has significant latitude in regulating those rights (*Garcetti v. Ceballos,* 2006 and *Tinker v. Des Moines Independent School District,* 1969). Congress enacts laws such as the Individuals With Disabilities Education Act (IDEA), and the U.S. Department of Education (DoE) issues regulations and enforces laws concerning student civil rights and privacy.

However, U.S. education is largely regulated by state and local governments. States establish how local school districts can be formed, establish educational standards, and create student and employee rights and responsibilities. Each state will have a cabinet office or state board to oversee and implement these laws. The state will specify what authority the local school board has for operating individual districts and schools, and will establish how local boards are elected or appointed. The local board, in turn, will issue its own policies on how its schools are run, and what rights and responsibilities students and school employees have. Most states permit school boards to collectively bargain with a local employee union, and enter into written agreement with the union over wages, hours, and terms and conditions of employment. Here are a few of the areas of law that school employees will be exposed to and may need to know: student records and privacy, child abuse reporting and investigation, tenure and employment rights, social media and technology use, leaves and disability, freedom of information, and government sunshine laws.

Let's illustrate this. Maintaining classroom discipline is an essential duty of a teacher. Most school boards adopt discipline policies regulating student conduct, outlining how discipline is established and enforced in buildings, and defining the roles teachers and other employees play. Several states have adopted statewide student discipline laws that local school boards, and therefore, individual employees must follow. For example, in 2015 the Illinois legislature mandated that local boards may not utilize zero tolerance policies and must establish procedures to ensure that alternatives to suspension are explored and exhausted before students may be removed from schools (Illinois Public Act 99-0456). The state also mandated professional development about student discipline for school employees and school board members. The state further required that the local boards must meet annually with a teacher advisory committee to review and assess the local discipline policy. Moreover, the U.S. DoE's Office of Civil Rights requires school districts to bi-annually report statistics regarding the extent of out-of-school and in-school suspensions and detailing how various racial demographics and special education students are disciplined in comparison to the general student population (34 Code of Federal Regulations §100.6, §104.61, & §106.71). Moreover, IDEA requires schools to make particularized determinations before disciplining special education students. Teachers may have learned practices on how best to implement student discipline in their classrooms, but they will be required to know their school's supports, the local school board policies and state laws as well as national requirements if a student is receiving special education.

The practice of using suspensions and detentions to discipline students who demonstrate inappropriate behaviors and violate a school's code of conduct has a long-standing history in American schools. Unfortunately, increasing suspension rates has not decreased incidents of improper student conduct and has only reinforced the school-to-prison pipeline for children who chronically misbehave in school (Schept, Wall, & Brisman, 2015), while not improving student deportment. The focus on punishment instead of remediation does not address the underlying reasons for maladaptive school behaviors and perpetuates the disciplinary cycle. Moreover, African-Americans, students with disabilities, and boys often disproportionately receive out of school suspensions and expulsions. (U.S. Government Accountability Office, 2018). Is there a better way to deal with students who chronically act out in school?

How do teachers become aware of the many legal rights and responsibilities that they have? They should look for professional development opportunities that their school district provides, and raise collective concerns if employees believe essential topics are not offered. The local or state union or other professional organizations may provide in-person or online training opportunities.

## Specific Questions to Guide Discussion

1. What is bullying? Harassment? Intimidation? What types of bullying have you observed? What is your state and district's policy regarding bullying? What are your school's procedures for bullying? Who can you speak to in your school to get additional support regarding bullying, harassment, and intimidation? Where and how do you report a bullying issue?

2. What are restorative practices? What does a restorative practice approach for classroom discipline look like? Are school suspensions and detentions effective ways to discipline students? What is the policy of your district in this regard? What procedures does your school follow to address student misbehavior? Who can you speak to in your school to get additional support regarding a student discipline problem?

3. What is the purpose of an acceptable use policy? What are some different ways that social media can be misused in schools? How can you effectively use social media to enhance learning and to improve communication among all stakeholders (i.e., students, families, colleagues, etc.)? Who can you speak to in your school to receive additional support regarding appropriate uses of technology?

## Productive Practices[1]

1. *Know and understand the law.* Be current about new or emerging legal topics and decisions.
2. *Report suspected child abuse (mandated reporter).* Teachers are classified as mandatory reporters under state child abuse and neglect laws. Be familiar with your school's policies and also understand that these policies don't relieve you, as a mandated reporter, from the legal responsibility to immediately report child abuse.
3. *Protect student safety.* Teachers play an essential role in the creation of safe and supportive learning environments for their students. Teacher awareness and preparation to follow school safety procedures are critical to every student's well-being.
4. *Understand due process rights and procedures for teachers and students.* Learn about your legal due process rights and what they mean. The due process clause of the 14th Amendment, provides that no state can "deprive any person of life, liberty, or property, without due process of law." Due process means that a teacher or student's legal rights as individuals should never be violated and one is entitled to fair treatment through the judicial system (Library of Congress, 2017).
5. *Maintain student and family confidentiality.* Teacher and student confidentiality is dictated by state and federal laws that protect health and school records. All stakeholders need to understand the guidelines of the Family Educational Rights and Privacy Act (FERPA) and the Health Insurance Portability and Accountability Privacy Act (HIPAA). FERPA is a federal law (1974) that protects the privacy of student records. HIPAA is a federal law (1996) that protects the privacy of an individual's medical records.
6. *Use appropriate disciplinary action.* Take time to understand the behavioral standards and management procedures in your school. Develop clear, positively-stated classroom behavioral expectations that you can consistently follow with your students. Be certain that your families understand and support these expectations, too.
7. *Be knowledgeable of students who have IEPs (Individualized Education Program) in your class.* Understand your responsibility regarding the implementation of the child's IEP in planning, instruction, and assessment.
8. *Maintain professional boundaries.* Boundaries refer to the verbal, physical, emotional, and social distances that teachers must maintain to ensure structure, security, and predictability in an educational environment. Usually, the boundaries that are crossed relate to role, time, and place (see National Association of State Directors of Teacher Education & Certification, 2015). Maintain the same professional boundaries with students and parents in online communications as you do in person.
9. *Engage in self-care and support your colleagues.* This includes understanding rights to leave and accommodations under federal and state laws such as the Family and

Medical Leave Act, Americans With Disabilities Act, state workers compensation laws, school code sick leave laws, and other state leave laws. Before you can care and support your students, you need to sustain your physical, mental and spiritual health.

10. *Read your collective bargaining agreement and school board policies.* Take time to read your collective bargaining agreement and the school board policies that affect your work and working conditions. If you have questions, ask school administrators or union leaders to clarify items that you do not understand.

## What Would You Do?

Ask your team or pair the following questions which link with the "Productive Practices" section. For suggested responses to these questions, see Appendix A.

1. What would you do if you are teaching a third-grade class and notice that one of your students has several bruises on the inside of her upper arms? You speak with her privately and ask her about them, and she appears uncomfortable and defensive but tells you that she got the bruises from playing football with her older brother. What do you do? Do you call the child's parents? Do you notify your principal? Do you look closer at the bruises to assess their severity? Do you call Child Protective Services?

2. What would you do if one of your tenth-grade English class students suddenly begins coming to class in dirty clothes and appears unkempt? In his journal writings, he reveals that his parents have been fighting a lot and his mother and four siblings have left their home and are staying at different friends' houses and that he is struggling to get to school each day. What do you do? Is this child considered homeless? If so, what do you do? Can you offer supportive services? Do students receive services if it is determined that they are homeless? Does your district have a homeless liaison?

3. What would you do if you notice that one of your sixth-grade students who has struggled with his weight since you first met him in first-grade seems to have become increasingly disengaged and withdrawn in your class? One day after recess you talk privately with him, and he informs you that several of the other boys tease him each day at recess and make fun of him because of his weight. What do you do? Is this bullying? Are you required to report this to anyone? Is a person's weight an identifying characteristic for a harassment and intimidation offense?

4. What would you do if the parent of a student with special needs asks for your personal email address and phone number so they can get advice over the summer on how to help their child? The parent and student text and email you several times. Later, the other parent announces they are divorcing and wants copies of all the

texts and emails. What should you do? What laws and policies do you want to know about? What might you have done differently?

5. What would you do if you are in your second year of teaching, you or your partner becomes pregnant, and you want to take off some extended time after the child is born? What are your concerns? What legal rights may come into play?

6. What would you do if you need to seek resources or legal assistance outside of your employer about a concern at school?

7. What would you do if you and your sibling, an engineer in a private company, are both arrested over the weekend for damage to public property after you both had too much to drink? How might your work rights and responsibilities be different?

## Reflective Professional Growth Activities

Consider these ideas or activities to facilitate and foster teacher growth and reflection in understanding teacher responsibility and the law. Select several ideas to help facilitate this reflection process. Remember that you know the teachers best so be sure to choose an activity that would be the most effective for them.

### *Idea 1: Harassment, Intimidation, or Bullying?*

Harassment, intimidation, and bullying (HIB) are pervasive problems in American schools that impact as many as 35% of a school's student population (Modecki, 2014). This reality warrants specific teacher training and expertise to mitigate the classroom impact of these types of maladaptive behaviors. In order to address behaviors that are considered harassment, intimidation or bullying, teachers first need to be able to define and identify these behaviors in the classroom, school, and community contexts.

Begin this activity by sharing the school and state-definitions of harassment, intimidation, and bullying (https://www.stopbullying.gov). Ask the pair or team to discuss the definitions with each other and then clarify any questions that they have. Once the teachers demonstrate an understanding of the definitions, then present them with various scenarios describing student behaviors. Working in groups, determine whether the behaviors described in the different scenarios constitute harassment, intimidation and/or bullying. Ask each pair or team to record their thinking on the handout (see Appendix B). Teachers should be ready to defend their responses.

## Scenario 1

Your third-grade student reports to you that at lunch recess several boys have been repeatedly calling him a "jerk." This upsets him and he would like you to address it. Does this scenario meet the definition of harassment, intimidation, or bullying? Please defend your response.

## Scenario 2

Two high-school students engage in an argument in the hallway that escalates, and one student calls the other student the "n-word." The student, who is African-American, then punches the student who called him a name. The students are then separated by staff members. Does this scenario meet the definition of harassment, intimidation, or bullying? Please defend your response.

## Scenario 3

Each day on the bus ride home from high school, a tenth-grade male student shares vulgar pictures of naked women with a female student who sits behind him. These pictures upset the female student. Does this scenario meet the definition of harassment, intimidation, or bullying? Please defend your response.

## Scenario 4

A middle-school, resource-center student shows you another general education student's Instagram account, which has the middle-school, resource student's face superimposed in a variety of unflattering memes with the word "retard" written across the image. These pictures upset the classified, resource-center female student. Does this scenario meet the definition of harassment, intimidation, or bullying? Please defend your response.

After the pair or team analyses the scenarios, encourage them to describe other similar situations that they have observed at their particular grade level. Teachers should then discuss whether these scenarios constitute harassment, intimidation, and/or bullying. Refer to the suggested responses for these scenarios that are posted on the second page of Appendix B.

> **Evidence:** Group or paired completion of Harassment, Intimidation, or Bullying? handout; Group suggestions of similar observed grade level scenarios; Participation in pair or group discussion.

## *Idea 2: Restorative Practices in Lieu of Suspensions and Detentions*[2]

Restorative practices offer an option for not only addressing student behavior concerns in schools but also dealing with the underlying causes of the behavior. These practices equip students with the capacity to accept responsibility for their actions and to choose more appropriate responses in the future. While restorative justice is reactive and deals with consequences of inappropriate conduct, restorative practice is a proactive system that develops human capacity building on enhancing the social capital of a school community. Relationships are the key to success. When teachers know their students, they are better able to help them navigate difficult situations and choose actions that successfully resolve issues in a manner that maintains the dignity of all involved parties.

As a classroom teacher, your exposure to school-wide student conduct and discipline concerns is generally limited to your classroom. To broaden this experience and view student discipline through the lens of a restorative practice perspective, contact your building principal and collect information about the last ten student behavior infractions and the associated consequences, absent the students' identifying information. After securing this information, work with your supervisor to see how these behavior/conduct infractions could be addressed via a restorative practices approach.

Teachers who use a restorative practices approach should pose the following conference questions when dealing with inappropriate student conduct. When interviewing individual student(s), keep a written record of the student's response to the following questions. You may also want to ask the student(s) to reflect in writing first before you discuss the responses together.

- What happened?
- What were you thinking about at the time?
- What have you thought about since?
- Who has been affected by what you have done? In what way(s)?
- What do you think you need to do to make things right?
- What impact has this incident had on you and on others?
- How will you react to similar situations in the future?

## *Examples of a Restorative Practice Approach in the Classroom*

Begin this activity by reviewing Case 1 as a pair or team. Using this as an exemplar, have teachers complete Cases 2 and 3. Identify the restorative practice actions for (a) student action, (b) restoration, (c) sanction, (d) treatment, and (e) desired outcome. Reference the Module 16 Glossary for definitions of these terms. Discuss your answers.

**Case 1**

***Student action:*** Students were rude to the school custodian, throwing trash on the ground in front of him and stating, "Just leave it there, it's his job to pick it up."

***Restoration:*** Students became the custodian's assistant for several days.

***Sanction:*** Students missed recess for those days.

***Treatment:*** By working with the custodian, the students gained an understanding of the hard work involved in maintaining a clean and safe school.

***Desired outcome:*** Students became helpers for the custodian and then encouraged other students to be respectful of this work and to help keep the school clean.

**Case 2**

***Student action:*** Two girls got into a fist fight during a handball game at recess.

***Restoration:***

***Sanction:***

***Treatment:***

***Desired outcome:***

**Case 3**

*Student action:* A school window was broken over winter break. The window was repaired before the school administrator determined that a third-grade student was responsible for the act.

*Restoration:*

*Sanction:*

*Treatment:*

*Desired outcome:*

> **Evidence:** Individual, pair or team identification of restorative practices elements (i.e., student action, restoration, sanction, treatment, desired outcome) in case studies 1, 2, and 3.

## *Idea 3: Social Media in the Classroom*

The ubiquitous nature of social media and technology in the classroom necessitates teacher knowledge and understanding on how to effectively incorporate its application to the educational process while still ensuring its appropriate use. The utilization of social media in the classroom can assist teachers in transforming the learning process to transcend the traditional school day and allows for collaboration among students on an almost continuous basis. The computing power contained in most of today's smartphones is significantly greater than that used in the computers that enabled astronauts to visit the moon and safely return in the 1960s. With this awesome power comes the possibility of misuse and even abuse.

With the proper training and understanding, teachers can help mitigate the potential negative consequences of the misuse of social media applications in a school-based setting. By establishing clear protocols for student-to-student and teacher-to-student communication, many of the potential pitfalls that often lead to the misuse of social media can be avoided.

Begin this activity by reviewing each situation and having teachers respond to the provided questions and decide whether each proposed action is appropriate for a classroom teacher. Suggested responses are found in Appendix D.

**Situation 1**

As a newly hired seventh grade English teacher, you want to establish a connection with your new students and solicit all the students' cell phone numbers and set up a group text message for each class to facilitate dialogue. Is this a good idea and an appropriate communication vehicle for a teacher? Please defend your response.

**Situation 2**

Your third-grade students just completed their authors' share session as a culminating activity for their first assignment in the new writers' workshop writing program. To celebrate this accomplishment, you take a group photo of the class with their writing pieces and post it on your Twitter account and Google classroom homepage. Is this a good idea and an appropriate way to celebrate your students' success? Please defend your response.

**Situation 3**

As a high school history teacher, you create a Facebook account with your class where students develop personas for key characters from history for specific time periods (e.g., the Civil War, World War II eras). The students develop character profiles and circles of influence based on historical information. The students excel on this assignment and demonstrate a robust understanding of the historical figures of each assigned time period. Is this an appropriate use of social media and assignment for high school students? Please defend your response.

**Evidence:** Participation in discussion and notes defending individual responses.

## Follow-Up, Monitoring, and Goal Setting

Depending on the idea chosen from the reflective professional growth activities, complete the following before you begin your next observation:

### *Idea 1: Harassment, Intimidation, and/or Bullying?*

- What criteria can teachers use to determine whether inappropriate student conduct is considered harassment, intimidation of bullying?
- When it is not clear if the incident meets the criteria under an HIB determination how will the teacher make the final decision?
- Can a single incident be considered harassment or bullying?
- How can teachers ensure that their students are aware of what behaviors constitute harassment, intimidation and/or bullying?
- What are you going to do proactively to reduce the occurrence of harassment, intimidation, and bullying in your classroom?

### *Idea 2: Restorative Practices in Lieu of Suspensions and Detentions*

- What are some activities teachers can use at the start of the school year to help establish positive relationships with their students?
- How can teachers enable students to interact with one another in positive ways to promote strong student-to-student connections and relationships?
- If your school employs a traditional punitive student code of conduct, what can teachers do to help facilitate a more proactive and positive approach to student discipline?
- Do you believe that implementing a morning meeting each day in your classroom can help to create a more nurturing classroom environment? Why or why not?
- How can you create a classroom atmosphere that embraces a restorative practices environment as opposed to a more traditional punitive method of discipline?

## Idea 3: Social Media in the Classroom

- Will you create a Twitter/Instagram/Facebook account for your classroom? Does your school permit such use or provide alternative platforms?
- How will you promote collaboration among students via social media in your classroom?
- What will you do to establish clear boundaries and expectations for the use of social media in your classroom?
- How will you address the potential of some students not having access to the Internet or social media resources?
- What will be your level of social media presence for your professional practice and how will you use it to leverage student learning?

# Resources

## Web Resources

### Social Media Classroom Infographic

This is a useful social media infographic clarifying expectations for teacher use of social media in the classroom.

Common Sense Education. (2017). *Protecting student privacy on social media: Do's and don'ts for teachers*. Retrieved from https://www.commonsense.org/education/sites/default/files/tlr-asset/document-2017-cse-classroom-privacy-infographic-0.pdf

### Ways Teachers Can Use Social Media in the Classroom

This Edutopia website provides an overview of how teachers can incorporate the effective use of social media resources in the classroom to enhance student learning.

Davis, V. (2015, February 19). *A guidebook for social media in the classroom*. Retrieved from https://www.edutopia.org/blog/guidebook-social-media-in-classroom-vicki-davis

### Teacher Guides on Social Media

This is an excellent resource for educators that provides links to teacher guides on social media applications in the classroom (e.g., Twitter, Google class, Pinterest), information on creating flipped classroom instructional models and keeping students safe online.

Edudemic. (n.d.). *The teacher's guides to technology and learning*. Retrieved from http://www.edudemic.com/guides/

### Examples for Using Social Media in the Classroom

This website provides specific examples on using Twitter and Facebook to foster more dynamic communication within a classroom setting and school community at large.

Lynch, M. (2017, October 11). *22 ways to use social media in your classroom*. Retrieved from www.theedadvocate.org/22-ways-use-social-media-classroom/

### Restorative Practices in the Classroom

This link explains restorative practices and provides strategies on how this approach can be incorporated into classroom practice in lieu of traditional student discipline practices.

Riley, E. (2017, March 17). *Implementing restorative practices in the classroom.* Retrieved from http://www.gettingsmart.com/2017/03/implementing-restorative-practices-in-the-classroom/

This website provides additional resources and a toolkit for teachers to use when implementing restorative practices in their classrooms.

The Schott Foundation. (2014, March). *Restorative practices: A guide for educators.* Retrieved from http://schottfoundation.org/restorative-practices

### The Heart of Learning and Teaching: Compassion, Resiliency, and Academic Success

The Washington State Office of the Superintendent of Public Instruction has published a manual on creating trauma sensitive environments. Chapter 2 reviews skills and self-care strategies that teachers can incorporate to maintain and support their personal health and well-being and avoid trauma fatigue.

Wolpow, R., Johnson, M., Hertel, R., & Kincaid, S. (2016, May). *The heart of learning & Teaching: Compassion, resiliency & academic success.* Retrieved from http://www.k12.wa.us/compassionateschools/pubdocs/TheHeartofLearningandTeaching.pdf

### Official U.S. Website for Bullying

This official government website provides a comprehensive reference on bullying, cyberbullying, prevention, and resources. The website provides an interactive map where one can "click" and learn about each state's anti-bullying laws and policies.

United States Government. (2017, September). *Facts about bullying.* Retrieved from https://www.stopbullying.gov/media/facts/index.html

### Discipline Disparities for Black Students, Boys, and Students With Disabilities

The U.S. Government Accountability Office (GAO) is an independent, nonpartisan agency that is known as the "investigative arm of Congress" or the "congressional watchdog." The GAO presents a report on the use of discipline disparities in schools. The report examines (a) patterns in disciplinary actions among public schools, (b) challenges that selected school districts report regarding student behavior and how they are approaching school discipline, and (c) actions taken by the Departments of Education and Justice to identify and address disparities or discrimination in school discipline. This searchable website includes many researched topics that are relevant to educators.

U.S. Government Accountability Office. (2018, April 4). *Discipline disparities for Black students, boys, and students with disabilities,* GAO-18-258. Retrieved from https://www.gao.gov/products/GAO-18-258

### Americans With Disabilities Act

The U.S. Department of Labor provides resources to assist with implementation of the ADA. This website provides a guide to the overall application of the Act. Significantly, it contains a wealth of resources regarding a variety of disabling conditions and how they can be accommodated in the workplace.

U.S. Department of Labor. (n.d.). *Americans with Disabilities Act.* Retrieved from https://www.dol.gov/general/topic/disability/ada

**Family and Medical Leave Act**

The U.S. Department of Labor Wage and Hour Division administers and enforces the FMLA. This website provides links to an overview of the Act, an explanation of qualifying events, fact sheets pertaining to specific issues in applying the Act, and links to formal rules and guidance the Department has issued to employees and employers.

U.S. Department of Labor. (n.d.). *Family and Medical Leave Act.* Retrieved from https://www.dol.gov/whd/fmla/?apartner=aarp

**Discipline and Policing Policies Harm Students of Color**

The mission of the National Education Policy Center is to inform discussions on educational policy through peer-reviewed research. Visitors to this research-based site can search for many educational topics of interest.

National Education Policy Center. (2017, June). *How discipline and policing policies harm students of color, and what can we do about it?* Retrieved from http://nepc.colorado.edu/publication/law-and-order

**Child Welfare Information Gateway**

The Child Welfare Information Gateway provides access to print and electronic publications, websites, databases, and online learning tools for improving child welfare practice that can be shared with families. The site also provides a searchable state resources tab to download PDFs of statutes for states and territories.

U.S. Department of Health & Human Services, Administration for Children & Families, and Children's Bureau. (n.d.). *Child Welfare Information Gateway.* Retrieved from https://www.childwelfare.gov

## *Videos*

**Restorative Approach to Discipline**

This video presents teacher, student, and administrator interviews in two Chicago Public schools that are implementing a restorative approach to student discipline (5:02).

Chicago Public Schools. (2014, July 18). *A restorative approach to discipline.* Retrieved from https://youtu.be/5r1yvyP141U

**Five Crazy Ways Social Media Is Changing Your Brain**

This video discusses ways that social media and the Internet affect one's brain (3:15).

Moffit, M., & Brown, G. (2014, September 7). *5 crazy ways social media is changing your brain right now.* Retrieved from https://youtu.be/HffWFd_6bJ0

**Know Me, Know My Name**

Nelba Marquez-Greene, a social worker and mother of a Newton school shooting victim, explains her cost-free way for educators to identify and contact children in danger of having no adult connections in the school (4:20).

Illinois Education Association. (n.d.). *Know me, know my name.* Retrieved from https://ieanea.org/resources/know-me/

### Making Student Discipline Reform Work

This informative video, presented at the IEA Representative Assembly by Deputy General Counsel Paul Klenck, shows how school employees can effectively work with a new state law (IL Senate Bill 100) regarding student discipline and ensure that it is implemented successfully in their schools (25:09).

Klenck, P. (2017, April 1). *Presentation IEA Representative Assembly*. Retrieved from https://vimeo.com/214050742

### Redefining Learning and Teaching Using Technology

In this TEDx Talk (2016, March 28), Jason Brown, Worldwide Microsoft Student Ambassador, advocates for the use of technology (i.e., smartphones and tablets) in classrooms to inspire and engage students of all ages (9:51).

Brown, J. (2016, March 28). *Redefining learning and teaching using technology*. Retrieved from https://youtu.be/AOTEQVYDPpg

### Reimagining Classrooms: Teachers as Learners and Students as Leaders

In this TEDx Talk (2015, October 13), Kayla Delzer, second-grade teacher from South Dakota and technology champion, speaks to the power of technology to transform the learning process for students (13:00).

Delzer, K. (2015, October 13). *Reimagining classrooms: Teachers as learners and students as leaders*. Retrieved from https://youtu.be/w6vVXmwYvgs

### I am Truly Sorry: Short Bullying Movie

This video shows the transition of a student from actively bullying a peer to demonstrating remorse and seeking to end the cycle after recognizing the effects similar behaviors were having on his sister (7:55).

Mormon Channel & Lightbulb Studios. (2016, February 11). *I'm truly sorry: Short bullying movie*. Retrieved from https://youtu.be/qcvTsFqptS8

## *Books*

### Using Social Media in the Classroom

This book serves as an excellent guide for websites and Internet resources that teachers can use to incorporate social media into their classrooms. The book discusses an overview of different types of digital technologies and offers advice on how to safely use them in the learning process.

Poore, M. (2016). *Using social media in the classroom: A best practice guide*. Thousand Oaks, CA: SAGE.

### Case Studies on Safety, Bullying, and Social Media in Schools

This book provides case studies that address critical issues occurring in our schools including, bullying, harassment, social media, and school safety. The case studies can benefit supervisors in providing appropriate vehicles to prompt faculty discussions on best practices in these areas.

Trujillo-Jenks, L., & Jenks, K. (2015). *Case studies on safety, bullying and social media in schools: Current issues in educational leadership*. New York, NY: Routledge.

### Social Media Wellness

Ana Homayoun, educator and author, provides parents, teachers, and students with a solutions-oriented guide that promotes healthy socialization, effective self-regulation, and overall safety and wellness in today's digital age.

Homayoun, A. (2018). *Social media wellness: Helping tweens and teens thrive in an unbalanced digital world.* Thousand Oaks, CA: Corwin.

### Restorative Practices for Positive Classroom Engagement

This book provides a practical blueprint for creating a cooperative and respectful classroom climate where students and teachers work through behavioral issues together. It is an excellent resource for teachers to help build classrooms that are welcoming, respectful, and dedicated to student achievement.

Smith, D., Fischer, D., & Frey, N. (2015). *Better than carrots or sticks: Restorative practices for positive classroom management.* Alexandria, VA: ASCD.

### Rethinking Behavior Management

This book provides practical advice for teachers to implement restorative justice classroom practices. It also contains documents that teachers can use to facilitate the restorative justice process in their classes.

Thorsborne, M., & Vinegrad, D. (2017). *Rethinking behaviour management: Restorative practices in schools.* New York, NY: Routledge.

### A Step-by-Step Implementation Guide for Administrators and School Personnel

Jim Sporleder, the former principal of Lincoln High School in Walla Walla, WA and featured in the movie *Paper Tigers*, together with school social worker Heather Forbes, provide a practical guide for school employees to implement an effective, compassionate approach to discipline.

Sporleder, J., & Forbes, H. T. (2016). *The trauma-informed school: A step-by-step implementation guide for administrators and school personnel.* Boulder, CO: Beyond Consequences Institute.

### The Legal Rights and Responsibilities of Teachers

This book presents reviews of federal and state law on teacher rights and responsibilities and discusses how local school boards and unions impact these laws.

Osborne, Jr., A. G., & Russo, C. (2011). *The legal rights and responsibilities of teachers: Issues of employment and instruction.* Thousand Oaks, CA: SAGE.

## Key Terms and Definitions

**Acceptable use policy:** School employees and students often must sign and agree to the school's terms (AUP) on appropriate use of school technology and devices, internet access, and email. Many schools have even broader policies on social media and network use that may even govern activity outside of the school day.

**Americans With Disabilities Act:** Individuals with a physical or mental impairment who, with or without accommodation, can perform the essential functions of their job are entitled to reasonable accommodations to perform their job, may be eligible for a modified work schedule, and may be eligible for a short leave to adjust or respond to medical changes.

**Board policy:** Local boards of education adopt policies that students, employees, parents and others must abide by. The boards can enact policies within the authority given to them by the state legislature and the policies must not conflict with state and federal legislation and court decisions.

**Bullying:** Any severe or pervasive physical, verbal, or conduct, including written or electronic communication or "cyber-bullying" that places a student or students in reasonable harm, interferes with academic performance or school participation, or has a detrimental effect on a student's physical or mental health. Bullying may take various forms including harassment, threats, intimidation, stalking, physical violence, sexual harassment, sexual violence, theft, public humiliation, destruction of property, or retaliation for asserting or alleging an act of bullying (Illinois Public Act 96-0952).

**Cyberbullying:** Federal and state legislation prohibit students from bullying other students through the use of electronic communication, which includes use of non-school equipment during non-school time. Cyberbullying typically is defined as severe or pervasive communication directed to a student to cause fear, interfere with academic performance, participate in school or have a substantially detrimental effect on the student's physical or mental health.

**Collective bargaining agreement:** Governing agreement between the board of education and teachers' association defining work parameters for all association members including, salaries, workload, health insurance, responsibilities, and expectations, working conditions, and grievance procedures.

**Confidentiality (FERPA and HIPPA):** Confidentiality is referenced in this module through the Family Educational Rights and Privacy Act (FERPA) and the Health Insurance Portability and Accountability Privacy Act (HIPAA). FERPA is a federal law (1974) that protects the privacy of student records. HIPPA is a federal law (1996) that protects the privacy of an individual's medical records.

**Conflict mediation:** The parties to a dispute work with a neutral party to generate solutions to the conflict.

**Family and Medical Leave Act:** Federal legislation requiring employers to provide employees with job-protected and unpaid leave for qualified medical and family reasons.

**Freedom of Information Act:** Federal and state legislation that allows for the full or partial disclosure of previously unreleased information and documents controlled by the government.

**Government sunshine laws:** Ensure that procedural practices are in place to grant the public access to and participation in board of education meetings and other governmental agencies.

**Harassment, intimidation, and bullying (HIB):** Harassment, intimidation or bullying can be defined as any gesture, written, verbal or physical act, or electronic communication, that can be perceived as being motivated by an actual or perceived identifying characteristic (e.g., race, religion, color, national origin, gender, sexual orientation, gender identity, mental, physical or sensory disability, etc.) or by any other distinguishing characteristic. It could be a single event in a series of actions.

**Individuals With Disabilities Education Act (IDEA):** Federal legislation that guarantees that students with special needs as defined in the legislation are provided with a free and appropriate education in the least restrictive environment possible in accordance with their individual needs.

**Intimidation:** The act of compelling or deterring someone through the use of fear and/or threats.

**Mandated reporter:** Designated persons (e.g., teachers, clergy, school staff) who are responsible for reporting suspicion of child abuse or neglect to designated authorities. All states have mandated reporting procedures in place. Failure to report suspected child abuse is punishable by law.

**McKinney-Vento Homeless Assistance Act:** Section of the Elementary and Secondary Education Act that defines student homelessness and provides protections to homeless students to help mitigate their situation and maintain consistency of their educational program.

**Restoration:** This term is used as part of a restorative practice approach used in schools. This approach emphasizes the restoration and reconciliation of relationships. The focus is on the healing process between the harmed individual, the affected community, and the offender rather than traditional punitive disciplinary practices that are often isolated and exclusionary in nature.

**Restorative practices:** Behaviors and practices that address inappropriate conduct in a manner that maintains the integrity of all involved parties while encouraging students to accept responsibility for their actions and mitigate any harm inflicted as a result of those deeds.

**Sanction:** This term is used as part of a restorative practice approach used in schools. During the restoration conference, the emphasis is on healing the relationship between the offender and the victim. Sanctions or punishments are often determined after a restorative conference is held between the offender and the teacher and possibly even the victim. Discipline shifts from isolated punishment to learning how to change one's behavior while in a relationship context.

**School board:** Elected officials possessing controlling authority over a school district who vote on recommendations of the chief school administrator and determine the policies and regulations that govern a school district.

**School-to-prison pipeline:** This term refers to school policies and procedures that directly or indirectly track students from the school to the criminal justice system. School-to-prison pipeline disproportionately represented groups include students of color, those who identify as LGBTQ, students with disabilities, and English language learners.

**Self-care:** A collection of strategies to prevent or alleviate the symptoms of vicarious trauma.

**Social media:** Technological applications that facilitate the creation and sharing of data, ideas, and other information via the world wide web and the Internet creating a platform for dialogue and expression across a wide audience.

## Notes

1. See, Individuals with Disabilities Education Act (IDEA), 20 U.S.C. § 1415(d). Productive practices are adapted from Burden & Byrd (2016) Methods for Effective Teaching: Meeting the Needs of All Students. *Teachers and the law,* Figure 2, p. 5. Also, adapted from the Model Code of Ethics for Educators (MCEE), National Association of State Directors of Teacher Education and Certification, 2015.
2. Adapted from Restorative Classroom Practices. (2018). *Restorative questions.* Retrieved from https://restorativeclassroomcircles.wikispaces.com/home (see Appendix C: Interview Report-Restorative Practices in Lieu of Suspensions and Detention Template).

# Appendix A

## *What Would You Do? Questions With Suggested Responses*

1. What would you do if you are teaching your third-grade class and notice that one of your students has several bruises on the inside of her upper arms? You speak with her privately and ask her about them. She appears uncomfortable and defensive but tells you that she got the bruises from playing football with her older brother. What do you do? Do you call the child's parents? Do you notify your principal? Do you look closer at the bruises to assess their severity? Do you call Child Protective Services?

   **Suggested Response to Question 1:** Teachers in 48 states are required to report suspected child abuse to state authorities and in some states to the local police departments as well (see Child Welfare Information Gateway, www.childwelfare.gov). A key aspect of this question is that teachers do not need to and should not investigate the reasons of the suspected abuse, for that is the role of the state child protective services agency. However, teachers should be aware that bruises on the inside of a child's upper arm are a telltale sign of abuse and not likely the result of an accident. Accidental bruises normally occur on the ankles, shins, wrists, lower arms, elbows, and under the chin. The principal should be informed as well, but the teacher should be the one who makes the call and many states mandate that the teacher makes the call. In addition, the parents should not be notified of your concerns at this point as this may compromise any possible investigation.

2. What would you do if one of your tenth-grade English class students suddenly begins coming to class in dirty clothes and appears unkempt? In his journal writings, he reveals that his parents have been fighting a lot and his mother and four siblings have left their home and are staying at different friends' houses and that he is struggling to get to school each day. What do you do? Is this child considered homeless? If so, what do you do? Can you offer supportive services? Do students receive services if it is determined that they are homeless? Does your district have a homeless liaison?

   **Suggested Response to Question 2:** Students who for any reason are no longer living in their regular homes and currently living in a temporary residence with relatives or elsewhere are considered homeless and entitled to protections guaranteed under Subtitle VII-B of the McKinney-Vento Homeless Assistance Act, reauthorized in 2015 by Title IX, Part A of the Every Student Succeeds Act (42 U.S.C. § 11431 et seq.) The McKinney-Vento Act also requires school districts to have a designated staff member who acts as liaison to coordinate services for homeless students. A key provision of the act requires school districts to allow homeless students to remain enrolled in their school of origin when it is in the child's best interest. This offers the students some degree of stability during a tumultuous period in their lives. Teachers should familiarize themselves with their district's policies and procedures for addressing the needs of students who are considered homeless.

3. What would you do if you notice that one of your sixth-grade students who has struggled with his weight since you first met him in first grade seems to have become increasingly disengaged and withdrawn in your class? One day after recess you talk privately with him, and he informs you that several of the other boys tease him each day at recess and make fun of him because of his weight. What do you do? Is this bullying? Are you required to report this to anyone? Is a person's weight an identifying characteristic for a harassment and intimidation offense?

   **Suggested Response to Question 3:** Students who are teased or made fun of due to a defining characteristic such as race, sex, religion, sexual identity, weight, and so on, are protected under state anti-bullying legislation and policies, and this would meet that criteria. Most states have specific procedures to follow for reporting and follow-up when incidents of suspected bullying or harassment occur. Please check the requirements in your state or local school district. Your school may have restorative discipline practices that should be implemented to help the harassing students understand their actions and take corrective measures. You may assess that you need to implement additional restorative practices in your classroom to ensure all students feel that they are welcome in the class community.

4. What would you do if the parent of a student with special needs asks for your personal email address and phone number so they can get advice over the summer on how to help their child? The parent and student text and email you several times. Later, the other parent announces they are divorcing and wants copies of all the texts and emails. What should you do? What laws and policies do you want to know about? What might you have done differently?

    **Suggested Response to Question 4:** Notify the principal or other administrator. Seek help from your union. Understand your responsibilities under your state's child protection act and the state agency hotline to call. Determine what state student records and privacy laws may be at issue. Study the district's social media or acceptable use policy for guidance. Discern whether you are responsible for actions taken over the summer. Do you have protections as an employee? Ask to what extent the state freedom of information act applies to these communications. The teacher should have sought administration advice before giving any summer contact information and should limit contact information to school-approved tools such as the school email address.

5. What would you do if you are in your second year of teaching, you or your partner becomes pregnant, and you want to take off some extended time after the child is born? What are your concerns? What legal rights may come into play?

    **Suggested Response to Question 5:** First, determine if taking off extended time will affect earning tenure. Ask if you are eligible for time off under the federal Family and Medical Leave Act. Determine how much time you can take and what benefits are available to you. Research if there are any state laws concerning new child leave. Find out if there is a provision in the collective bargaining agreement or board policy regarding taking extended time after the birth of a child.

6. What would you do if you need to seek resources or legal assistance outside of your employer about a concern at school?

    **Suggested Response to Question 6:** Most public school teachers are members of a local teachers' association that not only provides workplace protections under a collective bargaining agreement but also resources for legal concerns that arise in the performance of their teaching responsibilities. In addition, many state teachers' associations provide free job-related legal services and protections as a benefit of membership.

7. What would you do if you and your sibling, an engineer in a private company, are both arrested over the weekend for damage to public property after you both had too much to drink? How might your work rights and responsibilities be different?

    **Suggested Response to Question 7:** The teacher is a role model and may be disciplined if the school can show a connection to that role because of the teacher's behavior or publicity. The teacher will have due process rights, contract rights, and rights to representation during an investigation in most states. The engineer may not be subject to the same role-model standard. On the other hand, the engineer is likely an at-will employee and does not have constitutional, statutory, or contractual rights.

# Appendix B

## *Harassment, Intimidation, or Bullying?*

*Directions:* Read the four scenarios described below. In discussion with your pair or team, determine whether the behaviors in each scenario represent harassment, intimidation, or bullying. Defend your answers in the space provided. Be ready to share your thoughts.

### Scenario 1

Your third-grade student reports to you that at lunch recess a few other boys have been repeatedly calling him a "jerk." This upsets him and he would like you to address it. Does this scenario meet the definition of harassment, intimidation, or bullying? Please defend your response.

### Scenario 2

Two high-school students engage in an argument in the hallway that escalates, and one student calls the other student the "n-word." The student, who is African-American, then punches the student who called him a name. The students are then separated by staff members. Does this scenario meet the definition of harassment, intimidation, or bullying? Please defend your response.

### Scenario 3

Each day on the bus ride home from high school, a tenth-grade male student shares vulgar pictures of naked women with a female student who sits behind him. These pictures upset the female student. Does this scenario meet the definition of harassment, intimidation, or bullying? Please defend your response.

### Scenario 4

A middle-school, resource-center student shows you another general education student's Instagram account, which has the middle-school, resource student's face superimposed in a variety of unflattering memes with the word "retard" written across the image. These pictures upset the classified, resource-center female student. Does this scenario meet the definition of harassment, intimidation, or bullying? Please defend your response.

## Suggested Responses to Idea #1: Harassment, Intimidation, and/or Bullying?

### Scenario 1

Your third-grade student reports to you that at lunch recess several boys have been repeatedly calling him a "jerk." This upsets him and he would like you to address it. Does this scenario meet the definition of harassment, intimidation, or bullying? Please defend your response.

**Suggested Response to Scenario 1:** This would not meet the criteria of harassment, intimidation, and bullying because the behavior is not based on an identifying characteristic as defined in the legislation. Even if the conduct was based on identifying characteristics, the behavior would need to be pervasive or severe. This notwithstanding, the conduct is still inappropriate and warrants correction.

### Scenario 2

Two high school students engage in an argument in the hallway that escalates, and one student calls the other student the "n-word," The student, who is African-American, then punches the student, and they need to be separated by staff members. Would this meet the definition of harassment, intimidation and/or bullying? Defend your response.

**Suggested Response to Scenario 2:** This behavior would be considered an act of harassment, intimidation, and bullying because the use of the "n-word" is particularly vulgar and upsetting to students of color and race is one the characteristics identified in the legislation. Even if this was an isolated incident, the severity of the conduct and the physical violence would likely meet the legal standard of bullying.

### Scenario 3

While on the bus coming home from high school each day, a tenth-grade male student shares vulgar pictures of naked women with a female student who sits behind him on the bus. These pictures upset the female student. Would this meet the definition of harassment, intimidation, or bullying? Defend your response.

**Suggested Response to Scenario 3:** This conduct should be deemed harassment, intimidation, and bullying because the behavior is particularly offense to female students. While still inappropriate, showing other boys the images would not produce the same reaction indicating the behavior is motivated by the sex of the students, which is an identified characteristic in the legislation. However, if directed to another boy who may be considered to have non-traditional sexual preferences, the behavior may be considered bullying.

### Scenario 4

Your middle-school resource-center student shows you another student's Instagram account, which has his face superimposed in a variety of unflattering memes with the word "retard" across the image. These pictures upset the female student. Would this meet the definition of harassment, intimidation, or bullying? Defend your response.

**Suggested Response to Scenario 4:** This would be considered an incident of cyber-bullying where social media is used to willingly offend or inflict harm on another student using a computer, cell phone, or other electronic devices. The disturbing impact of cyber-bullying is that the offended party is often unaware of the offense and it can be shared with a vast audience very quickly. However, if the posting is done entirely off campus on non-school time, the "speech" will enjoy first amendment protection and the school may need to show that the conduct resulted in a substantial and material disruption of the educational environment.

# Appendix C

## *Restorative Practices in Lieu of Suspensions and Detention Template*

**Conference Report**

Student: _____ Date: _____

Keep a written record of each student's response to the following questions or ask the student(s) to reflect in writing first before you discuss the responses together.

1. What happened?

2. What were you thinking about at the time?

3. What have you thought about since?

4. Who has been affected by what you have done? In what way(s)?

5. What do you think you need to do to make things right?

6. What impact has this incident had on you and on others?

7. How will you react to similar situations in the future?

# Appendix D

*Suggested Answers to Idea 3: Social Media in the Classroom*

### Situation 1

As a newly hired seventh-grade English teacher, you want to establish a connection with your new students and solicit all the students' cell phone numbers to set up a group text message for each class in order to facilitate dialogue. Is this a good idea and an appropriate communication vehicle for a teacher? Defend your response.

**Suggested Response to Situation 1:** For teachers working with adolescent students, it is essential for teachers to establish clear boundaries that separate the teacher and the student. Sharing cell phone information with students and creating an environment for two-way dialogue blurs the boundaries between teacher and student and opens up the door for the possibility of inappropriate conduct. Other communication options exist that provide opportunities to share information with students that doesn't allow for dialogue such as the app Remind. Many schools provide guidance on when it may be appropriate or inappropriate to share text messages, such as allowing coaches to text students when practice may be cancelled due to bad weather.

### Situation 2

Your third-grade students just completed their authors' share session as a culminating activity for their first assignment in the new writers' workshop writing program. To celebrate this accomplishment, you take a group photo of the class with their writing pieces and post it on your Twitter account and Google classroom homepage. Is this a good idea and an appropriate way to celebrate the students' writing success? Defend your response.

**Suggested Response to Situation 2:** Social media application and websites provide excellent vehicles for communication and a forum to celebrate and share student successes; however, teachers need to be careful on what information is shared in a public forum. Most school districts have established procedures and protocols for securing parental permission about what information they will allow to be shared about their children via social media. Before posting any student information, teachers need to know what is permissible for each student in their class and act accordingly. If students are individually identified, the posting may be considered a "student record" and be governed by the state student records law.

### Situation 3

As a high school history teacher you create a Facebook account with your class where students develop personas for key characters from history for specific time periods such as the Civil War or the World War II era where they then develop profiles and circles of influence based on historical information. The students excel on this assignment and demonstrate a robust understanding of the historical figures of each assigned time period. Is this an appropriate use of social media and assignment for high school students? Defend your response.

**Suggested Response to Situation 3:** Social media platforms provide a motivating and engaging vehicle for students to engage in academic activities that otherwise may prove to be boring or of little interest to them. This assignment provides an appropriate vehicle for students to display their knowledge of historical eras and personas in an engaging manner that does not reveal any of their personal or identifiable information. You should monitor the account just as you would monitor classroom conduct for appropriate behavior.

# References

*Cleveland Board of Education v. Loudermill*, 470 U.S. 532 (1985).
*Garcetti v. Ceballos*, 547 U.S. 410 (2006).
Illinois General Assembly, Public Act 099-0456 (2016).
McKinney-Vento Homeless Assistance Act, Subtitle VII-B, reauthorized in 2015 by Title IX, Part A of the Every Student Succeeds Act (42 U.S.C. § 11431 et seq.).
Modecki, K. L. (2014). Bullying prevalence across contexts: A meta-analysis measuring cyber and traditional bullying. *Journal of Adolescent Health, 55*(5), 602–611.
National Association of State Directors of Teacher Education and Certification. (2015). *Model Code of Ethics for Educators (MCEE)*. Retrieved from https://www.nasdtec.net/page/MCEE_Doc?
Rehabilitation Act of 1973-Section 504, 34 Code of Federal Regulations §104.61 (2017).
Schept, J., Wall, T., & Brisman, A. (2015). Building, Staffing, and Insulating: An architecture of criminological complicity in the school-to-prison pipeline. *Social Justice, 41*(4), 96–115.
The Library of Congress. (2017). *14th Amendment to the U.S. Constitution.* Retrieved from https://www.loc.gov/rr/program/bib/ourdocs/14thamendment.html
*Tinker v. Des Moines Independent School District*, 393 U.S. 503 (1969).
Title VI of the Civil Rights Act of 1964, 34 Code of Federal Regulations §100.6 (1988).
Title IX of the Education Amendments Act of 1972, 34 Code of Federal Regulations §106.71 (2006).
U.S. Department of Health & Human Services, Administration for Children & Families, and Children's Bureau (n.d.). *Child Welfare Information Gateway.* Retrieved from https://www.childwelfare.gov
U.S. Government Accountability Office (2018, April 4). *Discipline disparities for black students, boys, and students with disabilities*, GAO-18-258. Retrieved from https://www.gao.gov/products/GAO-18-258

# MODULE 17

## Professional Dispositions

**LuEllen Doty**
*Elmhurst College*

**Jeanne White**
*Elmhurst College*

*Dispositions comprise habits of mind rather than mindless habits.*
—Lillian Katz

### MODULE DESCRIPTION

This module will provide information and resources about the development of the dispositions of an effective teacher. While there are many dispositions found in research which contribute to effective instruction in both collaborative and traditional teaching, this module will offer several examples of dispositions. Teachers should focus primarily on the dispositions required by their districts as well as those specified in this module that are appropriate to the context of the teaching placement in general, special education, and inclusive settings.

## Theory/Conceptual Framework

Professional dispositions are the attitudes, values, and beliefs demonstrated through both verbal and nonverbal behaviors as educators interact with students, families, colleagues, and communities (see Appendix B for example). Meidl and Baumann (2015) specifically define dispositions as the "observable patterns of behaviors of teachers driven by one's personal values and beliefs to benefit student learning and well-being" (p. 91). These positive, observable behaviors support student learning and development, and are needed for effective teachers to have an impact on student learning, as well as a sense of comfort and happiness in the classroom. Evaluations of teaching dispositions typically start in pre-service teacher education. Accrediting agencies and certification boards require teacher education programs to provide structure and opportunities for teacher candidates to develop and reflect upon the dispositions necessary to support and engage all students. The Council for the Accreditation of Educator Preparation (CAEP) requires institutions to evaluate the professional dispositions of future teachers based on observable behaviors in educational settings.

A frequently asked question revolves around the role and importance of dispositions in teacher education. Katz (1993) defines a disposition as "a tendency to exhibit frequently, consciously, and voluntarily a pattern of behavior that is directed to a broad goal" (p. 1). An effective teacher has not only professional skills and content knowledge, but also the beliefs and behaviors to meet the goal of helping all students learn. These dispositions, exhibited in the behaviors of teachers, foster student learning and are integrated in various contexts. How one teaches and the quality of that instruction stem from the beliefs and attitudes about each student and each student's individual learning process (Schussler, Stooksberry, & Bercaw, 2010). Teachers must develop self-awareness of their own beliefs and the impact of these beliefs on their practice (Hollins, 2015). Opportunities for reflection and self-awareness can have an impact on a teacher's developing practice. The delineation of behaviors and attitudes that indicate effective dispositions vary by state, district and teacher preparation program. These dispositions need to be introduced and defined early in a future teacher's career, and revisited throughout college and university coursework and field experiences, with ongoing opportunities for reflection and discussion (Cummins & Asempapa, 2013).

A common discussion reflecting the dispositions needed to help all children learn should revolve around general education teachers' acceptance of attitudes that support students including those with diverse abilities in their classrooms (McHatton & Parker, 2013). There is an increasing need for the skills necessary for effective collaboration between general and special education teachers, as well as an understanding of individualization and differentiation. Through structured coursework and field experiences, teachers build these skills and a sense of competence in implementing instruction and creating environments supporting all children. Jensen, Feinauer Whiting, and Chapman (2016) identified five dispositions found to support teaching children in a multicultural context: empathy, meekness, social awareness, inclusion, and advocacy. The researchers found strong support for the disposition of 'meekness' which was defined as teachers who are open-minded and seek out new opportunities to learn from students of diverse backgrounds.

## Specific Questions to Guide Discussion

1. How do dispositions (including your beliefs, attitudes, and actions) impact the process of becoming an effective teacher?

2. How have your perceptions about teaching at this level and with this group of students changed since starting this experience (and for your partner or team) since you started teaching? If so, why? What have you done as a response to those perceptual changes? If your perceptions have not changed, why do you think they have not?

3. Describe how your dispositions might have played a role in a recently taught lesson to help all students learn? Give some examples.

4. What dispositions will facilitate your continued collaboration work with your pair and/or team that can lead to more effective learning experiences for each student?

5. Are there any obstacles to becoming more collaborative? What strategies can you use to address these identified obstacles?

## Productive Practices

Supervisors can play an important role in helping preservice and inservice teachers to understand their professional responsibilities through the demonstration of selected dispositions in varied teaching contexts. Supervisors can facilitate the development of self-awareness and clarity for teacher educators as they develop dispositional areas (Schussler et al., 2010). The following productive practices can be used to accomplish this goal.

1. *Make sure dispositions are not left out of discussions and reflections.* Establish a consistent and continuing conversation where dispositions are assessed along with content knowledge and pedagogical skills. Take time to use this reflective process in an ongoing way to think about your practice, not just the content and skills shown at a particular time, but also your *growth and development* in these areas.
2. *Consider the selection of and reflection on field and teaching experiences that truly challenge your current beliefs, values, and actions.* Be open to new ideas and a variety of teaching styles demonstrated by veteran teachers. Use these experiences to establish lifelong dispositions for effective teaching, as well as effective collaboration.
3. *Establish ongoing, collaborative problem solving experiences in various contexts.* Discuss potential strategies and reflect upon those that were effective and those that were not. Consider and reflect upon the possible impact of your beliefs and actions on these experiences, during the planning process and after the experience.

## What Would You Do?

Ask your team or pair the following questions. For suggested responses to questions, see Appendix A.

1. What would you do if you notice a student is struggling with his reading yet has not been selected for the reading intervention program? How could you advocate for this student?

2. What would you do if a student said to you, "You don't know me, you don't know what my life is like, I can't do that..."?

3. What would you do if a student, after passing all the independent practice activities, failed the post assessment?

## Reflective Professional Growth Activities

Consider using these ideas or activities to facilitate and foster teacher growth and reflection. Select one or two ideas to help facilitate this reflection process that will help the teacher, pair, or team to understand the importance of professional dispositions. Remember that supervisors as instructional leaders should know their teacher, pairs or teams well, so be sure to choose a growth activity that would be the most effective for them.

### *Idea 1: Dispositions Related to Context for Learning*

With the use of think-alouds, provide opportunities to discuss and consider the viewpoints of others, as you explore the context of your students' lives (Hollins, 2015). How do you exhibit empathy toward the students rather than sympathy? How can you use each student's assets in your teaching?

**Evidence:** Notes related to the think-alouds, description of student assets that can be used in teaching with ideas for integration.

### *Idea 2: Dispositions Related to Planning*

Choose a sequence of lessons, taught collaboratively, from the previous week's instruction and discuss the planning and preparation process used. Perhaps try using the *Plus Delta* process to discuss how and if all students were challenged and engaged. The process, often used with collaborative teams, includes consideration of what happened, what went well (pluses), and what could be changed in future instruction (deltas). What contributed to each student's level of engagement and understanding of the learning targets? What should be considered for future planning?

**Evidence:** Annotation of lesson plan(s) with the ideas for change and improvement based on discussion.

### *Idea 3: Dispositions Related to Instruction and Assessment*

Choose a sequence of lessons, taught collaboratively, from the previous week's instruction and discuss the instructional strategies and assessments (formative and summative) used. Discuss how and if all students' needs were met. How did you check for understanding during the lesson? What adjustments did you make during the lesson and how did they contribute to improved student learning? Did your assessments accurately reflect how well your students met your objective? The *Plus Delta* process could, again, be used to facilitate the discussion.

**Evidence:** Annotation of lesson plan(s) with the ideas for change and improvement based on discussion.

### *Idea 4: Dispositions Related to Collaborative Teaching*

Discuss dispositions, such as collegiality and flexibility, as they relate to collaborative teaching. Include consideration of expectations for when collaborative teaching will occur with the pair at the start of the placement. Have the pair or team set a time each day to plan as well as debrief the collaborative lessons. When planning, be sure to focus on the impact on student learning and debrief the each teacher's development of self-awareness during the lesson.

**Evidence:** Document debriefing conferences regarding each teacher's understanding and self-awareness of their collaborative teaching skills (e.g., flexibility, communication, reflection).

## Follow-Up, Monitoring, and Goal Setting

Complete the follow-up questions for the selected reflective professional growth activity.

### *Idea 1: Dispositions Related to Context for Learning*

- What are your beliefs and attitudes toward the students in this classroom?
- What are the assets that students bring to this classroom?
- What do you have in common with the students? What are some differences?
- How can you advocate for your students?

### *Idea 2: Dispositions Related to Planning*

- What do you want your students to be able to do?
- Do you believe all of your students can achieve this objective? Why or why not?
- What supports do they need?
- What do you know about each student's strengths and weaknesses that can help you plan the lesson?

## Idea 3: Dispositions Related to Instruction and Assessment

- What type of instructional strategies will you use and why?
- How flexible are you during the lesson if it is not going the way you planned?
- How will you be responsive to each student's needs during the lesson?
- Are you open-minded when it comes to adapting or changing assessments so they match the strengths of the student (for example, letting a student use his native language to complete the assessment)?
- What changes will you consider for future lessons and activities based upon assessment results?

## Idea 4: Dispositions Related to Collaborative Teaching

- What are the challenges of collaborative teaching for each of the different co-teaching strategies?
- How would you rate your level of collegiality on a scale of 1-5 (5 being very collegial)?
- How are you demonstrating flexibility during planning, instruction, and assessment?

# Resources

## Books

**Framework for Teaching**

The framework for teaching is a research-based set of components of instruction that are grounded in a constructivist view of learning and teaching.

Danielson, C. (2007). *Enhancing professional practice: A framework for teaching* (2nd ed.). Alexandria, VA: ASCD.

## Modules

**An Introduction to Classroom Diversity**

Classroom Diversity: An Introduction to Classroom Diversity addresses teacher perceptions affecting instruction.

IRIS Center Peabody College Vanderbilt University. (2018). *Classroom diversity: An introduction to classroom diversity*. Retrieved from https://iris.peabody.vanderbilt.edu/module/div/

## Videos

**Cultural and Linguistic Differences**

This video is about cultural and linguistic differences and addresses stereotypes teachers might hold and their possible impact on teacher expectations.

IRIS Center Peabody College Vanderbilt University. (2018). *Cultural and linguistic differences.* Retrieved from https://iris.peabody.vanderbilt.edu/interview/ford_cul_ling_diff/

## Web Resources

**National Network for the Study of Educator Dispositions**

The Northern Kentucky University website includes their National Network for the Study of Educator Dispositions.

Northern Kentucky University. (2018). *National Network for the Study of Educator Dispositions.* Retrieved from https://inside.nku.edu/coehs/centers/educatordispositions.html

**Dispositions of the Effective Educator**

The School of Education at The University of Tennessee Chattanooga has identified eight dispositions with specific indicators that the effective professional educator displays.

The University of Tennessee Chattanooga. (2012–2018). The dispositions of the effective educator. Retrieved from https://www.utc.edu/school-education/studentresources/disposition.php

**Teacher Education Dispositions at Mansfield University**

This pdf links to the Teacher Education Dispositions document at Mansfield University.

Mansfield University. (n.d.). *Teacher education dispositions.* Retrieved on https://www.mansfield.edu/edspeced/upload/TeacherEducationDispositionsfinal208.pdf

## Key Terms and Definitions

**Dispositions:** Dispositions are the attitudes, values, and beliefs demonstrated through both verbal and nonverbal behaviors as educators interact with students, families, colleagues, and communities.

**Meekness:** Meekness is a quality a teacher has when the teacher is open to learning from their students, and who uses a variety of activities and opportunities for those learning experiences.

**Plus Delta Process:** The Plus Delta Process is a method for teams to debrief which includes consideration of what happened, what went well (pluses), and what could be changed in future instruction (deltas).

**Student assets:** Student assets are qualities that serve as an advantage or source of strength.

**Think-aloud:** Think-aloud is verbalizing out loud what you are thinking so others can be aware of your thought process.

# Appendix A

## *What Would You Do? Questions with Suggested Responses*

1. What would you do if you notice a student is struggling with his reading yet has not been selected for the reading intervention program? How could you advocate for this student?

   **Suggested Response 1:** You should talk to your cooperating teacher or colleague about the struggles you've noticed. Be specific and document what the student says or does such as: He substitutes a word that does not make sense. He does not use picture cues. Then ask the teacher/colleague how the referral process works and if there is anything else you can do to help document the student's strengths and needs.

2. What would you do if a student said to you, "You don't know me, you don't know what my life is like, I can't do that..."?

   **Suggested Response 2:** You can let the student know that you would like to get to know the student and offer some opportunities such as eating lunch together and allowing the student to pick some friends to join the two of you. Be a good listener and see if the student has any questions for you as well.

3. What would you do if a student, after passing all the independent practice activities, failed the post assessment?

   **Suggested Response 3:** First, find out if the format and delivery method of the post-assessment was appropriate for the student. For example, was it a math test that involved a lot of reading? Was it the first time an English Learner is taking a test in English? Then look at the problems that the student missed and see if you can pinpoint specific skills or concepts that need to be retaught.

# Appendix B
## R.E.A.C.H. Dispositions
### Elmhurst College Department of Education Professional Conduct Guidelines

Aligned with the Illinois Professional Teaching Standard *Professionalism, Leadership, and Advocacy* (9H, 9I, 9J, 9O, 9P, 9Q, 9R, 9S, 9T)

| | |
|---|---|
| **Responsibility** | **Demonstrates timeliness in course attendance and responsibilities.** Attends class, be on time, and stay for the duration of class.<br><br>**Follows syllabus guidelines.** Complete assignments on time, which is the beginning of class on a due date. Assignments are late if class is not attended or if there are technical problems. Work may not be faxed or e-mailed to the professor without prior approval.<br><br>**Communicates questions and concerns to the instructor.** Communicates in a timely and appropriate manner. Use instructor office hours or make an appointment to ask individual questions or discuss progress. |
| **Ethics** | **Practices academic integrity and honesty.** Assignments often involve collaboration and the use of multiple resources. Clearly cites ideas from other sources and acknowledges the assistance of others. Portions of assignments used for credit in different courses must be pre-approved by both professors and should be referenced clearly for dual credit on the cover page.<br><br>**Submits accurate accounts of field experiences.** Have them verified by a licensed supervising professional.<br><br>**Maintains confidentiality** in all field reports and discussions of fieldwork. Fabrication of field hours, experiences, or signatures or failure to notify the College or schools of your criminal background check status are violations of the College's *Academic Integrity Policy*. |
| **Attitude** | **Participates regularly and positively.** Active participation is expected during every class meeting. Electronic devices should not interrupt class or distract others. Set cell phones to vibrate or turn them off. Electronic tools are to be used for coursework or activities directly related to the class—not used for entertainment, personal communications, or other coursework during class meetings or in field settings.<br><br>**Respectful of others' contributions and demonstrates appreciation of diversity and new ideas.** Valuing of diverse ideas and beliefs is expected through courteous debate and dialogue as well as in respectful written evaluation and analysis.<br><br>**Responds positively to feedback.** Accepts feedback from instructor, mentor teachers, and peers in a positive receptive manner. Uses feedback from instructors and mentor teachers in course activities, course assignments, and field experience activities to improve coursework, teaching practices, and professional dispositions. |
| **Collegiality** | **Makes equitable contributions to group efforts.** Give your maximum efforts in promoting equitable group work and completing field experiences. Maintain commitments to classmates and professionals in the field.<br><br>**Collaborates with peers and school staff members and mentor teachers in a professional manner.** Take initiative in the field. Volunteer your time and share professional resources and responsibilities. Show appreciation for the time and efforts of others. |
| **Honor** | **Communicates high regard for the profession, educators, students, and parents.** Professional demeanor (e.g., conduct and attire) is expected in school settings. Honor the commitments of hosting professionals by providing details of all course assignments at the beginning of the term.<br><br>**View course assignments as opportunities to enhance content area knowledge and skills.** Demonstrate professionalism in formal class presentations. All written work must be word-processed and edited prior to submission. Use APA style. |

Elmhurst College Department of Education (2014). *REACH Dispositions: Policies and Procedures*. Elmhurst, IL.

## References

Cummins, L., & Asempapa, B. (2013). Fostering teacher candidate dispositions in teacher education programs. *Journal of the Scholarship of Teaching and Learning, 13*(3), 99–119.

Hollins, E. R. (Ed.). (2015). *Rethinking field experience in preservice teacher preparation: Meeting new challenges for accountability.* New York, NY: Routledge.

IRIS Center Peabody College Vanderbilt University. (2018). *Classroom diversity: An introduction to classroom diversity.* Retrieved from https://iris.peabody.vanderbilt.edu/module/div/

IRIS Center Peabody College Vanderbilt University. (2018). *Cultural and linguistic differences.* Retrieved from https://iris.peabody.vanderbilt.edu/interview/ford_cul_ling_diff/

Jensen, B., Feinauer Whiting, E., & Chapman, S. (2016). Measuring the multicultural dispositions of preservice teachers. *Journal of Psychoeducational Assessment.* https://doi.org/10.1177/0734282916662426

Katz, L. G. (1993, September). *Dispositions as educational goals.* ERIC Digest, EDO-PS-93-10.

McHatton, P. A., & Parker, A. (2013). Purposeful preparation: Longitudinally exploring inclusion attitudes of general and special education pre-service teachers. *Teacher Education and Special Education, 36*(3), 186–203.

Meidl, T., & Baumann, B. (2015). Extreme makeover: Disposition development of pre-service teachers. *Journal of Community Engagement and Scholarship, 1*(8), 90–97.

Schussler, D. L., Stooksberry, L. M., & Bercaw, L. A. (2010). Understanding teacher candidate dispositions: Reflecting to build self-awareness. *Journal of Teacher Education, 6*(14), 350–363. doi:10.1177/0022487110371377

MODULE **18**

# Supporting the Job Hunt

Courtney Miller
*West Virginia University*

*One important key to success is self-confidence. An important key to self-confidence is preparation.*
—Arthur Ashe

### MODULE DESCRIPTION

The transition from preservice teacher to hired educator can be an uncertain time. The pressures of finding a teaching position to demonstrate effective teaching skills can be overwhelming. This module provides guided questions, activities, and resources one can use to help support a teacher in the job hunting process. Some of the growth activities in this module are specifically relevant to the teacher candidate and the college/university supervisor.

## Theory/Conceptual Framework

Following graduation and certification/licensure in a specific educational program and/or content area, most preservice teachers plan to begin the process of job hunting. This process can be long and intimidating, even with the number of teacher shortages in the nation (Cross, 2017). Although teacher preparation programs have supplied preservice teachers with a toolbox of resources to support planning instruction and assessment, it is critical to also provide them with effective supports that will assist them in the job search.

The first part to successful job hunting is to understand how the employment process works. Although each state or local school district may have a different process, there are some similarities that are worth noting. First, the process will begin with the teacher locating open teaching positions. Some colleges or universities may provide teachers with the opportunity to attend career fairs. However, with technology so readily available, many school districts are electing to post their positions on the Internet. Teachers seeking employment can use a generic search engine, or choose to locate openings through teacher specific websites such as Teachers-Teachers (https://www.teachers-teachers.com/) or SchoolSpring (https://www.schoolspring.com/; Clement, 2012). After narrowing down job openings, they will then fill out a job application. While this may seem like an easy task, it is crucial to follow the steps entirely to ensure correct completion. Ayers and Senne (2011) stated that job applications should be proofread by outside individuals to eliminate errors. Additionally, the candidate should look over the job application with a seasoned professional such as a teacher or professor to make sure all components are filled out correctly.

For the job application, preservice teacher candidates could be asked to provide a resume and cover letter. A resume will provide the administration and/or hiring committee with information about the preservice teacher candidate. There are a number of things to consider while writing a resume. Teachers seeking employment should plan to write a one-page resume with bulleted points. The seven basic components of a successful resume include: personal data, career objective(s), education, teaching experience, related work experience, skills/expertise, professional organizations, and references (Quezada, 2004). Some teachers may elect to participate in a video resume that includes recorded lessons in addition to the seven basic components (Dendler & Edwards, 2011). The cover letter should reflect the teacher's personality, and also provide information specific to the job opening and school district (Clement, 2014). Carefully preparing these documents can assist the teacher for the next step of the hiring process: the interview.

Some individuals view the interview component of the hiring process to be the most stressful. The purpose of the interview is for the teacher and the hiring committee to meet face-to-face to discuss future employment. It is critical that the teacher candidate is fully prepared for successful interviewing. Behavior-based questioning has become a key factor in teacher interviews (Clement, 2013). Many hiring committees will ask interviewees a series of questions that allow them to answer based on their previous experiences and expertise. Teacher candidates should be mindful about how they answer the questions. Brosy, Bangerter, and Mayor (2016) found that long pauses between interview questions and answers had some negative impact on the hiring committee's decisions. Instead, anticipating these types of questions and practicing responses can help the teacher candidate to increase their confidence. Clement (2008) suggested that quick, direct answers are the most effective to yield positive hiring results.

While it is impossible to provide a contingency for every hiring process situation, it is imperative that teachers understand the procedures and are adequately prepared to begin the job hunt. For example, teachers can provide information regarding their collaborative teaching experience in both a general and special education setting. By providing teacher candidates with effective strategies and resources, they can begin to build their confidence and preparation that will hopefully help them to secure a teaching position in the future.

## Specific Questions to Guide Discussion

1. Describe a positive teaching experience you have had during your preservice or inservice teaching experiences. What made that experience stand out? What instructional skills and strategies did you demonstrate?

2. Describe the process that you use to reflect on your lessons while in process or after they have been taught. What made that experience stand out? What would cause you to change the course of a lesson? What did you learn from this experience?

3. Describe your ideal teaching position. Where is the location? What is the content area and/or areas of focus? What is the age of your students? What makes this teaching job fit your strengths and interests?

4. How do you feel about entering the job field? What makes you confident? What makes you nervous?

5. How prepared do you feel to participate in the hiring process? Have you ever completed a resume or a cover letter? Have you ever participated in an interview? Do you feel confident to complete online applications?

## Productive Practices

Use these practices to assist your preservice and inservice teachers with successful job hunting.

1. *Be prepared.*
   a. It is important to be confident when applying for teaching positions, but it is also important to be fully prepared for the process.
   b. Research teaching positions in several different settings to understand how the hiring process works. Ask questions regarding open positions to clarify any misunderstandings.
   c. Prepare a list of questions to ask during your interview about the position. Be alert and ask follow-up questions, if needed, to clarify the information and to show your interest in the position.

2. *Market yourself.*
    a. Identify your strengths and talents. Ask yourself, "What unique contributions can I make to the grade level and school?" and "What sets me apart from the other candidates?"
    b. Ask yourself, "How do I reflect on my instructional practice?" and "How can I improve my teaching?"
    c. Think about how you present yourself professionally. In the ever-evolving age of technology, make sure that you maintain a professional web presence or digital footprint. Ask, "Have I googled myself to see what information comes up?"
3. *Think ahead.*
    a. Think about what you will gain from potential teaching positions and how you will reach your professional goals within that district or setting.
    b. Ask yourself, "Am I willing to relocate? Do I feel more comfortable staying close to home?"
    c. Identify specific application steps that you will need to complete in order to meet job specifications.
4. *Reflect, reflect, reflect.*
    a. Reflect on your preservice or inservice experiences. Possibly video record a lesson to help guide your reflective practice. Be sure to include any parental consent needed to record and/or view lessons (see Idea 3 under "Reflective Professional Growth Activities" for more details).
    b. Reflect on the teaching positions that interest you. Ask yourself, "Why do these openings interest me? What is appealing about them?"
    c. Reflect on the different components of the hiring process: (a) determine personal needs, (b) research open positions, (c) prepare materials, (d) apply for position(s), (e) interview for positions(s), (f) follow-up on interview(s), and (g) reflect on individual performance. Ask yourself, "Am I prepared? Do I have all of my documents ready (e.g., sample lesson plans with student work, copies of the resume)? Do I have a prepared list of interview questions to ask? How should I follow up on the interview?"
    d. Reflect on your actions and consider what is important to address for the post-interview. Ask yourself, "What could I have done better? Did I maintain a professional disposition? How can I improve my chances of securing a position the next time? What did I do well? How could I build upon this experience?"

## What Would You Do?

Ask your team or pair the following questions. For suggested responses to questions, see Appendix A.

1. What would you do if an interviewer asked you a personal question you felt uncomfortable answering?

2. You are currently teaching sixth grade in an elementary school and would like to find a primary position. Your district does not have any primary openings. What would you do if you recently found a job posting for a second grade near your

home and see that the posting asks for three different reference letters? Should you ask your current principal for a letter of recommendation or is it preferable to keep your job search private?

3. You have decided to apply for several elementary positions in nearby schools. You have always heard that it is good to ask questions at an interview. What kinds of questions should you ask and where do you go to find out more about a school or district in preparation for an interview?

4. What would you do if you want to start looking for another teaching position but want to be sure that the salary will be higher in your new district? Where can you go to find this information? Is it rude to ask about salary during your interview?

## Reflective Professional Growth Activities

Consider these ideas or activities to facilitate and foster teacher growth and reflection. Select one or two ideas to help facilitate this reflection process that will help the preservice and inservice teachers on the job hunt. Remember that supervisors are instructional leaders and should know the teachers well, so be sure to choose a growth activity that would be the most effective for them.

### *Idea 1: Helping the Teacher Candidate to Research Job Openings*

Discuss with the teacher candidate their qualifications and job opportunities. Identify their interests and expectations for their first teaching job. Use one of the educator job opening search engines found in the "Resources" section (e.g., https://www.schoolspring.com/, https://www.teachers-teachers.com/) or have the candidate look specifically at local or state postings. Allow the candidate to search beyond their credentials for potential lifelong learning opportunities. After evaluating results, have the student further explore the specific districts or schools and list the openings in order of priority. Outline pros and cons for each job description and school district.

**Evidence:** The teacher candidate prepared a list of at least five to ten job openings in order of importance with pros and cons outlined for each school district and job description.

### *Idea 2: Complete a Job Application: Create a Resume and Cover Letter*

Use one of the desired job openings or find a posting and fill out the job application. Determine whether to complete the application on paper or online. Review the steps necessary in the application process. After completing the job application, create a resume and cover letter designed to address the requirements in the job posting. Use resume templates or sample resumes for reference. Write a cover letter specific to the job posting to ensure that it adheres to the position's guidelines. For sample resumes and cover letters, applicable to a variety of K–12 teaching positions, go to http://resumes-for-teachers.com. Develop a list of professional references that you can use in the hiring process. Be sure to notify these personal references that you are using their names on your application materials.

**Evidence:** Completed job application, resume, and cover letter following the job posting guidelines.

## *Idea 3: Video-Recorded Lesson and Reflection*

A key component of effective teaching is reflecting on your practice. Video record a single lesson or series of lessons from your preservice or inservice experience. Identify personal strengths and areas for improvement within the lesson. List ideas to improve the lesson and/or presentation during the teaching event. Use the checklist in Figure 18.1 to help guide your reflection. Be sure to add any additional components needed for successful reflection. It is helpful to view the teaching video first by yourself and then at least once together with the supervisor, pair or team to assist with the reflection process. The identification of teacher strengths and areas of improvement can help the teacher prepare for the interview itself.

**Evidence:** Videotaped lesson, completed checklist (Figure 18.1) with list of strengths and areas for growth.

| Lesson Component | Yes | No | Ideas for Improvement |
|---|---|---|---|
| Did you communicate your lesson objectives/outcomes to students through a lesson target sentence? | | | |
| Were you visible to each student? Did you speak loudly and clearly? | | | |
| Were the students engaged? What strategies were used to engage the students? | | | |
| Did you offer an adequate number of examples? | | | |
| Did you appropriately manage student behaviors? | | | |
| Did you differentiate your instruction by content, process, product or environment? | | | |
| Did you monitor student responses and progress throughout the lesson? | | | |
| Did you use various forms of assessment throughout the lesson (i.e., formative and/or summative)? | | | |
| Were you culturally responsive to student language, culture, and experience? | | | |

**Figure 18.1** Videotaped lesson reflection checklist.

## *Idea 4: Conduct a Mock Interview*

Conduct a mock interview to help the candidate to prepare for a real-life situation. Create a job posting that the job seeker can apply for and develop a resume and/or cover letter. Develop a list of behaviorally-based interview questions you can ask your candidate. Allow the candidate to look over the list of questions and discuss any questions or concerns. Discuss the importance of appearance and preparation before the mock interview. Help the candidate to generate a list of appropriate questions to ask after the interview. If desired, video record the mock interview and view it with the candidate. Reflect on strengths and weaknesses within the interview and develop a plan of improvement.

**Evidence:** A completed mock interview, generated list of 3–5 post-interview questions, and outlined list of strengths/areas for growth with a specific plan for improvement.

## *Idea 5: Lesson Database*

It is not uncommon for some interviewees to conduct a lesson in front of a group of students as a part of the hiring process. Have the candidate develop a lesson plan database with the most successful and effective lessons they used throughout their preservice or inservice teaching career. Be sure to include lesson plans that are differentiated in content, process of teaching, product or assessment, and/or environment.

**Evidence:** A compiled lesson plan database (online or in print) of at least 5-10 content area lessons. Lesson plans for collaborative teaching should also appear in the database.

# Follow-Up, Monitoring, and Goal Setting

Complete one of the follow-up, monitoring, or goal setting ideas based on the idea that you selected from the reflective professional growth activities section.

## *Idea 1: Research Job Openings*

- What websites did you explore while searching?
- Which website was the most helpful?
- What types of positions did you search?
- What information did you find in the job postings?
- Which job posting was most interesting to you? Which job posting was least interesting to you?
- What information did you find after researching the district and/or school?
- What are the pros of these teaching positions? What are the cons of these teaching positions?
- Why did you rate the positions in the list in that order?
- What next steps are you going to take to apply for these positions?
- Do you have any additional questions?

### Idea 2: Complete a Job Application: Create a Resume and Cover Letter

- What was the easiest part of completing the application?
- What was the most difficult part of completing the application?
- Do you have any questions regarding the job application process?
- Is your resume easy to understand and read?
- Does your cover letter meet the requirements addressed in the job posting?
- Are your documents written in a professional manner?
- Did you print the resume and cover letter on professional paper?
- Did you ask your references for a positive recommendation? Why did you choose these specific individuals as references?
- What did you learn about yourself and the hiring process during this activity?
- Do you have any additional questions?

### Idea 3: Video-Recorded Lesson and Reflection

- What were your strengths during the lesson?
- What were your weaknesses during the lesson?
- Did anything surprise you after viewing this lesson?
- How can you improve your effective teaching by viewing this lesson?
- Why did you choose to record this lesson?
- What did you learn about yourself after viewing this lesson?
- How can you use the information gained from this activity in the hiring and/or interviewing process?
- Would you like to record a second lesson to view and reflect? Why or why not?
- Do you have any additional questions?

### Idea 4: Conduct a Mock Interview

- How did you feel during the mock interview process?
- Did any part of the process confuse or worry you?
- Did you present yourself in a professional manner to the interviewer?
- Did you provide the interviewer with any additional documents needed?
- How confident did you feel during the interview?
- Were there any questions the interviewer asked you that made you uncomfortable?
- Did you give yourself enough time to answer the interview questions?
- Did you answer the interview questions fully?
- Did you maintain eye contact and a professional tone?
- Did you ask any follow-up questions?
- What did you learn about yourself after participating in this activity?
- How can the information gained from this activity help you in future interviews?
- Do you have any additional questions?

### Idea 5: Lesson Database

- How many lessons did you include in your database?
- Do you feel comfortable enough to teach a lesson "on the spot?" Some districts require teachers to teach a lesson as part of the interview process.

- What different types of content area lesson plans did you include in your database?
- Are there any similarities or differences in the lessons you chose for the database?
- Do you have enough variety in your lessons for the database?
- Do you think these lessons demonstrate your teaching effectiveness?
- What did you learn about yourself while you were creating your database?
- How will the information gained from this activity help you in the hiring process?
- Do you have any additional questions?

## Resources

### Articles

#### Getting a Job

This article discusses the group interview process and provides tips on how a candidate can stand out.

Cox, J. (n.d.). Getting a teaching job: Surviving a group interview. Retrieved from www.teachhub.com/get-teaching-job-surviving-group-interview

#### Improving Teacher Selection With Behavior-Based Interviewing

This article summarizes the interviewing practice of using behavior-based questions. The author includes sample questions and how to assess the answers.

Clement, M. C. (2008). *Improving teacher selection with behavior-based interviewing.* Retrieved from https://www.naesp.org/sites/default/files/resources/2/Principal/2008/J-Fp44.pdf

#### Hiring an Effective Special Education Teacher

This article provides lists and descriptions of characteristics shown by effective special educators. The author includes tips of what interviewers may be looking for during the hiring process.

Fenlon, A. (2008). *Hiring an effective special education teacher.* Retrieved from https://www.naesp.org/sites/default/files/resources/2/Principal/2008/N-Dp24.pdf

#### Behavior-Based Interviewing for Education Majors

This PDF offers sample behavior-based interviewing questions designed specifically for individuals in the education field.

Fort Hays State University Career Services. (n.d.). *Behavior-based interviewing for education majors.* Retrieved from https://www.fhsu.edu/career/documents/handout/educationbbi/index

### Modules

#### Dispositions of Teachers and Teacher Leaders

This module discusses the importance of teacher dispositions when preparing for the job hunt process. The authors outline four components of positive teacher dispositions including demeanor, interaction, commitment, and leadership.

Modules Addressing Special Education and Teacher Education (MAST). (2017). *Dispositions of Teachers and Teacher Leaders.* Retrieved from http://mast.ecu.edu/modules/dttl/

## Videos

### Traits That Employers Look For

This video outlines traits a school looks for when hiring new teachers.

Edutopia. (n.d.). *YES Prep Hires and Supports Great Teachers*. Retrieved from https://www.edutopia.org/stw-yes-prep-teacher-development-video

### Using Video to Improve Practice 101

This video provides helpful tips and tools that can be used to record and view your teaching. (Time: 4:38)

The Teaching Network. (n.d.). *Using Video to Improve Practice: Video 101*. Retrieved from https://www.teachingchannel.org/videos/videotaping-tips-for-teachers

### Using Video to Improve Practice: Do It Yourself!

A teacher demonstrates how using video reflection in the classroom can improve the effectiveness of teaching. (Time: 5:42)

The Teaching Network. (n.d.). *Using Video to Improve Practice: Do It Yourself!* Retrieved from https://www.teachingchannel.org/videos/improve-teaching-with-video

## Web Resources

### A+ Résumés for Teachers

This site lists many sample résumés and cover letters for various K–12 teaching positions.

Alstad-Davies, C. (2001–2018). *A+ résumés for teachers*. Retrieved on https://resumes-for-teachers.com

### K–12 Jobs

This website has teaching jobs and administrative school positions at public and private institutions.

K–12 Jobs (1997–2012). Teaching jobs and administrative school positions at public and private institutions. Retrieved from https://k12jobs.com/

### National Center for Education Statistics (NCES)

NCES is the part of the United States Department of Education's Institute of Education Sciences (IES) that collects, analyzes, and publishes statistics on education and public school district finance information in the United States.

U.S. Department of Education. (n.d.). *National Center for Education Statistics*. Retrieved from https://nces.ed.gov/

### SchoolSpring

This is a website that houses teaching and jobs in education for free.

PeopleAdmin. (2015). *School spring*. Retrieved from https://www.schoolspring.com/

**United States Department of Education TEACH**

Through this website, you can explore teaching as well as apply for positions to become a teacher based on different regions.

U.S. Department of Education. (n.d.). *Explore teaching*. Retrieved from https://www.teach.org/

## Key Terms and Definitions

**Behavior-based questions:** Questions used in interviewing that allow the interviewee to answer based on previous experiences.

**Cover letter:** A letter sent with a resume that highlights the features within your resume that are applicable to a specific job posting.

**Differentiated instruction:** Instructional strategies used within a lesson to meet the needs of all learners. Differentiation provides multiple opportunities to show student progress and achievement through changes in content, process, product, and/or environment.

**Group process interview:** A screening process where multiple candidates are interviewed at one time.

**Hiring committee:** A group of individuals involved in the job hiring process. Their responsibilities include reviewing applications, resumes, and cover letters, and participating in the interview by asking questions to the interviewee.

**Hiring process:** A step-by-step process that an employer takes to determine the best eligible candidate for the position.

**Job-posting:** Descriptions of teaching positions available online or in print that outline available positions and locations.

**Lesson database:** A number of effective lessons used by the teacher seeking employment as a means for completing the hiring process (such as teaching during the interview). These lessons differ in content areas and have been taught by the teacher during their preservice or teaching career.

**Mock interview:** A hypothetical interview conducted by the supervisor as the interviewer and the teacher candidate as the interviewee. Additional personnel may be included to replicate a hiring committee.

**Preservice:** A teacher candidate currently in a college or university teacher preparation program who is completing requirements for graduation and certification/licensure.

**Résumé:** A marketing tool that job seekers use to communicate their value.

# Appendix A

## *What Would You Do? Suggested Responses*

1. What would you do if an interviewer asked you a personal question you felt uncomfortable answering?

    **Suggested Response 1:** I would explain to the interviewer that I feel uncomfortable answering such a personal question but would be happy to answer questions pertaining to my qualifications for the job.

2. You are currently teaching sixth-grade in an elementary school and would like to find a primary position. Your district does not have any primary openings. What would you do if you recently found a job posting for a second-grade near your home and see that the posting asks for three different reference letters? Should you ask your current principal for a letter of recommendation or is it preferable to keep your job search private?

    **Suggested Response 2:** I would share my interests with my principal. It's important to build a relationship with your principal for multiple reasons, and in this case because they can offer valuable insight into the hiring process. They can write a letter of recommendation or refer you to other colleagues or districts who are looking for second-grade teachers.

3. You have decided to apply for several elementary positions in nearby schools. You have always heard that it is good to ask questions at an interview. What kinds of questions should you ask and where do you go to find out more about a school or district in preparation for an interview?

    **Suggested Response 3:** It's important to view the district and school's website. Look for important information about the school (i.e., a letter from the principal), read the handbook or discipline policies, and look over the school calendar. Try to gather as much information as possible about what they do, and as you are looking, create questions about the information that you find. For example, you may want to ask some of the following questions at the interview: "I noticed on your website that the 8th grade students completed a service-learning project at a local nursing home. Is there potential to get involved with service-learning? What other opportunities do the students have with service- learning in the local community?" It is important to ask questions about things that you are interested in becoming involved in and also any clarifying questions that you have about the specific position. For example, you could say, "I'm very exciting about collaborating with the other 3rd grade teachers. From the website, I noticed that there are 3 teachers. Are there opportunities for us to collaborate?" You can then follow up with, "Do you think that the team would be willing to collaborate?" Another question that you could also ask is, "What would the teachers say is the hardest thing about this position?" You want to design questions so that you have an understanding for the school and position to see if it's a good match for you.

4. What would you do if you want to start looking for another teaching position but want to be sure that the salary will be higher in your new district? Where can you go to find this information? Is it rude to ask about salary during your interview?

    **Suggested Response 4:** Sometimes this information is posted with the job description, so look there first. Teaching salaries in public schools are public information so you can use the Internet and search, "salary at XXXX in XXXX" to find information about the salary in that school or district. This is not something that you want to ask in an interview so try to avoid asking a question about salaries until you are in the final interview stage.

# References

Ayers, S. F., & Senne, T. A. (2011). Getting into the game: Helping preservice candidates find initial teaching positions. *JOPERD: The Journal of Physical Education, Recreation, & Dance, 82*(3), 19–31.

Brosy, J., Bangerter, A., & Mayor, E. (2016). Disfluent responses to job interview questions and what they entail. *Discourse Processes, 53*(5/6), 371–391.

Clement, M. C. (2008). *Improving teacher selection with behavior-based interviewing.* Retrieved from https://www.naesp.org/sites/default/files/resources/2/Principal/2008/J-Fp44.pdf

Clement, M. C. (2008). What women need to know about today's teacher job searches and interviews. *Delta Kappa Gamma Bulletin, 74*(4), 44–47.

Clement, M. C. (2012). Online teacher recruitment: An interview with two pioneers in the field. *Delta Kappa Gamma Bulletin, 78*(4), 30–33.

Clement, M. C. (2013). Hiring good colleagues: What you need to know about interviewing new teachers. *Clearing House, 86*(3), 99–102.

Clement, M. C. (2014). Purposeful professional communication by teacher educators: Helping candidates get jobs. *Delta Kappa Gamma Bulletin, 80*(3), 28–33.

Cross, F. (2017). Teacher shortage areas nationwide listing 1990–1991 through 2016–2017. Retrieved from https://www2.ed.gov/about/offices/list/ope/pol/tsa.pdf

Dendler, D., & Edwards, K. L. (2011). The tipping point: Mentoring the general music student teacher through the job-seeking process with a technology edge. *General Music Today, 25*(1), 27–32.

Quezada, R. L. (2004). From student teacher to teacher: Making the first cut (Part I). *Journal of Instructional Psychology, 31*(1), 75–85.

# About the Contributors

**Brooke Blanks, PhD**, is an associate professor of special education at Radford University. Dr. Blanks earned a BA in psychology from the University of Virginia and her MEd and PhD in specialized education services from the University of North Carolina, Greensboro. Prior to working in higher education, Dr. Blanks was a middle school special educator and reading specialist. She focuses on preparing general education and special education teachers to collaborate and co-teach in inclusive classrooms. She is particularly interested in pre-professional technology enhanced supervision and distance coaching in rural areas, especially rural Appalachia. Dr. Blanks is an active member of the Council for Exceptional Children.

**Bernard F. Bragen, Jr. EdD**, assistant professor, Monmouth University. Dr. Bragen earned a doctorate from Nova Southeastern University in educational leadership. His BS in management science/finance and MA in special education are from Kean University, with an additional MA in urban school leadership from New Jersey City University. He acquired additional post masters certification as a child study member in learning disabilities teacher consultant (LDT-C). He has taught secondary special education in a variety of grade levels and subjects in settings ranging from inclusion to self-contained. He also worked as an LDT-C, supervisor, assistant principal, principal, assistant superintendent, and superintendent in P–12 settings in Central New Jersey. Dr. Bragen began working as an assistant professor at Monmouth University in 2017. He specializes in educational leadership and is program director for the EdD program at Monmouth University. Dr. Bragen is an active member of the American Association of School Administrators, New Jersey Association of School Administrators, and the New Jersey Principal and Supervisors Association. His current scholarship focuses on school change and preservice teacher residency, clinical practice, and the impact of substitute teaching on preservice teachers.

**Ayanna F. Brown, PhD**, associate professor and associate chair of curriculum and professional development at Elmhurst College. Dr. Brown holds a BS from Tuskegee University in secondary education, language arts; MEd in curriculum and instruction; and PhD from Vanderbilt University in interdisciplinary studies: language, literacy, and sociology. Her research focuses on discussions of "race," contemporary African American studies, and discourse analysis. Her research has been presented nationally and internationally. She is an active member of several professional organizations and served as the 2013–2014 chair of the National Council of Teachers of English Assembly for Research. Brown is the co-editor of *Critical Consciousness in Curricular Research: Evidence From the Field* (2013, Peter Lang).

**Lisa Burke, PhD**, is a professor of special education at Elmhurst College in Elmhurst Illinois. Dr. Burke earned her BSEd and MSEd in special education from Northern Illinois University. She received her PhD from the University of Illinois at Chicago in special education with a specialization in literacy needs for students with exceptionalities. Dr. Burke was a special education teacher for 16 years before transitioning to higher education in 2001. She has experience working with students from elementary age through high school in a variety of special education service delivery options. Dr. Burke's research interests include literacy skill development for students with autism, the inclusion of students with exceptionalities in general education, compensatory abilities, and the use of learning strategies for students with exceptionalities.

**Debbie F. Cosgrove, PhD**, is an assistant professor and director of elementary education at Elmhurst College, Illinois. She holds a BA from Bethel University and an MA in educational leadership from the University of Illinois at Chicago. She earned her PhD from the University of Illinois at Chicago in curriculum and instruction. Dr. Cosgrove taught for 18 years in diverse public school settings in Grades K–6. She also served 18 years in public school administration in the roles of elementary principal, curriculum director, and assistant superintendent. She currently teaches courses to elementary education majors on curriculum, planning and instruction for primary grades, cross-cultural studies for teaching English language learners, teacher collaboration, and professional practice. She also facilitates advanced seminars for student teaching. Dr. Cosgrove's research interests include collaborative planning and instruction, culturally responsive pedagogy, supervision in collaborative teaching contexts, and school–college partnerships. She devotes much time and energy to supervisor development in order to support quality preservice teacher education. Dr. Cosgrove has presented at local, state, and national conferences and is a member of the American Association of Colleges for Teacher Education and the Association for Supervision and Curriculum Development.

**Linda Dauksas, EdD**, is an associate professor of education at Elmhurst College. She has a doctorate in instructional leadership from National Louis University. At Elmhurst College she is the director of the early childhood and special education programs. She teaches methods courses in curriculum and instruction, assessment, methods for early childhood special education and working with families and communities, and has published several articles on practices that enhance learning for young children. Before joining the faculty, she dedicated 30 years to teaching and leading programs for young children and families. Her current research centers on preparing responsive teacher candidates to work in high needs settings, including the development of family partnerships to enhance the growth and development of young children.

**LuEllen Doty, EdD**, is a professor of education at Elmhurst College and director of the Elmhurst Learning and Success Academy, a post-secondary program for young adults with disabilities. She has experience at the elementary through high school levels, as well as in the area of parent advocacy. Her pedagogical and research interests include transition and postsecondary experiences, early childhood special education, and applications of technology in special education. She is a member of the Council for Exceptional Children and the honor societies of Kappa Delta Pi, Omicron Delta Kappa, and Phi Kappa Phi, and has presented locally and nationally.

**Keri Haley, PhD**, is an assistant professor of special education at the University of West Florida. Prior to joining UWF, Haley worked as an exceptional student educator and ESE department supervisor in elementary and middle schools in the Tampa Bay area. She joined the special education field after her second of three children struggled academically with a learning disability. Her dissertation, based on personal experiences, focused on parent-educators who advocated for the rights of their own children with disabilities inside the school districts where they worked and their perception of related job security. Haley's research interests include parent–school relationships in special education, school–university partnerships, and special education preservice teacher preparation.

**Wendy Harriott, PhD**, is an associate dean for the School of Education and an associate professor in special education at Monmouth University. Dr. Harriott earned a BS in special education from Bloomsburg University. She earned a MS in special education with an emphasis in counseling from Marywood College. Her PhD was in special education with an emphasis on educational administration from The Pennsylvania State University. She has taught students with various disabilities in public middle and high schools in Pennsylvania. She has dedicated her career to improving teacher education and special education for Pk–12 teachers. She is an active member of the American Association for Colleges in Teacher Education (AACTE), the Council for Exceptional Children (CEC), the Teacher Education Division of CEC (TED), and the Association for Supervision and Curriculum Development (ASCD). She conducts presentations regularly for TED and AACTE.

**Mary Haspel, MA, BCBA,** is an instructor in the Department of Education at Monmouth University. She is a board certified behavior analyst as well as a certified special education teacher. Prior to working at Monmouth, she served as the autism and multiple disabilities specialist for the New Jersey Department of Education and conducted extensive training and guidance in the areas of behavior management and evidence-based practices for students with autism across the state. Her research areas include effective training modalities for teachers of students with autism, utilization of applied behavior analysis in public schools, and data-based home–school collaboration for the treatment of severe and challenging behaviors.

**David Hoppey, PhD**, is an associate professor and director of the doctoral program in educational leadership at the University of North Florida. David has taught courses to both special education and elementary education majors on best inclusive practices to meet the needs of students with disabilities as well as doctoral seminars on teacher education and special education. He also has worked extensively redesigning undergraduate and doctoral programs to include more clinically rich teacher preparation components. David's scholarship examines inclusive teacher education, special education policy, and school–university partnerships, including providing quality preservice teacher education, and ongoing, in-service teacher professional development.

**Paul R. Klenck, JD,** is an attorney practicing in labor, employment, administrative, and association law litigating cases before state and federal agencies, the Illinois Supreme Court, and courts throughout Illinois. He counsels school employees and unions on ways to best advocate for employee and student rights, and has presented at state and national conferences on issues such as student discipline, social media, ethics, and constitutional and statutory rights. He is a fellow in the College of Labor and Employment Lawyers. Paul has published papers for the National Academy of Arbitrators, American Bar Association, Illinois Public Employee Relations Report, and the AFL-CIO Lawyers Coordinating Committee. He served as deputy general counsel for the Illinois National Education Association (NEA) for over 22 years. He earned a BA in history at Northwestern University and his JD at DePaul University College of Law.

**Kathryn L. Lubniewski, EdD**, assistant professor, Monmouth University. Dr. Lubniewski earned a doctorate from West Virginia University in special education. Her BS in multi-disciplinary studies and MA in elementary education were also from West Virginia University. She acquired additional certification in multi-categorical special education and early childhood education. She has taught inclusion for reading and mathematics in Grades K–12, and has taught in a self-contained setting for Grades 9–12. Dr. Lubniewski worked as an assistant/associate professor at Elmhurst College for 6 years. She specializes in collaboration, differentiated instruction, and teacher training. Dr. Lubniewski is an active member of the Council for Exceptional Children, and American Association of Colleges in Teacher Education. Her current scholarship focuses on supervision in the collaborative context, differentiated instruction in the STEAM classroom, and how families utilize technology to communicate.

**Tracy L. Mulvaney, EdD**, is the assistant dean at Monmouth University. Dr. Mulvaney earned a doctorate in educational leadership from Northern Arizona University. She holds a BS in rehabilitation with a special education minor and an MA in special education, both from the University of Arizona. She achieved teaching certifications in special education and educational leadership (principal). Dr. Mulvaney started her career as a middle school cross categorical resource teacher. After 9 years of private consulting as an educational specialist for an Arizona company providing independent living services to youth aging out of the foster care system, she accepted a director position for a day school program for K–12 children with severe emotional disabilities. She also provided administrative oversight of the alternative school becoming the district's director of alternative education programs. Her current scholarship focuses on extended clinical practice, teacher residency programs, and using substitute teaching as a teacher preparation strategy.

**Kirstin Natale, MA**, is a graduate student from Monmouth University pursuing a master's degree in school counseling in the Department of Educational Counseling and Leadership. Her professional experience ranges from a special education setting to case management for nontraditional educational programs. She has co-taught classes in special education at Monmouth University in order to bring the perspective of a school counselor to the higher education classroom. Through graduate research assistantship supervision, Kirstin has published articles and presented research surrounding the topics of communication, technology, and education at international conferences. Further research interests include multicultural counseling within schools as well as the implications of communication in the educational setting.

**Megan Robinson, MEd**, is a special education teacher in Jacksonville, Florida. She specializes in teaching students with disabilities in the inclusive classroom setting. In addition to teaching, Megan is a doctoral student at the University of North Florida where her research is focused on collaboration between general and special education teachers, successful inclusive education for students with both high and low incidence disabilities, and building inclusive school culture through leadership.

**Theresa Y. Robinson, PhD**, is an associate professor and director of secondary education at Elmhurst College. Dr. Robinson earned a BS in biological sciences and secondary education and PhD in curriculum and instruction with an emphasis in science and environmental education from Southern Illinois University–Carbondale. She taught Grades 9–12 science in Chicago Public Schools. She has dedicated her career to preparing teachers to teach in culturally responsive ways and providing STEM professional development to Pk–12 teachers in the Chicagoland area. She is an active member of the National Science Teachers Association, American Association of Colleges for Teacher Education, and the Association of Teacher Educators.

**Jeanne White, EdD**, is a professor of education at Elmhurst College. She is certified in elementary education and general administration and was an elementary teacher for 12 years before joining the faculty in 2005. She has authored several articles and presented locally, nationally, and internationally on topics including elementary mathematics education, teacher leadership, service-learning abroad, and teaching math to English language learners. Her most recent publication is the book, *Using Children's Literature to Teach Problem Solving in Math: Addressing the Standards for Mathematical Practice in K–5, 2nd ed.* (2016, Taylor & Francis).

**Jaime L. Zurheide, PhD,** is an assistant professor at Elmhurst College. She holds an MA in learning and instruction from the University of San Francisco and a PhD in special education from the University of Illinois at Chicago. Dr. Zurheide taught for 9 years in urban public, charter, and therapeutic schools, primarily working with middle and high school students with emotional and behavioral disabilities. Her research interests focus on preparing teachers to more effectively work with students with challenging behaviors. Dr. Zurheide is an active member of the Council for Exceptional Children Teacher Education Division and the Council for Children with Behavior Disorders.

# Index

## A

Academic language, 64, 165, 167, 172, 190
Acceptable use policy, 217, 258, 269, 273
Accommodations, 14, 27, 61, 124, 165, 172–173, 193, 258, 269
Active listening, 26–27, 34–35, 238
Adaptations, 156, 168, 172
Adjourning stage, 4, 15–16
Advocacy, 72, 77, 91, 280, 287
Alternative teaching, (*see* Co-teaching models)
Americans with Disabilities Act, 259, 266–267, 269
Antecedent, 148, 151–152, 154–155, 157, 160
Antecedent, behavior, and consequence (ABC) data chart, 151–152
Assessment
    Alternative assessment, 119
    Behavior assessment, 150, 158–159
    Formative assessment, 11, 119–120, 163–165, 171, 173, 179, 189, 200, 234, 240
    Diagnostic assessment, 164, 173
    Direct assessment, 148–149, 160
    Functional assessment, 148–151, 154, 158–159, 160–161
    Indirect assessment, 148–149, 160–161
    Pre-assessment, 165, 167, 191, 201–203
    Self-assessment, 9, 12, 14–15, 18–20, 45–48, 51
    Summative assessment, 119, 164–168, 173–174, 189, 240
Asset, 56–57, 70
    Asset awareness, 43, 48
    Asset mapping, 71, 77, 88, 90–91
    Asset pedagogy, 43

## B

Behavior
    Baseline Measures, 153
    Behavior intervention plan, 48, 158, 160
    Behavior management, 107, 117–118, 269
    Behavior planning chart, 154–155
    Behavioral strategies by function, 155
    Functional behavior, 158–160
    Positive behavior(s), 131–137, 139–140, 142, 159
    Terminology reference guide for behavior plans, 154
Bloom's taxonomy (revised), 187, 189
Bullying, (*see also* Cyberbullying) 215, 217, 220, 222, 257, 259–261, 264, 266, 268, 270, 272–275

## C

Classroom
    Classroom culture, 100, 108, 215
    Classroom climate, 14, 97–99, 103–104, 109, 269
    Classroom arrangement, 98–99, 101, 103–105
    Classroom management, 6, 17, 59, 98, 105–109, 118, 180, 226, 238–239
    Classroom rules, 98, 100–101, 104–105, 110, 152
    Classroom routines, 99–100, 102
    Classroom transitions, 98–100, 102, 104–105, 109, 133, 135, 138, 142

Collaboration, vii-ix, 4–6, 8–10, 12–21, 26–27, 63, 85, 98, 109, 124, 177–178, 186–188, 225, 263, 265, 280–281, 287
    Collaboration self-assessment, 9, 12, 14, 18–21
Collaborative student teaching, vii, xi, 187
Collaborative teaching, vii, viii, 4, 6, 9–10, 12, 22–23, 114, 116–122, 125, 177–178, 182–184, 187, 190, 192–193, 197, 227–229, 283–284, 290, 295, 304
Collective bargaining agreement, 259, 270, 273
Community
    Community asset, 90
    Community asset mapping, 71–72, 78, 88, 91
    Community service, 77, 87–88, 90–92
Communication
    Communication skills, viii, 4, 6, 10–13, 23, 26–29, 34, 178
    Non-verbal communication, 16, 29, 35
    One-way communication, 35
    Reciprocal communication, 74, 78
Confidentiality, 258, 270, 287
Conflict mediation, 270
Consequence, 4, 102, 108, 143, 148, 151–152, 154–155, 160–161, 239, 261–263, 269
Cooperation, 16, 18
Cooperative learning, 99, 132, 134, 142, 202, 245
    Cooperative teaching, 35, 114, 123
    Cover letters, 294, 298–299
Co-Teaching, vii, xi, 5, 7, 9, 12–15, 113–118, 120–126, 137, 178–180, 182–188, 192–195, 218, 226–233, 245–246, 284
Co-Teaching models
    Alternative teaching, 114–115, 125, 188
    One teach, one assist, 114, 116, 119, 125, 179, 188, 192
    One teach, one observe, 114, 116, 119, 125, 137, 179, 188, 192
    Parallel teaching, 11, 114–116, 125, 188, 192
    Station teaching, 114–116, 125, 188, 192
    Team teaching, 114, 116, 125, 188, 192, 230
Critical consciousness, 42–43, 49–50
Critical friend, 227, 230, 233, 235
Culture
    Cultural brokers, 72, 74, 77, 79
    Cultural assets, 56, 58, 201, 203, 205
    Cultural capital, 56–57, 63, 84, 92
    Cultural competence, 40–41, 48–49, 56, 59, 63
    Cultural deficit model, 77
    Cultural frame of reference, 49
Culturally relevant pedagogy, 39, 43, 45–46, 48, 51
Cyberbullying, 215, 217, 220, 222, 266, 270

## D

Data mines/mining, 216, 221
Deficiency paradigm, 40, 49
Deficit perspective, 56–57, 63, 84–85, 92
Depths of Knowledge (DOK) model, 182, 184, 188–189
Differentiated instruction, 126, 165, 173, 199–200, 205–210, 299, 306
Digital citizenship
    Digital citizenship curriculum, 217–218
    Elements of digital citizenship, 212
    ISTE digital citizenship standard 3, 212–213
    Positive online presence, 218–219
Digital footprint, 213, 215–218, 221, 292
Disposition(s), 279–285, 287, 297
Diversity, 48, 62–63, 76, 83, 110, 284, 287

## E

Engagement, 70, 71, 73–76, 78–79, 81, 91, 98, 108, 132–134, 137–141, 226, 243, 269, 283
Ethnicity, 39, 41–43, 56, 63, 102, 110
Equity, 40, 43, 49, 62, 67, 176
English Language Learner (ELL), 63, 168, 181, 205, 271

## F

Family
    Family centered partnerships, 78
    Family engagement, 70, 73–76, 78, 81, 91
    Family visits, 73
    Multigenerational family, 78
    Nuclear family, 75, 78
    Sub-family, 78
Feedback, 11, 26, 35, 61, 66, 105, 110, 125, 132–133, 140, 142, 154, 164–167, 173, 179, 217–218, 226–232, 235, 245, 287
    Student feedback, 66, 132–133, 135, 166, 168–169, 175
    Teacher feedback, 114, 125, 164, 173, 226, 239, 241
Firewall, 216, 221
Forming stage, 4–5, 15–17
Funds of knowledge, 41, 47–48, 56–58, 60–61, 63, 65–66, 72, 78, 92

## G

Gradual release of responsibility, 115, 117, 119–120, 125–126

## H

Harassment, intimidation and bullying (HIB), 257, 259, 260–261, 264, 270, 274–275

## I

Instructional learning objective, 177, 181, 188, 190
Intrapersonal skills, 9, 12, 14, 18, 21
Interpersonal skills, 9, 12, 14, 18, 21
Interventions, 107, 109, 131, 140–141, 144, 147, 158–159, 172, 178, 282, 286

## J

Jobs
    Job applications, 290
    Job hunt, 290, 293, 297

## K

Kinship care, 78

## L

Law, 36, 49, 62, 92, 149, 212, 219, 222, 255–260, 266, 268–271, 273, 277
Learning standard, 58, 187–190, 193–195
Learning environment, ix, 29, 40, 106–107, 109, 173, 200, 202, 205, 207–208, 238–239, 258
Learning profile(s), 60–62, 66, 200–203, 205, 208
Lesson planning, 10, 28, 101, 119–120, 122, 177, 179–180, 183–184, 186, 193, 196, 205
Limited English Proficiency (LEP), 64

## M

Mandated reporter, 258, 271
Minority, 40, 64, 84–85, 92
Mock interview, 295–296, 299
Multicultural literature, 59–61

## N

Norming stage, 4, 6, 8, 14–17
Nuclear family, 78

## O

One teach, one assist, (*see* Co-teaching models)
One teach, one observe, (*see* Co-teaching models)
One-way communication, 35
Opportunity to Respond (OTR), 132–134, 14

## P

Pairs, vii, viii, ix, 4–6, 9–10, 13–14, 16–17, 55, 57, 100, 113, 117, 142–143, 163, 182–187, 197, 199, 226–233
Parallel teaching, (*see* Co-teaching models)
Peer coaching, 225–226, 228, 235
Performing stage, 4, 6, 15–16
Plus delta process, 282–283, 285
Problem solving, 9, 18, 20, 41, 109, 230, 232, 234, 281
Professional learning community (PLC), 230, 232, 234–235
Punishment, 110, 160, 257, 271

## R

Race, 39–43, 46–47, 56, 64, 270, 272, 275
Redirection, 133, 138–139, 142
Reflection
    Personal reflection, 21, 74, 123
Reinforcement, 11, 132–133, 137, 139, 142–143, 148, 154–156, 158, 160
Reproducible materials
    Advanced Organizer for Reflecting on Role in Collaborative Teaching, 118
    Collaboration Self-Assessment Survey, 19–20
    Collaborative Reflection on Lesson Planning and Learning, 196
    Communication Log, 37
    Communication Program Plan, 37
    Co-Teaching Core Competencies Observation Checklist, 246–249
    Culturally Relevant Pedagogy Teacher Self-Assessment Tool, 51
    Family Engagement Behavior Audit T-Chart, 81

Harassment, Intimidation, or Bullying Scenarios, 274–275
Getting to Know You Inventory, 65
Lesson Planning for Collaborative Teaching, 193–195
NEED-HEED-SUCCEED! Tool, 22
Peer Observation Protocol, 244, 250
Planning Protocol for Collaborative Teaching, 190–192
Quantitative Data Chart/Pre-Test-Post-Test, 175
R.E.A.C.H Dispositions, 287
Reflection Rubrics for Video Submission, 237–243
   Lesson introduction and closure, 237
   Classroom management, 238–239
   Assessment, 240–241
   Content delivery, 241–242
   Student engagement, 243
Reflective Data Chart to Analyze Opportunity to Respond (OTR) and Praise, 137
Resource Analysis Chart, 93
Restorative Practices Conference Report Template, 276
SHARE Worksheet, 245
Student Feedback Record Chart, 175
Student Learning Profile Chart, 66
Unpacking a Learning Standard, 189
Use of Communication Skills in Collaborative Teaching Contexts, 23
Videotaped Lesson Reflection Checklist, 294
Restorative practices, 257, 261–264, 266, 269, 271, 273, 276
Résumé, 32, 213, 290–291, 293–296, 298–299

## S

SAMR Model, 214–215, 218
School-to-prison pipeline, 257, 271
Service learning, 42, 47, 88, 90, 92
Social media, 27, 32, 88, 211, 213, 215–218, 221–222, 256, 258, 263–264, 265, 267–269, 271, 273, 275, 277, 306
Standards, 164, 172, 179–182, 184, 186, 188–190, 192, 201, 205, 211–213, 217–219, 242, 256
Station teaching, (*see* Co-teaching models)
Storming stage, 4–5, 9, 15–17
Students
   Student interest survey, 60–61, 201
   Student learning profile, 60–62, 66, 203, 205
   Student learning target, 180, 188, 193–195

## T

Team teaching, (*see* Co-teaching models)
Tiered lesson, 204–205, 208
Transition, 17, 98–100, 102, 104–105, 109, 133, 135, 138, 143, 145, 237, 243, 268, 289, 304
Translanguaging, 42, 49

## U

Universal Design for Learning (UDL), 165, 168, 171, 173, 206–207

## V

Video annotation, 229, 235

CPSIA information can be obtained
at www.ICGtesting.com
Printed in the USA
FSHW011205170120
66147FS